A European Expe[…]

This volume, a translation of th[…] letters of the Franco-Swiss merce[…] […]e-Louis-Henri Polier (1741–95), adds a ne[…] […] perspective to the debate on orientalism and establi[…] […] European rule in India. While European texts have generally been linked to the debate, the Persian literature has remained largely unintegrated. The book corrects this imbalance. A comprehensive introduction by two renowned experts in the field charts out Polier's formative years and life on the Indian subcontinent. It locates the collection of letters in their wider social and cultural milieux and also reconstructs the variety of social layers and networks that Polier's letters offer us. It brings out the complexities of the texture of Indo-Persian culture nurtured during Mughal rule which was being realigned into new categories of caste and religion by British orientalists and administrators.

Written at a time of critical transitions in north India, these letters depict Polier, who worked for the English East India Company as well as the Nawabs of Awadh and the Mughals, in interaction with a range of Indians from the emperor and nobles to ordinary trade agents and artisans in the bazaar. Also included in the volume are his personal letters written to his Indian wives, children, and domestic servants as well as letters to European and Company officials stationed in India.

Muzaffar Alam is Professor, Department of South Asian Languages and Civilizations, University of Chicago.
Seema Alavi is Professor, Department of History and Culture, Jamia Millia Islamia, New Delhi.

Title page of Polier's Album of Miniatures and Calligraphies

Colonel de Polier and his wife in France after his return from India in 1791.
Courtesy : Jacques de Polier

A European Experience of the Mughal Orient

The *I'jāz-i Arsalānī* (Persian Letters, 1773–1779) of Antoine-Louis Henri Polier

Translated and with an Introduction by
Muzaffar Alam and Seema Alavi

Liberté • Égalité • Fraternité
RÉPUBLIQUE FRANÇAISE
The Embassy of France in India

OXFORD
UNIVERSITY PRESS

OXFORD
UNIVERSITY PRESS

YMCA Library Building, Jai Singh Road, New Delhi 110 001

Oxford University Press is a department of the University of Oxford.
It furthers the University's objective of excellence in research, scholarship,
and education by publishing worldwide in

Oxford New York
Auckland Bangkok Buenos Aires Cape Town Chennai
Dar es Salaam Delhi Hong Kong Istanbul Karachi Kolkata
Kuala Lumpur Madrid Melbourne Mexico City Nairobi
São Paulo Shanghai Singapore Taipei Tokyo Toronto

with an associated company in Berlin

Oxford is a registered trade mark of Oxford University Press
in the UK and in certain other countries.

Published in India
By Oxford University Press, New Delhi

with the assistance of the Cultural Section of the
Embassy of France in India, New Delhi
as part of the
French Sources of Indian History Series

ISBN 13: 978-0-19-569187-0
ISBN 10: 0-19-569187-3

Typeset in Nalanda Baskerville
By Comprint, New Delhi 110 029
Printed in India at Pauls Press, New Delhi 110 020
Published by Oxford University Press
YMCA Library Building, Jai Singh Road, New Delhi 110 001

Dedicated to the memory of
Professor S. Nurul Hasan
and
to those engaged in the study of India's relations with Europe.

Contents

Acknowledgements

Our debts are many and varied. Years back Professor S. Nurul Hasan mentioned Polier's Persian correspondence to illustrate the significance of the Europeans' writings in Persian for a fuller understanding of eighteenth century India. We appreciated the value of this view in particular when for a brief period we taught together eighteenth century culture and politics as the Centre for Historical Studies, Jawaharlal Nehru University, New Delhi. As we delineated the diverse ways in which the Indian political culture was negotiated by the early British administrator, we realized that our story was incomplete without bringing to light the European view of the period. It is sad that, despite Professor Hasan's insistence, this work could not take off in his lifetime. It is our privilege to dedicate this work to his memory.

Christopher Bayly's enviable ability to link micro studies to a larger picture of European expansion helped us locate our story in a wider political and ideological context. Sanjay Subrahmanyam's command over the complexities of the East-West encounter is more than evident in our work. He commented on an earlier draft of the work and translated for us some relevant published French material. Our conversations with Neeladri Bhattacharya, Kunal Chakrabarti, and Dilip Menon helped us formulate and reformulate several issues raised in the introduction. Madhu Trivedi helped us to appreciate the art and craft of the period. M. Asaduddin, Mike Fisher, Marc Gaborieau, Farida Khan, Peter Marshall, Gail Minault, Sadhna Nathani, and Sandhya Sharma helped us in a variety of ways in preparing the penultimate draft of this work. G. Arunima, Meena Bhargava, Kirti Trivedi, Romila Thapar, Radhika and Ravi Vasudevan, and I.A. Zilli, have been our sounding board for this work.

In Paris, Francis Richard brought to our notice several Persian manuscripts of the eighteenth century French Orientalists, introduced us to the authorities of the Bibliothèque Nationale de France, Paris, and helped us generously in getting microfilms, slides and copies of the invaluable materials from the Oriental holdings preserved therein. Violette Graff arranged for us the help of scholars and institutions specializing in the history of the Huguenots in early modern France and Switzerland. R. Lardinois, Kapil Raj and Guy Deleury enlightened us about the French presence in eighteenth century northern Indian society. Kapil Raj also allowed us to profit from his. unpublished works on William Jones. Pierre-Edouard de Boigne introduced our work to the family of Polier from whom we got a great deal of relevant information.

It is our pleasant duty to acknowledge the support we received from Maurice Aymard and Jean-Luc Racine of the Maison des Sciences de l'Homme, Paris. They financed our visits to Paris, supplied us with a print out of the microfilm of the *I'jāz* and paid, on our behalf, the Bibliothèque Nationale for the slides of several other relevant materials. A generous subsidy from the Embassy of France in India helped improve the quality of production of this work. We acknowledge with thanks the help we received for this from His Excellency M. Claude Blanchemaison, the former Ambassador of France in India and M. Laurent de Gaulle, Cultural Attaché. In this connection, we are particularly thankful to Jean-Marie Lafont—who was associated with this work for some time and is expected to continue to be associated with us for our work on volume II of this work—for having expedited the dispatch of the copy of *I'jāz* from Paris as well as for obtaining the subsidy for publication. Alam would also like to take this opportunity to acknowledge the benefits he derived from his stay and work in Collège de France in association with G. Fussman, D. Matringe, and E. Olivier.

Our grateful thanks are due to the staff of the British Library, London, The Bibliothèque Nationale de France, Paris, for their efficient and ready response to our requests; Dr V. Enderlein, Museum for Islamic Art, Berlin, for sending us the colour slides of the selected miniatures and samples of calligraphy from Polier's album; Catherine Hieronymie, Aga Khan Foundation, for the ectachrome of the painting from the Prince Sadruddin Aga Khan collection, Geneva; M. Jacques de Polier, a young and dynamic descendant of our Polier, for the ectachrome of a portrait of Polier with his European wife and, for the imprints of the family emblems from the private collection of his family.

We cannot deviate from the customary practice of mentioning the various contributions our family members made to ensure the completion of this work, even though we know we do not have adequate words to acknowledge their support.

Finally we must admit, not just as a ritual, that we are solely responsible for all the errors and shortcomings that still remain in this work.

Note on Transliteration

In spelling and transliteration of the Persian, Arabic words, we have generally followed the system adopted by F. Steingass in his *Comprehensive Persian-English Dictionary*. A dot under 'd', 'r', and 't' as in *ḍak, chhakṛa* and *peṭh* represents the harder sounds of these letters in Hindi/Urdu.

We have, however, diverged from Steingass' system in the transliteration of combined words. In Persian combined words we have preferred to put a hyphen (-) between the first word (*muẓāf/mauṣūf*) and the letter *'i'* indicating its combination with the second (*muẓāf-ilaih/ṣifat*).

In Perso-Arabic combinations, the Arabic definite article *al* has been transcribed as *ul* and placed between two hyphens as in *amīr-ul-umarā*. This is aparently simpler than Steingass' *'u'l-'*, separates distinctly the three components of the combination, the two words joined together in *iẓāfat* by the article *ul*. We have thus written, for example, Asaf-ud-Daula and Qamar-ud-Din, whereas Steingass would have written Asafu'd-Daula and Qumaru'd-Din. Also, we have written simply Abul, 'Abdul and Zulfiqar instead of Abu'l, 'Abdu'l, and Zu'lfiqar. We have not used diacritical marks in writing the name drawn from Persian, Arabic, or Indian sources. In doing so, our principal consideration has been the convenience of the reader and more than that a concern for error-free printing. Over insistence on diacritical, it has been observed, entails for printers a heavy task which they rarely carry out satisfactorily. However, we have used the Greek spiritus asper (') and spritus lenis (') for *'ain* and *hammzah* respectively, where pronunciation of the words without these marks, we thought, would have been atrocious.

List of Maps and Illustrations

MAPS:

ILLUSTRATIONS: (B/W)

ILLUSTRATIONS: (Colour *between pp. 96 and 97*)

Title page of *I'jāz* with Polier's seal

de Polier

Comte de Polier

Two family emblems of Polier

Introduction

A significant feature of the eighteenth century in India was the rapidly changing character of European presence in the land. Europeans were no longer mere traders, mercenaries, travellers and missionaries; they were also settlers and power-builders who interacted with Indians, bought estates, married local women, and often left their progeny behind. Many Europeans in India also exhibited remarkable intellectual curiosity. They studied Indian society, wrote extensively about it, and made keen observations which threw light on the cultural interstices of the indigenous social fabric. Some of their observations were recorded in the local tongues, and in this manner there emerged a small body of literature different from that which existed in the market, in Persian and Urdu, adding a new genre to the existing Indo-Persian literary culture.

I'jāz-i Arsalānī, literally the wonder of Arsalān (Arsalān Jang was Polier's Mughal title), belongs to this group of eighteenth-century Persian writing. It contains about 2000 letters of the noted French adventurer Antoine-Louis Henri Polier (1741–95) who was in the service of the English East India Company almost throughout his career in India. Unfortunately, no proper attention has been paid to his work.[1] The present translation of volume I of *I'jāz-i Arsalānī,* together with a commentary situating it in the social and cultural milieu of the eighteenth century, is an effort to bring Polier centrestage within our historical understanding of the period.

Polier and His Works

Military engineer, architect and collector of oriental manuscripts, Antoine-Louis Henri Polier was baptized on 28 February 1741 at Lausanne, Switzerland. He was the younger son of Jacques Henri Polier and his wife Jeanne Françoise Moreau de Brosses, the family being French Protestants who had emigrated to Switzerland in the mid-sixteenth century.[2] Polier's parents were both French. They traced their ancestors to the eleventh century, when the family supposedly possessed a castle at Villefranche de Rouergue, in Aveyron province in south France, at the time when Comte Reimond de

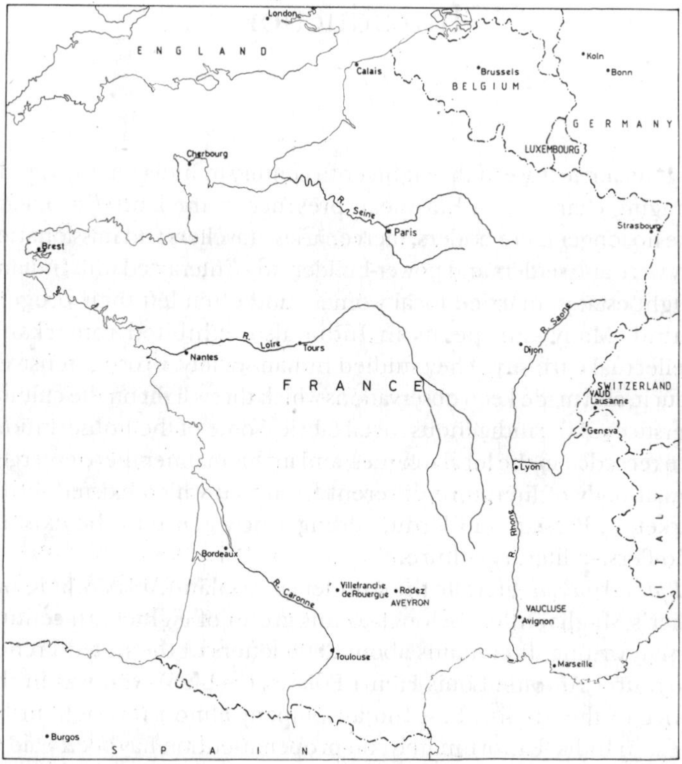

France/Switzerland and adjacent countries

Tolouse laid the foundations of that town. In 1214, a member of the family was believed to have saved the life of Louis IX during a fight with the English. He was honoured with knighthood and the coveted 'Order of the Cock'.[3]

The establishment of one branch of the Polier family, headed by Jean Polier in Switzerland, is often explained in terms of a migration provoked by religious persecution at the time of the religious wars that beset the last decades of the Valois monarchy in the sixteenth century. Another version is that Jean Polier arrived in Switzerland as interpreter and secretary of a French embassy to the Swiss League.[4] However, the aftermath of the celebrated St Bartholomew's Day massacre of 1572 in Paris, when Huguenots were killed with the connivance of the monarchy of Charles IX, seems to have changed the nature of Jean Polier's relations with France. In 1574, he applied for refuge in Lausanne 'on account of the massacres and persecutions for the Christian religion', and in April of the following year he was granted the status of burgher (bourgeois) in that city.[5] Polier's grandfather, Jean Pierre Polier (1670–1740), served in Prussia and played a key role in the Swiss cantonal wars of 1712, fighting for the Evangelical cantons against the Catholic ones. His great-grandfather held a number of significant martial offices, such as Lieutenant Colonel of the Militia, and became Burgomaster of Lausanne. He also displayed a literary talent which, when combined with his mystical inclination, helps explain the nature of his principal works on such subjects as the Apocalypse, the Jewish notion of the Messiah's imminent arrival, and the fall of Babylon.

There was thus a lively military and mercenary heritage, even before the departure of Polier's paternal uncle, Paul Philippe Polier (1711–58), to serve the English East India Company at Madras. There was an intellectual heritage to boot. Apart from his great-grandfather and grandfather, a notable intellectual was a great-uncle, Georges Polier (1675–1759), Professor of Greek and Moral Philosophy at the Lausanne Academy, later Professor of Hebrew and the author of a number of works of a religious nature. Of greater eminence still was a paternal uncle, Jean Antoine-Noe Polier (1713–83), brother of Paul Philippe, who made his mark as a Protestant pastor and correspondent of Voltaire and the Encyclopaedists.[6]

Notwithstanding this genealogy of intellection, the Polier who interests us swims to view in humdrum circumstances as a passenger in a sailing ship called *The Hardwick*, journeying to Madras in 1757 to join his uncle posted in that city. Having arrived in India Polier became a Madras cadet and sought active service under Clive against the French.[7] He served at Masulipatnam and Carnac in Bihar, and was then transferred to Bengal in 1761. Here he struck a long-lasting friendship with Warren Hastings, the British Governor General, and was appointed assistant to Thomas Amphlett, the chief engineer in charge of constructing Fort William. When Amphlett resigned, Polier was promoted to the post of chief engineer with a commission and the rank of captain lieutenant in the army. He continued in this position for more than two years.[8]

On account of the Company's increasing scepticism towards the French in India, Polier was then removed from his senior position as chief engineer. At the same time, the Company never managed to jettison his services entirely. He seems to have been able to cling to

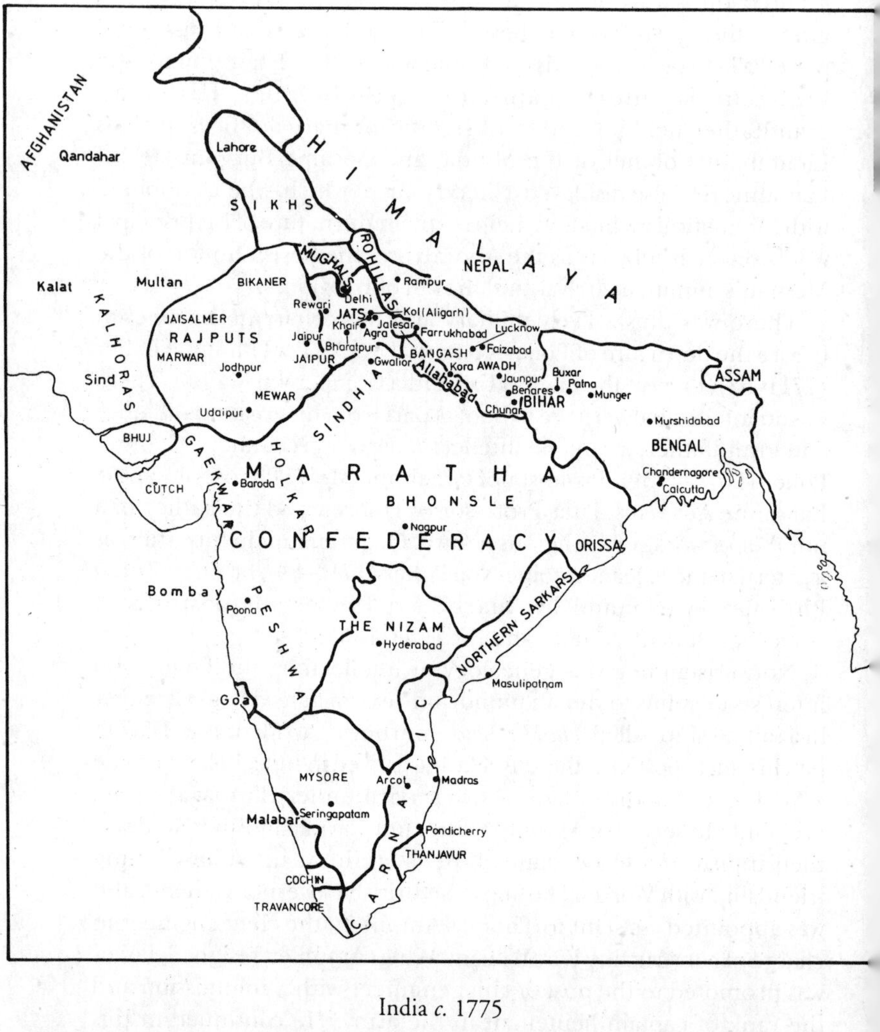
AFGHANISTAN
Qandahar
Lahore
HIMALAYA
SIKHS
ROHILLAS
MUGHALS
NEPAL
Kalat
Multan
BIKANER
Rampur
Delhi
KALHORAS
Rewari
JATS
Kol (Aligarh)
JAISALMER
Khaif
Jalesar
RAJPUTS
Agra
Farrukhabad
Lucknow
Jaipur
Bharatpur
BANGASH
Faizabad
MARWAR
JAIPUR
Gwalior
Allahabad
Kora
AWADH
Sind
Jodhpur
Jaunpur
Buxar
Benares
Patna
ASSAM
MEWAR
SINDHIA
Chunar
BIHAR
Munger
Udaipur
Murshidabad
BHUJ
GAEKWAR
HOLKAR
BENGAL
MARATHA
Chandernagore
CUTCH
Baroda
Calcutta
BHONSLE
Nagpur
CONFEDERACY
ORISSA
NORTHERN SARKARS
Bombay
PESHWA
Poona
THE NIZAM
Hyderabad
Masulipatnam
Goa
MYSORE
Arcot
Madras
CARNATIC
Malabar
Seringapatam
Pondicherry
THANJAVUR
COCHIN
TRAVANCORE

India *c.* 1775

Company employment one way or another, suggesting a wiliness and tenacity in line with that displayed by his French contemporary and friend Claude Martin, the adventurer-entrepreneur-architect who sank his roots deep into Lucknow. Like Martin, who clung on despite fierce hostility from jealous foes, Polier continued to act as a field engineer in the Company army and took part in the siege of Chunar in November 1764. In 1766 he was appointed a major and helped to quell the mutiny of white troops in Sir Robert Fletcher's brigade at Munger. But for all this, with his French origins Polier was handicapped. He was at this stage denied a rise beyond the rank of major.[9] It was only later in 1782, on Hastings recommendation, he was appointed Lieutenant Colonel.

It was because of this systemic block in his career that Polier agreed to be deputed into the survey department of Nawab Shuja-ud-Daula of Awadh. Here, in Awadh, Polier regularly supplied the Company with detailed news of the political developments in the region while assisting the survey and trade transactions of the Company. Simultaneously, in keeping with the general trend amongst Company officers, Polier created a niche for himself in Awadh society, amassing fortunes via private trade and by assisting Shuja-ud-Daula in military transactions—such as during the nawab's fight against the Jats, which involved a siege of Agra's fort. This streak of independence in Polier raised the hackles of several Company officials. Critics and opponents of Hastings, such as Edmund Burke and Philip Francis, pushed strongly for Polier's resignation from the Company, and their pressure proved irresistible. And so Polier resigned from Company service in October 1775. He did, however, survive deportation from India because of the solid economic stakes he had created for himself here. For a brief while he joined service with the Mughal Emperor Shah Alam. In 1781 he pleaded with Warren Hastings to be restored into Company service. Now, with Hastings' intercession, this was permitted and in 1782 Polier was allowed to stay on, initially in Faizabad, later in Lucknow with the rank of Lieutenant Colonel.[10] His fortunes seemed to have taken a turn for the better.

In Lucknow Polier developed an interest in collecting manuscripts and paintings. It was here in 1783 that he met the well-known British painters William Hodges and John Zoffany, with whom he developed a long-lasting friendship. Polier figures prominently in Hodges' famous painting 'Colonel Mordant's Cock-match' (1786) as well as in 'Claude Martin and his friends.'[11] It was during this period that the Indian artist Mehrchand, who enjoyed Polier's patronage, prepared

'Colonel Mordaunt's Cock Match', the Daylesford version, by John Zoffani, 1784–86, Lucknow.

'Colonel Antoine Polier with his friends Claude Martin, John Wombwell and the artist' by John Zoffani, 1786–87, Lucknow.

albums for him with miniatures and paintings that had a distinct European artistic imprint.[12] Again, it was in Lucknow that Polier arranged for a part of the *Mahābhārata* to be translated into Persian for the British orientalist Richard Johnson, a resident of the city.[13] Finally, it was in this period of his life that Polier developed an interest in the Hindu religion and dispatched to William Jones certain volumes of the *Vedas* that he had acquired from the Raja of Jaipur with the help of Khiradmand Khan Don Pedrose.[14] His notes in French for a book on Hindu mythology, prepared over these years in Awadh, earned him the honour in 1784 of being appointed a member of the Asiatic Society of Bengal.

Apart from collecting oriental manuscripts and miniatures during his stint in Awadh, Polier built up a fascinating library in Lucknow where his collection was maintained. The contents of this library, along with his other collections, were distributed between the Bibliothèque Nationale in Paris, the British Museum in London, the library of King's College at Cambridge, Eton College in London, the Islamic Museum at Berlin, and the Bibliothèque Cantonale of Lausanne—which also has a manuscript catalogue of 120 oriental works with annotations by 'Colonel Polier'. The French traveller Comte de Modave, who visited the Awadh court at Faizabad in 1774 where Polier was present, noted that the latter had a reasonably good command over the Persian language and an excellent knowledge of Urdu.[15] The Orme Collection in the British Library contains Polier's *Account of 'Begum Sombre'* (Begum Samru), the *History of Shah Alam II*, and the *Account of the Sikhs.*

In 1788 Polier returned to Europe after an absence of thirty-two years. Of this long period away he had spent a total of thirty years in India. On his return to Europe, at the request of William Jones, he deposited a collection of his manuscripts in England. He then moved on to Lausanne where, on 20 January 1791, he married Anne Rose Louis Berthoudt, daughter of Jacob, Baron van Berchem.[16] In India, Polier also had two Indian wives, identified within his Persian correspondence as his senior and junior wife.[17] These same Indian wives were identified as Johguenow [Jugnu] Begum and Zinnet [Zinat] Begum in Claude Martin's will. They were each bequeathed a pension of 10 sicca rupees per month.[18] By his European wife Polier fathered Pierre Ame'dee Charles Guillaume Adolphe, Comte de Polier. He had two other sons born of Indian women, and a daughter.[19] He maintained a full-fledged household in Faizabad, with his two

Indian wives and sons living under the care of his trusted Indian servant Lal Khan.

In 1792 Polier bought property in Rosetti near Avignon and settled there with his European wife, by whom he had another son. Here he is reported to have hosted parties in 'lavish Asian style' and adopted the ideas of the Revolution. His intellectual interests continued and he is said to have read the entire collections of his Lausanne library. Polier was pensioned on Lord Clive's fund with effect from 14th of March 1792. On the 9th of February 1795 he was assassinated by unidentified robbers. His wealth, accrued largely during his career in India, continued to be an asset to his family, which remained in the running for titles and honours. In 1828 Polier's older son by his European wife was accorded the status of Comte de Polier.

I'jāz-i Arsalānī

Polier's major work was a book entitled *Mythologie des Indous,* published and edited by his canoness (member of the Roman Catholic Order) in Paris in 1809. The preface by the canoness gives a kind of autobiographical note dictated to her by Polier. This has details of Polier's life in India, his contacts with the Indian élite, his search for the Hindu scripts—in particular the *Vedas*—which he finally acquired from Raja Pratap Singh of Jaipur on the condition that 'the texts would be bound only in silk and velvet'. The other work of equal interest by Polier is *I'jāz-i Arsalānī,* translated in the following pages, which is a compilation of letters. During his stay in Awadh and Delhi in the 1770s and early 1780s Polier was in touch with a large number of local people, with whom he often corresponded in Persian. These letters, compiled under the title *I'jāz-i Arsalānī,* were put together under Polier's instruction by his *munshī*[20] and are available in two volumes in the Bibliothèque Nationale, Paris. The title echoes Polier's Mughal title, Asralān-i-Jang, which was given to him by the Mughal Emperor Shah Alam and means 'the lion of the battle'. There are 1833 letters in this collection relating to the first phase of the period of Polier's stay in north India between Rabī' I,1187 AH (June 1773) and Ṣafar, 1194 AH (March 1780). Both volumes together, copied in *nasta'līq* and *shikast,* apparently by different hands, comprise 771 folios. Volume I consists of 445 folios with 13 lines on each page and is written upto folio 351 in *nasta'līq.* Volume II comprises 326 folios with 15 lines on each page and is written in *shikast.* The names of the adressees, sometimes also their locations, are written in red ink. In

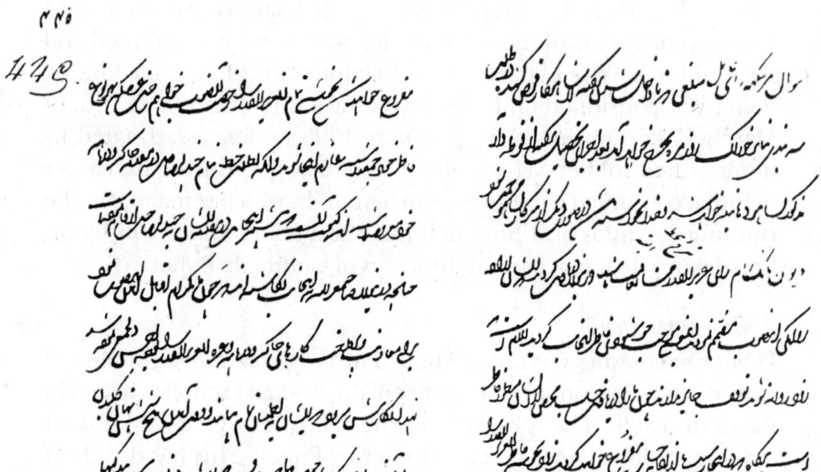

Two pages from *I'jāz-i-Arsalānī*

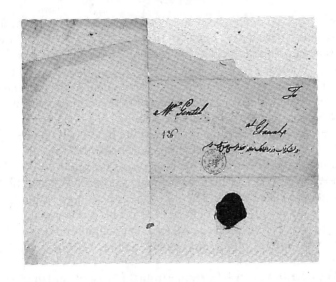

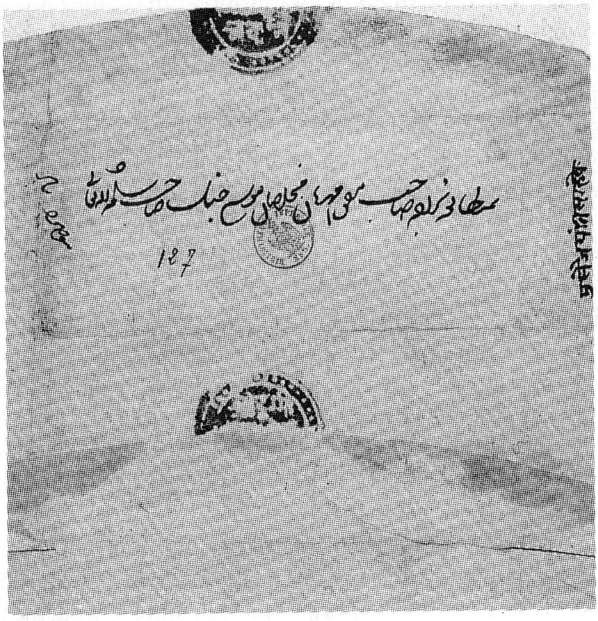

Covers of letters addressed to M. Gentil

some letters, as on folios 93–5 and 143–51, such headings are missing, even though from the content of the letters it is clear who they address. Each letter mentions the date of the *Hijra* era. In Volume I, often the time of dispatch is stated. The letters of Volume II, which pertain to Polier's service at the court of Emperor Shah Alam, also state the *julūs* (regnal) year, while others, particularly those relating to revenue or *jāgīr* matters, mention the *faṣlī* year as well.

Volume I is made up of letters from the time when Polier, as an agent of the East India Company, was associated with the Awadh court. He had joined the imperial service towards the end of this period and was assigned a *jāgīr* in *pargana* Khair, *sarkār* Kol (Aligarh) of the Mughal province of Agra. The folios towards the end of Volume I contain letters with details of Polier's problems and negotiations for imperial service and the grant of a *jāgīr*. The volume ends with copies of certain Mughal official documents such as *parwāna, muchalka, tamassuk* and *māl- ẓāminī.*

The addressees in the *I'jāz* range from the emperor and the Awadh nawabs to merchants, artisans and humble shoemakers. Among the rulers addressed are Shah Alam, the Mughal emperor; Shuja-ud-Daula and Asaf-ud-Daula, the rulers of Awadh and wazirs of the empire; Raja Chait Singh, the ruler of Banaras; Nawab Muzaffar Jang, nawab of Farrukhabad; Raja Ajit Singh, ruler of Riwa; Hafiz Rahmat Khan and his nephew; Nawab of Pilibhit in Rohilkhand; Raja Lalitsah, ruler of Srinagar in Garhwal; zamindars of Riwari, Khair, Anupshahar and sarkar Kol; and Raja Karan Singh, a Sikh chief. The nobles in Mughal state service who are addressed include Najaf Khan, Saiyid Lutf Ali Khan, Majd-ud-Daula, Raja Nawal Singh, Khan Muhammad Khan (a nephew of Hafiz Rahmat Khan), Nawab Murid Khan, Mirza Sulaiman Khan and Amin-ud-Daula (the son of Muzaffar Jang).

Polier wrote over a hundred letters to the *'āmils* of Khair and Riwari, where his *jāgīrs* were located. The other officials he corresponded with include Mufti Ghulam Hazrat, Amanat Khan (*faujdār* of Phulpur and Jaunpur), Mir Makhu Khan (*kotwāl* of Lucknow), Bhim Singh (*ḥawaldār* of Banaras), Muhammadi Khan (*'āmil* of Khalilganj), Hasan Ali Beg (*qil'adār* of Allahabad), Haidar Beg (*faujdār* of Kora), and Mirza Ubaidullah (*kumaidān*).

Traders, *mahājans* and trade agents also figure in the text, as do scholars, artists and artisans such as Maulavi Mir Haidar Ali; Mehrchand, the painter (*muṣawwir*); Mir Muhammad Azim, the binder (*jildgar*); and Mir Muhammad Salah, the seal engraver. Finally, the text includes letters to relations and attendants: Bibi Jawahar and Bibi Khwurd, his Indian wives; Baba John and Baba Antony, his sons; Lal Khan his attendant and domestic servant.

These Persian letters by Polier often generated a response from the addressees in Persian: unfortunately the replies are not included in the *I'jāz*. Most are lost, others scattered about. For instance, the Bibliothèque Nationale, Paris (Supplement Persian 1681, folio 12b) lists a letter from Najaf Khan addressed to Polier dated *Hijrī* 1191 regarding the *ta'alluqa* of Rewari, where Polier had a *jāgīr* and about which considerable correspondence exists in Volume II of the *I'jāz*. The names of Louis Perceret and Khiradmand Khan Don Pedro figure among the European addressees. Polier also wrote letters in Persian to Monsieur Gentil, though the *I'jāz* does not contain any of these. It does, however, refer to letters in *angrezī* (English) dispatched to Gentil.

Conforming with general practice in the Mughal empire, where the officials and nawabs employed *munshīs* (secretaries) to draft their letters,[21] Polier employed several who wrote letters on his behalf. Variations in style suggest that these were written by diverse hands. Indeed the different styles of compliment used in the letters to Polier's women in folios 95–159 tempt us to speculate that there was certainly more than one *munshī* involved in the preparation of the *I'jāz*. Some letters carry a sober way of addressing the recipient, suggesting dignity and distance in public life: *mukhaddara-i Parda-i'iṣmat-o-ḥayā, mastūra-i ḥajla-i'iffat-o-ṣafa, 'iffat panāhī* and *'iṣmat dastgāhī*. On the other hand, there are phrases in other texts expressing passionate attachment: *sarmāyạ-i muḥabbat-o-wafā* or *sarāpa muḥabbat-o-wafā*.

Only one of these *munshīs*, Kishan Sahai, uses his own name. This Kishan Sahai, who seems to have drafted most of the letters in Volume I, appears to have been a Kayastha from Bihar. He was employed by Polier as his *munshī* in Azimabad (Patna). He remained with Polier until about the beginning of 1776, with a brief leave of absence around the end of 1775 and early 1776. He wrote a preface to the *I'jāz* where he mentions his first meeting with Polier and his entry into the latter's retinue. There also figures a rather longish preface by him on folios 152–4, where he narrates Polier's desire that his letters be compiled in several volumes year-wise, with each volume possessing its own preface. Sahai indicates that this specific preface is for the volume of 1188/1774–5. There is no separate preface for any other volume of the letters over subsequent years, possibly because Polier was not free to closely supervise the preparation of the later volumes. It is also likely that Sahai left or died and that the *munshīs* who replaced him were not accomplished enough to write prefaces in the commonly accepted grandiose style.

Persian Inshā *and the style of* I'jāz-i Arsalānī

In its style and diction the *I'jāz* represents the eighteenth-century Persian *Inshā*. At the same time, Polier and his *munshī* preferred not to integrate herein all the features of *Inshā* as this evolved as an important genre of the Indo-Persian literary tradition. *Inshā*, which literally means the creation and construction of letters, documents and state papers, has been a part of the Muslim literary and politico-diplomatic world from the very beginning.[22] A brief history of *Inshā* as a genre is necessary here in order to appreciate the significance of the style of the *I'jāz*. By the eleventh century, when the élite court language of a number of non-Arab rulers in the Islamic East changed from Arabic to Persian, the Arabic *Inshā* format, which had acquired a verbose and hyperbolic slant since the time of the Abbasids, was accepted nearly wholesale by the first Persian *Inshā* maestros. There were, however, certain early Persian prose masters such as the Ghurid writer Nizami Aruzi Samarqandi (the author of *Majma'al-Nawādir*, better known as *Chahār Maqāla*), who also provided a different model for the perfect scribe, pleading the virtues of brevity, precision and clarity.[23]

As Persian literary culture evolved in India, Persian *Inshā*, with its characteristic emphasis on figures of speech, the free use of poetic imagination, and long convoluted addresses for addressees, formed a significant part of this. Amir Khusrau of Delhi, Ain-ul-Mulk Mahru (a noted noble of the Khalji Sultan of Delhi), and Mahmud Gawan (the Iranian *wazīr* of the Bahamani sultanate in the Deccan) were the most notable *Inshā* writers in the fourteenth and fifteenth centuries. Mahmud Gawan was not only an excellent composer but also wrote a treatise called *Manāẓir ul-Inshā* on the method of *Inshā*. Khusrau suggested that unless there were refined marvels and astonishing elegance (*badāi'latīf-wa-laṭāif-i-badī'*) in the *Inshā*—which he calls *ṭarz-i mutarassilāna*—the *Inshā* would not be of high quality. According to Khusrau, a significant task of *Inshā* writers (*or mutarassils*) is the 'sharpening of well-cooked Persian with pungent Arabic'.[24] Similarly, in the treatise by Gawan the emphasis is on forceful *bayān* (expression) when he discusses grades of *munshīs*. *Bayān* implied in almost all cases *bayān-i-muraṣṣa'* (ornate expression).[25] It was thus that

Samarqandi's suggestion—which was that the best speech ought to be brief and unequivocal—was overlooked in these redefinitions of ideal *Inshā*.

Ornate prose, in some ways, was also central to Mughal *Inshā*, this being a literary development out of an earlier predilection for simplicity. Timur is said to have appreciated a simple style in prose. The literary artifice and figures of speech that characterize *Inshā* literature are conspicuously missing from the official correspondence and documents of his period. Over time, however, the earlier preference for simplicity was overshadowed by the emergence of a kind of middle style.[26] While Babur advised his son Humayun to use plain words in writing so that he and his readers faced no trouble,[27] the *Inshā* masters at his and his son's courts were not entirely obedient. In some documents, such as the *fatḥnāmas* (victory letters) the anachronistic style of inspiring awe and invincibility continued. Again, in the time of Babur's grandson Akbar (1556–1605), the best known chronicler of this period, Abul Fazl (d. 1602), not only believed in communicating a message through his *Inshā* compositions but also a philosophy. Holding this view of style, he generated a new *Inshā* language which derived its ideological base from non-*Inshā* mystic literature.[28] A striking feature of this language was the use of phrases and combinations of words which, while not completely alien to the Persian language, had so far remained largely unused. At one level this resulted in what we know as *taṭhīr-i-fārsī*, or cleansing Persian of Arabic words.[29] Abul Fazal appears to have calculated that if he used the same old Arabicized phrases to communicate his new meanings, he would first have to contest the original meanings for which these phrases had been used. He thus looked for ancient Pahlavi words for his novel purposes. Verbosity and ornamentation resurfaced in his style, though not to the point of making his prose obscure or tautological.

Besides Abul Fazl, there were noted writers in Akbar's reign who influenced the Mughal *Inshā*. There was Abul Fazl's brother, Abul Faiz Faizi, better known for his poetry; and there were Hakim Abul Fath Gilani and Abul Qasim Namakin. In Faizi there is an emphasis on message and agenda (*mudda'ā*). In Gilani's letters the flavour of conversation is often discerned. Their writings are reasonably free of excessive metaphors and similies and follow the straight narrative style. Their styles are simple yet forceful.[30]

In the seventeenth century, in the wake of the decorative art of Shahjahan's time (1626–50), the balance achieved in Akbar's era appears to give way to the old hyperbolic trend. This was soon checked by Aurangzeb's (1658–1707) overwhelming emphasis on direct and plain prose.

Abul Barakat Munir Lahori (d. 1645) and Chandra Bhan Brahman (d. 1658) were the principal *munshīs* of Shahjahan's time. Munir is fond of rhetorical artifice and a diction in which meanings are subordinated to the grandeur of words, homonyms, and phonetic harmony. In the words of Momin Mohiuddin, his composition 'appears only a Love's Labour Lost', with meaning shrouded in a net of tropes and a haze of baroque phraseology. Munir also revealed a special liking for words with multiple meanings (*hazārān ma'ānī dar har'ibārat, hazārān nukta andar har ishārat*).[31] Brahman writes with greater ease and fluency even as he follows the model set by Abul Fazl. Interestingly, both he and Abul Fazl exercised a major influence on later Hindu *munshīs.*

Significantly, simultaneously with this ebb and flow in the development of the Mughal *Inshā* style, Babur's advice was never quite given up. Indeed, at the end of the seventeenth century appropriate language was thought of as that which was 'fluent, lucid, easy to comprehend and to be admired both by the high and the low' (*k͟hāṣṣ-o-'ām*).[32] The eighteenth century saw a large number of *Inshā* collections, many of which were collected by friends and relatives of the authors and were meant as models. By this time a kind of standardization in style and form is achieved. This process is accompanied by the emergence of a caste-like group of *munshīs* who write in Persian and who were employed by Indian rulers, nobility, and Europeans.[33]

Structurally, the principal constituents (*rukns*) of a complete letter are the titles (*alqāb*), salutations (*salām-i-taḥīyat*), and praise of the addressee, an expression of yearning for him (*ishtiāq*), and a desire to meet him (*ṭalab-i-mulāqāt*); these are followed by mention of the writer's own self, an account of his welfare (*i'lām-i-aḥwāl*), an eagerness to learn of the addressee's welfare, and miscellaneous news (*shauq-i istimā'-i ak͟hbār*). The core agenda (*mudda'ā*) of the communication is adjusted somewhere here in an extremely gentle manner, according to the prescribed norms (*ādāb*). The latter portion of the letter consists of requests and hopes (*iltimās* and *tawaqqu'*) for the continuation of correspondence. Finally, at the end is suffixed a *du'ā*—an invocation of prayers for the addressee. If the letter is written in reply to one received, then its first part comprises praise of the letter received (*ṣifat-i maktūb*), the date and time of its arrival (*ṣifat-*

i-zamān-i wuṣūl) and an expression of delight or gratitude (*ṣifat-i wuṣūl-i khiṭāb*) in keeping with the ranks of the sender and intended recipient. In a congratulatory letter, besides jubilation at the achievements of the addressee, the sender is expected to thank God and pray for the continuation and prosperity of that for which he has congratulated the addressee.[34]

This format was generally followed in the Indo-Persian *Inshā*, and in the *I'jāz-i Arsalānī* nearly all the letters follow this pattern. There are, however, striking differences in the words and phrases preferred, depending on the content of the letters and corresponding to the individual writer's varying appreciation of received diction. Thus, in many epistolary collections, the *mudda'ā* may be in plain language but the rest of the contents may well be in ornate language, rich in verses and adorned with Arabic adages. *Inshā-iMādho Rām*, an eighteenth-century collections, is one such example. Madho Ram chose ornate titles for his addressees.[35] On the other hand, Anand Ram Mukhils, the leading eighteenth-century litterateur, often used very simple *alqāb* of everyday conversation. Indeed, in some of the treatises on the ideal *Inshā*, compilers often mention and recommend appropriate verses from the *dīwāns* of the master poets for citation by the *Inshā* writer so as to reinforce the emotions expressed in prose within the letters.[36]

The letters which comprise *I'jāz-i Arsalānī* are generally in a direct style. The prose is simple, elegant, free from turgidity and a heavily Arabicized phraseology, and uninterrupted by verse quotation. This has no adverse reflection on the competence of the writer, Kishan Sahai. As a matter of fact, his command over the language seems to be unusual. The letters (*'arẓdāshts*) addressed to Shah Alam, the *tahniyatnāmas* to Shuja-ud-Daula and Asaf-ud-Daula, and the two prefaces in the volume are extraordinarily rich in vocabulary without being tedious.

Krishan Sahai's style seems to have been guided by Polier. It is difficult to say how much Persian Polier knew, but it is significant that he examined these letters, instructed Kishan Sahai to make a volume, lent his own name to the collection, and wished that it should be read as an achievement and not as a routine compendium. Polier appropriated in a significant way, as we will see below, the Mughal Persianate lifestyle, and thus diluted his European identity. His interventions in the indigenous cultural world were considerable, and these letters in *I'jāz-i Arsalānī* represent one expression of Polier's larger cultural negotiations—in this case with the prevailing literary local styles. For example, in contrast with contemporary letter-books, which are organized addressee-wise, the *I'jāz* collections are arranged chronologically. And therefore, in the way that we would use a Mughal letter-book carrying the name of a nobleman (even if not a single letter had been drafted by him) as an important source for writing the social and cultural history of this period, Polier's letters are an important text within the study of India's cultural encounter with the West.

Eighteenth-Century India's Encounter with the West

The English Company's Continental Underbelly

Constructions of British India and a colonized 'other' as mere narrative productions within the vast political discourse of colonial domination are now being questioned. The colonized 'other' and the colonial experience as a whole are being located in more pliable cultural interface and material as well as discursive negotiation between Britain and India. But while British 'Self' and Indian 'Other' are no longer binary opposites, a reified image of the former as culturally definable and politically demarcated does persist. 'Britishness', projected as a Protestant political identity fashioned during the eighteenth-century Anglo-French conflict, is taken as given and then contrasted with, for example, the 'Frenchness' of a hostile and Catholic France.[37] *I'jāz-i Arsalānī* makes us reconsider the notion of such an unadulterated Britishness within Britain's colonial success. It implicitly questions the view that the British were alone in the vanguard of imperial expansion in India, and it qualifies the reified image of the British emerging from new researches on the making of British identity.[38] At least in India, British imperialism depended on and derived from a range of Europeans, of which Polier was a representative.

In eighteenth-century India, Anglo-French rivalries notwithstanding, an informal network of Europeans, dominated by Frenchmen, was in operation, furthering the English Company's imperial project. These men included engineers, architects, watchmakers, mechanics, painters, traders, and surveyors who often worked in tandem with English Company officials. While the Company did not hesitate to use Frenchmen to its political advantage wherever it thought this expedient, it expressed concern at their presence, particularly in the courts of regional rulers. A large number of Europeans worked for the indigenous polities, often switched jobs, and exchanged information between native rulers and the Company. According to an English military officer, Colonel Galliez, there existed around 200 Europeans in Awadh alone in the year 1775.[39] The large French presence in no way implied a tension-free relationship between them and the English. At the level of official policy there was complete animosity towards the French, matched with a desire to cleanse them out of India. In fact, one of the important points of dispute between the English Company and Nawab Shuja-ud-Daula of Awadh was the large French presence in his *Nawābī*.

Immediately after the battle of Buxar, as Company inroads into upper India took priority and the Company began to erode the military organization, arsenals, and factories of indigenous rulers, Frenchmen commanding critical military set-ups in Awadh also became the target of its fury. For instance, pressure for the dismissal of the military commander Monsieur Gentil, in the service of Nawab Shuja-ud-Daula of Awadh gained momentum.[40] Gentil was called the 'secret agent' of the French Company and his continuous service with Shuja-ud-Daula was seen as 'inconsistent' with the latter's friendship with the English.[41] In 1774, under pressure from the Company, Shuja-ud-Daula was forced to dismiss Gentil from his service.[42]

In 1771, Gabriel Harper, the British Commandant in Awadh, complained to the Company administration about Nawab Shuja-ud-Daula maintaining Frenchmen in his service despite repeated requests to 'discharge such a set of useless people'.[43] Harper perceived the French presence in Awadh as a point of dispute between the English Company and Shuja-ud-Daula. He was incensed at the Nawab's reply stating: 'he knew of no disputes between the English and the French nations; and that if there was any I should acquaint him, that the latter were admitted by the former to reside in many places of the Company districts.'[44] Harper was annoyed that whereas at the time the Nawab had become an ally of the English Gentil had been the only Frenchman with him (and had been pardoned by the English officers of various crimes because of his association with the Nawab), subsequently the number of French in Awadh had swelled.[45] Harper appealed to the Company to come up with a solution to 'put a stop to such tribes of these Frenchmen remaining in the service of an ally whose fidelity ought always to be suspected.'[46] The following year the president of the select committee of the Company reinforced Harper's view castigating Frenchmen—in particular Monsieur Gentil—as 'secret agents of the French Company' who needed to be turned out.[47]

It was again with the intention of monitoring the movements of Frenchmen in upper India that the Company resolved in 1771 to issue passports to officers who were proceeding upcountry on service. Commanding officers were to apply for such passports to the Company.[48] At the same time, the select committee of the Company decided to block fresh inflows of the French from Bengal into Awadh by making it mandatory that 'no Europeans shall be allowed to pass out of the province to the westward without the *parwāna* of country government.' Orders to this effect were issued by the *nāib ṣūbadār,* Maharaja Shitab Rai to officers of the government.[49] From 1772 the Company moved in the direction of making inventories of Frenchmen in the service of Nawab Shuja-ud-Daula.[50]

With this curb on fresh inflows of Frenchmen into Awadh and upper India, the Company mounted pressure on Shuja-ud-Daula to discharge those he nurtured in his service. Veiled threats of snapping their alliance with Shuja-ud-Daula were issued if he continued to encourage the 'natural enemies' of the English.[51] However, the French menace in upper India continued. N. Middleton, British Resident at Awadh, continuously reported to Hastings the Nawab's reluctance and hide-and-seek policy over the dismissal of Frenchmen like Monsieur Gentil and Madec.[52] On being informed of the presence of Madec in Awadh, Hastings wrote to Middleton making the Company's position very clear:

> I desire you will inform the Vizir that you had it in strict injunction from me to remonstrate against every instance of such encouragement given to the subjects of the French nation, especially such as have been guilty of treachery towards ours and to declare to him that while he betray that attachment to enemies of the English, I consider my engagements to assist him against his [enemies] as suspended.[53]

Despite all such efforts the French continued to find employment not only in Awadh but in the service of rulers like the Mughal general (*amīr-ul- umarā* and *mīr-i-ātish*) Najaf Khan, who controlled revenue bearing territory around Delhi as well. Najaf Khan was reported to have clandestinely employed Frenchmen in his service. The Company viewed this with concern, being of the opinion that in the face of any war between it and the French these Indian powers would assist the French. This was very clear in the correspondence between Middleton and Hastings over the dismissal of Frenchmen employed by Najaf Khan. Middleton expressed concern to Hastings that, in view of Company orders, Najaf Khan had only expelled those Frenchmen who were of no consequence to him, the only exception to this rule being Madec, who was first dismissed but then reinstated after a discreet interval. Even more alarming was the case of the Frenchman, Daniel du Jarday, who had become Najaf Khan's confidant and was given a salary of Rs 1000 a month, and who was reported to be living clandestinely on the *jāgīr* of Major Polier to avoid the direct glare of the Company. Middleton wrote: 'Dejardu it is confidently reported is empowered to treat with him on the part of the French nation and through whom he is supposed to carry on a correspondence with Mr. Chevalier.'[54] His intelligence reports suggested that 'the object of Dejardu's negociations [sic] is said to be to effect an alliance between Nudif Cawn and the French nation and to engage his assistance in a war now meditating against the English in India.'[55]

Middleton's fears were not unfounded, for Frenchmen in Awadh were not entirely free-floating mercenaries. Many had direct contact with the French Company in Chandernagar and had held important positions in its military establishment. For instance, an official of the French settlement in Chandernagar, in a significant Persian letter to Shuja-ud-Daula, makes a strong case for retaining of Monsieur Gentil in Awadh on the grounds that 'he is reliable, has been an important commandant in the French army, and the French Company has full trust and confidence in him. From such a person you should not expect anything but welfare'.[56]

The French Company's threat to the English notwithstanding, French networks continued in Benares, Mirzapur and the eastern provinces, to the persistent annoyance expressed by Company administrators. In 1768 Raja Balwant Singh of Benares reported that one Monsieur Cononje was resident in Mirzapur for the sale of French merchandise and carried on a lucrative trade there. The raja allowed his goods to pass without duties and his French agents (*gumāshtas*) were allowed to stay because of the approval of Shuja-ud-Daula: a *dastak* of Shuja-ud-Daula forbade the raja to interrupt the trading activities of Frenchmen.[57] Balwant Singh promised the Governor-General that, now that he had Company instructions to flush out the French, he would have the man seized. In the 1790s, Jonathan Duncan, British Resident at Benares, reported more such French networks in his region. He tightened Company surveillance on the French and began to restrict Europeans from taking contracts for indigo, from establishing vats within four to seven miles of existing ones, and forbidding the construction of new vats without Company permission.[58] So intense was the Company's distrust of the French that even common Indians who associated with them were not spared. In an interesting incident, the Nawab of Bengal was told that all Indian servants of 'French kothis' in the region would be punished if they did not quit their jobs. Muhammad Ramzan, a *jamā'adār*, paid no heed to this order and was penalized.[59]

Of course the English Company's anxiety over non-British Europeans did not prevent it from using to their own political advantage all information, surveys, cartographic and topographic work that they could gather from such people. In 1791 Jonathan Duncan transmitted to Edward Hay, secretary to the government, a map and journal reference which he needed and had extracted from a French resident of Mirzapur, Monsieur Devil Maublin. He wanted to know if the board desired him to get further information.[60]

It was perhaps on account of the pragmatics of governance that the British appreciated the need for an inclusive continental presence within the early phase of their rule in India, a necessity which may have been accentuated by reverses suffered across the Atlantic. Also, by now the 'White Mutiny' had shaken the Company's faith in English officers and possibly encouraged it to broaden its officer cadre to include other Europeans. This is suggested by Polier himself in his memoirs, dictated to his cousin Canonness in Paris. Commenting on his joining Lord Clive's army in Calcutta he says:

> . . . promoted to the rank of Major, I joined his army, and he gave me the command of the Cypayes, the body of Indian troops who were a part of the second brigade; and as he had particularly attached me to his own person and since he honoured me with his confidence he gave me the charge of looking to those of the officers of his army who, unhappy with his operations, conceived of dangerous plots to undermine them.[61]

Administrative need created a compromise between theory and practice in the English Company's relationship with the French. In 1778 Middleton—the most vocal opponent of French presence in India—found it politically expedient to recommend Claude Martin's continued residence in Awadh because:

> I have found him very active and serviceable in equipping Major Hannay's corps which I could not have been able to have fitted out tolerably without his aid and whether the Nawab chuses to employ him or not he will always be useful both to Col. Leslie and myself especially if any considerable part of the stores are to be furnished by Vizir. . . I should think it would be the best plan both for His excellency and the Company as he has plenty of materials

in his store houses at Faizabad which will be otherwise squandered away in useless and ridiculous purposes.[62]

Another important case in point was Polier. The Company's ambivalence towards him was evident very early, when he was used as a spy to supply Hastings with information about Frenchmen resident in India.[63] At the same time, British residents like Middleton were angry at the role Polier played in encouraging French trading and espionage activities. It was at this time that Middleton complained that the Frenchman du Jarday was staying clandestinely on Polier's *jāgīr* to escape the Compnay's legal ambit.[64]

Company officers had reason to be suspicious of Polier and his French contacts. Comte du Modave, in his account of this period, mentions the curious episode of a French Company official, Jean Baptiste Chevalier, who managed to get hold of confidential plans detailing the defences of Fort William in Calcutta by using a Frenchman who frequented Polier's house. Chevalier achieved this by bribing a mestizo who was copying out these plans and elevations under the directions of a major. As Modave notes:

> . . . a small sum of money was enough to settle the matter. The wretch betrayed his master and his duty and handed over all the papers that were in his charge to Monsieur Chevalier. The governor of Chandernagore applauded this action like a victory, without thinking that those who engage others to commit a perfidious act share the shame that is attached to such a dishonest act, in the view of honest men.[65]

Yet Hastings' soft corner for Polier continued. His personal attacks on Frenchmen like Madec were conveyed in a careful manner to his subordinates 'lest they should hurt Major Polier'.[66] By 1777 Middleton appeared reconciled to the idea of not merely having Polier around to assist the Company but also to him being allowed to operate through a galaxy of Frenchmen who worked in tandem with him. In a letter to Hastings on the killing of one such French commandant of Polier called Lauzun—who was killed on duty when he attempted to subjugate a *paragana* of Polier which was part of his *jāgīr*—Middleton refers to the episode as a 'very heavy misfortune' for Polier.[67]

Resentment among Company officers and their suspicion of Polier resurfaced time and again. During the Rohilla war of 1774, Colonel Alexander Champion, commandant of the Company's forces, complained to Hastings that 'neither the president at the Nabob's court nor Major Polier, who is also in the Nabob's court thought proper though an officer in the army, to show me any part of the respect which it was his duty to have manifested.'[68] In an ongoing correspondence over Polier's apparently poor conduct, Hastings defended Polier and wrote back:

I would willingly attribute the present deviation from both to some misapprehension or other cause which when explained may palliate his offence and as I have hitherto entertained an esteem for Major Polier as an officer and gentleman, I shall be happy (should you find this to be really the case, or should Major Polier make such reparation as you can with propriety admit of) that you will at parting show him some proof of your reconciliation.[69]

These were hiccups; Polier continued to help the Company in a variety of ways, such as, most crucially, political espionage.[70] In 1774 he informed Hastings that despite the Company's order prohibiting recruitment of Frenchmen, the Nawab of Awadh continued to employ the French mercenary Madec.[71] He also spied for the Company's indigenous allies, like the Nawab of Awadh, even while reporting the latter's political activities to the Company. The reports he sent to Nawab Shuja-ud-Daula from Agra (Akbarabad), where he had been dispatched to assist Najaf Khan lift the siege of the fort, were remarkably detailed and perceptive. They included military and technical details of the fort and a scientific assessment of its vicinity:

I inspected the entrenchments along the southern wall of the fort on Saturday, the 2nd of Ẕīqa'da. The fort wall resembles the one of the Allahabad fort. But it looks very vulnerable near the Bengali Tower. There is no moat below; and the door opening on the river side which is used continuously by people is adjacent to it. In my assessment if we prepare our entrenchment (*damdama*), with ten to twelve cannons, next to it and bombard from there, the wall would probably break. We can then storm the fort through the gate. I will investigate into it further tomorrow and write to you.[72]

From Agra Polier daily transmitted copious information on the transactions and negotiations between Najaf Khan and the Jat leaders who had beseiged the fort. To safeguard against leakages of confidential matters, he often dispatched his trusted agent, Mir Muhammad Husain Ata Khan, to the nawab so as to get the news narrated verbally.[73] One letter to Shuja-ud-Daula illustrates very vividly the meticulousness with which every detail of political development in Agra is reported:

I have sent you the report of the developments here until the 1st of Ẕīḥijja. Mir Muhammad Ata Khan will give you further details. Yesterday night Dan

> Shah met Najaf Khan and was with him for some time, standing with folded hands, seeking forgiveness for his offences. Najaf Khan said he had already forgiven him, whereupon Dan Shah requested for the conferment of the Raj upon Kheri Singh; permission to sell the grain to pay the arrears to the troopers; his own appointment and a number of other irrelevant and unacceptable demands. Najaf Khan said that he would accept his demands to the maximum reasonable extent only if he surrenders the Delhi gate to his people. He [Dan Shah] agreed that the following day after he digs out the bones of Jawahar Singh interned inside the fort, [he] would hand over the Delhi gate and join him [Najaf Khan] with all his brothers and *sardārs.* He then left and entered the tent which he had erected on the bank of the river adjacent to the *retī* [river bank] wall. Since the day Dan Shah came out of the fort and met Najaf Khan he has not returned to the fort; and on his request the people of Najaf Khan have been deputed to protect him. Today, the 3rd of Ẕīḥijja, one of Najaf Khan's men who had already entered the fort came out and reported that Dan Shah was engaged in digging out the bones of Jawahar Singh. I have just received the news that the kotwal of the city is building a bridge over the moat leading to the fort gate. I will report the subsequent developments to you.[74]

Similarly, Polier played a key role in informing the Company of political developments at the Rohilla quarters and in negotiating a political settlement at the time of the 1774 Rohilla war. In this war the English Company and Shuja-ud-Daula were pitted against the Rohilla leader Hafiz Rahmat Khan. In a letter to Hafiz Rahmat Khan he reiterates that the English Company desires to establish cordial relations with the Rohillas, but that 'there is no proof as yet of the cordial relations that you profess to have with the English. I hope you will regard me as a sincere friend in all cases and keep in touch with me.'[75]

His work at this time involved collecting vital information about the movement of Rohillas for the Company. For this purpose he alerted his agents, who were stationed in the friendly territory of the Nawab of Awadh. In a letter to one such agent, Mir Waliullah Khan, he says:

> I noted with appreciation that the mischievous Rohillas have advanced further, the Nawab has deputed a contingent for their chastisement, and that the battle is about to commence. Keep writing to me and continue to send the reports about the army and the Nawab's camp without fail.[76]

In Benares he exhorts Raja Chait Singh to keep him regularly informed of his well-being. In a letter to the raja he makes his political intent clear: 'You should rest assured that I shall always work for the betterment of your affairs. You should entertain no doubts about my intentions.'[77] In the Benares region he regularly collected information on fordable river bridges and the feasibility of military surveys and campaigns.[78] Finally, he assisted Company surveyors such as Captain Cartier, who had been deputed to survey land in the Benares, Jaunpur, Phulpur, and Faizabad sectors. In a series of letters to Raja Chait Singh and to local zamindars and *faujdārs* of the raja, he demands their-co-operation in the survey operations of Company officials.[79]

Most of Polier's European contacts were in the service of Shuja-ud-Daula, but they were also close to him. Many of them owed their positions in Awadh to him. Don Pedro de Silva, with the title of Khwaja Khiradmand Khan, a Portuguese physician in the service of Raja Pratap Singh of Jaunpur, was one such agent.[80] Pedrose transacted in Awadh solely through Polier, who made full use of the latter's fluency in both Persian as well as English, and with his skill had several books in Persian translated into English.[81] Polier would buy books from collectors and pass them on to Pedrose to translate.[82] Oshra Gora Mistri was another important agent of Polier in the service of Shuja-ud-Daula. He looked after Polier's commercial interest in his *sarkār* and supplied him with bridles and saddles and kept track of goods that Polier sent back to be stored in his *sarkār*. The other important agent, spy and friend of Polier was the famous 18th century Jesuit Padre, Wendel. Wendel again was in Shuja-ud-Daula's service and thus in close contact with Polier. Polier obtained for him a village as *āltamghā* from Najaf Khan and saw to it that he was able to effectively combat difficulties in getting revenue from the *jāgīr*.[83]

Padre Wendel and Khwaja Pedro worked in league, spying for Polier and clandestinely supplying him vital political information from upper India. They generally wrote to Polier in Persian. Strategically, whenever purveying extremely confidential information, they switched to a European language. This is evident from a letter from Polier to Pedro: 'I received your letter on the 19th. You have written that since it was not appropriate to write certain things in Persian you wrote in a European language (*ba-khatt-i-Firangī*) to Padre Wendel, and that he would write to me accordingly. I will try to do his work at my convenience whenever he will write to me'.[84] Often, perhaps for similar reasons, Polier wrote letters in English to his agent Oshra Gora Mistri.[85] That this network of espionage was geared towards helping theEnglish was evident in 1761, when Shuja-ud-Daula's plan to march towards Bihar was leaked to the English by Padre Wendel.[86]

Polier was friendly with the well-known Frenchman in Awadh, Monsieur Gentil. He instructed Ijaz Raqam Khan, his agent in Awadh who had complained of slackness in the preparation of newspapers (*purzahā-i akhbār*), to take advantage of Gentil's presence and 'make it a point to record the daily news and hand them over to Monsieur Gentil so that they reach here without delay'.[87]

But the friend who assisted the Company the most was Claude Martin, the famous French soldier-surveyor who was in the service of the Company. The text is replete with instances of Martin's survey operations and his efforts to draw a map of the Agra fort so as to assist the Company fight the Jats. Besides these well-known Frenchmen working with Polier, there was an assortment of European cooks, watchmakers, organ mechanics and soldiers whose services were constantly made use of.[88]

These European contacts reinforced the British suspicion of Polier. In a letter to Hastings, Middleton expressed his suspicion of Polier's role in the event of an Anglo-French war. He said he had intelligence reports suggesting Najaf Khan's offers to Frenchmen to join his service, which he thought were a clear indicator of Khan's tilt towards the French. Middleton was particularly concerned by du Jarday's clandestine residence on Polier's *jāgīr*, and this put Polier in a spot over the Najaf Khan issue.[89] British unease over using Polier and his European contacts for their political advantage was best reflected by their initial denial to him of the rank of lieutenant colonel because he was not one of them.[90] The title was granted to him late in his career through the efforts of Hastings, for which Hastings earned a lot of flak from his enemies.[91]

Colonial Identities in the Eighteenth Century: English or French?

Polier's French origins notwithstanding, his loyalty to the English Company was unquestionable. Indeed, he gave an exemplary display of this when he landed in India in the thick of the Anglo-French war and started his career by fighting against the French and for the English armies on the coast of Orissa.[92] Later, he supplied vital information to the Company on the activities of his French friends in India: Madec, and Gentil.[93]

In the *I'jāz-i Arsalānī*, Polier's own identification with the English is absolute. This suggests that identity is to be construed in this context not so much in terms of national identity but as a professional and linguistic identity. Like the English, Polier could speak and write the English language. Both he and the English were learners of Sanskrit and the Urdu *zabān* (language), and often used the same pandits and *munshīs*.[94] Polier refers to himself as an *angrez*, a term which, literally, connoted an Englishman. In a letter to Nawab Shuja-ud-Daula complaining of delay in the issue of instructions granting him audience at the Lucknow court he says:

O Lord, I have travelled a long distance and have lived here on the instructions of Nawab Imad-ud-Daula, governor Hastings for five months, but I am still deprived of your kind attention. All the other Englishmen who came here have been fortunate enough to be blessed with your favours, but you did not enquire about my welfare. My English comportment (*ṯīnat-i-angreziya*) does not bear with this. How can I live here without your kindness. It is difficult for me to stay here now even for a moment.[95]

Polier does not stop at identifying himself culturally and politically with the English: he extends the ambit of this overarching English identity to include his other European associates and friends. For instance, the Frenchman Claude Martin is continuously referred to by him as an English *ṣāḥib.* This is evident in several letters of complaint he writes to Najaf Khan about an episode in which Martin was humiliated by Najaf Khan's men at the time when he attempted to survey and draw a map of the Agra fort. Expressing his anger at Martin's treatment, Polier describes him as 'an English *ṣāḥib* from Calcutta' who has been unnecessarily troubled despite Najaf Khan's 'relations of faith and confidence with the English'.[96] The reference to Martin as an Englishman is repeated in all letters of complaint sent to Najaf Quli Khan, the principal military chief of Najaf Khan. Martin is addressed as 'Captain Martin *Bahādur sardār-i-angrez*'.[97] In these letters Polier argues that to humiliate the 'Englishman' (*sardār-i-angrez*) Martin *ṣāḥib* is to sully the dignity of the English presence as a whole.[98]

Polier's identification with the predominantly Protestant English may have had something to do with his being of similar faith, and moreover with having been born in a family that had lived as part of a minority in Catholic France. In fact, his acceptance of service in the English Company and his identification with the *angrez ṣāḥibs* perhaps derived quite considerably from the eighteenth-century French intellectual environment in which his Protestant family had been at the receiving end of Catholic onslaught. France had become a religious cauldron waiting to explode from the time Martin Luther was excommunicated by the Pope in 1520 and Calvin migrated to Geneva in 1541. In 1598, Henri du Bourbon, a Protestant prince, inherited the crown after his conversion to Catholicism. He enforced the famous Edict of Nantes—i.e. religious peace—which heralded a period of religious toleration. A phase of respite for Protestants was inaugurated in which they received special status, even as Roman Catholicism continued as the religion of the state. However, with the assassination of Henri IV and the coming to power of his son Louis XIII and grandson Louis XIV, the so-called reformed religions once again received a blow. The Edict of Nantes was revoked in 1685 and the one and only Catholic faith became compulsory for all. It was at this point that thousands of Protestants fled the kingdom, seeking refuge in Switzerland, the Netherlands, England and Prussia. Those left behind faced unprecedented violence and a torture which continued until the second half of the eighteenth century. It was over this that Polier's family migrated to Switzerland.[99] In this context, the English Company's friendly overtures and Polier's reciprocation are likely to have been coloured by his strongly Protestant religious feelings.

Polier's identification of himself and his continental associates as English was of course—and more importantly—expedient. The English had acquired considerable power in the region and it was always beneficial to function under their overarching political and cultural umbrella. Identification with the English would certainly have furthered Polier's private trade and other transactions with indigenous rulers, for whom in this context the national distinction between white Europeans may not have seemed significant since such a distinction was being successfully obliterated by Frenchmen and at least partially accepted by the Company. Polier's drive to identify with the English is explained most clearly in one of his letters to Shuja-ud-Daula. Here, to ensure for himself the special care of the nawab, he reminds the nawab of the cordial relations that the nawab has maintained with English officers, among whom he includes himself:

> It is absolutely necessary for me to submit to you, even though I cannot say it elegantly because I do not know Hindi, that there is a strong bond of cordiality and friendship between you and the English officials. I have been here in [your] service for the last nine years and the Governor has asked you to take special care of me. Obviously, we derive strength from your favours. If we receive your favours we gain in strength and if, God forbid, we are deprived of them we lose our stature. I hope that I will continue to be in your service and it will be my privilege to execute in all humility the orders of your Highness.[100]

This recourse to identification with the English Company and its economic and political interests is again evident when Polier exhorts Najaf Khan to act against his officials who, despite his orders, have created hurdles in Polier's trade:

Just consider the labour put into escorting the goods to you. And in this there was no personal interest involved except considerations of friendship. Above all, nothing belongs to either of us—but the reputation of the English is the link between us. In such a case such treatment was not appropriate.[101]

The personal and political motives for such identification are reinforced by the fact that the overarching 'English' identity which emerges in the text appears to be selective. For instance, the Frenchman Madec is never identified in the text as 'English'. Polier is not on good terms with Madec, and in a letter to Najaf Khan he comments harshly on Madec:

Further, the day I met you in Akbarabad [Agra] we also talked about Madec. I hope you remember what I told you about him. Now I learn that you have developed a relation with him, and have also obtained a *jāgīr* for him. This is contrary to what we discussed the other day. Since I am your friend I should warn you that if *Ṣāḥib-i-Kalān* [Warren Hastings] hears about it he will be very unhappy.[102]

So, Madec is not really an Englishman because he is not of Polier's camp. But there is more to this. Within the interstices of Polier's linguistic and religious identification with the English there coexists his assertion of a very distinct European identity. Polier shared with Frenchmen in Company service their dream of the establishment of a French empire in India. Indeed, for many such the British empire was perceived as a tolerable substitute for the French empire that, sadly for them, had failed to materialize. In their minds the memory of Dupleix and the other French Generals in India continued to constitute the reference point against which they judged English officers. This is articulated by Gentil who, in a significant passage, creates a direct link between Hastings and Dupleix. He fears that the former's recall to England is detrimental to the interest of the British empire in the same way as the latter's return extinguished French imperial designs in India: 'His recol [sic] is the ruin of the British dominion in India as was the case of the great man Dupleix whose example he followed and whose recol had also lost the crown of France its dominions in that country'.[103]

Polier too never forgot his 'foreign birth'. This is evident from the fact that his tendency to identify himself with the English figures mostly in letters written to indigenous rulers and ordinary people. In his English letters to Sir William Jones, Warren Hastings and Sir Joseph Banks (President of the Royal Asiatic Society and a trustee of the British Museum) he makes a distinction between Englishmen and

Europeans and identifies himself with the latter. In a letter to Joseph Banks—wherein he discusses the procurement of a copy of the *Vedas* from the Raja of Jaipur in order to gift it to the British Museum—Polier projects himself as a European:

Since the English by their conquests and situations have become better acquainted with India and its aborigines—the Hindoos— the men of science throughout Europe have been very anxious of learning something certain of these sacred books which are the basis of Hindoo religion and are known to India and elsewhere under the name of the Baids. . . I made it also my business, particularly to inquire for those books, and the more so, as I found that doubts had arisen in Europe of their very existence.[104]

He again identifies himself as a European when he reports the raja's surprise at 'what use we Europeans could make of their holy books'. The raja was told that 'It was usual with us to collect and consult all kinds of valuable books of which we formed in Europe's public libraries. . .'[105]

This letter to Banks ends with a reassertion that his gesture in presenting the *Vedas* to the British Museum should be viewed 'as a small token and tribute of respect and admiration from one who though not born a natural subject, yet having spent the best part of his life in the service of this country, is really unacquainted with any other.'[106] At the time of entry into Awadh's service he is a European: 'thus I accepted a post of architect and engineer that he [Hastings] procured for me with Soujah A'doula [Shuja-ud-Daula] who was looking for a European who was capable of taking charge of the buildings and fortifications that he was proposing to make in his state'.[107] Thus Polier asserts his English identity selectively even though he is very conscious of the difference between him and the English on account of his European background. For its part the Company was also always eager to remind him and other Europeans of their foreign origins. The pretext—as Polier himself calls it—of his foreign origin was always available for use against him.[108] Indeed, between 1760 and the 1770s a number of battles and intrigues were carried on within the English Company over the issue of officers of foreign origin who were accused of lacking 'patriotism'.[109]

On the one hand, Polier's English letters to British officials reinforce the argument that his effort at donning an English identity was basically for the consumption of indigenous rulers and the local populace. On the other hand, we cannot discount the fact that a generalized equation of all Europeans with 'Englishmen' may have been rather commonplace in eighteenth-century India and was, in the *I'jāz*, merely being articulated as such by Kishan Sahai.

Yet, not all Persian writers of the eighteenth-century perceive Europeans as *angrez*. In fact, many are aware of separate groups of Europeans—*firangīs*—and the variations within these. Khwaja Abdul Karim Kashmiri, author of the eighteenth-century text *Bayān-i-Wāqi'*, distinguishes between the French (*Frāncīs*), the English (*Angrez*), the Dutch (*Wolandez*), and the Portuguese (*Purtagez*). He says that their manner of pronouncing the syllable '*za*' indicates the group's specific connection with each different country,[110] and observes that 'Europeans dress and live in accordance with the customs of their own country. Here also they have built churches, they are good craftsmen and many Bengālīs have learnt their crafts from them.'[111] So, while the *I'jāz* seems to open up questions on the role of the *munshī* as an agent in the formulation of European views on the people and politics of India, Polier's *munshī* does not seem sensitive to the variety of European presence in India revealed in a writer such as Kashmiri.

Shopping in the Oriental Bazaar

The similarity between relatively enlightened English administrators and Europeans like Polier was reflected in their engagement with the book bazaar of eighteenth-century north India. Both were fascinated by the range of books that they discovered in the collections of indigenous rulers. Maintaining large libraries of precious literary, scientific and historical manuscripts appeared to be a hallmark of high aristocratic life in the region. From the Nawab of Awadh to the Raja of Jaipur, all had rich holdings of oriental books.[112] These collections ranged from oriental manuscripts in Arabic, Persian and Sanskrit to Arabic translations of Greek and Latin manuscripts. In 1784, Warren Hastings was delighted to find, in the Vizir's Library at Lucknow, Arabic translations of about 15 important works of Greek astronomers, scientists, mathematicians like Euclides and Archimedes. He noted that an equal number of books were reported lost.[113]

The range of astronomical and mathematical manuscripts in the Benares raja's holdings, and the scientific sophistication with which the local observatory functioned, provoked a thoroughly impressed Reuben Burrow, the eighteenth-century British mathematician and astronomer, to write a provocative report titled 'Hints concerning some of the advantages derivable from an examination of the astronomical observations at Benares'.[114] So enthused was Burrow that he described India as the 'parent of the sciences',[115] and called Englishmen oblivious of these scientific treasures 'Huns and Barbarians'.[116] He was of the view that there were many more manuscripts recording the observations of Indian astronomers in the possession of natives, and that these could be obtained through good relations with them. Burrow speculated a high degree of communication and interaction between Indians and Greeks, and a commonality of symbols of superstition between Persia, Rome and India (bull, ox, cow, sun, moon), which in turn suggested a degree of interaction between the East Indies and the Jews—who also worshipped the calf.[117]

This interest among eighteenth-century Indian rulers in the books and manuscripts of neighbouring cultures and the Hellenic world was a continuation of the Islamic intellectual legacy into which, by the sixteenth and seventeenth centuries, Indian traditions of learning had been incorporated. Indeed, this insatiable quest for knowledge of other cultural and intellectual traditions had derived from the Qur'ān, which gives paramount importance to the acquisition of learning. Early Muslims had demonstrated extraordinary energy in rediscovering the achievements of the ancient world in astrology, astronomy, mathematics, alchemy and chemistry. This process received a fillip with the spread of Islam into the Christian world, when Greek philosophers and thinkers like Aristotle and Plato began to be mentioned in Arabic and Persian literature along with Islamic theorists.[118]

Mutual interest and interaction between the Islamic Orient and the West as is known resulted in major Arabic works, the Arabicization of Hindu numerals, and significant improvements upon Greco-Hellenic texts. Ibn Sina and al-Farabi were forerunners among the Muslim scientists. The former's medical texts *al-Qānūn* and *al-Ḥāwī* were prepared in Arabic and translated into Latin, and these remained the prescribed medical texts in Europe until the mid-nineteenth century. Indeed, from the twelfth century, new Latin translations of Arabic scientific texts began to spread in Europe. Spain, the civilizational bridge between the Islamic world and the continent, was the first recipient of this literature. The crusades accelerated this interaction.[119]

When Islam entered its Indo-Islamic phase, the scientific and religious intellectual traditions of India were also incorporated into the evolving Muslim scientific tradition. Thus we have evidence from the fourteenth-century of Muhammad Tughlaq's courtiers with unusual accomplishments in Hellenic logic and philosophy. His successor, Firuz Tughlaq, is credited with encouraging several scientific devices. Later, in the Mughal period, a number of Sanskrit works were translated into Persian. In the field of medicine there were efforts at blending Perso-Islamic ideas with *Āyurveda.* Most Mughal emperors extended their patronage to leading scientists of their time: Fatullah Shirazi of Akbar's reign and Shaikh Sadullah and Mulla Abdul Hakim of Shah Jahan's reign were known teachers of science. Sanskrit, Turkish and Arabic texts on science, law and religion were also translated into Persian during the Mughal period. Part of this scientific drive was reflected in Persian renderings of the ancient Hindu scriptures and related texts: these included the *Rāmāyana, Mahābhārata, Bhagvadgīta,* the *Upanishads* and the *Nalopakhyana.* Hindu scholars—pandits—were actively involved in these translations.[120] Jai Singh's astronomical treatise, *Zij-i-Muḥammad Shāhī,* drew on the writings of the fifteenth-century Central Asian Timurid prince Mirza Ulugh Beg.[121]

At another level this literary and intellectual ferment, the large number of libraries under the control of local rulers, the compilation of odes, poems and literary verses to honour the famed, the promotion and translations of texts, the buyers and sellers of books, and the demand and production of paper that the literary activities generated–all this pointed to the important role the book bazaar and its economy played in shaping the cultural life of regional polities. If the maintenance of libraries came to signify power and status, the gifting of prized manuscripts, and the compositions of eulogizing odes and verses connoted gestures of loyalty, friendship and honour in India's pre-colonial society. It was with these notions of proper conduct that people expressed their feelings for Europeans and Britishers who, from the mid-eighteenth century, increasingly became part of Indian society. Hastings, probably the most popular of the British administrators, was the recipient of many odes and literary verses extolling his rule. In 1784, natives of Benares called Sewnat (Shiv Nath), surnamed Tarka Bhoosan (Bhushan), Haree Dew (Hari Dev), surnameed Tarka Bkees, Gokool (Gokul) surnamed Beedya Lankan (Vidyalankan), and Kalee Das, (Kali Das), surnamed Seedyant (Sidhant), composed an ode in the Sanskrit language glorifying Hastings' rule and presented it to him.[122] Hastings continued to receive verses of admiration from Indian rulers like the Nawab Wazir of Awadh even after he had returned to England.[123] The Nawab Wazir wrote to Hastings : 'My body is here, my soul is in the bosom of my friend. The world imagines my soul is with my body.' He exhorted Hastings to return to India since the prosperity of the Company depended on him.[124] Nawab Asaf-ud-Daula is said to have presented a collection of the original Arabic translation of Greek books on mathematics, science and astronomy to Hastings in 1784.[125] Similarly, we have evidence of the Raja of Jaipur gifting the *Vedas* to Polier as a gesture of goodwill.[126]

The social signification attached to books and manuscripts is evident from the fact that during wartime indigenous rulers protected their libraries. Among a conqueror's ultimate triumphs was the control or pillage of the literary collections of the vanquished. That the English Company was sensitive to this cultural signifier is evident from its records, where the militarily strong Tipu Sultan's ultimate collapse is often described via the British takeover of his rich library. In 1799, a gleeful Charles Wilkins wrote to Hastings: 'The papers have told you and that truly, that the captors of Seringapatinam have reserved Tipoo's library for the Company's repository. Could any intelligence have come more opportunely for my causes?'[127]

It would be pertinent to suggest that prior to the arrival of the English Company there existed in northern India a vibrant tradition of collecting manuscripts and of engaging pandits and *munshīs* to translate religious and scientific texts into Persian. This, as we argued above, marked a continuity with the Islamic intellectual legacy which, from the seventh century, was characterized by promoting the translation and collation of a wide-ranging series of texts from diverse intellectual traditions. If pre-colonial rulers, in particular the Mughal emperors, relied on indigenous men of learning for the translation of Sanskrit texts into Persian, their motive for such an exercise also derived from a desire to create greater understanding and social harmony between local groups. This they saw as a prerequisite for a stable empire. In the introduction to a Persian translation of the *Mahābhārata,* Abul Fazl described Akbar's intention in sponsoring the translation:

He [the Emperor] noticed the increasing conflict (*nizā'*) between the different sects of the Muslims (*farāiq-i-millat-i-Muḥammadi*), on the one hand, and the Jews and Hindus (*Juhūd-o-Hunūd*), on the other, and also the endless show of repudiation of each other's [faith] among them. The sagacious mind [of His Excellency] then decided on translation of the revered books of both the communities (*fariqain*) so that with the blessing of the most honoured and perfect soul [the Emperor] of the age, they both refrain from hostility and dispute, seek truth, find out each other's virtues and vices and endeavour to correct themselves.[128]

The English Company in the Book Bazaar

From the middle of the eighteenth century, English Company administrators came into direct contact with this oriental intellectual bazaar and its literate community of pandits and Persianate scholars.[129] The Company's sensitivity to the social nuances of the book bazaar was most evident during the course of its transition to a formidable political power at this time, for in this period the book bazaar of upper India experienced very significant changes, induced by the Company's rise to ascendancy. The indigenous patrons were sucked into its fold by the Company, which was fast emerging as the new centre of political power and patronage. As the Company spread its administrative networks up the Ganges valley, influential English *ṣāḥibs* became the new centres around which the indigenous literary bazaar began to reconfigure itself. As C.A. Bayly shows, in the increasing absence of local patrons, Muslim and Kayastha *munshīs* readily flocked with their literary arsenals to the new English and European *ṣāḥibs*, seeking sustenance to continue their traditional occupation.[130] Often these people offered administrative texts to British officials in order to teach them how to go about their business.[131] From Sanskritists like Charles Wilkins and William Jones to administrators like Warren Hastings, Jonathan Duncan and Company officials, to professionals like Reuben Burrow—all benefit from this. Under the aegis of this new patronage, even if the community of indigenous scholars and translators remained the same, the intentions of their English and European patrons were different from those of their pre-colonial patrons. Native texts needed to be collated and translated not merely for social harmony and to bridge the distance between indigenous religious and ethnic communities, but for a variety of reasons concerning both the reinforcement of English political power in India and the European and English rediscovery of their intellectual and cultural past in India. The life and works of English Sanskritists such as Charles Wilkins, Warren Hastings and William Jones, and of officials like Reuben Burrow illustrate this trend.

Charles Wilkins, a Company civil servant and the first European to master Sanskrit, camped in Benares at his own request to learn that language.[132] In 1783 Hastings induced the supreme council to grant Wilkins leave of absence from his other duties on full salary to continue his studies in Benares.[133] The pandits of Benares, who had a history of assisting earlier rulers (such as Mughal prince Dāra Shikoh) with translations of Sanskrit texts,[134] extended their co-operation to Wilkins as well. Wilkins became an instant hit with local Brahmins, who brought their texts and offered their skills for his use. With their help he managed to undertake and successfully complete a series of important translation projects for the Company.[135]

Wilkins' favourite pandit Ca'shyna'th (Kashinath), who taught him Sanskrit and helped him with his translations, benefited in several ways from this association. His friendship with Wilkins brought him power and status in the new political configurations that the English were setting up in north India. Being Wilkins' pandit brought him to the immediate notice of other Company officials who used his contacts and linguistic expertise in identifying and selecting other qualified pandits for their translation work. Thus, in 1785, William Jones selected Goverdhan Caul (Kaul) Pandit for his translation of the Hindu law books, the latter having brought a certificate from Kashinath. Jones wrote to Wilkins: 'Goverdhan Caul Pandit has just brought a certificate of his qualifications to which I see the respectable signature of Ca'shyna'th, your pandit: if I give my voice in favour of Goverdhan it will be owing to the testimonial of the good man, who brought me 3 daisies at Benares, and of whose learning, since you employ him, I can have no doubt.'[136] Kashinath's power and status can be gauged from the fact that he was included in the committee of two to three 'learned pandits' that Jones invited to examine fresh pandit recruits.[137] In the context of this bonhomie between Kashinath and his English masters, it is not surprising that after settling down in Benares, a happy and satisfied Wilkins reported to Hastings that 'His habitation is becoming the resort of the learned men of Kasee.'[138]

Indeed, Hastings' patronage to the pandits and *munshīs* provided a larger umbrella for the reconstitution of the book bazaar and the literati that serviced it. As Robert Traverse argues, the orientalism of Hastings' regime was part of the bedding down of the Company government in Indian society both through the construction of colonial knowledge and by creating links between officials and Indian élites.[139] Hastings established contact with local learned men to translate and thus 'know' the administrative and legal texts of India. Despite initial opposition from the court of directors on account of the expense involved, Hastings managed to give the go ahead to Francis Gladwin, who completed a translation of the *Ā'īn* during Hastings' governor-generalship. A triumphant Hastings wrote to the court of directors about the significance of Gladwin's work: 'The work would prove of the utmost utility to the Company and would also aid in the promotion of the knowledge of Indian literature.'[140] Hastings' intention was clearly in sharp contrast to that of Akbar who, according to Abul Fazl, had had the *Mahābhārata* translated for the purpose of maintaining social harmony between Hindus and Muslims and other groups.

Alongside translations of Mughal texts, Hastings engaged pandits and *munshīs* to prepare the Hindu (Gentoo) law code and translations of the *Hidāya*.[141] As the patron figure for the pandits of north India, he established long-lasting contacts with a number of learned Hindus, beginning with the pandits who compiled the Hindu code. He was later able to persuade Radhakanta Sarman, 'a Brahmin of distinguished abilities, and highly revered by the Hindus in Bengal for his erudition and virtue', to produce an exposition of history based on the Puranas, which was translated into Persian. Radhakanta was given a grant of land worth Rs 1200 before Hastings left India. Another treatise on Hindu learning was translated from Sanskrit into Persian and compiled at Hastings' direction by a *munshī* called Karparam (Kripa Ram).[142]

Alongside this patronage of Hindu learning, Hastings, who had learnt to read Persian and speak Urdu, became an enthusiastic collector of Islamic art and literary culture.[143] When he eventually sold his collection to the East India Company it contained 190 volumes in Persian and Arabic, as well as Sanskrit and Hindi items.[144] The Arabic and Persian manuscripts ranged from works on history, grammar and medicine to an extensive collection of poetry graced by a magnificent illuminated *Shahnāma*, copied in 1560, and the *Kulliyāt-i-Sa'dī*.[145]

The same was true of William Jones, who relied on the intellectual labour of a range of pandits and Persianate scholars, whom he referred to as 'my private establishment of readers and writers'.[146] These included Tafazzul Husain Khan Kashmiri, Mir Muhammad Husain Isfahani, Bahman Yazdi, Ali Ibrahim Khan Bahadur (his well-known Sanskrit teacher pandit), Radhakant Sarman,[147] Ramlochan (his sixty-year-old teacher from Nadia), and his *munshī* Brahman.[148] In fact Jones was in contact with scholars of Persian even prior to his arrival in India in 1783.[149]

The British quest for indigenous texts and knowledge of India accelerated in the 1770s and 1780s as the Company's territorial expansion and political responsibilities increased, and as it came in the grip of a financial crisis at home and in India. It became imperative to ensure a regularity of revenue collection from India. For this purpose 'knowing the country' became a pressing necessity. The process went full steam after 1784 when, in the words of C.A. Bayly, the phase of 'constructive imperialism' began to tie the Company's India government with the British state.[150] In this 'authoritarian era of Hastings', as P.J. Marshall calls it, the search for Oriental texts gathered momentum.[151] It was this purposeful and authoritarin political tenor of the Company that shaped its intervention in the indigenous book bazaar of the eighteenth century. This drive to gain knowledge of the country followed a specific intellectual trajectory. Englishmen like Hastings, Wilkins and Jones belonged to the Oxonian élite of the eighteenth century that was obsessed with classical thought and scripture; indeed their education had been dominated by the study of Greek and Latin.[152] In India, their understanding of the country was shaped by this education and training. Sanskrit seemed to them to have the same relation to vernaculars that Greek and Latin had to contemporary European languages.[153] This perspective made them rely heavily on their subcontinental counterparts—Brahmins who knew Sanskrit and *ashrāf maulavīs* and *munshīs* who were adept in Arabic and Persian. Concomitant with this was their indifference to ordinary folk and the subaltern classes, whether at home or in India.[154] Their understanding of Indian society was thus largely based on scrutiny of classical Sanskrit texts, more specifically those they commissioned their Brahmin collaborators to translate. This also meant that their intervention in the book bazaar was guided by their relatively restricted intellectual gaze. This was most clearly evident in their interest in Indian legal texts. Between 1773 and 1775 about fifty legal treatises were produced for the British, compiled by 'pandits, translated into Persian by Zain ud-Din Ali Kasai and then to English in 1776 by Nathaniel Halhed as the Code of Gentoo Law.'[155]

British orientalist intervention also received impetus from the late-eighteenth and early-nineteenth-century conception that Europe would undergo a second Renaissance by studying the Orient, especially via Sanskrit and the *Vedas*, analogous with the study of Greek as the cause of the first Renaissance.[156] And so India and Sanskrit became the centres of a new Orientalism spearheaded by Charles

Wilkins, Warren Hastings and William Jones, and this was stimulated by the setting up of Asiatic societies in Europe and by the establishment of the Asiatic Society of Bengal at Calcutta, where British Sanskritists built up a large repository of Oriental collections.[157] The Company's dominant and overwhelming intrusion into the indigenous book bazaar, spearheaded by these Sanskritists, distinguished itself from pre-eighteenth century English forays and those of contemporary Europeans by its claims of 'knowing the country' through linguistic mastery of its 'mother' language, namely Sanskrit.[158] This interest in Sanskrit worked as a vanguard in the book bazaar, and had specific implications for the particular brand of Orientalist knowledge it generated. Hastings and Jones were of the view that knowledge of native languages was essntial for a 'reconciliation' of the people of England with the natives of Hindustan.[159] This reconciliation was to be with people that they saw clearly as either Hindus or Muslims. Thus they were of the view that indigenous learning was compartmentalized into the Hindu brand, written in Sanskrit, and the Islamic variety, recorded in Arabic and Persian.[160] This meant that they began to cut into a carefully crafted Indo-Islamic intellectual legacy which had a six-hundred-year-old history in India. The intellectual debates between Hindu and Muslim 'learned men' and British officers on matters of legal rights and privileges increased, at one level, the need to master Indian languages and unravel the mysteries of Oriental texts.[161] At another level it led to Muslims and Hindus being linguistically identified with Arabic and Persian, the language of Islamic texts, and Sanskrit, the language of Hindu texts. British interest in Sanskrit thereby calcified identities on religio-linguistic lines, and compartmentalized the book bazaar along religious denomination.[162]

Even as British reliance on Brahmins and *maulavīs* segregated indigenous learning, their suspicion of 'native' interpreters and translators remained constant. This suspicion prompted Jones to make Indian classical languages, especially Persian, accessible to Company officials. In 1771 he published *A Grammar of the Persian Language* for the use of Company officials. He made his intent clear in the preface: 'It was found highly dangerous to employ the natives as interpreters, upon whose fidelity they could not depend.' In 1782, for similar reasons, he published a literal metrical translation of a summary of the laws of inheritance according to the Shafi'ī school, Ibn-al Mulaqqin's *Bughayat al bāhith* and *Jumal al mawārith* for the use of Company officials.[163]

None of this affected the vibrancy of the bazaar. British Residents in Awadh like Middleton encouraged local transcribers, writers and collectors to satiate Hastings' appetite for Oriental texts. In 1781 Middleton gave an indication of the local expertise to which he had easy access when he sent a copy of the 'Ranjo-Turrunggheenee' (*Rājtranginī*), 'written as neatly as the shortness of the period in which it has been done and the number of different hands employed upon it would admit.' He offered that, if Hastings desired, another copy could be made with more care and in the handwriting of one man: 'I will not take more than a month or 6 weeks to complete it.'[164]

As news of the bazaar spread, men of linguistic skills often came from the distant Christian world seeking employment and dreaming of making fortunes. In 1779 the Pera of Constantinople sent to Hastings one Mr Diego Talamas, son of the chief interpreter of the holy land, bearing a letter of recommendation to assist him when seeking employment in India. This Talamas was said to be a 'perfect master of Arabic, Turkish, Greek, Armenian languages and also of French and Italian.' He came to India on account of the 'disagreeable and critical situation back home.'[165]

The Missionary Shoppers

A small number of Evangelical missionaries who appeared in India in the late eighteenth century—primarily due to the pressures exerted by Wilberforce, a personal friend of Pitt and Charles Grant, director and for many years chairman of the East India Company[166]—added a different kind of vibrancy to the indigenous book bazaar. These missionaries conducted a more indirect, camouflaged proselytizing exercise, pushing vociferously for the spread of English education in India. This was meant as the entry point by which indigenous societies were to be exposed to Christianity and thus freed from their own stifling and anarchic religions.[167]

In pursuing this exercise, missionaries like MacKinnon—who arrived in India in 1781 and toured north India—claimed they 'could not discover one article of dupical [sic] taste of the knowledge of mathematical truth or of genuine moral or religious principle in any class not in any individual of the human species born and educated in Hindustan or even in all Asia.'[168] Paradoxically, though MacKinnon attributed this absence of rational knowledge in India to the narrow intellectual vision of its people, which he argued was instilled by the restricted confines of their own language and texts, he appended to his observations a list of Arabic translations of Greek texts on rational sciences, mathematics, astronomy, etc. which he found in the library of the Nawab of Awadh in 1784. He also suggests awareness of the intellectual legacy of Indian Islam, observing that

although the Musalmans studied and acquired the Greek language at a former period yet the Koran has always prevented them from tasting the productions of the inspired poets, orators and legislators to the conception of which a knowledge and study of mythology as well as correct classical taste were necessary.[169]

These observations indicated that the missionaries were not unaware of the intellectual contours of eighteenth-century indigenous society. Yet, they made a strong case for the need to teach Indians the English, Latin and Greek languages and introduce Greek classics into the the local book bazaar[170] To this effect MacKinnon compiled a grammar of the English language, the rules and instructions of which were in the Persian language and character. This book was published in 1791 at the expense of the proprietors of the *Calcutta Gazette*, Harrington and Morris. He also compiled a version of this grammar in the Bengālī language, though it was never printed. MacKinnon obtained full support and encouragement for his activities from the government, and his efforts bore results: 'I can produce instances of individual natives who have acquired a competent knowledge of the English language by the help of my grammar.'[171] He was of the view that fuller results would be obtained only by the 'perusal of classical books'.[172] To this end he wanted Claude Martin's will to be interpreted in such a manner that his institution at Lucknow—with its collection of Greek and Arabic manuscripts—be converted into a seminary for the learning of the language and literature of the Greco-Hellenic and English world. He strongly protested against the Awadh administration's effort to sell off Martin's library.[173]

This missionary emphasis on Greco-Hellenic texts inadvertently resurrected the intellectual legacy of the Islamic world from which the eighteenth-century book mart derived its characteristic hue and which was of relatively little interest to British Sanskritists. Due to the seventeenth-century transition from Arabic to Persian as the language of the literati and administration, Arabic translations of several Greco-Hellenic texts were cheaply available at this time in north India.[174] Missionary intervention in the bazaar for books gave impetus to the market for such texts, which was in any case fast losing local patrons on account of the Company's political drive.[175]

Shoppers with a Difference: Reuben Burrow, Gentil and Polier

If the missionaries inadvertently resurrected the Islamic intellectual legacy in the book bazaar, and British Sanskritists began to compartmentalize indigenous learning into linguistically defined Hindu and Islamic categories, the introduction of private adventurers and entrepreneurs, both British and European, added a non-sectarian synthetic dimension. This circuit of men, none of whom claimed linguistic expertise in Sanskrit, Persian and Arabic, included most notably the distinguished British mathematician and astronomer and member of the Asiatic Society of Bengal whom we have mentioned, Reuben Burrow (1747–92),[176] and Frenchmen such as Polier, Madec, Gentil and Martin. For this galaxy of men, knowing the languages of India, collecting its texts, and promoting the work of translation was as important as to 'know the people'—as it had been for British Sanskritists. In fact Burrow, who arrived in India in 1783 at the suggestion of Henry Watson, the chief engineer of Fort William, to pick up whatever he could, lamented the Company's lack of interest in the study of Sanskrit. He argued that after Wilkins no serious effort had been made by the Company to undertake translations from Sanskrit. He was of the view that sales of translated works in Europe were low and that therefore the Company's inducements for such works had remained low-key. He strongly suggested to the Company that the Sanskrit language be promoted and direction given for the discovery, collection and translation of whatever was extant of the ancient works of the Hindus. From this effort would emerge their history and their scientific theories, which would benefit Europe. He interested himself in Hindu astronomy and expressed his keenness to visit the pandits of Benares in order to obtain the 'ancient literature of the Hindoos'.[177]

However, there were important points of difference between Burrow and the British Sanskritist Orientalist. First, the link between certain languages and religious identities were nowhere narrowly and rigidly demarcated in Burrow's thought. Sanskrit as the language of only the Hindus and Persian as well as Arabic as the language of only Islamic texts and Muslims were not views that Burrow held. This also meant that Hindu and Muslim texts and traditions of learning were not viewed by him as neatly defined and compartmentalized. In his report on the Benares observatory and the astronomical knowledge of the Brahmans of Benares, Burrow makes it very clear that

Brahmanical knowledge is heavily influenced by the Greco-Arabic learning traditions of the Islamic world.[178] Second, linguistic expertise was not projected as the only requirement to know the people and politics of the country. Instead, knowledge of indigenous people was, implicit in this view, best acquired through interaction with not only Hindu and Muslim learned men but with a range of people, cutting across communities, who were seen as embodiments of the heterogeneous cultural layerings that constituted indigenous knowledge. *I'jāz-i Arsalānī* has information about indigenous society being derived from not only literate Hindu and Muslim élites, but from a cross-section of people who are never identified within religious categories. Similarly, Burrow's *Journal* describes encounters with all kinds of people as he travelled upcountry from Bengal and Bihar, conducting astronomical surveys and carrying out his search for manuscripts of traditional scientific learning. Even though he was looking for the Sanskrit manuscripts of 'Hindus', the *Journal* has fascinating accounts of his dialogue with indigenous mathematicians, astronomers, and rajas who often gifted him their astronomical manuscripts. These encounters fed his search for manuscripts of indigenous learning, but he evinces no appetite for denominating these astronomers, mathematicians and cooperative rajas in religious terms. The manuscripts that he collects in the name of the indigenous scientific literature of the 'Hindus' range from Sanskrit books to the *Ā'īn-i-Akbarī*. The latter was gifted to him by the ruler of Rampur, Faizullah Khan, who said that 'He had a book containing many latitudes and longitudes, which he would make me a present of, if I would accept it.'[179]

Free from the constraints of providing the requisite knowledge that would help tide away the Company's financial deficit and tighten its grip on the administration, men like Burrow and Polier generally, offered a more flexible and negotiable forum for interaction with the locals, unmediated by 'learned' men. Thus Burrow recommended to Hastings a regular astronomical survey to serve as a foundation for the geography of India, showing scant appreciation of the early surveys done by Company surveyors like James Rennell who had relied considerably on information derived from 'Hindu' and 'Muslim' learned men.[180]

In a letter to Warren Hastings written in 1783, Burrow explains his quest for the restoration of the texts and books of this ancient civilization. He says his quest is driven by the fact that he found in the works of ancient philosophers, thinkers and mathematicians (like Archimedes and Apollonius) a brevity and clearness of investigation and methodical superiority that he found lacking in the writings of modern thinkers. This, he says, convinced him that 'if the elegance and perspicuity of the ancients could be combined with the certainty and expedition of the moderns, mathematical knowledge might be greatly improved and exploited.'[181] Enthused with this spirit he left his family back in England and set off towards India:

> As I looked upon it as of some consequence to the world and was by this time convinced of the possibility of the existence of several of those manuscripts supposed to be left, I concluded that the best method of answering every purpose would be to go to the East Indies for a few years.[182]

He planned to visit Arabia, Persia, Tartary and other parts of the world later and then return to England to 'employ the remainder of my life in publishing such things as I might meet with and finishing such of my own productions as should not be precluded by those I might chance to discover.'[183] Burrow asked for Hastings' assistance in this endeavour but was convinced of going ahead with his plans anyway because, as he said, 'India was the parent of the sciences' and Europe was still ignorant of its literary treasures (except for the translation of the Code of Gentoo law).[184]

For men like Burrow Indian texts were not essential for purposes of good governance, nor was theirs the curiosity of a connoisseur about Indian civilization. It was a much wider, all-embracing intellectual interest—reminiscent of the Renaissance attitude—in which India was relevant for a better understanding of the origins of European civilization. More important was the fact that underneath their quest for texts of the history, natural sciences, astronomy and mathematics of the 'Hindus' lay a more general sensitivity about the historical process that had gone into their making. Burrow suggests a strong awareness of the Islamic intellectual legacy which underlay the Indo-Persian literature available in the local book bazaar. He is very clear that these 'Indian' texts reveal a distinct Greco-Roman imprint—a cultural strand which had become part of the Islamic intellectual ambit since the eighth century—as well as a Persian and Arabic intellectual flavour. He is convinced that the mathematical and astronomical manuscripts of Arabian mathematicians (who incorporate the learning of Greek mathematicians like Archimedes and Euclid) are all to be found in the Indies.[185] He observes that the Brahmins of Benares used algebraic formulae which derived from a familiarity with the Netwtonian doctrine of 'series' to compute eclipses, and that this knowledge was a consequence of interaction with Arabic treatises in their possession.[186] Through the Arab manuscripts they had gained familiarity with the thirteen books of the Greek mathematician Diophantus. Seven of his books were lost, but the remaining six were in circulation.[187]

Thus, to a large extent the quest for oriental manuscripts by men like Burrow was informed not so much by administrative and political concerns as by the cultural experience of rediscovering European texts in their original, or first Arabic or Latin translation, in the Orient. This was an intellectual hunt triggered by sensitivity to the historical processes that shaped the spread of Islamic civilization across parts of the medieval Euopean world. Of course, the rediscovery of these texts had a commercial dimension as well: they fetched the discoverers lucrative profits in the markets of Europe.

Burrow argued that, in view of the intellectual imprint of the larger Islamic world on Hindu manuscripts and the similarities between the religious and political traditions of ancient Egypt and Hindu civilization, it was evident that the latter was constituted of layerings of different cultural encounters which dated to antiquity.[188] With this more synthetic understanding of Hindu civilization, Burrows moved beyond the narrow geographical and cultural confines which British Sanskritists had sketched for it. Indian civilization was seen as integral to the cultural rythms of the ancient world. Even though we do not have more illustrations from other European writings, it will not be unfair to speculate that such a thinking may have made men like Burrow pivots for the promotion of a more syncretic and outward-looking Hindu learning in eighteenth-century north India. For Burrow 'the histories, the poems, the traditions and the very tables of the Hindoos might therefore throw light upon the history of the ancient world and particularly upon the institutions of the celebrated people from whom Moses received his learning and Greece her religion and arts.'[189]

Even as Burrow locates indigenous learning as an interaction with the larger intellectual world of Islamic civilization, he cannot escape segregating Hindu and Muslim learning entirely: linguistically he identifies it exclusively with Sanskrit and its producers and consumers as primarily Hindus. For all this seeming ambivalence and confusion, the fact remains that Burrow familiarized Hastings with his larger view of Hindu learning and presented him with memoranda on Hindu astronomy in order to suggest that there was much that the West could profitably learn from it.[190]

Englishmen like Burrow were assisted in their quest for a more broad-based and all-encompassing Hindu intellectual tradition by like-minded Frenchmen. One important French contact of Burrow was Monsieur Gentil. This Frenchman was in the service of Nawab Shuja-ud-Daula. In 1772 Gentil brought with him from the coast of Coromandel astronomical tables of the Brahmins of Tirvalour. He passed these on to Burrow, along with his illustrations of their mode of calculation.[191] Gentil's discovery generated interest in the English astronomers' circle and led one of them, Bailey, to examine certain astronomical tables which had been recovered from Siam as far back as 1687. This work, with his inferences and remarks, was considered with much attention at Edinburgh.[192] The partnership of men like Burrow and Gentil in such exchange of knowledge was of some significance, specially as Gentil worked for a French patron, Anquetil Duperron, and thus represented a rival power. What they were creating was a shared perspective on the elements that constituted Indian history and civilization.

Gentil's interests were apparent during his stint in Awadh; he spent twelve years at Faizabad as a captain in the French service, representing French interests. Shuja-ud-Daula honoured him with the title of Mudabbir-ul-mulk Rafi-ud-Daula Gentil Bahadur Nazim-i-Jang and revenue amounting to 50,000 livres in the form of *jāgīr.*[193] It was at the behest of Duperron that he searched out manuscripts of Indian texts, including the Upanishads, of which Duperron was to publish a Latin translation at Strasbourg in 1801.[194] Significantly, Gentil had sought out the Persian translation (*entitled Sirr-i-Akbar*) made of the Upanishads by Dara Shikoh in the seventeenth century, for his patron's use. He also supervised the production of a manuscript atlas of the chief provinces of the Mughal empire, using information drawn in part from Abul Fazl's *Ā'īn-i Akbarī*)[195] On his return to France he put down his *memoires sur l'Indoustan,* which were published in 1822 after being reworked by his son. Earlier, in 1778, on the occasion of his audience with Louis XIV at Versailles, he presented the monarch a summary history of India (the *Abrege historique des souverains de l'Indoustan*) based on the early-seventeenth century Persian chronicle of Abu'l Qasim Hindushah (better known as 'Ferishta').

The siege of Benares by the English seems to have pushed Gentil to amass some of the masterpieces to be found in India—coins,

Specimen of calligraphy *(naskh)*

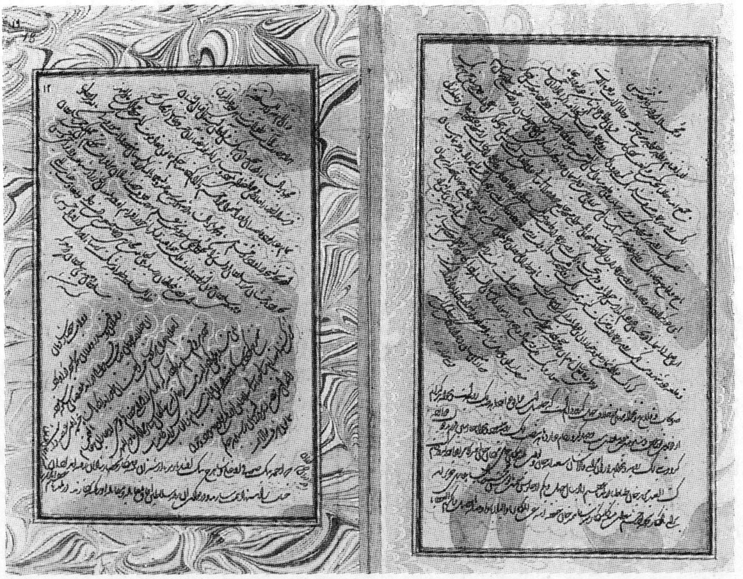

Specimen of calligraphy *(shikast)*

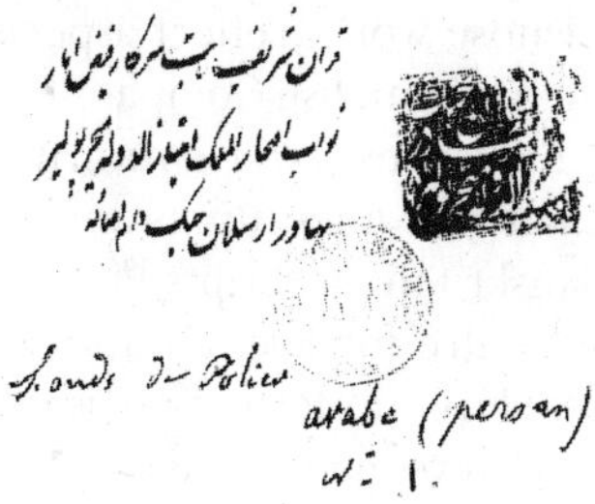

Polier's seal on the cover page of a copy of Qur'an

A page from Qur'an with Persian translation

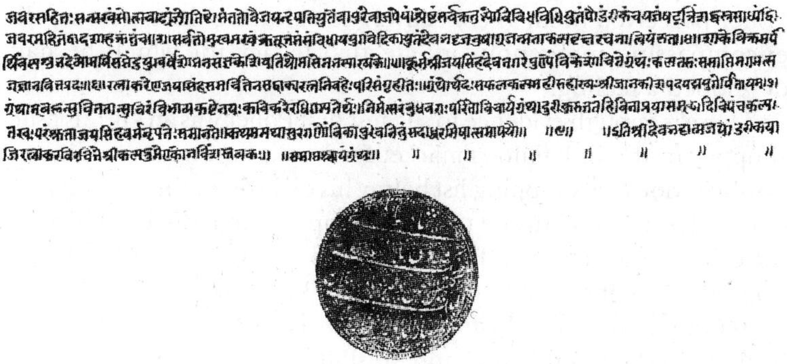

Polier's seal on the last page of Sanskrit text

miniatures and oriental manuscripts. He also hired three artists who worked with him for ten years and whose works reflect aspects of court, city and countryside. In 1775, when the English Company forced the nawab to sack all Frenchmen, Gentil was exiled. He returned to France financially ruined but with cases full of paintings and more than a hundred Persian, Urdu and Sanskrit manuscripts.[196]

Pondicherry emerged as a major centre for French interest in oriental manuscripts and miniatures. Here, under the aegis of the Jesuits, many translations of Indian texts were made. And there is the instance of Father Tieffenthaler, who travelled in the Indo-Gangetic belt, lived in Narwar as the bishop of a parish (comprising a few French-speaking Catholics), and was keenly interested in geography. When he settled in Lucknow he sent maps and geographical descriptions to Duperron, who had them edited in Berlin in 1791.[197] Such exercises were curtailed after the 1733 French defeat at the hands of the English.

Polier's Orient

An important constituent in the Burrow–Gentil network of knowledge transmission that transcended political rivalries was Polier. In the manner of Burrow and other such Europeans in India, Polier showed sensitivity towards the more syncretic and assimilative Islamic intellectual legacy that the Mughals had nurtured. He did not compartmentalize indigenous texts into Hindu and Muslim categories. Both the *Vedas* and the *Qur'ān,* as well as Persian manuscripts like the *Gulistān-i-Sa'dī,* were equally sought after by him. Polier perceived them as collectively constituting the syncretic, all-encompassing indigenous intellectual legacy for which he had developed a feeling.

There is enough evidence to suggest that Polier was an enthusiastic shopper in the indigenous market for books and manuscripts, yet nowhere does his shopping list betray his division of this market into one for Hindu and Muslim texts. This impression is discernible from the oriental collections of Polier, amassed during his career in India, housed in his library at Lucknow, in the Bibliothèque Cantonale of Lausanne, and in the British Museum. He never seems to make distinctions between Hindu and Muslim texts.[198]

Rather, Polier's collection reflects his appreciation and acceptance of the Islamic intellectual legacy which the Mughals promoted and which had by the seventeenth century come to constitute the dominant

Mughal literary culture. In the manner of Mughal literary repositories, Polier collected a nice mix of books on Islamic theology, religious texts like the *Qur'ān* and *Ḥadīṣ* (tradition) and, alongside, Persian translations of Greco-Hellenic manuscripts on reason, rationality, logic, science and astronomy. Later divided between the libraries of Eton College and Kings College, Cambridge, the collection included several copies of a Persian translation of the *Qur'ān*, Traditions of the Prophet compiled by Ataullah al-Shirazi and Muhammad al-Farabi, and collections of prayers for Shī'as such as the *Aḥkām-i Ziyārat-i Ḥaẓrat Imām Ḥusain*. Also included were manuscripts on the principles of governance, Persian manuscripts on Islamic law—such as two volumes of the *Fatāwā-i-'Ālamgīrī* and the *al-Sirāj al Munīr*. Arabic and Persian manuscripts on Sufism such as Muhammad Al-Ghazali's *Kīmiyā i-Sa'ādat* and Dara Shikoh's *Majma' al-Baḥrain*, and the Arabic manuscript of '*Awārif al Ma'ārif* of Suhrawardi were also found here.[199] The Kings College Collection also held Arabic manuscripts of Islamic theology like the *Iḥyā-i-'ulūm al-Dīn*, being a work comprising the system of medieval theology by al-Ghazali; and *Ufq-i Mubīn*—a treatise on the Muslim faith by Mir Baqir *Dāmād*. Polier's catalogue reveals that like the Mughals he too did not see any contradiction between collecting Persian and Arabic manuscripts of the *Qur'ān, Ḥadīṣ* on the one hand and being enthusiastic about the Persian translation of the *Mahābhārata* and other Hindu texts.[200] This list is testimony of Polier's inheritance of a world-view in which the indigenous intellectual tradition is all-encompassing and uncompartmentalized. Persian translations of Sanskrit religious and scientific texts exist here without giving any sense of being 'Hindu' texts. His successful hunt for the *Vedas* indicates that he viewed this text as an integral part of the Indo-Persian intellectual tradition. He went to great efforts to translate the *Rāmāyana* and the *Gīta*, his pandit Ramachandra reciting these texts to him while he himself translated them into French:

> I took Ramchand home; he never left me, I plunged into the work and I wrote under his dictation... the complete system. What it was originally, its variations—very different from the ideas of it that one forms in Europe... Like a majority of Europeans I had believed Hindus to be polytheist, but I see now the base of the mythology is an invisible being... eternal supreme and the source of all else.[201]

Polier's collection of historical text was also quintessentially Mughal in its eclecticism. It included: Arabic and Persian manuscripts of general histories of the world like *Ṭabaqāt 'Abd al-Karīm* or *al Ṭabaqāt al Maḥmūd-Shāhiyyah,* a general history brought down to 905 AH; *Mir'āt-al 'Alam* by Bakhtawar Khan, composed for Alamgir and brought down to his time; *Muntakhab-al-Tawārīkh* by Hasan Kaki of Shiraz which is a universal history down to 1060 and many others of this genre.[202] To these more general histories were added several books on the history of the larger Islamic world which included Persia and Central Asia. The books on Persian history included *Tārīkh-i- 'Ālam Ārā* by Fazli Isfahani, an account of the affairs of the Safavids; the *Tārīkh-al-Mu'jam fi āṣār-i Mulūk al 'Ajam,* the history of the Kings of Persia; the *Dīwān-i-Āhī* (the Dīwān of Jalal Asir of Isfahan) and *Sharḥ-i-Zij -i-Ulughbegī* being the commentary on the astronomical tables of Ulugh Beg by Abd ul-Ali bin Muhammad Husain Barjanzi.[203] Finally, the collection had a rich component of Persian books on the history of India. These included both the general histories of the Sultanate [204] as well as the chronicles, treatises and histories such as *Tūzuk-i-Jahāngīrī,* the Persian version of *Tūzuk-i-Bābarī;* [205] *Akbarnāma,* the *Ā'īn-i-Akbarī, 'Ālamgīrnāma* of Muhammad Kazim; *Farrukh Siyarnāma,* being the history of Farrukhsiyar; *Bayān-i-Wāqi'* also called *Tārīkh-i Nādirī* by Abd al-Karim of Kashmir.[206]

In short, Polier's location of Indian literary culture and civilization within a larger intellectual legacy and the historical contours of medieval Islamic Empires suggest an understanding of Indian society more complex and nuanced than that of both his contemporaries and even of Burrow. Burrow, like Polier, seems to have viewed Hindu culture as heavily influenced by Greco-Hellenic and Islamic traditions; but he also saw Sanskrit as the language of Hindus and thus their texts as linguistically cordoned off. In the 1780s Polier too, under the influence of William Jones, drifted towards learning Sanskrit and engaged himself in getting the *Mahābhārata* translated. Yet he remained more solidly a believer of and cultural shareholder in the larger tradition of an Indo-Islamic ethos.

Polier's Intervention: Arts and Crafts

A good example of Polier's sensitivity to Mughal cultural practice was his patronage of local painters, who provided him miniatures of local historical figures and rulers. Mehrchand of Faizabad was one such.[207] In the manner of Mughal patrons, Polier commissioned portraits of èlites irrespective of their religious and caste background, with only their names written behind the paintings. Of these he ordered about 96. This neutrality contrasts with British commissionings, where the caste and community of the subject was always stated at the bottom or back of the paintings.[208] In the manner of the Mughals, Polier took care over the aesthetics of their bindings and in the making of these albums. In a letter to Mehrchand he writes, 'The decorator should decorate on the reverse of the bindings,'[209] and in another he says:

> Call the binder and ask him to prepare three albums for them according to their different size. . . an excellent artistic touch should be given to the parchment paper on the paste board (*pushta-i waṣlīhā*). Then note down the name of the person at the back of each portrait on a separate piece of paper, to be [finally] written on the pasteboard. . . [210]

Under his Persianate veneer Polier was subtly influencing artistic and literary styles. Art historians have noted a distinct European imprint on the paintings of Polier's artist Mehrchand.[211] Mehrchand had no formal training in the European technique (as had Awadh artists like Nivasi Lal), yet under his aegis new styles of miniature painting evolved in Awadh which were a mixture of indigenous and European art. The method adopted was gouache: a mixture of minerals, vegetable and animal pigment mixed with gum Arabic, often embellished with gold and silver, was applied to a paper or cloth support.[212] The greatest range of Mehrchand's works originally assembled for Polier are to be found in the Hamilton Albums at Berlin. This collection includes several which were part of Polier's collection at Lausanne and were bought by William Beckford in 1802.[213] One of these albums, comprising Mughal portraits in the Hamilton Collection, was presented to Polier by Emperor Shah Alam in 1181 Hijri (1767–68). No special occasion is mentioned in the album for the conferment of this gift, but Polier's important position in Calcutta may have been an incentive for the gift.

That Polier was not content merely to preserve these Mughal portraits and left his own imprint on them is evident from the portrait of the Mughal prince Khusrau—labelled in this collection as 'Khusro—the unlucky'. On the right margin of this painting there is Persian handwriting, identified as Jahangir's; on the lower margin of the painting there is writing in French, identified as that of Polier. In these early collections Polier wrote in French, whereas in the later acquisitions his comments are invariably in Persian.

Three other albums put together by Polier include two comprising Mughal calligraphy, dated 1776 and 1780–84/5. These were possibly done during his stay in Delhi. One of them includes two beautiful calligraphies by Dara Shikoh. It is possible that these were passed on to Polier because they were being protected by the emperor's family. It is noted in this album that Polier possessed them from 'six years before'.[214] An important letter by Polier to Mehrchand indicates that these albums were probably dispatched to Lucknow for restoration by professional artists. Polier gives instructions to Mehrchand for payments due on account of the repair of the *qit'as* (calligraphed verses). He instructs him to 'keep all the albums (*muraqqa's*) and calligraphed verses in one box carefully fixed so that they are safe from the dust and do not get damaged in transit.' Further, he is advised to 'load them together with the boxes for the Persian books and fix them there [tightly]' and bring them along with him to Delhi.[215]

Finally, Polier's collection includes an album of miniatures of Indians and Britishers. This was probably put together during his long stay in Lucknow, where he commissioned local artists like Mehrchand to produce portraits of local rulers and Englishmen. Interestingly, the portraits that Polier commissioned Mehrchand to draw include those of Shuja-ud-Daula, Hindu rajas, and British officials like Warren Hastings. These portraits appear to be inspired directly by the works of the English portrait painter, Tilly Kettle, who visited the Faizabad court in 1771–72.[216] It is possible that the requisition of portrait paintings by Polier encouraged local artists to learn from Kettle as well as other English artists who visited the region.

Polier's corrspondence with his craftsmen, who were scattered about north India, indicate his perpetual dissatisfaction with their made-to-order preparations. Particularly interesting in this context are letters of complaint to his craftsman Mir Muhammad Azim for not making the *'amārī* and *ḥauda* conform to his taste and requirements.[217] An angry Polier describes the problems with the *'amārī*: 'The *'amārī* that you have sent is very small: its roof and the planks used are thin, and the narrowness has made it inconvenient. The *ḥauda* which is being prepared should not be like this. It should be strong, spacious and convenient to ride.'[218] When, despite his instructions, the *ḥauda* does not conform to his style, he says:

> I had asked you to prepare a *ḥauda* because the *'amārī* that you had earlier sent was small by two *girah* (about four inches) and was inconvenient to rides. The new *ḥauda* that has now arrived here is big by two *girah* and has an inconvenient wooden back support. Further, you have got it knitted with cane which is difficult to find everywhere. You should have used *nivar* which is easily obtainable. It is strange that you have not followed my advice.[219]

Again, in a series of orders to the same craftsman, and to Mir Muhammad Salah, the engraver, and to Muhammad Azim, the binder, Polier sends specific design instructions for engravings, ornaments and seals which suggest he was attempting to improvise on the prevalent styles. For instance, Mir Muhammad Azim is asked to engrave the motif of a fish and a lion on the handle of a knife. Fish motifs on artifacts were a common feature in Awadh, but the introduction of the lion seems to be Polier's introduction; or alternatively an idea he shared with Claude Martin, who used the lion motif as a reminder of Lyons, his birthplace. Similarly, very specific instructions for the stitching of the *shamiana* (canopy)—its colour combinations and patterns—are dispatched to a craftsman at Lucknow:

> The upper part of the *bichūba* [small tent without the wooden poles] under the flap of the bigger tent should be of white cloth with multicolour prints. The inside of the tent should be made of only the printed cloth. As for the *qanāt* [walls of the tent] Manik Ram had instructed you earlier to make it of four parts but now I think you should make them of six parts with each part measuring 15 yards. . . The floor mats (*shaṭranjī*) should be pink and blue in colour. . .[220]

These letters to craftsmen, giving instructions on minute details of colour, design and styles and relating to items ranging from the '*amārī* and the *hauda* to mats, tents and ornaments, stand out in their precision and intricate detail. Such details are frequently repeated in letter after letter addressed to the same craftsman over a period of time. The letters suggest that Polier is introducing new designs in the craft bazaar, a process which the craftsmen are taking time to adjust to and at which Polier is impatient. The letters indicate Polier's obsession with high standards of perfection and irritation at craftsmen who do not conform to these.

Modifications to existing artistic styles is again evident in the realm of architecture, where Polier's instructions to his agent, Oshra Gora Mistri, for the construction of four houses and the layout of their gardens, though rich in minute details, reflect the same anxiety and impatience as his letters to the craftsmen.[221] Here, Polier insists that his *ḥavelī* must have concrete walls and a concrete floor.[222] He sends specific instructions and material from Lucknow for the construction of the *bāradarī*.[223] The most clear instruction for the emulation of the European style bird-houses comes in a letter to Oshra Gora Mistri, where the latter is instructed to construct bird-houses on the pattern of those in Monsieur Gentil's house: 'The partridge house should be modelled on the one in the house of Monsieur Gentil. It should have small windows with wire nets. The house for the water fowls should have a small concrete tank for bathing and drinking purposes.'[224] Rosie Llewellyn-Jones' work on Nawābī Lucknow suggests that Asaf-ud-Daula's taste for European architectural patterns was probably due to the influence of French advisors like Polier.[225] The clearest of Polier 's interventions lies perhaps in horticulture; he makes local gardeners plant European saplings in his garden. In a letter to Oshra Gora Mistri he writes: 'The European seeds which had been sown earlier have not sprouted at all. Hand over the remaining seeds to the gardeners and ask them to take appropriate measures. The sowing of the European seeds and the planting of the grape saplings should be done as per my earlier instructions.'[226]

The Eighteenth-Century Library of Social Categories

British ideas about Indian castes, races and ethnic groups are viewed as having developed out of a dialogical process between colonial and indigenous society.[227] In a recent book C.A. Bayly has attempted to locate this colonial discourse within its specific social and political context. He dates its emergence to the early-nineteenth-century shift from 'affective' knowledge informing Company rule to the setting up of 'knowledgeable institutions': the army, revenue, legal and educational establishments.[228]

Early British institutions, particularly the army, were indeed central to the evolution of colonial discourse on caste, race and community. But the setting up of the Bengal Army—to which Polier belonged—indicates that the British understanding of indigenous social identities itself emerged in the late eighteenth century as a consequence of military recruitment. The variety of British notions about indigenous people derived from the specific social and political context in which the military traditions of the Bengal Army were entrenched. The tenor of this colonial discourse was heavily influenced also by the personal ideological dispositions of individual British and European military officers and their engagement with the socio-cultural context in which they were posted. The regional diversities from which the Company recruited its different regiments provided critical arenas in which the British either successfully located and plugged into local networks of 'knowledgeable institutions' that had already initiated new identity formations in the region, or else failed to do so.

The former process was evident in the Gangetic plains where the high-caste defined armies of the Benares Raja, Chait Singh, provided Warren Hastings the model which conformed to his own Brahmanical notions of social hierarchy. Alongside, the peasant base of the raja's regiments also corresponded to the general British experience with yeomen soldiers in their own armies. The eighteenth-century development of the discourse on caste was a consequence of military recruitment which used to its full advantage the indigenous military traditions which had already begun to shape caste identities in the region.

The British failure to make adequate use of local networks of knowledgeable institutions was most clear beyond the Gangetic plains, in the Jungle Tarai. Here, such institutions were either not easily accessible or else incomprehensible because of being different from the mainstream overarching Brahmanical tradition for which early British administrators had developed a textual feel. In this fringe area, realizing the inadequacy of caste as a sociological tool for understanding the tribal polities of the region, the discourse on the Indian 'savage' and the 'civilizing' mission of the British began to be articulated through military recruitment. The vocabulary of this discourse derived solely from the personal ideological dispositions of Augustus Cleveland, the first British Collector and architect of the Hill Corps in the Jungle Tarai.

Finally, in the post-Mughal capital of Lucknow and the important erstwhile Mughal *ṣūba* of Awadh, the social identifiers continued to be the caste-and community-neutral categorizations that the Mughals had popularized in the region. Here, the Company's French officers appropriated these identifiers with relative ease because of their own familiarity with marking status and identity in terms of an individual's relationship to court societies. Thus Polier appeared to reflect a greater sensitivity to the processes of identity formations, based on an individual's relationship to court society, that the Mughals had unleashed in the Gangetic plains. Polier's cultural world as gleaned through the *I'jāz* stands in sharp contrast to that of his English contemporaries. Yet, the cultural contour he defines for himself does not stand in isolation. In Company officialdom his vision is stringed together with those of other Company officials, like Hastings and Cleveland, who do not necessarily share his world-view. Together, these diverse perspectives constitute a sociology of colonial knowledge which is in the making in this early period of British rule. The *I'jāz*

MYTHOLOGIE

DES INDOUS;

travaillée

par

Mdme. la Chnsse. de Polier,

sur des Manuscrits authentiques apportes de l'Inde

par

feu Mr. le Colonel de Polier,

Membre de la Societé Asiatique de Calcutta.

Tome premier.

A ROUDOLSTADT,
a la librairie de la cour, et.

A PARIS,
chés F. Schoell, Libraine. Rue des Fossés
St. Germain l'Auxerrois No. 29.
1809.

Title page of the first edition of *Mythologie des Indous*

Sati (painting)

thus represents one important form of cultural negotiation with indigenous society.

Polier and the Indian Social Categories

In the core areas of the erstwhile Mughal empire Mughal categorizations of society continued into the colonial period. In the Agra–Delhi–Awadh region Polier appropriated the prevalent language and culture of the imperial court. In the *I'jāz*, vocational identities are the primary identifiers of people. Polier's appreciation as well as reprimands to people are couched in the elitist, urbane but caste-and community-neutral vocabulary which had gained currency under the Mughals. Thus 'gentlemanly' behaviour, 'candour', and 'loyalty' (*maḥabbat, khulūṣ, ikhlāṣ, sharāfat*) are preferred phrases which occur in the text and, as in Mughal times, they here connote proper conduct. Polier appears to continue the pre-colonial cultural value code and identity markers—which the British understood differently and eventually transformed.[229]

Polier's European background made him give importance to court culture, and this coincided with the prevailing methods of expressing an individual's relationship to the court. He was also impressed by the politics of a minority Muslim ruling house which strove to co-ordinate varied ethnic and religious groups so as to sustain its rule. The Mughal policy of compromise and cooperation with indigenous social groups was bound to appeal to someone who himself belonged to a minority, both in France and in India.

Polier's political and trading agents are a nice mix of Christians, Hindus and Muslims from upper north India, Bihar and Bengal. The absence in the text of allusion to their religious, caste or community identity gives the impression that Polier was indifferent to these sorts of differences that may have existed between them. Dīwān Manik Ram, Polier's trusted agent, is a Bengālī. The text does not refer to his linguistic, ethnic, regional or religious identity, whereas his professional title, *Dīwān,* is always prefixed to his name so as to establish his identity in vocational terms. The same is true of Ras Bhihari Sarkar and Nidhiram Sarkar, his agents in Awadh and Faizabad. In the text Shiv Prasad, the *gumāshta* of the *kothī* of Awadh, and the *gumāshtas* Ram Sunder Datt and Kali Prasad, of Faizabad, and Mayachand Sahu of Agra, are as trusted, appreciated and reprimanded as his Muslim trading partners—Mir Muhammad Azim in Awadh, Mir Sulaiman Khan in Patna, Mirza Abdullah Beg *kumaidān* in Agra, and Mir Muhammad

Husain Ata Khan and Mir Waliullah Khan in the Farrukhabad area. When suggesting the names of two recruits to be enlisted as *kumaidāns* he makes his recommendation on the basis of their intelligence and experience.[230] In a letter to Mir Sulaiman Khan he makes his observations about local people in caste-and community-neutral terms:

> There is nothing new to report, but I have observed that people here are of a strange nature and are not trustworthy. When they observe someone's rising fortune they praise him keeping their hand on the head. But when someone is cursed with divine wrath the whole world puts its foot on his head.[231]

Several of these letters show that Polier's image of local people is based on their relationship to success and power, not on their status within the *varna* hierarchy. His preferred language of appreciation or reprimand for these deploys a vocabulary which identifies them in terms of the professions they pursue and relates to them on professional grounds. Their conduct is judged by using the urbane and upper-class notions of 'proper conduct' which the Mughals had popularized in the region: gentlemanliness, trustworthiness, loyalty, intelligence and honesty. Dereliction of duty means to Polier a violation of the norms of 'intelligence', 'candour' and gentlemanliness' that constitute 'proper and good' conduct. He reprimands Mir Muhammad Azim, the craftsman of Lucknow, for the undue delay in the preparation of the orders placed for various goods: 'I sent several letters to you but none of them has been acknowledged by you, nor has there been any information regarding the preparation of the things [that were ordered]. This is not commensurate with your intelligence (*īn ma'nī khilāf az dānāi īshān ast*)'.[232] Mayachand Sahu, an agent, is admonished when he delays the dispatch of goods from Agra: 'There cannot be any justification for the delay in getting ready such a small order. Clearly then, you are issuing false statements which does not behove a *mahajan* (*ba'īd az shīwa-i-mahājanī*)'.[233] Finally, when he dispatched a substandard consignment he is told: 'The goods that you sent were useless (*nākāra-i-mahaz*). I had thought that you were a clever (*fahmīda-o-hushiār*) person, and to prepare such [useless] things is not becoming of a man of your intelligence and wisdom (*dānāi-o-farāsat*)'.[234] He lashes out at a craftsman thus: 'The embroiderer (*naqqāsh*) is a bastard (*harāmzadgī*) and will be punished (*sazā, tambīh-i wāqi'ī*) accordingly.'[235]

Significantly, Jats and Rohillas are the only two social groups identified as ethnic categories and stereotyped according to their racial/community type. Even though British ethnographers in India, such as Robert Orme, had begun to discuss ethnic stereotypes as early as the mid-eighteenth century, yet they had classified their ethnic types on climatic and dietary factors.[236] In Polier's text, war and the battlefront constitute the context in which Jats and Rohillas are seen as a community and stereotyped as 'cheats' and 'plunderers' (*qaum-i-Jāt-hama-hā-ghanīm wa daghā-bāz-and*) 'doomed' and 'accursed'.[237] This categorization emerges when Polier is assisting Najaf Khan in breaking the siege at Agra, where the fort had been taken over by Jats.[238] In another letter to Manik Ram he calls Jats robbers and disrupters who have blocked a road leading to Delhi.[239] He similarly castigates the Rohillas, who are fighting the armies of his master Shuja-ud-Daula in 1774, as 'mischievous' (*shaqāwat pazoh*) Rohillas'.[240] Their leader Hafiz Rahmat Khan is portrayed dispprovingly by playing upon the three basic letters, *ḥa, fa* and *za,* of his name, i.e. Hafiz, which means the one who provides security, is (ironically) the 'insecure (*nā maḥfūz*) Hafiz'.[241]

This categorization of Jats and Rohillas is similar to the Mughal image of these social groups. *Taẕkirat al-Salāṯīn Chaghtā* and *Bayān-i-Wāqiʿ*, the eighteenth-century Persian texts, bracket Jats with robbers (*rahzanān-wa-jātān*) and call them the 'misguided community' (*ṯāifa-i-ẕālla-i-Jātān*). They are also referred to as the 'accursed ones' (*makhāẕīl*), betrayers (*harāmkhor*) and robbers, and referred to as the 'faithless ones' (*Rohīlā-i-bedīn*).[242]

Polier's vocational categorization of his own associates is distinct from his use of the Mughal classification of Jats and Rohillas as ethnic types, and this latter happens when he joins the service of Shah Alam in Delhi. Once in Delhi, Polier shows sensitivity to the regional identities that had begun to assert themselves from the early eighteenth century. In a letter to Manik Ram, reporting on the affairs of the Delhi court, he writes: 'Here in Delhi the Kashmiris are in control (*darbār-i-Kashmīriyān ast*). And I have neither a Kashmiri nor Bengali. If you find people like that who can manage my work then send them.'[243] Here he appears to have appropriated the eighteenth-century Mughal categorization of ethnic types. He also seems to have continued with the indigenous image of these communities: Bengālīs and Kashmīrīs are projected as diligent, Jats and Rohillas as plunderers and robbers.

His image of Jats and Rohillas seems to have come about as a consequence of his close association with the armies of Shuja-ud-

Daula and Najaf Khan, which he led against the Jats and the Rohillas. Like the Mughals, he seems to be aware of clan-and community-based social stratifications in Indian society.[244] And in the manner of the Mughals, he prefers to transcend these primordial identities for his own political advantage. In an important letter to Manik Ram, referring to an earlier request for finding a competent person he says: 'You have written that no competent Bengālī is available there. The man should be reliable and it is not necessary that he should be a Bengālī. Send a person you know well and about whose competence everyone is convinced.'[245] In other words, while Polier has definite views on varying social identities, he maintains a kind of all-embracing Mughal *élan.* His scepticism of rigidly defined caste and community classifications by British Orientalists like Jones and Hastings is evident in his letter to Sir Joseph Banks, written from London in 1789. In this letter he implies clear disagreement with the notion that Brahmins hoard their learning:

> . . . How little a dependence is to be placed in the assertion of those who have represented the brahmins as very averse to the communication of the principles of their religion—their mysteries and holy books. In truth I have always found those who were really men of science and knowledge very ready to impart and communicate what they know to whoever would receive it and listen to them, with a view of information, and not merely for the purpose of a thing to ridicule.[246]

In this same letter Polier wonders how religious books were handed over so easily to a European and the transaction sanctified in a society, where according to the texts, only the Kshatriyas are permitted to hear these being read.

This emphasis on professional attributes and an expected code of conduct deriving from ones vocation rather than religious or caste identity makes Polier's text stand in contrast to the writings of his British friends and contemporaries such as Warren Hastings, Charles Wilkins and Sir William Jones. Polier's relations with his local informants are also more personal and contrast with the more restrained contact Hastings maintained with pandits and scribes. Hastings, in a letter to Elijah Impey, Chief Justice of Calcutta High Court, introducing his pandit, says: 'Be so good as to allow him a chair, as I treat him with a respect which I do not commonly show to gentleman withor [sic] shirts and jackets.'[247] In contrast Polier says: 'I thus quit Calcutta, to go to Faizabad, residence of the nawab and, on establishing myself there, I took on the customs and the usages of the Indians with whom I lived.'[248]

The 1780s represented a distinct intellectual shift both in Europe as well as in India. While in France the debates of Enlightenment philosophers proffered the religion and custom of 'Hindu' India to critique the old regime, in India political and administrative compulsions of governance compelled Orientalism to tear apart the composite Indo-Persian tradition into Hindu and Muslim components for streamlined legislation. The establishment of the Asiatic Society of Bengal in this decade and the emphasis on Sanskrit learning to 'know the Hindu religion' exclusively was a new and culturally divisive intellectual trend of the period. Polier could not remain entirely isolated from its influence. He realizes belatedly the importance of Sanskrit for knowing the religion of Hindus. In a personal notice that he dictated to his cousin, and which he is said to have revised and corrected,[249] and which was published by this same cousin, Chanoinesse de Polier, he says:

> As the course of my researches on this matter [namely on the Sikhs, etc.] brought me in due time to the Indous [Hindus], and to the religion of this people that is indigenous to India, I found myself embarrassed on a great number of points, and greatly astonished that after such a long stay in India (where I had spent more time with the natives of the land than with the Europeans), I still knew so little, and so poorly, the basis of their primitive mythology. However, nothing is so common as this ignorance. First, because on arriving in India, we bring to it ideas that are taken from travellers' accounts which, with few exceptions, merit little faith for, since most of them have neither the time nor the desire to make a profound study of this system, the little that they have seized upon is so muddled, and a mix of the true and the false, that one can hardly find the thread. Second, because the Indians who are educated and in a position clearly to set out the prodigious chaos of this mythology are such rare beings, that one is easily discouraged. When one begins such a study without the advantage of possessing the Sanskrit, or sacred tongue of the Indous, which the pandits or savants so constantly draw upon in their usual discourse that it is difficult for me to follow them in their conversation, even though I have a deep knowledge [je possede a fond] of the common tongue of India, called Moors by the English, and Ourdouzebain by the natives of the land.[250]

Yet, Polier's interest in Sanskrit as a conduit for knowledge of Hinduism was not of the British Sanskritist brand. Unlike the latter, he views the acquisition of this knowledge as an integral part of understanding Indo-Persian tradition. He is more dispassionate and disinterested in his quest than were the Orientalists and the administrators. He is more like the Mughals, who promoted Persian translations of Indian classics, both religious and secular, and for whom appreciation of Indian traditions were often regarded as a preferred and enviable part of high learning.[251] The boundaries of knowledge in the Mughal world, as the compilation of *Tuḥfat al-Hind* and several lexicographical works indicated, had extended much beyond the narrow confines of 'pure' and unalloyed Islam or Persian. Siraj ud-Din Ali Khan Arzu (d. 1756), a Mughal philologist, had assiduously established the affinity between Sanskrit and Persian. [252] Polier's appreciation and interest in Brahmanical scriptures was thus a part of this legacy.

Casting the Mughals: The English and the European Way

The British Orientalist understanding of Indian people and politics on caste and community lines was structured mainly on their image of the Mughals. Eighteenth-century British historians, revenue officials, ethnographers and cartographers shunned the Mughal regime as despotic and abstracted from Indian society. They were thoroughly biased against the social and cultural impact of this Indo-Persian period. In fact, the ills of Indian society which the British were all set to 'correct' were attributed to the rapaciousness of the Mughals.

The British military officer and scholar Robert Orme who arrived in India in 1742 and wrote the *Fragments of the Mughal Empire* was one such Briton. Orme based his account primarily on the Persian manuscripts and histories of Mughal historians. Yet, in the *Fragments* the Mughals are projected as 'licentious', 'corrupt', 'pleasure loving' and 'cruel'.[253] Such images of the Mughals proliferated in British accounts of the late eighteenth century–early nineteenth century.[254] British officials like Philip Francis and James Grant, while deliberating on the Company's revenue policy, further reinforced this imagery in their reports.[255]

The image of the Mughals as callous and despotic provided a justification for Company rule. By the early nineteenth century British Orientalists began to translate select passages from Persian manuscripts to reinforce their portrayal of tyrannical Mughals and cement their rule in India. Elliot and Dowson's, *History of India as told By its Own Historians*, exemplified the culmination of this trend. Elliot's preface attached to Volume I of the series makes the British motive very clear: 'Tyranny and capriciousness of the despotic rulers of

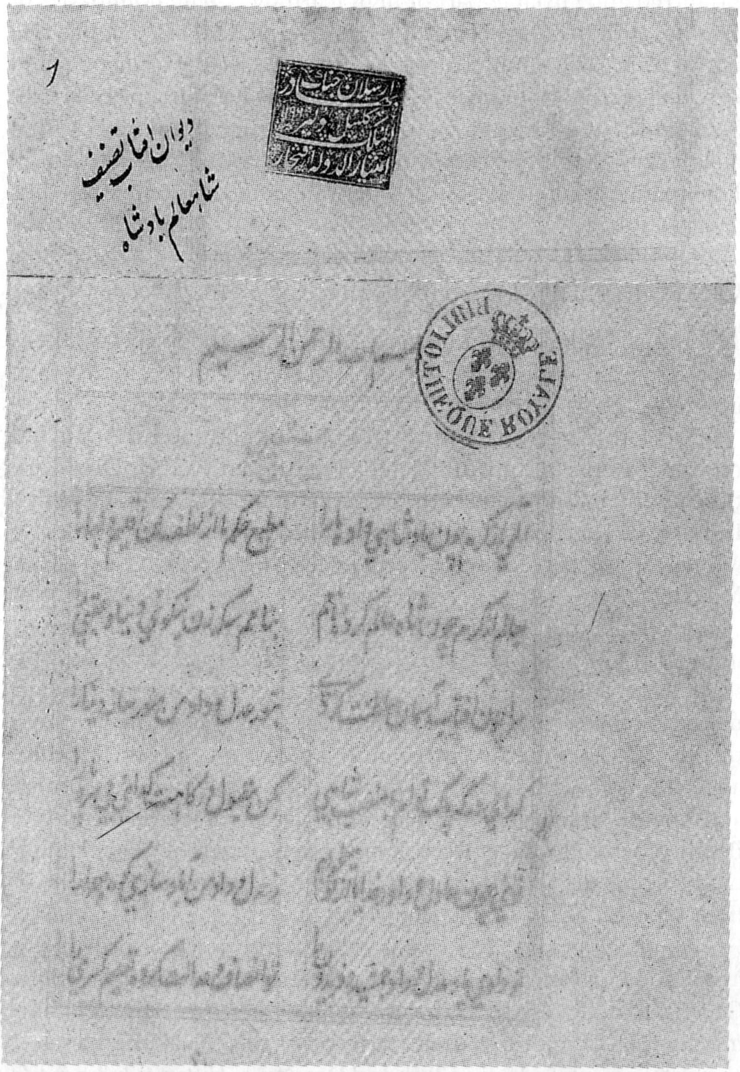

A page from a collection of the poems of Shah Alam II.

medieval India was discussed; in that way it would make the Indians shudder at their immediate past and hail the British regime as a blessing.'[256] While selecting passages from Persian and Arabic texts, Elliot and Dowson concentrated on tales of intrigue, woe, deception, war, fire and famine. There are no references to the cultural and social life in medieval India in these volumes. For instance, from the *Kitāb-ul-Hind* of Albiruni we have an extract of less than four pages, and this too relates to the kings of Kabul.

A vast majority of authors chosen by Elliot and Dowson for their series are Muslims: their eight volumes have only five non-Muslim authors. By this means an image of the decadence of pre-colonial India is built around Muslim authors of predominantly Persian manuscripts. It is as if Muslims and texts other than those in Persian were separate from the cultural and political tradition of the period covered in these volumes.

The image of the Mughals that emerges in Polier's narrative on Shah Alam II[257] and in the *I'jāz-i-Arsalānī* is that of a humane, benevolent, sensitive regime entrenched in Indian society and politics. Neither the text on Shah Alam nor the *I'jāz-i-Arslānī* were 'official reports'. Polier wrote the history of Shah Alam at his own behest. The text has an extremely intimate narrative style, obviously written by one who was personally acquainted with the people and issues he wrote about, and by one who plays some part in the story he relates.[258] The history of Shah Alam II was based on information collected by Polier during his stay at the court of Delhi. Much of this information he passed on to friends who requested it.[259]

Polier's tone in the Shah Alam narrative is mild and lacks the derogatory tone of contemporary British historians. The emperor is projected as 'gracious', 'grave', 'reserved in public' and 'benevolent'.[260] The Marathas, in their numerous forays against Shah Alam, are always referred to as 'insolent' and the humiliation of Shah Alam at their hands condemned.[261]

Polier does not project Shah Alam as a perfect king. He is said to have faults but these are attributed to 'his fondness of flattery, however gross, and the too unreserved confidence he places in his ministers'. In fact Polier discusses the politics of intrigue at Delhi with reference to Shah Alam's minister Abdullah Khan and his chief advisor Ahsan-ud- Daula.[262] These two Mughal officials and Polier were always at cross purposes. Abdullah Khan had regarded Polier as a threat to his power during the latter's brief employment at the Delhi court. He had dissuaded the emperor from allowing Polier to raise a contingent of troops[263] and had deliberately given Polier a *jāgīr*, in lieu of salary, in the recalcitrant *pargana* of Khair in the Agra *ṣūba*. This had caused immense hardship to Polier.[264]

In fact the only time Polier detracts from his reverential stand towards Shah Alam is when he is reminded of the great influence his personal enemies, i.e. Abdullah Khan and his colleagues, have over the Emperor: 'This shows a great weakness in the King and it must be confessed that it has more than once, been carried to inexcusable lengths and which appear the more extraordinary as it cannot be said to be for want of good sense or knowing better.'[265]

Polier's accounts of political transactions in Awadh are similarly based upon an image of a benevolent Nawab circumscribed by a rapacious court. He views court intrigues as the source of all problems in the region while eulogizing the Nawab.[266] The same trend is reflected in Polier's account of Najaf Khan.[267] It is significant that Polier wrote the history of this unsuccessful eighteenth-century regional power. This is a break from the British norm of history writing, which is obsessed predominantly with the Mughals and the more important regional principalities like Awadh.

Polier's text also views the emperor as the cultural representative of a bygone era. The hyperbolic phraseology used exclusively for addressing the emperor is one indicator of what his person connotes for Polier. In the *'arẓdāshts* to the emperor, Polier addresses the emperor invariably in the accepted conventional style:

The loyal slave Major Polier who has the honour of kissing the threshold of your service (*zamīn-i k͟hidmat balab-i-adab bosīda*) is present with his *'arẓdāsht*. It is submitted that I have been your sincere and devoted well-wisher for the last fourteen years and have been endowed with your boundless graces. I have always desired that the affairs of the state get strengthened with every passing day.

He goes on to say that he has conveyed to Asaf-ud-Daula the need to take care of the interest of the empire, and he hopes that the emperor will reciprocate.[268] The same benevolent image of the emperor and his *wazīr* Majd-ud-Daula is projected in the letters which he writes to Nawab Asaf-ud Daula regarding political negotiations in Delhi for the grant of the *wizārat* to the Nawab:

The Nawab, i.e. Majd-ud-Daula is your well-wisher and the *k͟hil'at*, the *qalamdān* and the *chārqab* are ready. The matter of *peshkash* is left to you. However, there is no doubt that here at the imperial court there are heavy expenses. I have thus come to know that the expenditure is three times more than the income. Despite all this, Majd-ud-Daula has procured the *wizārat* for you. And the Emperor is willing to bear with the [financial] difficulties for the sake of your happiness.[269]

Polier adopts a similarly polite tone in his description of the Awadh nawabs whom he views as the '*k̲h̲ānazāds*' (traditional servitors of the Mughals).[270] The use of this expression indicates an unusual familiarity with and appreciation of Mughal values and tradition. His letters to the nawabs follow the pattern of his '*arẓdāshts* to the emperor. Each letter is prefixed with compliments and an expression of pride at being in correspondence with these exalted nawabs.

Polier: A Persianate Mughal Noble

Polier created a niche for himself in Mughal Indian society. He lived like a Mughal noble with a *jāgīr* in the *pargana* of Khair in Agra district.[271] He was also involved in lucrative commercial activities in Agra, Delhi and Awadh[272] and had sprawling houses in Lucknow and Faizabad.[273] He viewed any threat to his little world with concern. The activities of Shah Alam's nobles, the intrigues of Asaf-ud-Daula's courtiers and the raids of Najaf Khan impinged at different points of time on Polier's personal status and fortunes.[274] Thus he felt the need to eulogize them to safeguard his interests in the region.

Polier identified not only with Mughal court culture but with the entire Indo-Persian ethos that this court represented. In letters to his agents stationed in a range of towns and *qaṣbas* over north India, Polier places orders for household items, food and clothing which reflect an acquired, élite and urbane taste for Indo-Persian culture. Almost every item listed in his demand slip is associated with the upper echelons of indigenous urban society: silver vessels, betel-leaf holder (*pāndān*),[275] a *ḥuqqa*,[276] '*amārī* , and palanquins.[277] Also included in this list are rings made of engraved precious stones,[278] gold and silver laces (*gota* and *kinārī*),[279] and Pashmina shawls, *masnad* and a *razāi*.[280] Polier asks incessantly for food items associated with the urban upper crust: these included items like sweet pickle (*murabba*),[281] green mango pickle in oil (*achār*),[282] cinnamon (*dārchīnī*) and other Indian spices, vinegar, Indian berries (*phalsa*)[283] and different kinds of tobacco.[284] Polier needed these both for his personal use as well as gifts, and for his private trade.

Polier's Persianate lifestyle was rendered complete with his acquisition of two Indian wives, and by his preference for the indigenous

Unani system of medicine for the treatment of his son by one of these wives.[285] He adhered to this system of treatment and shows sensitivity to the cultural nuances which shaped social conduct towards indigenous practitioners of medicine.[286] He displayed an appreciation for indigenous dance and singing (*raqṣ-o-surūd*) forms as well, and got his sons tutored by professional teachers in these forms.[287] In these numerous ways Polier demonstrates his familiarity with the Mughal process of identity formation and their relationship with political power. The politico-cultural identity of the élite had come to be defined in reference to their relationship with Mughal power. Over a period of time this evolving Mughal identity had developed a social code of conduct of its own, as well as related concepts like 'loyal' and 'gentlemanly' behaviour in which performing one's duty in the interests of a political master was sacred. Polier's appropriation of these élite concepts and behavioural patterns is reflected in his sensitivity towards the cultural signifiers that had come to connote high status in the Indo-Persian set-up, but also spelt out in the package of social etiquette that he advocated to his wives and family members. In a letter he wrote to the mother of his senior wife over the issue of an altercation between his junior and senior wives—in which the latter physically manhandled the former—he made the cause of his anger very clear:

> She [your daughter] calls her [the junior *bībī*] 'her slave' (*kanīz-i-khwud*). [Imagine] what honour (*ḥurmat*) will be left if I call your daughter her slave. It is loathsome (*nāmunāsib*) for women to come out of their seclusion (*parda*), not to speak of running out from their own house to that of others and raising a commotion. Shame. This is far from decency (*az sharm-o-ḥayā dūr ast*)![288]

In keeping with the customary resolution of such problems within polite society, Polier adds:

> It seems that you have not understood my nature. I swear that if there is any harm (done) to the junior *bībī* or to her pregnancy I will finish both of you there and then and will never see your faces again. It is in your good that as soon as you receive this letter you take her [junior *bībī*) immediately to the place where she was. Otherwise in the event of any negligence you will face the consequences.[289]

On his arrival at the Delhi court in the year 1776 he was honoured by the grant of *nazr* and *khil'at* by Shah Alam. In a letter to Manik Ram reporting on these ceremonies, Polier attributes to them the cultural meanings that they were meant to connote:

I offered thirty-six *asharfīs* as *nazr* to the Emperor and to the Princes; the Emperor honoured me with a *khil'at* of seven pieces and fixed the turban jewels and the turban ornaments (*jīgha-o-sar pīch*) with his own hand. He thus elevated me to the sky. A pearl necklace (*malā-i-marwārīd*) was also put around my neck and I was presented with a sword, an elephant and a horse. Again, in the evening I was presented with special *ulūs-i-khaṣṣa*. In sum, the honours that I have received from the Emperor and the affections (*dostīhā*) received from the Nawab are abundant.[290]

These numerous examples make apparent Polier's immersion within Mughal cultural norm and political ritual. His life appears in sharp contrast to the lives of his British contemporaries, who understood differently, and who obliterated and eventually transformed the pre-colonial understanding of indigenous groups—a whole world of rights and privileges and political rituals.[291]

Between the 'Self' and the 'Other'

Phrases like 'I will make you happy' or 'I am looking after the interests of' were commonly used within the work culture of non-European societies. They connoted certain extra-economic exchange patterns between individuals that were based on personal friendship, family association, previous indebtedness and past gratitude. These networks of social and cultural relationship, in which each individual had a relative power position, intermeshed with the cultural patterns of social behaviour that had percolated from the court. Bernard Cohn has shown how Mughal political rituals of *nazr* and *khil'at* served to integrate the individual and his prestige value into that of the court culture. He also argues that the British reduced these cultural patterns of behaviour to economic exchanges.

Polier's text not only has an abundance of the phraseology of a pre-colonial work ethic and of its political rituals, but also its correct usage in the appropriate contexts. In his text the phraseology he deploys connotes the cultural meanings that is meant to suggest in the Indian context. For instance, in the instructions issued to Ras Bihari Sarkar, his agent and the keeper of his *ḥavelī* in Faizabad, Polier sends reminders asking him to be careful when conducting business. Almost as an incentive he adds, 'I have told him [Mr Loyd] about you. He will be very kind (*bisyār mehrabānī*) to you'.[292] This could have a range of meanings: obligations, money, favours, etc. The text is replete with such ambivalent phrases as 'He will be kind to you', or 'I will make you happy';[293] an oft mentioned phrase is 'the work of Mir Ṣāḥib [is like] my own work',[294] even 'there is no difference between you and me'.[295] In his letter to Nawab Majd-ud-Daula he says 'I feel privileged to hear that I should consider your exalted house as my own.'[296]

Polier appears to have understood the primacy of the oral word that characterized transactions in pre-colonial India. In a case regarding the payment of elephants purchased from Mir Sulaiman Khan on behalf of Najaf Khan, he writes to his agent Sayid Niyaz Ali Khan:

Najaf Khan is expected to be back soon from the imperial court. If you are free you can come here and talk to him personally so that the matter is settled soon. Direct conversation (*gufta-i-rū-ba-rū*) resolves matters in a way in which correspondence (*nawishtan-i-khatt*) can never do. I reiterate that the work of Mir Ṣāḥib is [like] my own work (*kār-i-Mīr Ṣaḥib kār-i-khwud*).[297]

In keeping with the work culture of eastern societies Polier values trust based on friendship and the power positions of individuals in society. In an angry letter to Najaf Khan written about some discrepancy in the amount of *tankhwāh* he says: 'I am shocked and venture to ask you as to why you trusted Major Hang who had never been your friend. For his sake you have completely neglected our old friendship'.[298]

Polier appropriated the Mughal traditional norm of expecting a certain level of behaviour and action from nobles stationed at a distance from Delhi. As he says, *zuhūr-i īn ma'nī khusuṣan az sardārān-i'umda nihāyat ba'īd ast* (such an act is rarely expected in particular from nobles of high standing). The importance of friendships in work relationships is stressed in a letter to Maharaja Rana Chhatrapat:

I am happy to hear from Captain Martin about your fine qualities and your friendship for me. Nothing in this world is superior (*sharīftar*) than the ties of friendship (*rawābiṭ-i-dostī*). So do consider me equally eager [for your friendship]. I will be happy to receive your letters regularly.[299]

Once again when Don Pedrose asks Polier about the price of a book that the latter had sent him he is reminded that 'the word price does not exist in the world of friendship (*ba'ālam-i-dostī ḥarf-i-qīmat darmayānīst*)'[300]

The text is also replete with examples which indicate that Polier is aware of narrowly treading between two different cultural patterns of work ethic. In a letter to Shuja-ud-Daula complaining of his inability to recover money from the *tankhwāh jāgīrs* assigned to him at Allahabad and Benares, he flaunts the distinct cultural world to which he belongs: The realization from there also is postponed. Therefore I have earned a bad name among my own people (*abnā-i-jins*) since I had assigned the *tankhwāh* in both places to Mr. Scott and there has been a discrepancy.'[301] The correspondence around the siege of Agra fort reveals Polier's efforts to demarcate himself from the East. He is disgusted at the working style of Najaf Khan's soldiers and people which he continuously contrasts with that of Europeans. He writes to Shuja-ud-Daula:

I can calculate completing a task within a given stipulated time only when things are done the way (*ẓābiṭa*) we [Europeans] do amidst our own people (*darmayān-i-ma mardum*). Nobody cares for orders (*ḥukm*) here; everyone is in conflict (*ẓidd-o-mukhālafat dārand*) with the other; nothing is done in a coordinated manner (*bil-ittifāq*).[302]

In short, the *I'jāz-i Arsalānī* makes us understand several significant cultural dimensions of India's early European encounter. Indigenous curiosity towards the newcomer was matched by European romantic fascination for the vanquished, as well as by an urge to 'know' the people and their politics. This generated a hierarchy of knowledge, deeply informed by indigenous knowledgeable communities, and often peppered by the urge to reinforce the political power and control of the English East India Company over the local population. European understanding of eighteenth-century India contested with English Orientalist underpinnings of colonial rule, even as it came to be uneasily accommodated within British officialdom. We have analysed some of the questions pertaining to the cultural turmoil generated by India's encounter with European colonizers during this period. A careful study of this text, as well as similar eighteenth-century Persian texts by Europeans will, we hope, enable us to unravel many more issues relevant to a fuller understanding of this crucial phase of Indian history.

The letters in the *I'jāz* throw new light on relations between the Europeans, the Mughals, and the Awadh court. Rich in details of cultural and economic transactions, Polier's own interest in private trade, which he carried on with agents scattered in the major cities of northern India, make these letters an important source of information to discern not only changing trade routes in the period, but also the nature and extent of commercial networks which tied together a large number of small towns and market centres. At the same time, these letters represent a rich source base for piecing together a picture of changing land relations and the links between landed magnates and the Mughal centre during the period of transition. The significance of *I'jāz-i-Arsalānī* as a source for the economic and social history of the eighteenth century prompts us to bring to view these letters in what we hope is an adequate English translation.

A Note on Translation

A word about our translation would be in order here. This is not a word to word translation. We have preferred a summary translation of the text without ignoring any substantive part of its contents. But the exclusion of the adjectives and the embellishments of the original Persian text have not been done at the cost of clarity or compromise with the substance of its contents. We present below the literal translation of a letter to Maharaja Nawal Singh to give to our readers a flavour of the kind of style which Polier picked up from the indigenous tradition, and which was approved and modified by his *munshī*. The literal translation is followed by our rendering of the same.

To Maharaja Nawal Singh,

Maharaja *ṣāḥib*, the benefactor of friends, may you prosper and be safe. A cheer-inducing letter of yours highlighting the reinforcement of degrees of [your] love and sincerity together with an *'arẓī* addressed to the high and exalted nawab reached here, bringing added joy to [my] heart, full of manifest concerns [for you]. As its contents comprised the splendours of friendship it brought cheers to the senses that appreciate sincerity. Further, Manik Ram, my honoured friend also gave the details of your welfare. Since in the world of appearance union of hearts is a thing rare and matchless, it is good that the bond of love is regulated and strengthened from either sides.

The situation here is that due to the chaos and confusion in the wake of every day journey I could not have chance to present the *'arẓī* of that friend to His Highness. I also feel that it is proper to submit this case when His Highness is cheerful. Therefore at the time of camping when he is delightful, the *'arẓī* will be submitted and your case will be brought to the notice of His Highness in the most appropriate way. It will then be written to that friend about the entire proceedings. The basis of the task will also be set right in consultation with Nawab Zulfiqar ud-Daula and then you will be informed, and you will also know about this from Manik Ram's letter. It is necessary that until we embrace each other you should regularly write to me the good news of your welfare so it may induce joy to my heart.

We have rendered the literal translation as follows:

To Maharaja Nawal Singh,

I am delighted to receive your letter with an *'arẓī* for the Nawab. Manik Ram also apprised me of your welfare. I am sincere to you but at the moment because of travels I could neither present your *'arẓī* to the Nawab nor tell him anything about you. When he camps and is relaxed I will bring to his notice the case in an appropriate manner. I will write to you whatever transpires. I will also set right your case in consultation with Najaf Khan. You will know more from the letter of Manik Ram. Keep writing until we meet to embrace each other. 29 Ẕīḥijja 1197.

Our readers will notice that in the translation of letters like the above our rendering of the *mudda'ā* has been reasonably close to being faithful, even if it is not a word to word translation. However, in the translation of the congratulatory letters in which celebration is the *mudda'a,* and where Polier, conversant with the demands of such occasions, allows his *munshī* to excel in figurative and grandiose language, we have preferred to give only a synoptic rendering. Such letters are very few in the *I'jāz-i-Arsalānī,* the bulk of which comprises letters of the type sent to Maharaja Nawal Singh and discussed above. However, a specimen of the congratulatory letters is given below. A word to word translation of this letter, an *'arẓdāsht* to Emperor Shah Alam, would be as follows:

Having solemnly performed the proprieties of salutation and obeisance to the lord of the age, the King of the world, the shadow of God, the gate of whose palace is embellished with tapestries and curtains look like the galaxy, at the exalted court of whom the angels reside, the one who adorns the imperial throne, is the world conquering sovereign, the King of the land and time, the deputy [caliph] of God eternal, the target of allegiance, may his country and power last forever, this faithfully devoted servant sincerely prays for his day and night ascent to royal dignities and submits that since the fore-crushing, awesome and invincible authority of His Majesty is ever increasing, the fort of Akbarabad, the abode of the Caliphate, which raised its head aloft and boastfully vied with the tall mountains in strength and height, has been brought in full control of the friends of the mighty state with the support of the grace of the real benevolent and the blessings of the splendid power of the true goal of devotion and fealty. Its walls and towers were raised to the ground with a few shots of a small cannon devised by the worthless (servant), despite the shortage of the materials of warfare and the non-availability of instructions to subjugate a fort. As the divine benedictions and support become manifest, the beseiged gave up the thread of patience, sought refuge under the victorious standard and appealed for their life to be spared.

I am proud of being in praise to the almighty and of the ever rising imperial fortune that such a strong and impregnable fort, surpassing in strength and grandeur over all the other forts of earth, has been [re]captured. The sound of the proclamation of this fresh victory and the fame of this immeasurable triumph echoed all around in the world scaled even the height of the sky. The wide sheet of the age has been cleaned up and freed from the cruelty and oppression of the tyrants. The cry of pleasure and happiness filled the ear of the age with thrills of joy; the rouge of success and felicitation added beaming mirth to the face of the world.

May God ever endow the slaves and the servants of this august angels-inhabited court with such victories regularly, one following another. May the sun of wealth and fortune keep shining and the splendour of the magnificent authority be ever aglow.

Our summary of this letter is as follows:

Salutations and compliments. . . with the grace of God and the fortune of His Highness, following the strategies which I chalked out, the fort of Akbarabad, comparable in strength and height to the mountains, has been reduced, the inadequate war material notwithstanding. I am proud and thankful to God for this, the announcement of which has travelled all around. The world has been saved from the oppression of the tyrants. May you achieve many similar victories.

Such renderings of the text are few. This is because there are only some letters that follow this convoluted and hyperbolic pattern. Further, Kishan Sahai's prefaces are in verbose style. The opening preface has been incorporated in the translation of the text. The second preface which is much longer, extravagant and grandiose in style has been summarized in the translation of the text. This is because we thought that a verbatim translation of the preface would not have been compatible with the genial tenor of our translation. A word to word translation of the second preface is as follows:

The freshness of the spring of speech and the blossoming flowers of this colourful garden [the world] are in praise of the impeccable layout of existance. They acquire freshness from the streams of His bounty and benevolence. The new delicious wines owe their maturity and colour to the breeze of His unbounded munificence. The drops of the rain of His munificence keep alive the hopes of the people in distress in this dark and dusty world; and the flowers of desire in the gardens of hearts are in full bloom in the fragrance of the gentle breeze of His grace and generosity. It is on the branches of truth and purity that the nightingale is singing in the sweetest voice the songs of His thanks. The parrots are also chanting the praises of His benevolence. The fabulous rare bird with its wings of fantasy and imagination soars high only to appreciate His inaccessible height. The fast running footman of reason in the vast plain regrets its inability [to run further], stops and remains just as a particle of dust on the path. Speech fails to offer [anything] to explain even a single letter of the tomes of His mysteries; the pen has no power to write [even] a single word about the volumes of His account. Indeed, how can our withered reasons, afflicted with smeared ignorance and stupidity dare to understand or raise its head? How can human temperament, tired, blistered and wounded step ahead in this desert full of thorny bushes. Indeed it is not even proper for the incomplete, defective and flawed human reason and intellect to try to comprehend Him.

I, in keeping with my limited capacity and skill, am presenting from an assembly where success prevails an achievement entitled *I'jāz-i Arsalānī*, which is adorned with the jewels of virtue, evenness of freshness, and is resplendent with fresh meanings in a manner that would be the envy of heaven. The letters in this collection were written on behalf of the gracious, generous and blissful master, who is like the full moon in the sky of wealth and triumph, the brilliant sun in the sky of glory and generosity, a rose bed in the gardens of magnanimity and munificence, a spring in the woods of purity and piety; one who does away with injustice and cruelty from its root, demolishes the foundation of adversity and calamity, a friend of the master of the throne of the country, the learned—wise in possession of the devices to capture the fort, the valiant swift-paced in the battlefield, protector of the world, master of sciences, crusher of the basis of haughtiness and afflictions, the shark in the sea of bravery, the lion in the jungle of valiance, the pearl in the ocean of wisdom, the music of the gems of administrative skill, the sun in the sky of learning and excellence, with brilliant shining conscience and gracious resolve, Iftikhar ul Mulk, Imtiaz ud-Daula, Major Polier Bahadur, Arsalan Jang, may the shadow of his grace and favours last for ever and extend everywhere.

The sky having picked up [the light] from the rays of his shining advice is endowed with the stars busy in praise [of God] for the unbounded wealth and the world having benefited from the table of his kindness, blessed with fortunes, is engaged in prayers for his favours. The [stretches of the] world [provide just] a narrow and inconvenient space for the passage of his noble steed of resolve; the entire wealth of both this world and of the world hereafter is just like the worthless chips of silver for his generosity. In the battle the heart of the lion-hearted melts in terror of his dreadful sword. The light of the candle of his soul nourishing assembly, the moth, quenches its burning bosom with elixir. Under his protection the lions are safe in their dens, the spear of his anger pierces into the chests of the enemies like the tongue of the pen. His benificence bestowed upon the ants the wealth of Solomon. With the hubhub of the spring of his generosity the garden of the colourful world has pushed off the autumn of the unfulfilled desire. By looking at his shining visage, the evening of the edifice of hope obtains the morning like night. The mirror in the sky is illumined with the light of the gilded crescent at the top of his standard. He therefore ordered these letters, written to those friends steadfast in their faith and one with him in sincerity, to be collected and compiled.

After, I, the sinful, collected the letters drafted by me with my humble pen for the period of Rabī ‘I, 1187 and the end of the year, and each page of this volume became illumined with the light of the glance of the master whose countenance shines like the sun, it was ordered that all the majestic and auspicious epistles be compiled in volumes: year-wise each commencing with an appropriate preface. Therefore on the first of this Muḥarram, the beginning of 1188 when the bestowal of wealth, fortune and joy to the world from all covering grace and increasing beneficence of that benevolence has commenced, I began this achievement of distinction, the marvellous volume of wonder and thus gathered the eternal fortune; a matter of pride both for this world and the world hereafter and brightened my face with the magical rouge of his unlimited favours. Since I, this worthless Kishan Sahai, knows that the execution of the task of the management of affairs of the world, of the description of truths and the economy of the domain of the belles-lettres, and subjugation of the cities of subject matters, ideas and the seige of the fortress of styles, are difficult, rather impossible simply with human efforts, I seek help from the grace of [God] the matchless benefactor and the friends and colleagues, considering the kind and liberal master, the conqueror of the forts, [provider to] the key to the doors of time and hope that the readers will not deprecate this. They will ignore the shortcomings or weaknesses in the style and usages which arise because of my limitations. They [readers] will, like a generous river, with two kinds of waves, clear this by removing the defects of the style and thus give to it a real purity and excellence.

If the *I'jāz* is generally free from such verbose passages, a major reason is Polier's constant supervision of the drafts that were made before its appearance so that he was able to claim full authorship of the Persian text. Its title, *I'jāz-i-Arsalānī* which means the 'wonder of Arsalan' [i.e Polier himself] is reminiscent of Amir Khusrau who also referred to his prose by the title meaning 'the miracle of Khusrau (*I'jāz-i-Khusrawī*). The possible allusion to Khusrau by Polier was in all probability, to provide his own work the aura of significance and authenticity within the mould of Islamic letters.

NOTES

1 P.C. Gupta (ed.), *Shah Alam and his Court by A.H. Polier,* Calcutta, 1989.

2 The first immigrant was a certain Jehan (Jean) Polier from Ville Franche (Rouergue) He was in a list of supplicants before the Syndics and council of Geneva on 5 December 1553. Paul F. Geisendorf (ed), *Livre des Habitants de Geneve,* vol. I (1549–1560), (Geneva: Droz, 1957), pp. 28–9.

3 Interview with the family of Jaques de Polier, Paris, June, 1998.

4 Eugene and Emily Haag, *La France Protestante,* vol.8, Paris: Cherbuliez, 1858, pp. 274–83.

5 'Liste des refugies francais a Lausanne', in *Bulletin de la Societie de I' Histoire du Protestantisme,* vol. 21, 1872, p. 476.

6 On Voltaire, his contemporaries and India, also see Sylvia Murr, 'Les conditions de l'emergence du discoursesur l'inde au siecle des Lumieres', in Marie Claude Procher (ed.), *Inde et Litterature,* Collection purusartha 7 (Paris: EHESS, 1983), pp. 233–84. Educated at Leiden where he defended a thesis in 1739 comparing the purity of Arabic, Polier's essay on the

Messiah did find a place in Voltaire's philosophical dictionary. See article 'Polier' in *La France Protestante*, pp. 278–9, collated with the article 'Polier' from the *Dictionnaire historique et biographique de la suisse*, vol. v, Neuchatel: DHBS, 1930, pp. 313.

[7] Bengal Past and Present, 1910, p.176; V.C.P Hodson, *List of Officers of the Bengal Army1758–1834*, London, 1946, part III, p. 546.

[8] Hodson, *List*, p. 546

[9] Ibid.

[10] Home Misc/90, pp. 91–2.

[11] M. Archer, *India and British Portraiture, 1770–1825*, London, 1979.

[12] *I'jāz*, vol. I, ff. 37a, 256b, 388b & 389a; also see V. Enderlein and R. Hickmann, *Indische Albumblaiie, Miniaturen und Kalligraphien aus der Zeit der Moghul-Kaiser*, Gustav Kiepenheuer Verlag, Leipzig and Weimar, 1979.

[13] A. Ethe, Catalogue IOL, vol. I, Oxford 1903, no. 1940, p.1086.

[14] *I'jāz*, vol. I, ff. 81b, 82a, 172b, 173a, 213b, 214a, 231b, 232a, 387b and 388a for Polier's early contact with him.

[15] J. Deloche (ed.), *Voyage en Inde*, Paris, EFEO, 1971, p. 77.

[16] Hodson, *List*, p. 546.

[17] *I'jāz.*

[18] L/AG/34/29/12. Last will and testament of Claude Martin, pp. 122–51. Article 29, p.140

[19] *I'jāz*, vol. I, ff. 147b and 148a, vol. II, f. 15b.

[20] The only known manuscript copy of the work is preserved in the Bibliothèque Nationale, Paris, Edgar Blochet, catalogue des Mannerite Persans, de la Bibliothèque Nationale, Tome I, nos. 713–14, Paris, 1905, Supplement Persan 479 et 479A. See also G. Colast et Fr. Richards, 'Les Fonds Polier a la Bibliothèque Nationale', *Bulletin de l' École Française d' Extrême-orient*, LXXIII, 1984, pp. 110–23

[21] Bhupti Rai (*Inshā-i-Roshan Kalām*, Maulana Azad Library, AMU, Aligarh MS, Abdus Salam Collection 10939), Bhagwan Das (*'Azīz ul-Qulūb*, Aligarh MS, Abd-us-Salam 188/54) and Lala Awadhi Lal (*Manṣūr ul-Maktūbāt*, Lucknow University Library MS) for instance were such *munshīs* who wrote the letters respectively on behalf of Ra'd Andaz Khan, *faujdār* of Baiswara in 1698–1702, Muhammad Khan Bangash, founder of Farrukhabad Nawābī, and Safdar Jung, the second Nawab of Awadh.

[22] For a survey of the history of *Inshā*, see I.A. Zilli, 'Development of *Inshā* Literature till the End of Akbar's Reign', in M. Alam, F.N. Delvoye and M. Gaboreau, *The Making of Indo-Persian Culture: Indian and French Studies*, Delhi, 2000, pp. 309–49.

[23] Nizami Aruzi Samarqandi, *Chahār Maqāla*, ed. Muhammad Qazwini and Dr M. Moin, Tehran University Press, 1334 *Shamsī*, pp. 19–23, English tr. E.G. Browne, London, 1899, pp. 22–5.

[24] See *I'jāz-i-Khusrawī, risāla*, I, pp. 66–8.

[25] Zilli, 'Development of *Inshā*'.

[26] Muhammad Taqi Bahar, *Sabk Shanāsī or Tarīkh-i-Taṭawwur i-Naṣr-i Fārsī*, vol. III, Tehran, 1319, p.199
[27] *Babar nāma*, English tr., p.627
[28] Momin Muhiuddin, *The Chancellery and Persian Epistolography under the Mughals*, Calcutta, 1971, pp. 181–3
[29] Muzaffar Alam, 'The Pursuit of Persian: Language in Mughal Politics', *Modern Asian Studies*, 32, 2, 1998, pp. 317–49.
[30] See *Ruq'āt-i Abu'l Fatḥ Gīlānī*, ed. M. Bashir Husain, Lahore, 1968; *Inshā-i-Faiẓī*, ed. A.D. Arshad, Lahore, 1973; and *Munsha' āt-i-Namakīn*, ed. I.A. Zilli, unpublished, Department of History, Aligarh Muslim University, Introduction by editors.
[31] Momin, *The Chancellery*, pp. 221–34; see also S. Abdullah, *Adabiyāt-i Fārsī mein Hinduon kā Ḥiṣṣa*, Lahore, 1967.
[32] Sujan Rai Batalvi, *Khulāṣat ul-Makātib*, cited in S. Abdullah, *Fārsī Zabān-o-Adab*, Lahore, 1977, p.303
[33] N.H. Zaidi, '*Inshā*', in S.F. Mahmud and S.W.H. Abidi (eds) *Tāīkh-i Adabiyāt-i Musalmanān-i Pakistan-o-Hind*, vol. 5, *Fārsī Adab*, III, Lahore, 1972, pp. 242–51.
[34] Riazul Islam, *A Calendar of Documents on Indo-Persian Relations*, vol. I, Karachi, 1979, introduction, pp. 10–16.
[35] *Inshā-i Mādho Rām*, ed. Maulavī Qudrat Ahmad, Lucknow, 1260 A.H./ 1844.
[36] N.H. Zaidi, '*Insha*', citing *Inshā-i Khalīfa*, pp. 249–50.
[37] L. Colley, Britons, *Forging the Nation 1707–1837*, Yale, 1992.
[38] Ibid.
[39] Col. Galliez to Fort William, 12 February 1775, Secret Consultation (SC), 24 February 1775–8.
[40] SC 67, ff. 387 & 385.
[41] President to Shuja-ud-Daula, 15 May 1772, (SC) 1772–73, pp.164–5.
[42] Persian Correspondence 1772–75, June 1, 1774, pp. 347–8. Enclosed with a copy of the *parwāna* written to Monsieur Gentil.
[43] G. Harper to Fort William, Faizabad, 16 December 1771, SC 1772–73.
[44] Ibid.
[45] Ibid.
[46] Ibid.
[47] President of SC to Shuja-ud-Daula, 15 May 1772, SC 1772–73, pp.164–5.
[48] A. Champion to R. Barwell, Bankipore 29 December 1771, SC 1772–73, ff. 14–5. Champion was of the view that the Commanding Officer of the brigade himself issue the passports to his men who were moving out into the country. This he thought would be a less cumbersome procedure.
[49] R. Barwell, Patna to A. Champion, 26 December 1771, SC 1772–73, ff. 13–15.
[50] Fort William to Harper, 10 January 1772, SC 1772–73, f. 11.
[51] Fort William to Robert Barker, SC 1772–73, f. 31, 10 January 1772.

[52] Ad. Ms. 29135, Middleton to Hastings, 23 September 1774; Ad. Ms. 29134, Middleton to Hastings, 11 March 1774.

[53] Hastings to Middleton, 30 September 1774. Hastings Papers Ad. 29135.

[54] Ad. Ms. 29138, Middleton to Hastings, 25 March 1777, Lucknow; du Jarday was an *ijāradār* in the Doab area from 1778–87. For details on his activities see S. Nurul Hasan, 'Du Jardin Papers: A Valuable Source for the Ecnomic History of North India, *IHR*, vol. 5, nos 1–2; for a copy of the *parwāna* to Du Jarday and a *maḥẓar* relating to his *ijāra* in *pargana* Secundra and Marahara, see also Bibliothèque Nationale, Pairs, Persan Supplement 1581 and 1582 respectively; for a *parwāna* from Farrukhabad to Du Jarday dated 11 Ṣafar 1201, see *I'jāz*, vol. II, f. 61a.

[55] Ibid.

[56] Bibliothèque Nationale, Paris, Persan Supplement, 1584, f. 45a.

[57] Balwant Singh to Govenor-General., 22 March 1768, tr. of Persian letters received 1767–68, no. 98, p. 336; see for similar *dastaks* of Nawab Shuja-ud-Daula to facilitate the passage of Polier's goods from Faizabad to Azimabad; and Nawab Asaf-ud-Daula's *dastaks* to Polier for the safe passage of his goods, in Bibliothèque Nationale, Paris, Persan Supplement 1581; this manuscript also includes *dastaks* of the Awadh Nawabs issued to other Frenchmen like Louis Perceret for facilitating their trading activities.

[58] Residents Proceedings of Benares, Basta no. 42, Register no. 9, June 1795, Duncan to Barlow, 21 June 1795.

[59] Bibliothèque Nationale, Paris, Persan Supplement 1605.

[60] Duncan to Hay, 8 March 1791, Residents proceedings of Benares, Basta no. 31, Book no. 42, March 1791.

[61] Preface to *le Mahabharata,* cited in S. Subrahmanyam, 'The career of colonel Polier and Late eighteenth century Orientalism', *Journal of the Royal Asiatic Society,* 2000.

[62] Ad. Ms. 29140, Middleton to Hastings, 14 February. 1778; for details on how the Company made most of Claude Martin's presence, see Rosie Llewellyn-Jones, *A very Ingenious Man: Claude Martin in Early Colonial India,* Delhi, OUP, 1991.

[63] Hastings to Middleton, 30 September 1774, Ad. Ms. 29135.

[64] Ad. Ms. 29138, Middleton to Hastings, 25 March 1777.

[65] Jean Deloche, ed. *Voyage en Inde du Comte du modave, 1773–1776: Nouveaux memoires sur I'etat actuel du Bengale et de l'Indoustan,* Paris, EFEO, 1971, p.77.

[66] Hastings to Middleton, 30 September 1774, Ad. Ms. 29135.

[67] Ad. Ms. 29139, Middleton, to Hastings, Lucknow, 2 November 1777.

[68] H Misc/221, p.41.

[69] Ibid., pp. 20–1. Ad. Ms. 29135, f.250.

[70] Hastings Papers. Ad. Ms. 29135, f.250.

[71] Ad. Ms. 29135, f.250.

[72] *I'jāz,* f. 46a. See also ff.45b–46a, 47a, 48a, 56b, 60a, 64b, 65b, 66b, 67a, 70b, 71a and 72a, 75b, 76b.

[73] Ibid., f.75b.
[74] Ibid., f.76a.
[75] Ibid., f.29a.
[76] Ibid., f.129a.
[77] Ibid., f.5b
[78] Ibid., f.9a.
[79] Ibid., ff.8b, 14a, 15b, 18a.
[80] Ibid., ff.12b, 59a
[81] There was a general demand for Portuguese transcribers in 18th century India. Ad. Ms. 45432, f.17, Anderson Papers; for their employment in Fort St. George specifically, see Ad. Ms. 16265, f.14.
[82] *I'jāz*, f. 245b.
[83] Ibid., ff. 156b, 215a, 245b.
[84] Ibid., f. 87a.
[85] Ibid., f.39a
[86] A.L. Srivastava, *Shuja-ud Daula of Awadh, 1754–1775*, 2 vols, Agra 1961, 1974, vol. I, pp. 107–8, 148.
[87] *I'jāz*, ff. 64a and 58a.
[88] See *I'jāz*, ff. 49b, 400b, 402a., Ad. Ms. 29135, f. 254.
[89] Ad. Ms. 29138, Hastings Papers, ff. 257–63.
[90] Preface to *Le Mahabharat et le Bhagavat of Col. de Polier*, rept. with an introduction by G. Dumezil, Paris, 1986, p. 15.
[91] Ibid., p. 18.
[92] Ibid., p. 14.
[93] Ad. Ms. 29135, ff. 220, 250.
[94] Preface to *Le Mahabharat*, pp. 20–1.
[95] *I'jāz*, f. 17b.
[96] Ibid., f. 161b.
[97] Ibid., f. 162a.
[98] Ibid., f. 163a.
[99] Preface to *Le Mahabharat*, p.1. It is important to note here that in the latter half of the 18th century French philosophers, like Voltaire, openly challenged the Catholic church and the state. In 1787, the Edict of Toleration was introduced by Louis XVI and his councillors only two years before the revolution. The edict recognized the existence of 'non-Catholics' in France and granted them for the first time the right of having a registrar for birth, marriage and death, other than the parish priest.
[100] *I'jāz*, f. 39a.
[101] Ibid., f. 186a.
[102] Ibid., f. 194b.
[103] Hastings papers, Ad. Ms. 39903, f. 38.
[104] Ad. Ms. 5346.
[105] Ibid.
[106] Ibid.
[107] Preface to *le Mahabharata*, cited in Subrahmanyam, 'Career of Colonel Polier'.

[108] Ibid., p. 7.

[109] Ibid., p. 7. A prominent case is that of William Bolts, author of the celebrated *Considerations on Indian affairs*, who was in all probability born in Germany, ironically at least some of Bolt's opponents who accused him of a lack of 'patriotism' were themselves of Dutch descent; as was the case with his arch enemy Harry Verelst as also Henry Vansittart.

[110] Khwaja A.K. Kashmiri, *Bayān-i-Wāqi*,' ed. K.B. Nasim, Lahore, 1970, p. 161.

[111] Ibid.

[112] Ad. Ms. 13828, f. 312 and Ad. Ms. 5346.

[113] Ad. Ms. 18828, f.312.

[114] Ad. Ms. 29233, ff.263-275.

[115] Ibid., f. 263.

[116] Ibid., f. 263.

[117] Ibid.

[118] In Firdausi's *Shāhnāma* and Nizami's *Sikandarnāma* we come across Alexander's queries to Aristotle and the latter's response. See for details Muzaffar Alam, 'Akhlaqi Norms and Mughal Governance', in Alam et al., *The Making of Indo-Persian Culture.*

[119] Howard R. Turner, *Science in Medieval Islam: An illustrated Introduction,* Austin, 1995, repr. Delhi, 1998.

[120] M.T. Targhi, 'Orientalism's Genesis Amnesia', *Comparative Studies of South Asia, Africa and the Middle East*, 1996, vol. XVI, no. 1, p. 4.

[121] Turner, *Science in Medieval Islam.*

[122] Ad. Ms. 39891. This was later translated by Charles Wilkins.

[123] Ad. Ms. 29170, f. 421.

[124] Ibid.

[125] Ad. Ms. 13828, f. 312.

[126] Ad. Ms. 5346.

[127] Ad. Ms. 29177, f.158.

[128] *Mahābhārat,* Persian translation by Mir Ghiyas ud-Din Ali Qazvini, ed. S.M. Reza and N.S. Shukla, vol. I, Tehran, 1358 *Shamsī*, Abul Fazl's introduction, pp. 18–19.

[129] For the dialogue between British Orientalists and Persian and Indian scholars, see also Targhi, 'Orientalism's Genesis Amnesia', pp. 1–14.

[130] C.A. Bayly, *Empire and Information: Intelligence Gathering and Social Communication in India 1780–1870,* Cambridge, CUP, 1996, chapter II.

[131] Ibid.

[132] For his request to be stationed in Benares on account of the availability of Brahmins there to help him in translation work, see Ad. Ms. 29167, f. 296.

[133] P. Marshall, 'Warren Hastings as Scholar and Patron', in A. Whiteman, J. Bormley and P.G.M. Dickson (eds), *Statesmen, Scholars and Merchants: Essays in 18th Century History presented to Dame Lucy Sutherland,* Oxford, 1973, p. 249.

[134] Targhi, 'Orientalism's Genesis Amnesia', p. 4.

[135] IOL Catalogue of European manuscripts, 2 vols, vol. II, p. 1172. Wilkins sent a translation of the *Bhagvadgita* to Hastings who was so impressed by

it that he persuaded the Company to publish it in 1784. He also published a translation of the *Hitopadesa* in 1787, Sanskrit grammar in 1808 and the work on Sanskrit roots in 1815. He was also the first to apply the methods of the printing press to the Sanskrit, Arabic and Bengali alphabet, himself designing and cutting the types from Hallhed's *Bengali grammar* published in 1778. See also J.C. Marshman, *Life and Times of Carey, Marshman and Ward. Or a History of the Seerampore Mission*, vol. 2, London, 1859.

136 Jones to Wilkins, 1785, Ms Euro. C27. Memoirs of life, Writings and Compositions of William Jones, and letter from Jones to Wilkins, 1804.

137 Ibid.

138 Ad. Ms. 29163, Wilkins to Hastings, Benares, 11 April 1784.

139 R. Traverse, forthcoming Cambridge Ph.D. thesis on Warren Hastings.

140 Hastings to Court of Directors, 23 October 1783, Bengal. Letters Received, E/4/41, British Library, London.

141 Hastings to Court of Directors, 21 February 1784, E/4/41, Bengal. Letters Received, British Library, London.

142 Marshall, 'Hastings as Scholar and Patron', p. 250.

143 He and Henry Vansittart were said to be the only Englishmen in Calcutta in the early 1760s who 'undertook a little Persian', *A Translation of Seir Mutakherin*, 4 vols, Calcutta, 1902–3, vol. I translations, preface, p.1. John Shore later said that Hastings had a proficiency in Persian; Lord Teignmouth, *Memoirs of the Life : Writings and Correspondence of Sir William* Jones, 1807, p. 297.

144 P. Gordon, *The Oriental Repository*, 1835, p. 4.

145 Persian Ms. in IOL, Ms Eur. D543, p. 7.

146 G. Cannon (ed.), *The Letters of Sir William Jones*, Oxford, 1970, vol. II, p. 798.

147 Targhi, 'Orientalism's Genesis Amnesia', p. 5.

148 Kapil Raj, 'Manufacturing Trust: William Jones and the Anglo-Indian Administration of the East India Company's Indian Territories', mimeograph, p. 1.

149 Ibid.

150 'The first age of global imperialism, c.1760–1830', *Journal of Imperial and Commonwealth History*, vol. 26, no. 2, May 1998.

151 P.J. Marshall, 'Empire and Authority in the later Eighteenth Century', *Journal of Imperial and Commonwealth History*, vol. 25, no. 2, January 1987.

152 See R.M.Ogilvie, *Latin and Greek: A History of the Influence of the Classics on English Life from 1600 to 1918*, 1964, ff. 46; J. Lawson and H.Silver, *A Social History of Education in England*, 1973, pp 217–18.

153 Raj, 'Manufacturing trust', p. 15.

154 Ibid

155 J.D.M. Derrett, 'Sanskrit Legal Treatises compiled at the instance of the British', *Zeitschrift fur vergleichende Rechtsuissen schaft*, 63 (1961), p. 72–117.

156 Raymond Schwab, *The Oriental Renaissance*, New York 1984.

157 See T. Trautmann, *Aryans and British India*, Sage, New Delhi. 1997, p. 26; R. Rocher, 'British Orientalism in the Eighteenth Century: the Dialectics

of Knowledge and Government', in Carol Beckenridge and Peter van der Veer (ed.), *Orientalism and the Post-colonial Predicament*, Delhi, OUP, 1994.

158 Trautmann, *Aryans*, p. 14.

159 Letter to Scott, 9th December 1784, Ad. Ms. 29129, f. 275.

160 See, for example, the translation of the *Hidāya* for codifying Muslim law, and the Sanskrit *Manusmritī* for the Hindu law.

161 Bayly, *Empire and Information*, chapter IV.

162 See also G. Cannon, 'Oriental Jones: Scholarship, Literature, Multiculturalism and Humankind', in *Bulletin of the Deccan College*, vol. 54–55 (1994–95), pp. 3–22. Here Cannon clearly distinguishes between Jones Muslim texts (Persian and Arabic) and the Indian texts (Sanskrit).

163 Raj, 'Manufacturing trust', p. 19.

164 Ad. Ms. 29151, Middleton to Hastings, 30 November 1781, f. 437.

165 Ad. Ms. 29143. The Pera of Constaninople to Hastings, 8 March 1779.

166 E. Stokes, *The English Utilitarians and India*, Delhi, OUP, 1959, repr. 1992, p. 28.

167 Charles Grant, 'Observations on the state of society among the Asiatic subjects of Great Britain, particularly with respect to morals and on the means of improving it, written in 1797 for the Court of Directors', published in the Parliamentary Papers 1813, vol. x, p. 31.

168 Ad. Ms. 13828, f. 308.

169 Ibid., f. 309.

170 Ibid., f. 306.

171 Ibid.

172 Ibid.

173 Ibid.

174 Anderson Papers, Ad. Ms. 45432, f. 15.

175 The ease with which books in Arabic could be had very cheaply is evident from a letter of R. Chambers to David Anderson who had sent him a catalogue of books to enable him to make his pick. Chambers writes that his *munshī* tells him that, 'there are now few buyers of Arabic books—that I may probably get the whole library for Rs 1000 or less.'He was willing to buy the entire library if the books could be had at so small a price. Ad. Ms. 45432, R. Chambers, to D. Anderson, 28th May 1776, f. 15.

176 Dictionary of National Biography (DNB), C.E. Buckland, London, 1906, p. 64.

177 Ad. Ms. 29233, ff. 237, 238.

178 Ibid., f. 268.

179 IO Maps MS (5). *Journal* contains a long description of his survey and of the people with sketches of Cheduba (85f/9).

180 Ms 29233, f.237. Burrow's recommendations had to wait until 1787 because Hastings left India in 1785. In 1785 on Watson's recommendation Burrow was appointed Mathematician Master to the Engineer officers at Fort William. Watson helped him get the permission for the astronomical survey on grounds that due to its absence repetitious surveys were being conducted at additional expense to the government. See also

R.H. Phillimore, *Historical Records of the Survey of India*, vol.I (18th century), Dehradun, 1945, p. 157.

181 Ad. Ms 29159, from Burrow to Hastings, 12 June 1783.

182 Ibid., f. 380.

183 Ibid.

184 Ad. Ms 13828, f. 312.

185 Ibid., ff. 273–4.

186 Ibid., f. 269.

187 Ibid.

188 Ad. Ms 29233, f. 238.

189 Ibid.

190 Memoranda for Hasings, Ad. Ms. 29233, ff. 207, 263.

191 Ad. Ms. 29233, f. 237.

192 Ibid.

193 Francis Richard, 'Jean Baptiste Gentil collectionneur de manuscrits persans', *Dix-huitieme siecle*, no. 28, pp. 91-110.

194 Duperron was the son of a Paris-based grocer who was able to become a student of Paris University and disciple of the jansenists. He departed for India in 1755 with the express intention of searching out ancient manuscripts which he hoped to translate by learning the relevant languages in India itself. He returned to France in 1762 after a long stint in Surat where he lived with the Parsis and wrote about them. For a standard account see R. Schwab, *Vie'd Anquetil-Duperron, suivie des usages civils et religieux des parses par Anquetil-Duperron*, Paris, 1934; Jean-Luc Kieffer, *Anquetil-Duperron: l'Inde en France au XVIIIe siecle*, Paris: Belles-Lettres, 1983.

195 Susan Gole, *Maps of Mughal India: Drawn by Colonel Jean -Baptiste -Joseph Gentil, Agent for the French Government to the Court of Shuja-ud-Daula at Faizabad*, 1770, New Delhi, Manohar, 1988.

196 In 1799 the Bibliothèque Nationale, Paris deputed Anquelil Duperron to prepare an inventory of his paintings. Guy Deleury, 'L' ingenieur Polier', *Reveue des Meur Mondes*', October et. November, 1986, p. 302.

197 Ibid.

198 In 1788 an English Company civil servant, Edward E.Pote, bought in India a collection of more than 550 Persian and some Arabic manuscripts. Half of these he donated to Kings College and the other half to Eton College, UK. These manuscripts had formed part of the oriental library of Polier. His seal 'Major Polier, A.H. 1181' and his autograph 'Anthony Polier' is inscribed on a large number of these manuscripts (Catalogue of the oriental MS in the library of Kings College, Cambridge, called Pote (Kings), Oriental Mss; and Catalogue of the oriental Ms in the libarary of Eton College, by D.S. Murgolionth, Oxfrod, 1904. Poliers' oriental collection also included about 42 other volumes of Arabic, Persian and Sanskrit manuscripts which his heirs later deposited with the Imperial Library at Paris (Catalogue of Pote (Kings) oriental Mss, p.3; The Bibliothèque Cantonale of Lausanne has a manuscript catalogue of 120

oriental works with annotations by Polier (A392, Letters, Autographs, Manuscrits, Documeats, Historiques etc. Catalogue General).

199 Eton catalogue, pp. 7–9.

200 Kings catalogue, pp. 19–20.

201 Guy Deleury, 'L' ingenieur Polier', p. 306.

202 Eton catalogue, p. 21.

203 Kings catalogue, pp. 6, 17.

204 Ibid., p. 7.

205 Ibid., p. 10.

206 Eton catalogue, pp. 23–4.

207 See for orders placed to him, *I'jāz,* f.37b.

208 Mildred Archer and Toby Falk, *India Revealed: The Art and Adventures of James and William Fraser 1801–35,* see section on Company Drawings, pp. 90–136, London, 1989.

209 *I'jāz,* f. 258a.

210 Ibid., f. 256b.

211 M. Trivedi, 'Encounter and Transition: European Impact in Awadh 1765–1856', in A.J. Qaisar and S.P. Verma (eds) *Art and Culture: Endeavour in Interpretation,* Delhi, 1996, pp. 17–48. Trivedi argues that the depth in some of Mehrchand's paintings is delineated by diminishing the scale in the objects and distinct landscape.

212 Madhu Sharma, 'Culture and Society in the Kingdom of Awadh', unpublished Ph.D. thesis, Aligarh Muslim University, Aligarh, 1977.

213 See for details, V. Enderlein and R. Hickmann, *Indische Albumblaiie,* p. 6. After Beckford's death they passed on to his sister who married a Hamilton (in Scotland) gentleman, Alexander Marquis. This is how the collection reached Hamilton Palace, Scotland, and were named as Hamilton Albums. It was in 1882 that at an auction with the help of exchange of material between British Museum and the Berlin Museum, the Hamilton collection was acquired by the Berlin Islamic Museum.

214 Ibid., p. 6.

215 *I'jāz,* f. 398a.

216 Toby Falk and Mildred Archer, *Indian Miniatures in the IOL,* London, 1981, p. 135.

217 *I'jāz,* ff. 23a, 24a, 26b, 96b and 117b.

218 Ibid., f. 96b.

219 Ibid., f. 117b.

220 Ibid., f. 22b.

221 Ibid., ff. 24b, 31b, 40a, 55b, 101a, 115a.

222 Ibid., f. 31b. The other houses there appeared to have had mud walls.

223 Ibid., f. 31b.

224 Ibid., f. 40a.

225 Rosie Llewellyn-Jones, 'Lucknow, City of Dreams', p. 54, in Violette Graff (ed.), *Lucknow: Memories of a City,* OUP, Delhi, 1997. She indicates that Nawab Shuhja-ud-Daula employed Polier to superintend the building at

Faizabad in 1773. He was asked to draw a plan for banqueting house in Faizabad and a palace in Varanasi. But Polier's employer was dead by the time the plan was complete. Asaf-ud-Daula also asked to prepare plans for some border forts. But these could not be completed because Polier was recalled to Calcutta.

226 *I'jāz*, f. 31a.

227 E. Irschick, *Dialogue and History*, Delhi, 1995; Breckenridge and Van der Veer, *Orientalism and the Postcolonial Predicament;* for the initiation of this debate, see Edward Said, *Orientalism*, London, 1995.

228 Bayly, *Empire and Information.*

229 Barnard S. Cohn, 'Representing Authority in Victorian India', in *An Anthropologist among the Historians and Other Essays*, OUP, Delhi, 1987.

230 *I'jāz*, f. 80b

231 Ibid., f. 35a.

232 Ibid., f. 52b.

233 Ibid., f. 126b.

234 Ibid., f. 135a.

235 Ibid., f. 63b. For other such examples see also ff 86a, 87a, 209b, 214a.

236 R. Orme, *Historical Fragments of the Mughal Empire, of the Morattoes and of the English Concern in Indostan from the year MDCLIX* (reprint 1974), p. 303.

237 *I'jāz*, ff. 132b, 173b, 359b.

238 Ibid., f. 72a.

239 Ibid., f. 359b.

240 Ibid., f. 129b.

241 Ibid., f. 165b.

242 Muhammad Hadi Kanwar Khan, *Tazkirat al-Salāṭin Chaghtā*, ed. M. Alam, Bombay, 1980.

243 *I'jāz*, f. 369a.

244 The awareness of indigenous rulers about the caste and ethnic stratifications of rural society is also revealed in the observations of the Awadh *'āmils* and officials posted in the Rajput *zamindarīs* of Benares. See F. Curwen's translation, of *Balwantnāma*, Allahabad, 1857.

245 *I'jāz*, f. 382b.

246 Ad. Ms. 5340.

247 Ad. Ms. 16262, correspondence of Elijah Impey, Governor-General 1780–82, f. 169; cf Marshall, 'Empire and Authority', pp. 118–19. He argues that beneath the veneer of Hastings benevolence there was a lot in common between him and the anglicist Cornwallis.

248 Sanjay Subrahmanyam, 'Notes on Colonel Polier Arsalan Jang', p. 11.

249 Preface to *Le Mahabharata* pp. 14–21.

250 Preface to *Le Mahabharata* cited in Sanjay Subrahmanyam, 'Notes on Colonel Polier Arsalan Jang'.

251 Polier's different understanding of India created a clash between him and his British colleagues during the survey of upper India. Unlike Rennell and his team, Polier did not confine himself to Hindu and Muslim 'learned

men' to gather information. Polier is said to have disappointed both Hastings and Rennell in the matter of surveys of Awadh. Even two years after his arrival in Awadh he had still not sent the reports to them. See Jones, *Claude Martin*, p. 56. For an overview of survey operations in these years, see H. Edney, *Mapping an Empire: The Geographical Construction of British India, 1765–1843*, Chicago, 1997; Kapil Raj promises to work on a comparative study of Rennell and Polier's surveys.

252 Siraj-ud-Din 'Ali Khan Arzu, *Muthmir*, ed. Rehana Khatoon, Karachi, 1991, p. 221; see also S. Abdullah, *Mabāḥiṣ*, 1, Delhi 1968, pp. 70–1.

253 Robert Orme, *Of the Government and People of Indostan*, reprint, Lucknow, 1971, p. 17.

254 Home Misc/191. This file has another account by Robert Orme entitled 'A History of the Military Transactions of British Nation in Indostan from 1745'; also see W. Franklin, *The History of the Reign of Shah Alam, the present Emperor of Hindustan*, London, 1798.

255 W.K. Firminger (ed.), *Fifth Report, Analysis of the Finances of Bengal*, pp. 172–3, 475–6, vol. I, Calcutta, 1917.

256 K.A. Nizami, Supplement to Elliot and Dowson, *History of India as Told by its own historians*, vol. II, Delhi, 1981, p. 1.

257 P. Gupta, *Shah Alam and his Court.*

258 Ibid., p. 1.

259 Ibid., p. 2.

260 Ibid., p. 67.

261 Ibid., p. 30.

262 Ibid., p. 30–1.

263 Ad. Ms. 29138, Hastings Papers, f. 34.

264 Gupta, *Shah Alam and his Court*, p. 69.

265 Hastings Papers, Ad. Ms. 29138, f. 34.

266 Orme Ms. OV 91, pp. 89–94.

267 Orme Ms. OV 274, ff. 1–161.

268 *I'jāz*, f. 230a.

269 Ibid., f. 367b.

270 Ibid. f. 253a.

271 *I'jāz*, vol. II; Ad. Ms. 29138, f. 39.

272 Ibid., ff. 35–6.

273 Jones, *Claude Martin.*

274 For the problems with the zamindars on his landed estates for which he continuously sought the intervention of the Emperor and the Nawab of Awadh, see also Ad. Ms. 29135, f.254 and Ad. Ms. 29138, ff. 34–8; for flights with Major Hannay's estate managers, see Ad. Ms. 16264, ff. 25–6.

275 *I'jāz*, f. 118a.

276 Ibid., ff. 22a–24a.

277 Ibid., f. 23a.

278 Ibid., f. 5b.

279 Ibid., ff. 20b, 21b, 35b.

[280] Ibid., f. 359a.
[281] Ibid., f. 177a.
[282] Ibid., f. 99a.
[283] Ibid., f. 177a.
[284] Ibid., f. 33a.
[285] Ibid., f. 141b.
[286] Ibid., f. 141b.
[287] Ibid., f. 147b and 248b and 249a.
[288] Ibid., f. 106b.
[289] Ibid., f. 106b.
[290] Ibid., 365b.
[291] Cohn, 'Representing Authority'.
[292] *I'jāz*, f. 52b.
[293] Ibid., f. 95b.
[294] Ibid., f. 159b.
[295] Ibid., f. 258b.
[296] Ibid., f. 362b.
[297] Ibid., f. 159b.
[298] Ibid., f. 175a.
[299] Ibid., f. 177b.
[300] Ibid., f. 245b.
[301] Ibid., f. 192b.
[302] Ibid., f. 50b.

POLIER'S LETTERS

(*I'jāz-i Arsalānī*)

Praise and glory be to the creator who blessed the ignorant, who have failed in their endeavour to comprehend Him in this world of appearance, with skill to earn their livelihood; and gratitude and thanks for the divine beneficence which generously opened the doors of the fortunes to those who [roving in]* the vast stretches of knowledge and intellect have been completely incapacitated and drained of their power to speak and discern.

After this it is submitted that when the faithful Kishan Sahai presented himself, in the auspicious city of Azimabad, to the generous and gracious nawab—the commander of the exalted titles and honours, the bright fortune in the imperial cavalcade, the glittering mirror in the banquet of wealth and munificence, the brilliant conscience as the sun, the protector of the Christian faith, the patron of the law of the prophet, the lord of justice and equity, the judicious appraiser of the worth of the noble natured, the principal support of the edifice of glory and triumph, the shining lamp in the assemblies of unity, religion and divinity, the knower of the secrets, the chamber of the hidden realities, the recipient of Divine mysteries, the essence of the illustrious English house, the ocean bestowing treasures and pearls, the matchless jewel of the land of the Firangis, the master of fortunes resolutely firm in generosity—Iftikhar ul-Mulk [the pride of the country], Imtiyaz ud-Daula [the distinction of the state] Major Polier Bahadur Arsalan Jang [the brave lion in the battle]—he accumulated the capital of endless pride, accredited by him [Polier] to earn the virtue of being at his service and thus store the sublimities of servility through the excellent means of his secretaryship.

The rays of his kindness illumined this worthless particle while his generous care turned this dirtied dust into the collyrium of worthy eye (and thus lent me a respectable identity). Since the letters which he sent to the high statured *amīrs*, exalted Khans and other friends were drafted in elegant and pleasing style, these are [hereby] compiled into a volume at the instance of the sun-like grandmaster [Polier]. It is hoped that the learned, the skillful who appreciate the styles of art and writing and who promote [this skill] would be kind and generous to suggest improvements and corrections to free this volume from errors and blemishes and [thus] allow the wild young steed like pen to gallop some distance.

* Editorial insertions in the text have been placed within square brackets.

Folio 2b. To Nawab Shuja-ud-Daula.

I took leave of Imad-ud-Daula, Governor Hashtin [Warren Hastings] *Bahadur ṣāḥib* and reached Azimabad [Patna] where I stayed for some time to rest. A week later I arrived in Benares. Since I am very keen to pay my respects to you I look forward to meeting you. But some important matters have delayed my departure for four to five days. However, I am eager to have audience with you and hope to arrive in the court very soon.

Earlier I had written a letter to you from Murshidabad and had been waiting to hear from you until I reached Benares. Since I did not hear from you I am sad and feel deprived. 17 Rabī‘ I, 1187, Benares.

Folio 3a. To Raja Gobind Ram, resident of Calcutta.

I have received your letter in which you have enquired about my visit to this place, and mentioned about the letter to Nawab Ikhtiyar-ul-mulk, Middleton *ṣāḥib.*

Having left that place [Calcutta] I reached Azimabad. I stayed back to attend to some important work here. Now I am planning to proceed ahead. The delay in writing to you was caused because of the demise of my old *munshī.* I have appointed another *munshī* and in future my letter will reach you regularly along with the letters enclosed in the envelopes for the *ṣāḥib* [through the Company mail]. I hope you will keep in touch. I have nothing more to say. 8 Rabī‘I, Azimabad.

Folio 3b. To Nawab Shuja-ud-Daula.

I have [now] been honoured with having had the audience with you. I had asked Manik Ram Bose to submit to you the details of my requirements. Apparently, he could not muster enough courage to communicate the same to you, perhaps his submissions were not attended to. It so happens that the goods I had brought with me were ruined because of incessant rains and the lack of proper accommodation for me to stay. Meanwhile, I came to know that you have ordered the construction of a new house for me, but that will take a long time. I have been deputed to be in your service by Imad-ud-Daula. It is thus strange that I have still not been provided a proper place to stay in, and am left [virtually] in the open field to face the ordeal of rain and storm. I do not know what I should write to Ịmad-ud-Daula. Gernail *ṣāḥib* has certainly been nice enough to offer me a place in the *ramna* (hunting houses). But since I have come here for your work it is not appropriate that I stay anywhere without your direction.

1. Polier watching a nautch

2. The young emperor Akbar in the Royal Garden

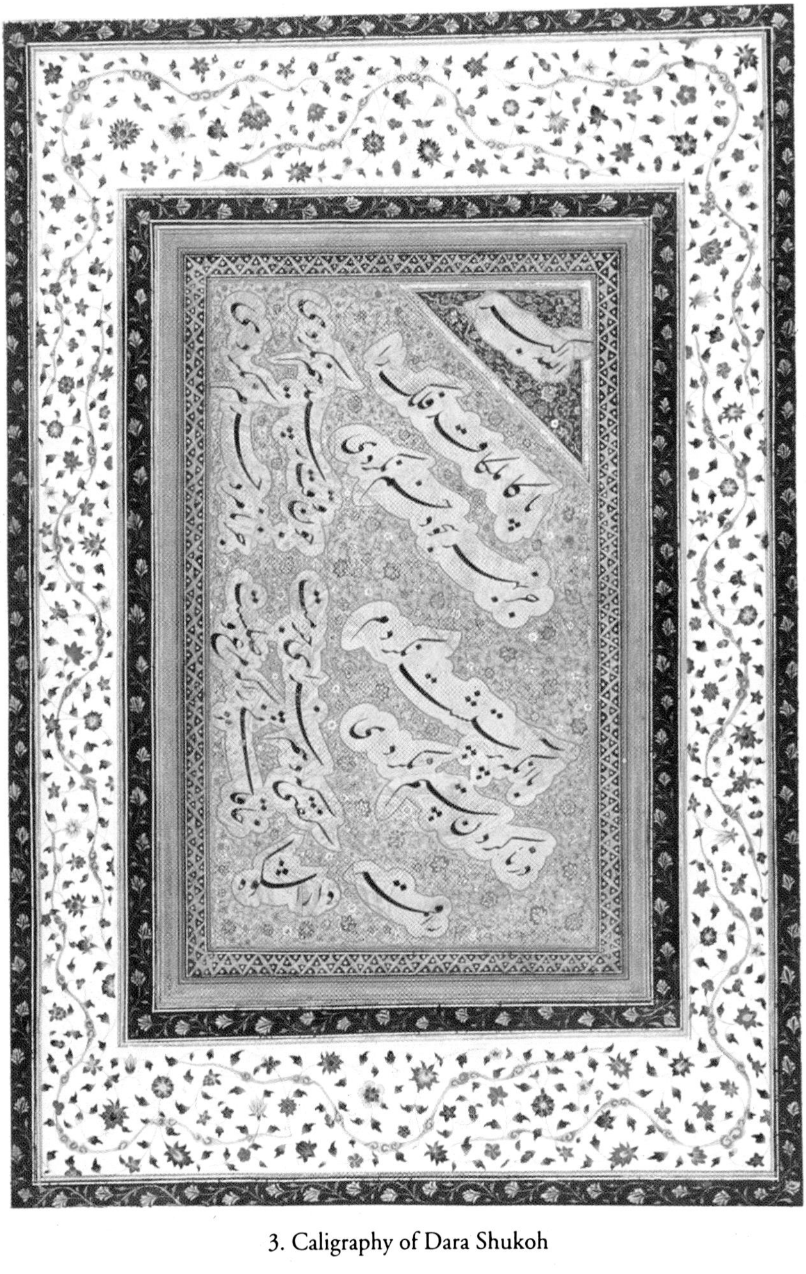

3. Caligraphy of Dara Shukoh

4. A Holy man

5. Princess at fireworks

6. Meeting at the well

7. Female musician

8. *Vibhāsa Rāginī*

I hope that you will soon issue orders for some accommodation until the construction of the new house is completed. 8th Rabī'II, *ramna*, Faizabad.

Folio 4b. To Raja Gobind Ram, resident of Calcutta.

I have received your letter in which you have mentioned about your meeting with the Governor, [Hastings] and about your earnest but unsuccessful efforts [for me]. Since nothing can be achieved without the help of God one can only look for his grace and help. At the moment matters here are also not being carried out to my satisfaction. When it is done I will let you know. So be patient. Patience is the key of relief. It is important that we keep in touch. 12 Rabī'II, Lucknow.

Folio 5a. To Mir Muhammad Azim, the binder.

Since I have had the pleasure of meeting you often in the past, I now wish to meet you again. I will appreciate if you take the trouble of travelling and reaching here. 16 Rabī'II, Faizabad.

Folio 5b. To Muhammad Salah Khan, seal engraver.

I had sent you a piece of ruby. It was certainly not of the best quality. So if you find a good piece—better in colour, cut and size—it will be preferable. Otherwise, take this one to the polisher of precious stones (*hakkāk*) and have the legend that I sent you engraved on it in an elegant way. Send this [engraved stone] back to me as I need it at an early date. 16 Rabī'II, Faizabad.

Folio 5a. To Raja Chait Singh, son of Raja Balwant Singh.

Ever since I reached here I have not heard from you. I am therefore anxious about your welfare. I hope you will keep me regularly informed about your well-being. Rest assured that I shall always work for the betterment of your affairs. You should entertain no doubts about my intentions.

I gathered from Mousseau Gentil *ṣāḥib* that you like the essence of *dārchīnī*. I am sending you a small quantity of the same. If you want more I will send it along with the goods which will be sent to you subsequently. I have given Manik Ram the details of this place. He will write to you. Have faith in me. May the days of [our] unity last forever. 27 Rabī II, Faizabad.

Folio 6a. To Raja Chait Singh.

I am happy to receive your letter. I was a bit worried about your welfare and had written to you a letter which must have reached you by now. I was delighted to hear from Manik Ram about your excellent qualities. I am sincerely concerned about your affairs and it is my heartfelt desire that these are managed appropriately.

The Nawab [Shuja-ud-Daula] is planning to set out in the direction [of Benares] at his advice. I am also accompanying him. When we reach there I will discuss matters with you and accordingly (*ba ḥasb-i ṣalāḥ-i hamdīgar*) I will do my best to get the things done properly. The rest you will know in detail from the letters of Manik Ram. 15 Jumāda I, Faizabad.

Folio 7a. Reply to Mufti Ghulam Hazrat Ahmad, resident of Lucknow.

I have received the letter that you sent me at Faizabad. I will indeed be delighted to meet you personally. I intend staying here permanently (*sukūnat-i dāimī*), but at the moment I am accompanying the Nawab to Benares. Until we meet, you must keep writing to me.

Regarding your enquiries about some of the English *ṣāḥibs*, Graham *ṣāḥib* and John *ṣāḥib* have passed away, and the other *ṣāḥibs* have left for *wilāyat*.

I have written to Muhammad Azim, the binder who often met me when I was there, but I have not received his reply. Could you please find out about his welfare and write to me? Jumāda I.

Folio 7b. To Raja Chait Singh.

The relatives of Jugal Kishore, agent of Gokul Chand and Ramchand Sah, who look after my business are going from Benares to Lucknow. I am writing to you so that you can arrange ten dependable *piyadas* from amongst your troops to escort them. They should be instructed especially to look after the safety [of these men] on their way upto Shahzadpur. 23 Jumāda II, Benares.

Folio 8a. To Raja Chait Singh.

I am delighted to receive your reply to my letter. Tomorrow has been fixed for our departure, but as yet none of your palaquin and luggage carriers have reached here. We need forty persons to carry our luggage and the palanquins. Your people here have made no arrangements. They require strict instructions. Their wages will be paid as per our agreement. 23 Jumāda II, Benares.

Folio 8a. To Raja Chait Singh.

Though I had intended to follow the order of the Nawab to leave along with his retinue, I have stayed back to meet some friends. I am very keen to meet you but I have no time. At any rate, love relates to the heart and is not dependant upon physical meeting. The Nawab has issued strict orders regarding the goods that had been stolen on the way. But since I am your friend I did not consider it necessary to report. At the time of his departure the Nawab had issued strict instructions to the *yasāwal* [state messenger] to apprehend the thieves and recover the goods. I have therefore sent the *yasāwal* to you along with the list of the [stolen] goods. Dispatch the thieves as well as the goods to Faizabad before my arrival there and inform the Nawab. 25 Jumāda II, 1187.

Folio 8b. To Raja Chait Singh.

Captain Cartier arrived in Faizabad following an order from Hastings to journey through the country and to survey the lands for the Company. From there he intends to set out for *chakla* Kora and the other districts [in the neighbourhood]. He requires carts and people to carry the goods. I am writing to you to arrange money for the same. The people should be dependable and the carts and oxen should be strong enough to avert any problem on the way. Send me also a *parwāna* in the name of the *'āmils* of the *maḥāls,* to be handed over to the Captain, so that they refrain from giving him any trouble on his way. 25 Jumāda II, handed over to Captain Cartier.

Folio 9a. To Amanat Khan, faujdār of Jaunpur and Phulpur.

I and the other English *ṣāḥibs* left Benares and arrived in Phulpur. Here we were informed by *harkāra* that the bridge of Jalalpur as well as two or three other bridges which happen to be on our way have been damaged and are unpassable due to floods. I therefore write to you to immediately dispatch masons and carpenters, along with the requisite equipments, with strict instructions to repair the damaged bridges immediately. The boats should also be available on the spot. We should not be made to wait for their arrangement on our arrival. This should be treated as urgent. 27 Jumāda II, Wednesday, sent with a *harkāra.*

Folio 9b. To Nawab Shuja-ud-Daula.

I left Benares two days back and arrived in Jalalpur where I was taken ill because of the humid climate. I wanted to reach you at the earliest but the floods and the non-availability of boats kept me there for four to five days. After great difficulty I have now reached Jaunpur. Though I am keen to meet you, I will have to stay here for sometime because of my weak health. I will start from here as soon as I have recovered. The letter of Mushirul-Mulk Murad-ud-Daula, Mr. Middleton Ikhtiyar Jang which I received here on my way has been sent to you and will reach you soon. (May the sun of your power grandeur keep shining.) 7 Rajab 1187, Jaunpur, dispatched with Dhotal Singh, *dārogha* of *harkāras.*

Folio 10a. To Chait Singh.

I have received here, in Jaunpur, your letter in response to mine. You mention that you have enquired into the case of the theft with care; but since the incident took place in a border area, the *'āmil* there is appointed by [and thus is accountable to] the Nawab. The fact is that the incident took place in *Sarāi* Khatia which lies in your jurisdiction. Notwithstanding the Nawab's strict instructions, I have refrained so far from taking any unpleasant step against you because of my sincere concern for you. I believed that you would not indulge in unmerited delay tactics, but I am astonished to discover that you are engaged in mere correspondence. I have genuine friendly feelings for you. I therefore think that whenever the matter is brought to the notice of the Nawab I should not utter a word but in your praise. It is necessary that the stolen goods along with the thieves be sent to Faizabad before I reach there. This will cement the bonds of our friendship. Following indisposition I am stationed in Jaunpur for a while. 9 Rajab, 1187, dispatched with Dīwān Manik Ram Bose.

Folio 10b. To Nawab Murid Khan.

Our friendship needs no ritual formalities. I have sent you a watch. Please acknowledge its receipt. 17 Rajab 1187, dispatched with Muhammad Jafar *chūbdār.*

Folio 11a. To Mirza Abdullah Beg, kumaindān.

I received your letter along with the details about the horses. I have ordered the horses from Aqa Husain in *wilāyat* [Afghanistan]. I came to know from Hurmat Khan that you have bought them from another dealer (*saudāgar*). Well, today the Nawab has requisitioned all the horses. It will be good if you also bring all the horses with you so that the matter is decided in his presence. 21 Rajab 1187.

Folio 11b. To Sulaiman Khan.

On the 15th of Rajab I received your letter in which you have enquired about the broad cloth (*bānāt*) and the instructions regarding its sale. The receipt of all the *thans* of the broad cloth which were acquired by Mushtaq is with you. The other forty-four soiled *thans* are kept in the custody of Manik Ram for sale. We have not been approached by any buyer yet. You will be informed as soon as they are disposed off.

The horse that you require for your personal use has not yet been found. This time the dealers did not bring good breed horses because of the rains. However, I am looking for a good horse for you, and as soon as I get one I will send it to you.

In the meanwhile I have sent ten *mans* of high quality rice by boat. My men will receive it in Calcutta and bring it to you in Charchara (?). 25 Rajab 1187.

Folio 12a. To Nawab Shuja-ud-Daula.

You have ordered that the *ḥavelī* of Basant Khan be made my residence. I will obey your order but there is no privacy in the *bāradarī* of that house even if it is not absolutely un-habitable. The roof is still incomplete and the attached small quarters are damaged in several places. For the time being the tiled roof will do but repair is necessary. A reliable person should be instructed to arrange for proper repairs. It is not appropriate that I approach you again for this matter. Lime, bari(?) and bamboo which are available would be required for the repair. 26 Rajab 1187.

Folio 12b. To Mir Sulaiman Khan.

I have sent twenty-six *mans* of fine rice by boat to the *ṣāḥib* in Calcutta. Out of this, ten *mans* are from me, while sixteen *mans* are from Ashur Beg Khan. He [the *ṣāḥib*] will send the rice to Khwaja Pedrose from where it will reach you. I have also enclosed a letter of which this letter is a copy. 28 Rajab 1187.

Folio 13a. To Ghulam Hazrat Ahmad Mufti, resident of Lucknow.

I have received your letter in which you have mentioned your indisposition and the fact that you could not trace Muhammad Azim, the binder. May you recover soon. At the moment the Nawab is leaving for Lucknow and I am also accompanying him. We hope to meet you there. Keep in touch. 29 Rajab 1187.

Folio 13a. To Dulichand sāhūkār.

I was delighted to meet your *gumāshta* Kanjimal and to hear from him about your fine qualities. I will try to get your work done as per your wish. At the moment I have asked your agent to do something which you would know about from his letter. I hope that you will do what he writes about and thus contribute to the enhancement of our business. 1 Sha'bān 1187, handed over to Kanjimal.

Folio 13b. To Raja Chait Singh about the case of Shihab Khan, son of Lal Khan.

Shihab Khan, who is in the service of the Nawab, has purchased Makhdupur, etc., the two villages there. Some people, out of greed, are unjustly interfering with his servants. Since you are the *mālik* [master] of that place I will be happy if you could warn them so that they desist from such acts. You should also ensure that in future no one dares to indulge in any mischief like this and no harm is done to their goods and possessions. 7 Sha'bān 1187.

Folio 14a. To Amanat Khan (faujdār of Jaunpur).

Following a demand from the Nawab, I have sent Raso Sarkar with a *dastak* to bring from Jaunpur 680 *thans* of pattu belonging to General *ṣāḥib.* Please arrange whatever carts and carriers Raso Sarkar requires for this purpose. You may recover the due wages and the cartage charge from him. 9 Sha'bān 1187.

Folio 14a. To Raja Hindupat regarding the case of Captain Cartier.

Captain Cartier, who has been appointed by the English Company to survey the lands in your jurisdiction, has left for his destination along with the troopers of the Nawab. Please ensure that Cartier is provided with every thing that he requires and that no excesses are committed. You should not get unduly alarmed at Cartier's arrival; take it rather as an opportunity and try your best to arrange the things he needs at a reasonable, price. This will please me and Nawab Imad-ud-Daula Hastings Bahadur. 12 Sha'bān 1187.

Folio 15a. To Amanat Khan, faujdār of Jaunpur.

A boat from Sultanpur, laden with tents, wine and other goods of the Company, reached Jaunpur along with the army. But it disappeared after its departure from Jaunpur together with the other boats and the army. It is not clear whether the boat returned to Sultanpur, or proceeded further towards the east or is still stationed in Jaunpur. Please enquire about this. If it is still there take care of its safety and inform me immediately. Or find out if it has returned to Sultanpur or is headed towards the east. 12 Sha'bān 1187.

Folio 15b. To Maharaja Ajit Singh, zamindar of Rewan.

Captain Cartier, appointed by the Company to survey the land in your jurisdiction, has left along with two companies of the Nawab's troops. He [Cartier] is a fine man. He will pay for whatever he needs. He will also ensure that none of his troopers commit any excesses. Do not get suspicious of him. Be nice to him. This will help sort out matters easily and will please the Governor and me. 12 Sha'bān 1187, Faizabad.

Folio 16a. To Shaikh Diyanatullah.

Half *man* of white vinegar (*'arq-i-na'nā'*) along with the list of expenses sent with Ilah Bakhsh *piyāda* reached me in time. Send two more *mans* of vinegar matured in your presence and a bit better and more pungent (*tund-tar*) so that it can be used for pickles, etc. Muhammad Azim, whom you tried to locate in vain, reached here a few days ago. He will be back [in Lucknow] after two or three days. This is for your information. 15 Sha'bān 1187, dispatched with Ilah Bakhsh, *piyāda* of the Shaikh.

Folio 16b. To Nawab Ṣāḥib.

The soldiers appointed with Captain Marsack arrived on the 20th. I also learnt further about their condition from Manik Ram. The soldiers do not have shirts, caps, and trousers. You know it well that no work can be carried out without these items, particularly in view of the road condition. I therefore request you to arrange for 100 *tonths* and three sangs and shirts from the *sarkār* so that Captian Marsack can set out for his work. On their return, the caps and trouser that are leftover will be deposited back[to the *sarkār*]. 21 Sha'bān 1187, dispatched with a *harkāra* from Faizabad.

Folio 17a. To Diwan Manik Ram.

A *hundī* of Rs 900 has been sent to you. Since the *hundī* is in the name of Manik Ram Gangoli you must procure the receipt of the money from him. Hand over the money to him after that. One letter in the name of Mirza Abdullah Beg *kumaindān* and three *chuktī* [clearance papers mail] *dāk* are being sent herewith. 23 Sha'bān 1187, Mianganj, 1 *pahar* night.

Folio 17a. To Mirza Abdullah Beg, kumaidān.

I received your letter regarding the dispatch of horses for Nawab Imad-ud-Daula Governer Hashtin [Hastings] and your returning to him the money for their cost. There is no harm in your meeting the *ṣāḥib* [Hastings] and personally returning the money to him. Do as he wishes. I have sent you the *dastak* of *rāhdārī* for eighteen more horses. 23 Sha'bān, 1187, Miyanganj, at night.

Folio 17b. To Diwan Manik Ram.

There was a watch among the items stolen which belonged to Richi *ṣāḥib.* You should therefore deposit Rs 500 with him towards its cost along with the casket and the letter for him, that I sent you. Send me as soon as possible the cotton bags that Piru handed over to you for stitching. 24 Sha'bān, 1187 Nawabganj, 4 *gharī* of the night.

Folio 17b. To Nawab Shuja-ud-Daula.

On my arrival in the city yesterday I sent my man to seek your permission for an audience with you at the court. You promised to issue instructions for the same today. Today, in response to his [my man's] repeated requests you said that I could meet you in the camp tomorrow. O Lord, I have travelled a long distance and have lived here on the instructions of Nawab Imad-ud-Daula Governor Hastings for five months, but I am still deprived of your kind attention. All the other Englishmen who came here have been fortunate enough to be blessed with your favours, but you did not enquire about my welfare. My English comportment (*tīnat-i-angreziya*) does not bear with this. How can I live here without your kindness. It is difficult for me to stay here now even for a moment. However, I still hope to receive your beneficence. 26 Sha'bān.

Folio 18a. To Nawab Shuja-ud-Daula.

Since there is an agreement between you and Nawab Imad-ud-Daula [Hastings] that you would arrange for troopers required to accompany the *ṣāḥibs* [English officers] in charge of the survey and measurement of land, I repeatedly appealed to you to apoint two companies and fifty horsemen to accompany Marsack *ṣāḥib.* The soldiers who arrived here have not been paid their emoluments for three months. This may lead to dereliction of duty on their part and in desperation they may commit excesses on the peasantry (*ri'āyā*). As submitted to you earlier, the companies are short of three *havaldārs* and thirty troopers and that they have neither their shirts nor caps. I hope you will issue orders for the supply of the same and sanction money for the payment and thus earn the goodwill of *Ṣāḥib-i-Kalān* [grand *ṣāḥib*, Hastings]. Further, the fifty horsemen that you said you would dispatch on your return to Lucknow have not yet arrived. You may issue orders for their dispatch as well.

Since you had instructed the grain merchants (*baqqāls*) not to do anything without your orders I had sent word to you through Ilich Khan to order the *baqqāls* to accompany the companies. The order may be issued and dispatched. In response to my letter an order was issued yesterday directing me to arrive at the court and meet you. I think servitude (*bandagī*) is not dependant on my personal audience with you. Since nothing is being done despite my requests it is necessary that you instruct your officials to carry the work at the earliest.

Lambert *ṣāḥib* has written to me that you have ordered two horses for me and that he would get them on reaching Lucknow. He must obtain these horses from you and send them to me. 27, Sha'bān 1187, Bagh Yaqut Khan, Lucknow.

Folio 19a. To Mufti Ghulam Hazrat Ahmad.

I received your letter in which you have regretted your inability to come for reasons of ill health. I am happy to meet Shaikh Nur-ud-Din and learn from him about your welfare. Do come as soon as you recover. Consider my house as yours. 29 Sha'bān, Lucknow.

Folio 19b. To Nawab Shuja-ud-Daula.

It is the fourth day since my letter was presented to you. No reply has been received so far. Your instructions in the matter are awaited. 1 Ramẓān, Tuesday, sent with Rai Kishan, *chūbdār.*

Folio 19b. To Diwan Manik Ram.

On the 2nd of Ramẓān I received your letter through the *harkāra* stating that the money you sent to Richi *ṣāḥib* was returned to you, after being kept with him for some time, due to the problem of the Patna currency (*ṣarf Aẓimabadi*). Why did he accept the money and if it was of no worth why did he keep it with himself [for some time] before returning it? Anyhow, you should try to reach here at the earliest. When you arrive in Lucknow find out about the progress regarding the preparation of the tents and see that they reach us soon. The bags of cotton have also not yet arrived. Send them immediately. 2 Ramẓān, Purwa.

Folio 20a. To Diwan Manik Ram.

I had written to you earlier about the preparation of the tents. Consider the matter urgent and have them sent at the earliest. It is difficult [to live] here without an additional tent. A parasol (*shāmyāna*) is also required. If you plan to reach here early you may bring them with you. Otherwise, have them sent before your departure. The cotton bags are still to reach here. Send also a small *Diler Khānī* spade/shovel (*pāl*) which is required for Didar Bakhsh. 4 Ramẓān, 1187, Madarpur, 3 *kos* away from Jajmau, sent with a *harkāra* at night.

Folio 20b. To Mir Muhammad Azim.

Nawab Shuja-ud-Daula is soon to set out for Kanauj. If you are already prepared to reach there, well and good. Otherwise [wait a bit], I will write to you from Kanauj where we will stay for sometime.

Have two rings,of the style I mentioned, made out of the precious stones I handed over to you and send them to me. Ensure that the other things that you have to bring with you are ready. Bring also a few *thāns* of silver lace (*kināri*) enough for three *peshwāzs* and 100 big oranges. See that the tents are ready and sent here soon. 6 Ramẓān, Monday.

Folio 21a. To Diwan Manik Ram.

I have not heard about your departure yet. Since most of the work here is dependant upon your arrival you should try to reach here early. The Nawab will leave for Kanauj in two days time and will stay there for sometime. So you should proceed for Kanauj immediately after your arrival in Lucknow. 8 Ramẓān, Tuesday, sent with a *harkāra.*

Folio 21a. To Ras Bihari Sarkar.

I received your letter in which you report that Scott *ṣāḥib* has objected to and stalled the dispatch of the 376 *thans* of *pattu* [coarse woollen cloth] which you had acquired from him. Since the *ṣāḥib* had petitioned to me earlier, you should hand over to him whatever he wants and give him a list of the items transacted so that he reaches here soon. See to it that there is no further delay in sending the *dastak* of *rahdārā*. 8 Ramẓān,Tuesday, village Madarpur, three *kos* before Jajmau.

Folio 21b. To Diwan Manik Ram.

Since *Karānī ṣāḥib* [the manager of the household] is leaving for Calcutta from Faizabad, hire two boats for him and instruct the boatmen that on arrival in Calcutta they contact the *ṣāḥib* who is looking after my business there. You get the goods loaded and come back. Give him [my man] 50 rupees *Arcoti* for expenses. In case Manik Ram has already left for this place then whosoever is there may act accordingly. 8 Ramẓān 1187.

Folio 21b. To Mir Muhammad Azim, Lucknow.

I received your letter along with hundred oranges and two pieces of sugar candy. The candy is too oily and is not white. Get seven to eight *mans* of white candy, unmixed with oil, ready and send two pieces of it to me as specimen. When my men reach there [Lucknow] they will take it [sugar candy] to Calcutta. I would appreciate if you could also send hundred more oranges after twenty days.

You have not written anything about the ring. Write about it in detail along with the reply to this letter. Write also whether the two precious stones that you have acquired are of better colour and quality.

Get laces of different colours for three *peshwāzs* and send them to me. Note that one *peshwāz* requires six yards of *gota* [gold laces] and thirty yards of *kinārī* [silver laces]. 12 Ramẓān, Pitam Sarai 1 *pās* night has passed.

Folio 22b. To Saiyid Muhammad Aẓim, Lucknow.

Please send at an early date the tent which is being prepared under your supervision. The upper part of the *bichuba* [small tent without the wooden poles] under the flap of the bigger tent should be of white cloth with multicolour prints . The inside of this tent should be made of only the printed cloth. As for the *qanāt* [walls of the tent], Manik Ram had instructed you earlier to make it of four parts; but now I think you should make them of six parts with each part measuring 15 yards. In addition to this, I request you to get a large size *qanāt* ready. The floor mats (*shaṭranjī*) should be pink and blue in colour, and of such sizes that one of them is fit to be spread under the small tent without the poles and the other pair on the floor under the flap. Pitam Sarai, 12 Ramẓān, 1 *pās* night.

Folio 22b. To Mir Muhammad Azim.

Get the four worn out mirrors [kept with you] polished and then hand them over to Monsieur Gentil who has arrived in Lucknow. Also see that the tent is prepared soon and is dispatched here. Along with the new tent, which you will send through Saiyid Muhammad Khan, send also a strong and stable cot with beautifully carved legs and knitted with *nivar,* two to three reams of Kashmiri paper and three to four reams of Lucknowi paper. I had earlier written to you about the Nawab's departure to Kanauj. Having spent some time there he is now proceeding towards Etawah. Send the book also with the paper. 13 Ramẓān, Sunday, written at night and sent by a *harkāra.*

Folio 23a. To Mir Muhammad Azim.

I had written to you earlier about the four mirrors you had acquired in Lucknow. Get them polished and keep them in a wooden box, wrapped in white paper to protect them from the dust while they are in transit. Send them [mirrors] to me along with a knife which has a lion and fish engraved on its handle. You had mentioned earlier about an Indian gun available for sale. Settle the price for this gun, buy it, clean and oil it and then send it with the other goods to Faizabad. Ensure that the person who carts these goods prepares an inventory for them. In case you cannot procure the gun send the mirrors, the knife and ½ *ser kasis* [Martial vitriol] and look around for a proper gun. I had earlier mentioned to you about 200–300 arrows. Acquire hundred of these of good quality and send them.

Send the details of the *'amārī* [the canopy of the elephant] that is being prepared there: what kind of *'amārī* is being put together; and how much of it is still to be completed. Since the *ḥauẓa* [canopy] of my *sawārī* is light in weight, small and useless, place an order for a *ḥauẓa* also with the person who is making the *'amārī.* The *ḥauẓa* should be strong, elegant and spacious. Once these items are ready keep them with you. I will write to you whenever I need them.

Send me the specimen of the fine cloth with golden thread work for the *peshawāz.* I will write about its purchase only after I have made my choice. If you need any money I will send you the *hundī* from here. Send some of these things to Faizabad; you can bring the others when you come here.

Get also the following items ready from the artisans noted for their fine work: two big size handkerchiefs with self-coloured print; one hookah pipe made fully of *bādla*; one *zanjīra* made of golden thread (*kalābatūn*) of high quality; one ornamented coloured hookah of Rs 15 with a silver chillum having an elegantly polished cover. Further, if you manage to acquire the animal skins and other items I had asked for from Farrukhabad please send them also. 16 Ramẓān, Wednesday, sent with the *harkāra.*

Folio 24b. To Mir Muhammad Azim.

I had written to you earlier about the preparation of the sugar candy. Get the following ready: two *mans* of oil-free pure white candy and ten *ser* of mango pickles. Send these with Ajab Singh *harkāra,* who has brought the letter to Faizabad. There should be a minimum of one *man* sugar candy and it should not exceed two *mans.* Similarly, there should be a minimum of six to seven *ser* mango pickle and it should not exceed ten *ser.* Also send ten to twenty *ser* of good quality white vinegar for the pickles. 16 Ramẓān, Wednesday, Makanpur, in the night.

Folio 24b. To Oshra Mistri Gora.

I received your letter containing the details regarding the preparation of the garden and the land. Give maximum possible attention to their preparation and also to the arrangement of the trees. Manik Ram has written to Sayidi Alam about the gardeners who came from Azimabad. These Azimabad gardeners should work according to the advice of the local gardeners.

It is not necessary to prepare a concrete wall. Build four good houses: one for me, another for Marsack *ṣāḥib,* the third one being the *ḥavelī* for Bībī *ṣāḥib* [wife], and the fourth one for *karānī ṣāḥib.* The houses should have concrete platforms.

Two gardeners who came from Azimabad had been paid their wages there itself. They should now be paid after two months. It is necessary to note the date of their departure from Azimabad. As for the instructions for sowing are concerned, ask the gardeners to sow the seeds in time. But withold the sowing of the musk melon and water melon seeds for the moment. I have in mind the case of your emoluments; rest assured that I will present your case to the Nawab at an appropriate time.

Manik Ram should also write to Sayidi Alam about the grape saplings. Plant good quality saplings there. Look around also for fine quality saplings of plums, peaches and other good fruits, and procure them even if they are available at high prices.

Arrange reasonable accommodation for the European (*firangī*) whom Falak *ṣāḥib* has sent from Azimabad. Arrange also for a *sawārī* if he needs one and send him here soon with a *harkāra.*

Finally, a boat with three boxes containing parts of a musical instrument is arriving from Calcutta. Bring them carefully to the house to be assembled by the watchmaker (*gharīwala ṣāḥib*) after which the instrument should be wrapped in a cloth to protect it from the dust. Keep me regularly informed about the condition of the house. 17 Ramẓān, Thursday, 5 *kos* from Makanpur towards Etawah, night, dispatched to Faizabad with Diwan Manik Ram.

Folio 26a. To Nawab Muzaffar Jang (son of late Nawab Ahmad Khan Bangash).

Sahib Rai and Permanand, brothers of my agent Jugal Kishore, who reside in Farrukhabad are being troubled by an Afghan. I urge you to summon the Afghan and Sahib Rai and enquire into the case. In case of unwarranted interference by the Afghan, you should chastise him so that he does not think of this kind of mischief in the future. I shall be happy if you could help these brothers and attend to their requirements regularly. 20 Ramẓān, Monday, near Pila.

Folio 26b. To Mir Muhammad Azim.

I recieved your letter of 17 Ramẓān on the 21st. I also received two specimen pieces of the sugar candy, out of the eight *mans* that you have had prepared, and two jars of pickles. I had written to you that the sugar candy should be of high quality, oil free and crystal clear, but the specimen candy is not clean and is too oily. The pickles are fine but you should still look around for a better variety, made of several [fruits and vegetables].

I understand that the initial payment for the ruby has to be made and the remaining amount is to be adjusted in monthly payments as was the case earlier. You are aware of the deal and should act on your own accord. I am not in favour of buying the four *nargas* [square tents], and the small (*bīchūba*), tent without the poles. The tent being prepared under the supervision of Muhammad Saiyid Khan should be completed and sent soon.

Similarly, the *'amārī* should be dispatched as soon as it is ready. The cushions and its spread should be of the same colour as the lining, which itself should be done elegantly.The inside of the frills should be made of silk threads and the outer face of golden threads.

The laces and the rings should be sent whenever they are ready. I have written to Makhu Khan the *kotwāl* [of Lucknow to help you].

The money you have asked for is not being sent since we are in a hurry at the moment. It will be sent to you later.

You have written that the four mirrors and saddles are available for Rs 1500. This price is not acceptable to me. Buy them at the price you had procured them earlier, but you know better. We require two to four mirrors but some more details are awaited which I will let you know when we meet.

Send the lace for one *peshwāz* through the same *harkāra* immediately. You have responded to some cases about which I had written to you earlier. Please do write and clarify the details about the ruby. Send me at an early date four *ser* of dry and fine quality Multānī or *Amānat Khānī* tobacco. I have given Re 1 to the *harkāra*; you can include it in his account. 21 Ramẓān, Monday night.

Folio 27b. To Mir Makhu Khan, kotwāl of Lucknow.

Since the things which I had ordered are being prepared at the house of Mir Muhammad Azim, you should attend to his requirements. The work for my orders requires artisans of different kinds. Instruct your people to arrange for whatever he needs without any delay. 21 Ramẓān, Monday night, sent with the letter of Mir Muhammad Azim.

Folio 28a. To Raja Gobind Ram.

You have written to me about not having recieved replies to the two letters you had sent me. I replied to you as soon as I received your letter. I am perfectly all right and pray for your welfare. Keep in touch. 22 Ramẓān, Tuesday.

Folio 28b. To Shah Muhammad Riza Pīrzāda.

I received your letter. I had not received any letter from you earlier otherwise I would have written back to you. I will write to Mr Law about the refusal of Holasi and other *mahājans* of Bihar to return the money you had deposited with them, and about your request to me to send a *parwāna* regarding this matter. You should meet him and apprise him of the details. He will do the needful to retrieve your money. 23 Ramẓān 1187.

Folio 28b. To Nidhiram Sarkar.

One *chuktī* in the name of Captain Marsack *ṣāḥib* has reached here.

Apparently he has left from Faizabad. The *chuktī* [clearance paper] is being sent to you to be sent there. 26 Ramẓān.

Folio 29a. To Hafiz Rahmat Khan.

Your letter, together with the communication of the Governor *ṣāḥib*, has been received. But the reply is delayed because it was not possible to write back to you promptly.

I am your sincere friend and would like to have a cordial relationship with you. I had presented your case to the Governor *ṣāḥib* and I understand that you have received his reply. However, as a precautionary measure I am also writing to you. There is no proof as yet of the cordial relations that you profess to have with the English. I hope that you will regard me as a sincere friend and keep in touch with me. 4 Shawwāl 1187.

Folio 29b. To Khan Muhammad Khan (nephew of Hafiz Rahmat Khan).

I received your letter. There was delay in writing to Hafiz Rahmat Khan because I had not received any letter about him from the Governor in Calcutta. Now that instructions have come from Calcutta, I have sent my letter to Hafiz Rahmat Khan which should reach him soon. Since the English always desire cordial relations, I hope that he will also strive for the same. 4 Shawwāl.

Folio 30a. To Raja Kalyan Singh, zamindar of Rampur Budh Painth.

I received your letter from Niranjan Das *vakīl*, along with the *kharīṭa* for the Nawab [Shuja-ud-Daula]. I came to know from Mir Muhammad Husain Ata Khan about your fine qualities. I have presented your *kharīṭa* to the Nawab. The reply will be sent through the *vakīl*. Reach the court and rest assured that everything that you want will be done properly. 4 Shawwāl

Folio 31a. To Mir Muhammad Azim.

I had earlier sent you a *hundī* of Rs 500 written by Raghu Chand to be encashed at the shop of Nain Sukh. I am sending you another *hundī* of Rs 500 to be encashed at the same shop. You had asked for Rs 1000. You should now ensure that payment for my orders is made to the concerned party. For the last twenty days I have not received any letter from you. We hope to stay for sometime in Etawah where we are camping at the moment. Get my orders ready and send them here along with the *'amārī* and its cover.

I learnt from Monsieur Gentil that the shield and saddle you had acquired were good. I have written about them to a friend in Calcutta. Keep dillydallying the terms of the purchase until I hear from Calcutta. My tent with Muhammad Sa'id Khan is ready. Ask him to send it soon. The pickles you had sent were fine, but the sugar candy was too oily. 5 Shawwāl 1187.

Folio 31a. To Nawab Shuja-ud-Daula.

Today a strange incident took place. The men of the *sarkār* belonging to the *paltan* of Latafat Ali Khan quarrelled with my men, beat them up and arrested them. The encounter ended only with the intervention of some other people. My people have been instructed not to pick up quarrels with the people of the *sarkār,* and if they do they would be punished. Whenever excesses committed by my people were brought to my notice I took appropriate action. It was not necessary that 300 people fight and attack my men with swords. I have sent my people along with those from the *sarkār* to you. Whatever is just should be done. I feel such an incident was inappropriate because there is no conflict between the English Company and you and I am here alone in a country of strangers courtesy your kindness. It will be difficult for me to live in your court if you do not take proper care of me, and if the people of the *sarkār* persist with these raids and go unpunished. 6 Shawwāl 1187.

Folio 31b. To Oshra Mistri Gora.

I had replied to your letter earlier and learnt about your welfare from Monsieur Gentil. I had also written to you about the construction of the four houses: one for me; one for Marsack *ṣāḥib*; one for Bībī *ṣāḥib* and one for *karānī ṣāḥib.* Your letter informs me that the floor of the courtyard of the *ḥavelī* has been made of concrete; that while this is fine the mud wall in your judgement is inadequate, and that it will be better if it can be made of concrete. Please do whatever you feel is appropriate. But construct my house first with concrete floor and walls. Later you can do whatever you consider best for the other houses.

The European seeds which had been sown earlier have not sprouted at all. Hand over the remaining seeds to the gardeners and ask them to take appropriate measures. The sowing of the European seeds and the planting of the grape saplings should be done as per my earlier instructions. The letter of Sayidi Alam in the name of Muhammad Bashir Khan regarding the completion of the roof of the *bāradarī* will reach you .The materials needed for the construction are with Sayidi Alam. Obtain these from him and start the construction. Sayidi Alam will pay the expenses of the masons, gardeners, and the artisans. In case you do not receive payment from him write to me. Your work should be done without any delay or disruption in the management of my establishment there.

Captain Martin *ṣāḥib* and Captain Brooke will be reaching Faizabad from the east. Arrange their accommodation if they come to my *ḥavelī*, look after their requirements in a manner which should please them. The palanquin and the other goods which they would bring for me should be kept properly in the *ḥavelī*. Keep the turkey and the duck that they are bringing for me in a clean place along with my other birds. Arrange for their feed and see to it that they are safe from harmful animals.

I remember your work and will do it in time. 7 Shawwāl.

Folio 33a. To Mir Muhammad Azim.

I have not heard from you for the last twenty-two days. Send the things I ordered immediately because I need them urgently. You should send the wine carton that I left in your house before the army departs from here. I wonder if you received my letter in which I had asked for some tobacco. Please dispatch immediately five to six *sers* of *Amānat Khānī* or Multanī tobacco. Do not make excuses for not writing because nobody from my *sarkār* met you. You are my agent and will be suitably paid for all the expenses you incur in arranging for the things I order. 7 Shawwāl.

Folio 33b. To Mir Sulaiman Khan.

I received your letters in which you have complained about my not replying to your letters written from Azimabad, Murshidabad and Calcutta. I have not received any of these letters. But I believe you have received two to three of my letters which I had sent to you together with ten *mans* of rice that you had ordered. I am enclosing herewith copies of these letters.

As for the two horses that you have written about, please note that I record the orders of friends in my diary (*kitāb*) so that I do not forget to fulfil them on time. You had earlier asked for one horse and now you want two. I am looking around for these and hope to find them in two months time.

I wonder if you are aware of the contents of the letter which I received recently from Lutf Ali Khan who is in the army of Nawab Najaf Khan. I am sending you excerpts of this letter on a piece of paper. If I find the book you mention with Agha Rahim I shall send it to you forthwith. Keep in touch. I am your sincere friend and always your well-wisher. 4 Shawwāl 1187

Folio 34b. To Mir Sulaiman Khan.

I had written to you earlier about the developments here. There is nothing new to report but I have observed that people here are of a strange nature and are not trustworthy.

When they observe someone's rising fortunes they praise him keeping their hand on the head.

When someone is cursed with divine wrath the whole world puts its foot on his head. 11 Shawwāl 1187.

Folio 35a. To Raso Sarkar, Faizabad.

Find out the details of the following: what goods I possess there along with the latest additions; what goods will reach later; what items have been sold and are still to be sold. Send me all this information in confidence so that I can ascertain how reliable and loyal you are. Once you have recorded the above information hand it over to Gora Mistri who will send it to me along with his own letter.

Folio 35a. To Oshra Gora Mistri, Faizabad.

Hand over personally the letter that I have written to Raso Sarkar. Enclose and seal his reply with your own hand and send it to me. 11 Shawwāl 1187.

Folio 35b. To Mir Muhammad Azim, Lucknow.

I have received your letter. I have sent you a *hundī* of Rs 500 in addition to one of a similar amount that you received earlier. Acknowledge its receipt. I am sending back the *gota* and *kinari* that you had sent as they are useless. Send [new stock] only if you can procure better ones. There is some confusion about the three rings which you mention having dispatched to me through the same *harkāra* [who brought the letter]. I have not received any ring. I had written to you earlier to procure a shawl for Monsieur Gentil from Khwaja Karim *saudāgar* and dispatch it to me. You have not mentioned anything about it in your letter; you have forgotten even the name of Khwaja Karim.

You have not completed even half the work that I had assigned to you. You have not reported what you have done and what you intend to do; there is no information about the tents and the *'amārī* that is lying incomplete in the house of the embroiderer (*naqqāsh*). The embroiderer is a bastard—he said he would finish the work within twenty to thirty days but he has not yet completed it. Please be strict with him and have it sent soon. You have not replied to my queries regarding the orders I had placed. However, I promptly send you whatever money you require. I do not know why you take time to fulfill my orders.

I have received the inventory of goods, the specimens of the *kārchūbī* and two hundred pieces of lace that you have sent. I did not like the sample of *kārchūbī* and have therefore sent it back to you. The colour of the cloth should be fast and enduring, it should be without borders, and with only flower designs. It should also be beautifully textured like *kimkhwāb*. Send me a sample first and place the order only often my approval. 11 Shawwāl.

Folio 36b. To Oshra Gora Mistri, Faizabad.

I received your letter. I had earlier received two of your letters in which you had referred to the letter of Muhammad Bashir Khan, addressed to Sayidi Alam, regarding the preparation of the garden, the buildings and the house, as well as the monthly wages of the gardeners. Obtain the necessary items, like the wooden beams, from Sayidi Alam for the preparation of the garden, the *havelī* and a house for Manik Ram. Inform me if Sayidi Alam makes any excuses in meeting your requirements. [In such case] I will arrange them from here. The work should not get delayed. I have written to arrange the money that you will require for this [work].

Muhammad Azim has written to me about the tea (*chāh*). I am sending you the keys of the [tea] chests kept there since I do not have tea here. Open the tea chests, take out the tea leaves, and fill them in four dry bottles. Send them along with the key with the same *harkāra*. Ensure that the chest is carefully locked and kept back [in the same place]. Send also one saddle along with three bridles out of the seven or eight kept there. 11 Shawwāl.

Folio 37a. To a painter (muṣawwir) in Faizabad.

The portrait of the Nawab [Shuja-ud-Daula] that you had sent for me has been held back by Monsieur Gentil for himself. Make a similar portrait and keep it for me. You shall be generously rewarded when I reach Faizabad if you do my work with due care and attention. 11 Shawwāl.

Folio 37b. To Nawab Shuja-ud-Daula.

I have heard strange things about the two companies of troopers appointed with Captain Marsack. At a distance of twelve *kos* from Faizabad, all the troopers threw down their guns and demanded their emoluments from him. He told them that if he had the money he would have given it to them. He told them that in Tanda he would collect it from the *faujdār* and pay them. However, in Tanda the *faujdār* had no money. Consequently, the troopers threatened not to go further towards Benares with him. Somehow the commotion was controlled, and Marsack summoned the rival *ṣūbadārs* of the two companies and enquired about the reasons [of the incident].

The *ṣūbadārs* said that when the companies were being set-up, the officials of the Nawab, ignoring their protestations, substituted their troopers with the bastard and useless soldiers of Awadh who do not obey their orders. A hapless Marsack then proceeded towards Benares. Two *kos* before Benares the troopers demanded half of whatever money he possessed at the moment, while their monthly salary would be paid in Benares. Marsack then distributed Rs one hundred of the Rs two hundred that he had on him. Upon which they [soldiers] apparently repented and sought forgiveness for whatever they had done. Even though some troopers did not join the commotion, it is quite likely that they will attack Marsack if they believe that this is the way through which they can get their emoluments.

Your Excellency may remember that in Benares the Governor had told you in my presence that four to five English officers under the leadership of Major Polier would visit the country for the Company's survey work. It was also agreed that as and when soldiers to accompany these officers would be required, you will arrange them. The English troopers were not sent along with these officers to avert the danger of damage to your country. Two months after my return from Benares to Faizabad I had informed you that Marsack *ṣāḥib* will require two companies of troopers and some horsemen on the day he arrives. However, the soldiers were arranged only two months after the arrival of Marsack. If I had known of your intentions I would have written to the Governor in Calcutta to arrange for troops from there. Now that the situation has deteriorated so much I do not know how to account for the same. 12 Shawwāl 1187.

Folio 39a. To Oshra Mistri Gora.
I am enclosing along with this letter another letter in English. From this you will know which chest is to be sent to me here in my camp. The chest contains glasses. Wrap them up carefully in cotton and send them to me. 16 Shawwāl.

Folio 39b. To Nawab Shuja-ud-Daula.
It is absolutely necessary for me to submit to you, even though I cannot put it elegantly because I do not know Hindi, that there is a strong bond of cordiality and friendship between you and the English officials. I have been here in your service for the last nine years and the Governor has asked you to take special care of me. Obviously, we derive strength from your favours. If we receive your favours we gain in strength and if, God forbid, we are deprived of them we loose our stature. I hope that I will continue to be in your service and it will be my privilege to execute in all humility the order of your Highness. 22 Shawwāl 1187.

Folio 40a. To Oshra Gora Mistri.
I received your letter of 14 Shawwāl. I had earlier sent you the letter of Muhammad Bashir Khan addressed to Sayidi Alam who will help you in your work. Otherwise you write to me and I will act accordingly. Sow the seeds in whichever way you feel is best, and take care of the grapevine. Prepare bird houses for the partridges, water fowls and the other birds. The partridge house should be modelled on the one in Monsieur Gentil's house. It should have small windows with wire nets. The house for the water fowls should have a small concrete tank for bathing and drinking purposes. Look around for [other] variety of partridges and water fowls and bring them whenever you find them. The house for *Karānī ṣāḥib* should be made ready soon. 20 Shawwāl.

Folio 40b. To Mir Muhammad Azim.
I had received your letter on 11 Shawwāl but have not heard from you since then. There has been no news [from you] regarding the tent and the other things I had enquired about. Tell Muhammad Sa'id Khan that if I wanted I could have had the tent made here. I do not know when they will complete it. You had written that you will dispatch the tent on Id day. But I am dismayed because it is 20 days after Id and I have not yet received it. I require paper for daily use: get ten reams of Lucknow white paper and five reams of high quality, expensive paper of large size. Get some ink also. Send [these items] with the *harkāra* soon. 2 Shawwāl I.

Folio 41a. To Mirza Najaf Khan, Akbarabad [*Agra*].
I received your letter. I am sorry for replying late. However, I assure you that I have immense regard, love and respect for you and had always wanted to consult you regarding the fort. As directed by the Nawab [Shuja-ud-Daula] I am in Akbarabad with a contingent of the Awadh army. I hope to join you [in your camp] in a few days time. 23 Shawwāl, Akbarabad.

Folio 41b. To Mirza Abdullah Beg kumaidān, Akbarabad.
I was delighted to receive your letter along with the letter of Najaf Khan. You had written of the availability of Turkish horses there. Obtain them and keep for me six horses for the chariot and two for riding purposes. The horses for riding may be of any colour but those for the chariots should be brownish red or greenish grey. I hope to join you very soon.

A letter from Mr Cockrell addressed to you had arrived. I redirected it to Lucknow twice in the past. If it comes back again I will keep it with me and give it to you when we meet. I will also hand over to you the money which Mr Cockrell owes you. 23 Shawwāl.

Folio 42a. To Nawab Shuja-ud-Daula.
In accordance with your order I am here in Akbarabad. I have dispatched the drafts of two letters to you in the hope of getting them back under your seal: one addressed to Mirza Najaf Khan and the other to Mir Saiyid Ali. Orders may be issued that the troopers deputed with me should arrive with gun powder and other ammunition. 23 Shawwāl.

Folio 42b. To Najaf Khan.
I received your letter enquiring about my programme. On the 24th I had been directed to proceed to Akbarabad. I will set out on the 25th and have the pleasure of meeting you. 24 Shawwāl, night, Etawah.

Folio 42b. To Lutf Ali Khan.
I received your letter, along with that of Najaf Khan, in which you have mentioned about your intention to leave for Shahjahanabad [Delhi] to collect the salary so as to pay for the elephant. I have been directed by the Nawab [Shuja-ud-Daula] to leave for Akbarabad and I shall depart tomorrow, the 25th, and reach there soon. Do not leave for Shahjahanabad until I am there. 24 Shawwāl, Saturday evening, Etawah.

Folio 43a. To Diwan Manik Ram.

I received your letter. A total of only one hundred horsemen and one company troopers arrived here. Please dispatch the remaining horsemen and also the falcons. I have also written to you repeatedly about the turbans of the robe of honour. I had earlier sent you a box with the cloth for the *khil'at*, four packets of shawl and one bottle of perfume. Keep the turban in this box (*pitāra*) and send them along with the Indian gun to Dr Clue in Azimabad. Get the list that I have kept in the box copied out by Mr Lloyd and paste it on the box. Give accurate accounts of all of these to Lloyd *ṣāḥib*.

Secondly, hand over all the *pattūs* and *kurtīs* [shirts] to the *khānsāmān* and get their receipt. I will not bother you much because I will be preoccupied with my own work for the next ten to twenty days. But I insist that you make Mr Lloyd understand [everything] clearly and after that reach here as soon as possible. Send whatever money you have with Mir Husain Ata Khan as it may be needed for my expenses here. Also see that the guns are wrapped in covers, tied properly with a rope and sealed; the other items should also be sealed. The papers which are needed here—like the one on which the Nawab Wazīr had signed in Benares, should be put in a cover and sent here.

I have also written a letter to Dr Clue *ṣāḥib*—this is to be forwarded to him along with the things being sent to him. Send the goods, which could not be sold in Akbarabad because of the turmoil, through a reliable person to Monsieur Gentil. Lloyd *ṣāḥib* had requested for a *dastak* to obtain grain from Mirzapur. Apply to the Nawab for the same and send it to him [Lloyd] after finding out which grain he wants. 25 Shawwāl 1187.

Folio 44b. To Najaf Khan.

I received your letter enquiring about my camping place. Today, ie. the 28th of Shawwāl, Wednesday, I have reached Katra Azmat Khan, near the river bank, and have camped here. I do not intend to go further because I am tired. I hope to meet you soon. 28 Shawwāl, Akbarabad, night.

Folio 45a. To Nawab Asafjah Shuja-ud-Daula.

I left the army on the 25th and entered the city on Friday the 1st of Ẕīqa'da. Here, I stationed myself in the *havelī* which is adjacent to the populated area. The same afternoon I enquired about the condition of the fort and bombardment of the people inside and about the efforts of our fighters. I inspected three entrenchments. Our soldiers have positioned themselves along the moat—just below the fort wall. But I do not think there has been any effective effort [on the soldier's part]. I will write to you tomorrow after inspecting the other sides. 1 Ẕīqa'da, Friday, Akbarabad, *ḥavelī* Rai Shivdas, night.

Folio 45b. To Nawab Shuja-ud-Daula.

I inspected the entrenchments along the southern walls of the fort on Saturday, the 2nd of Ẕīqa'da. The fort wall resembles the one of the Allahabad fort. But it looks very vulnerable (*nākāra*) near the Bengali Burj [Tower]: There is no moat below, and the door opening on the river side which is used continuously by people is adjacent to it. In my assessment if we prepare our entrenchment (*damdama*) with ten to twelve cannons next to it and bombard from there, the wall would probably break. We can then storm the fort through the gate. I will investigate into it further tomorrow and write to you. 2 Ẕīqa'da 1187 [Shawwāl is a misprint here].

Folio 46a. To Nawab Shuja-ud-Daula.

I had written to you about this fort yesterday, the 2nd of this month. Today during an inspection in the afternoon I discovered that there is a tunnel near Shāhburj, which leads to the fort wall. We have achieved nothing so far. I will inspect [the site] again tomorrow.

It has been decided that we erect the entrenchments, of twelve to thirteen cannons. We will work the whole day and night to collect the necessary equipments [for the entrenchment]. We believe that it should be ready by early afternoon when the bombardment will commence. A catapult is required to throw the heavy stone and the *gola* into the middle of the fort. The large catapult which is in Lucknow may please be sent for this purpose. One more thing is needed to break the door—I do not remember its Hindi name but in the *firangī* language it is called pitard. I remember that it is probably in Lucknow and have written to Monsieur Gentil. He will tell you what it is called in Hindi. I hope that we will have the favour of getting it from you to break the door. 3 Ẕīqa'da, Sunday, Akbarabad.

Folio 46b. To Nawab Shuja-ud-Daula.

I had written to you earlier about matters relating to the fort. I inspected the entrenchments yesterday, the 5th of Ẕīqa'da. One of these with six cannons, near the Bengālī Tower, had been prepared; another one with two cannons was made ready yesterday night. Today, one more entrenchment, with four cannons at a gap of one pistol shot, has been prepared. However, the equipment for the battle is inadequate and if we commence in this state we will run short of material; this will damage both your as well as my reputation. The task can be carried out satisfactorily if six or [at least] four more cannons along with 3000 cannon balls are arranged. I must add that this is the only way this [task] can be performed.

At the moment there are thirteen to fourteen small cannons with 300 cannon balls for each which are inefficient. Further, no one here is of any use except Nawab Najaf Khan, and whatever advantage accrued from the entrenchment was solely because of him.

It is rumoured that Dan Shah has sent his letter (*'arẓī*) to you stating that he would vacate the fort if you send reliable mediators. If this [rumour] is true it is better to wait for some time. I shall act according to your advice. 6 Ẕīqa'da, Wednesday, mid-day.

Folio 47b. To Oshra Gora Mistri.

I read your letter. As desired by you I wrote to Bashir Khan to advice you. Do as Sayidi Alam suggests as far as the wages of the masons are concerned: the payment would be from the day the *parwāna* was issued. I will write to you further about this later.

The flower beds that you have laid out in the garden are fine. Manik Ram told me that the musical instrument has reached you. Keep it protected from dust, etc. and [see to it] that no one except the watch-maker and you touch it. My *k͟hānsāmān, Gora* Steward, is coming along with Brooke and Martin *ṣāḥibs.* Send him here when he arrives, along with one packet of *chāh* [tea], thirty to forty bottles of *madira* [wine] and ten to twenty bottles of brandy. As for the clerk (*navīsanda*) that you had written about, Manik Ram has also written to the *sarkār* about it. [At the moment] let Nidhi Ram and Raso Sarkar do the clerical works. 7 Ẕīqa'da, Thursday afternoon.

Folio 48a. To Nawab Shuja-ud-Daula.

Earlier in my letter (*'arẓī*) of 6 Ẕīqa'da I had written to you about the preparation of the entrenchment near the Bengālī Burj. But on inspection today, i.e. the 7th of this month, I found no work done because of the non-availability of workers (*beldārs*). You said that following an imperial order 400 *beldārs* had been deputed for the work. [But] Nawab Najaf Khan tells me that none of them reached here. The work could have been done even if there were 200 *beldārs*; [now] despite Najaf Khan's order the work is not being done satisfactorily. Since my own people are not here I feel helpless. I have sent you three to four letters requesting you to send *qumbāra* [catapult] etc., [but] I have received no response from you. Your orders are awaited. 7 Ẕīqa'da, Thursday.

Folio 48b. To Nawab Shuja-ud-Daula.

I had written to you earlier about the state of affairs here till the 7th of this month. In the meanwhile, I am privileged to have received your letter (*'ināyat-nāma*) sent through Muhammad Ilich Khan. Today, the 8th of this month, I summoned Mir Saiyid Ali and learnt from him that 100 *beldārs* are available and that the arrangement would be made for the additional labourers required for the purpose. Subsequently, in the afternoon I decided to inspect the entrenchments.

Mir Saiyid Ali will be entrusted with one entrenchment with four cannons, work for which will begin this evening, to be made ready by tonight or tomorrow. The bombardment will commence tomorrow early in the morning. Yesterday Najaf Khan had suggested removing the entrenchments as there was hope for negotiation. But in my opinion, the negotiation will be precipitated when we hit the besieged. At any rate I am trying to carry out the task in keeping with your order. 8 Ẕīqa'da, Friday.

Folio 49a. To Najaf Khan.

I summonned Mir Saiyid Ali and directed him to prepare the entrenchment near the Bengālī Burj. I therefore hope you will provide him with all the necessary materials, and direct your people to be present at the big entrenchment. 8 Ẕīqa'da, Friday.

Folio 49b. To Najaf Khan.

Our people have captured an elephant near the fort wall. I do not know if it belongs to you or to the people inside the fort. Let me know if it is yours so that it may be returned to you. 8 Ẕīqa'da, Friday.

Folio 49b. To Oshra Gora Mistri.

Make arrangements at the *ḥavelī* for the accommodation of Munshī Hasan Riza Khan, who is leaving for Faizabad. 8 Ẕīqa'da.

Folio 49b. To Oshra Gora Mistri.

I received your letter in which you mention about the troubles created by Saiyidi Alam in the laying out of the gardens, the structure of the buildings, etc. For the moment tell him that he should have informed us earlier if he thought the work was unworthy. Do not approach him any more and arrange the expenses from my establishment (*sarkār*); let Saiyidi Alam go to hell.

I note that you have kept the organ which came from Calcutta safely. I have written about it to Mr Sangster, the watch-maker. I have received an order regarding your salary from the Nawab [Shuja-ud-Daula], but let me know the following: from where did you receive and how much was your earlier salary? How much money do I owe you? Up to which day have you been given the salary? The money cannot be received without [my having] these details. Rest assured that you will receive your salary as soon as you write [to me] these details.

I appreciate that Raso Sarkar is doing the work [assigned to him] in all earnestness. You had mentioned that he had sent a letter to me through a *harkāra*. Write the name of the *harkāra* because I have not received this letter, and tell Raso Sarkar to keep doing his duty with dedication and sincerity—he will be duly rewarded. 10 Ẕīqa'da, Sunday, 2 watches of the day. Handed over to Mayaram *harkāra*.

Folio 50b. To Raso Sarkar.

I received your letter (*'arẓī*). You have mentioned that you had sent a letter earlier with the *harkāra*. Let me know the name of that *harkāra* since I have not received that letter. Keep doing the work with promptness and sincerity. Rest assured that your interests will be taken care of. 10 Ẕīqa'da, Sunday, enclosed with the letter of Gora Mistri.

Folio 50b. To Nawab Shuja-ud-Daula.

I had earlier sent you six letters. Only two of these could elicit response from you, which I received in these four to five days. The remaining four [letters] with my request for catapult etc. remain unanswered. I do not feel confident enough to go ahead if I do not get any response from you.

I had sent you a daily account of the battle front. I feel let down before you because of the false statements (*darogh-gūi*) of the Hindustani people (*mardum-i Hinsdustān*). I wrote to you that the entrenchments would be ready because Mir Saiyid Ali had said that 100 *beldars* were available and that the entrenchments would be prepared quickly. [However], when I entrusted the work to him only 16 *beldārs* came for work; as a result nothing could be done by mid-night and I am being accused of misleading because of the lies of these people. The entrenchments could finally be prepared only with the effort of Najaf Khan's people. I can calculate completing a task within a given stipulated time only when things are done the way (*ẓābiṭa*) we [the Europeans] do amidst our own people. Nobody cares for orders (*ḥukm*) here; everyone is in conflict (*ẓidd-o-mukhālafat*) with the other; nothing is done in a coordinated manner (*bil-ittifāq*).

I have received a letter (*chithī*) from the Governor *ṣāḥib* directing me to send Marsack *ṣāḥib,* who had come to survey the land, back to Calcutta. Accordingly, I have written to Marsack that the two companies of troopers and horsemen, deputed by you on him, be directed to join the army here. 11 Ẕīqa'da, Monday.

Folio 51b. To Nawab Shuja-ud-Daula.

When I was leaving for this place I had seen a garden being laid out for you in Etawah. [Since] beautiful narcissus are available here, I have acquired 168 plants and am sending them through a *harkāra.* These plants are already big, and I hope that they will flower soon and bring delight to you. 13 Ẕīqa'da, Wednesday evening, sent with Hira *harkāra.*

Folio 52a. To Mir Muhammad Azim, Lucknow.

I received your letter on 11 Ẕīqa'da, but you have not given enough information. I sent several letters to you but none of them has been acknowledged by you, nor has there been any information regarding the preparation of the things [that were ordered]. This is not commensurate with your intelligence (*dānāi*). Despite your assurances that the *'amārī* would be ready within ten days, it is still incomplete. This extent of delay and negligence (*ihmāl*) is not proper. Since I do not know how long I will stay here you should take the road of Nana Man which is a quick and problem free route to reach here.

I had instructed you that the *harkāra* who carried the letter should be sent back immediately. It has now been twenty-two days since I wrote to you but they have not reached here, nor have you written anything about them. This is strange since a prompt response to the letter is expected. Delay on your part makes things difficult here. 15 Ẕīqa'da, Friday.

Folio 52b. To Mir Muhammad Azim.

I had written to you about the preparation of the *ḥuqqa* to which, strangely enough, you have not responded. Buy at an appropriate price and bring here for my assessment the mirrors which Monsieur Gentil had inspected in Lucknow, and about which I had instructed you to dillydally the transaction. 15 Ẕīqa'da, Friday, sent on Sunday.

Folio 52b. To Raso Sarkar.

I have received two of your letters and appreciate your sincere service and concern for me. In the meanwhile Lat *ṣāḥib*, my *karānī*, left for Faizabad and I hope he has [now] reached there. Take care of him and familiarize him with the rules of sale and purchase in retail as well as in bulk. I will appreciate if you are careful in the dealings of my business. Keep supplying the necessary information. I have told him [Lat *ṣāḥib*] about you. He will be considerate towards you. 16 Ẕīqa'da, Saturday, sent on Sunday, the 17th.

Folio 53a. To Shiv Prasad, gumāshta of kothī of Awadh.

I received your letter (*'arẓī*) in which you have written about your being imprisoned. Apprise my *karānī*, Lat Ṣāḥib, who is reaching Faizabad to take stock of my business, with the exact details of your situation, and help him understand the state of the business there. Though I am concerned about your well-being, I could not go through the details of your imprisonment. However, I will write to Lat Ṣāḥib to obtain the details and settle the matter judiciously. Rest assured that no one can harm you if you are not at fault. 16 Ẕīqa'da, Saturday, dispatched on 17th, Sunday.

Folio 53b. To Najaf Khan.

I have received your letter (*mihrabānī-nāma*) regarding the case of your servant, Mir Imam Bakhsh. As a matter of fact your associates are [like] my associates (*wābastahā-i ān ṣāḥib wābasta-i mukhliṣ*). He will be forgiven and reinstated. I have told him to accompany me during my visit to you. 17 Ẕīqa'da, Sunday.

Folio 54a. To Oshra Gora Mistri.

I have received three letters with details about the developments there. As I wrote to you earlier regarding Saiyidi Alam's mischief, do not ask him for anything in future, and arrange for the necessary expenses from my *sarkār*. The mischief and breach of trust on Saiyidi Alam's part is all too evident.

Apprise my *karānī*, Lat *ṣāḥib*, who has gone there to take stock of my business, of the precise details of the business. He is my sole agent and will do whatever he thinks is appropriate. Ask Raso Sarkar also to give him all the details. Get the details about the betel nuts and the other goods in writing for him. I have written to Shiv Prasad also. Tell him to familiarize Lat *ṣāḥib* with everything and you tell Lat *ṣāḥib* about his services.

You had written that Marsack *ṣāḥib's* house was nearing completion except the floor which was still under construction. That is fine. Once you are free from this, expedite the construction of Bībī *ṣāḥiba's* house. Remove the logs which the *kotwāl* of the bazaar has piled at the door of the *ḥavelī* so as to avert the danger of fire. I will think of a way out (*tadbīr*) to deal with the untoward behaviour and irregularities (*bid'at-i ghair ma'mūl*) of the *kotwāl* towards the shopkeepers around the *ḥavelī* and write to you later.

Build the houses for the pigeons and the ducks wherever you think appropriate. Now that my agent (*mukhtār-i kār*), Lat *ṣāḥib* is there, take necessary action for the appointment of the four *harkāras* as per his instructions and write to me. I had written to you earlier that I have received the order for your salary from the Nawab [Shuja-ud-Daula], but the payment cannot be made without the following details: write [to me] from where you got your salary earlier? Upto which time [did you receive it]? and what arrears are due? I am sending some cuttings of narcissus and some cypress plants to you. As per the suggestions of the gardener keep the cuttings and plant the cypress saplings in the garden. Take special care to keep the ducks, turkey and other birds which have come from Azimabad in a safe place. 17 Ẕīqa'da, Sunday, sent the same day.

Folio 55a. To Oshra Gora Mistri.

My *karānī*, Lat *ṣāḥib,* is in Faizabad to take care of my entire business and assess the situation there. [I] am writing to tell you that you should tell him everything relevant and never deviate from his advice. Complete the house of Bībī *ṣāḥiba* quickly and cunstruct a house for the residence of Lat *ṣāḥib* without any delay. 17 Ẕīqa'da, Sunday, sent the same day.

Folio 55b. To Oshra Gora Mistri.

I have sent to you through Nathi *harkāra* two caps made of golden *bādla*, some cypress plants, narcissus cuttings, and one packet of the seeds of *asharfī* flowers along with one gardener by the name of Narain. Plant these plants according to the gardener's advice in whichever

part of the garden you like. Seeds will be sown in season. The emoluments of the gardener have been fixed at Rs 6 per mensem and he has been payed one month's wages in advance. The caps are for my son. Following is the list of the things sent:
Cypress—218
Plums—7
Motia—26
Narcissus cuttings—1000 in 4 bundles
Gul-i-asharfī [calendula] seeds—1 packet
Golden *bādla* [brocade] caps—2
17 Ẕīqa'da, Sunday, sent with Nathi *harkāra.*

Folio 56a. To Raso Sarkar.

Karānī ṣāḥib is reaching Faizabad for my work. You should remain in attendance on him and give him whatever information he requires. Follow his advice and never deviate from his suggestions. You will be honoured for your loyal and sincere service. u.d.

Folio 56a. To Shiv Prasad, gumāshta of the kothī in Awadh.

Let my *karānī,* Lat *ṣāḥib,* who is the sole agent for all my business in Faizabad, know all the accounts and the entire situation regarding the sale and purchase of the goods. Be in attendance on him and keep informing him daily. Your interest will be taken care of in return for your loyal service. 17 Ẕīqa'da, Sunday, sent on Sunday.

Folio 56b. To Nawab Shuja-ud-Daula.

I had written to you earlier whatever I had noticed here. The latest is as follows: I had submitted [to you] the very first day that without 400–500 cannon balls for each cannon, and the same amount of gunpowder, the fort could not be recovered. At that time I thought the equipment was available—Mir Saiyid Ali had also said that for each cannon there were 300–350 cannon balls [available]. I thought that the only thing left was the preparation of the entrenchments. The entrenchment was prepared with great difficulty in a period of eight days. When I inspected the materials at the time of execution of the task I discovered that there were approximately only 150 cannon balls for each cannon. What can I do when these people give such [false] statements about [the state of] their own affairs. The people inside the fort also want the capture of the fort to be delayed until [the time] my army departs from here. The delay in the recovery of the fort would add to the strength of the Jats.

However, the fact is that the people inside the fort are not willing to fight. One day 400 people shouted from the top of the fort wall, but they were prevented from going ahead by some leader—perhaps a Jat. If the seige of the fort is tightened, the fort could soon fall, and the report that we get from the Jat side will be belied. I believe you will understand this. I have also made it absolutely clear to Najaf Khan that without four hundred to five hundred cannon balls the task can never be carried out. He has promised to arrange them in four days time.

I will report to you whatever happens subsequently and will follow your guidance. The delay of five to six days in sending you [information] was because I was ashamed of writing to you without setting things right. [But] because you have [now] written I am writing [back]. Following the recall of Marsack by the Governor sahib I had written to him to return the soldiers deputed with him to the [Nawab's] army. I had submitted this to you. Now I hear that he has been reinstated and have therefore written to him to keep these soldiers with him. This is for your information. 8 Ẕīqa'da, Monday night.

Folio 58a. To I'jaz Raqam Khan, in the army of the Nawab Shuja-ud-Daula.

[No] new letters have been received [here]; I know nothing about the developments [there]. But since the day you were appointed on my suggestion for this work with Monsieur Gentil, the news is received on alternate days. You must under all circumstances be present at Monsieur Gentil's and keep recording the daily news so that the information is available here. 18 Ẕīqa'da, Monday night, sent with the *dāk* through Mayaram *harkāra*.

Folio 58a. To Khiradmand Khan.

I am delighted to receive your letter and am as keen to meet you as you are to see me. On my arrival here I discovered that I am deprived of the pleasure that I had had there when I met you [regularly]. Keep in touch. 19 Ẕīqa'da, Tuesday.

Folio 58b. To Mir Sulaiman Khan.

I received your letter and learnt that you have received [only] ten *mans* of the rice I sent you through Khwaja Pedrose, but have not received another sixteen *mans* of the same which I sent through Ashur Beg Khan. I will find out the reason for this; you should also enquire [into the matter]. Possibly the boat with [Ashur Beg's] consignment reached Murshidabad.

[Further], I will write to you how much of the soiled broad cloth entrusted with Manik Ram has been sold. If all of it has been disposed of it is fine, otherwise its disposal will now be conducted as Khawaja Aratun advises.

The Rs 1000 that you have written about will be given to Ashur Beg Khan whenever he asks for it. I have already sent the *dastak* for the payment of one camel and two horses, and if you need another one [*dastak*] it will be arranged. You will know from the letter of Lutf Ali Khan that Najaf Khan has directed that the payment of the elephants will be made in Azimabad. At the moment Lutf Ali Khan has left for Shahjahanabad. This is just for your information.

I searched for the two horses that you required but at the moment there are no good horses available—none of the horses acquired are worthy of being sent to you. The search is on and I will send them to you as soon as I get them. Keep me informed about your health and welfare. 20 Ẕīqa'da, Wednesday, Akbarabad.

Folio 59a. To Gora Mistri.

I received your letter of 12 Ẕīqa'da on the 20th. The news about me is as follows: I left the [Nawab's] court on the 1st of Ẕīqa'da and entered Akbarabad where I am engaged in efforts to recover the fort. May God help us in this. I have repeatedly written to you about Saiyidi Alam and I write again to forbid you to ask him for anything. If he [Saiyidi Alam] refuses to give anything arrange for whatever is necessary from my *sarkār*: the payment for the fruit trees and grape plants, as also the emoluments for the gardener and sweeper.

I have received the order for your salary from Nawab Shuja-ud-Daula. But it is not clear from where you received your salary earlier? How much I owe you? and how much you have [already] got? Write back these details and rest assured that the payment will be made. Do not get distracted from your duty; anyone who disturbs or interferes in your work will be punished.

Earlier, on 11 Shawwāl, I had written to you asking for three bridles and one large saddle. Send them through Store *ṣāḥib* because I have not yet received them. The boat which carried the English organ from Calcutta is also carrying a bag of clothes and seven bottles of medicine. Keep these bottles safely and send the bag of clothes with anyone coming here. 20 Ẕīqa'da, Wednesday, night.

Folio 60a. To Najaf Khan.

This morning I inspected the entrenchments and discovered that my advice has not been followed—I found them as they were earlier. The two jute bags of mud that are kept there are of no use. Because of them the mouth of the cannon will remain inside, whereas the place for keeping the cannon should be so made that the cannon mouth projects out. Only then is there enough space for manipulation at the time of firing. The entire entrenchment should be redone. It is strange that in these four days the things to be done have not [yet] been done and those which were not necessary have been accomplished. I feel that you should appoint one person incharge of the entrenchment, with instructions to follow advice, and not use his own mind [act on his own]. I do not want even a single cannon ball or little bit of equipment to be wasted because we have an inadequate quantity of the same. It is for this purpose that the entrenchment should be entrusted to somebody.

An envelope containing instructions is enclosed herewith. I hope you will attend to this task since I do not know who the commander is and which work is to be done by whom. Instruct the *dārogha* of the *topkhāna* for the works related to the cannon and the other leaders for whatever you deem appropriate. I had suggested that one opening of the small entrenchment, with four cannons, should face the small fort gate situated on the left side of the Bengali Burj, and the other two openings be directed towards the Bengālī Burj. However, at the moment only the opening facing the small fort gate is arranged. Do send the *beldārs* so that the place for the cannons and the entrenchment are correctly positioned. So far the battle has been postponed because of the inadequate preparation. Now it is advisable to launch the battle because you say that every thing is ready. Any further delay would be detrimental for us.

By this evening two cannons should be stationed where the Zulfiqar cannon was placed, while this cannon should be shifted to the front entrenchment with four cannons. It is also necessary to station two cannons of the paltan of Mir Saiyid Ali there. It is the [right] time to launch the attack. Things, like cannon and gunpowder must be ready at the front entrenchment so that when required we do not have to get them from any other place.

Yesterday you had suggested that one man would go inside the fort [for negotiation]. My suggestion would be that no one—friend, acquaintance, servant, or for that matter any person should go inside the fort at the moment. If you consider this advice our work will be easier. I suggest this both because [I regard] your work as my own, and also for the successful execution of the task.

The arrangement of the entrenchment should be as follows:

(1) There should be one *sardār* in the *morcha* where four cannons have been placed. Two of these cannons, meant to break the bastions of the wall along the Bengali tower upto the gate lying on the left, should be from the army of Nawab Shuja-ud-Daula. The other two cannons, to be used at the time of the attack for hitting the upper portion of the fort wall at the place from where the people look out, would be from the *paltan* of Mir Saiyid Ali.

(2) There would be another *sardār* for the big *morcha* with ten cannons: of these four [cannons] would be from the army of the Nawab and six from the army of Najaf Khan.

(3) Another *sardār* would be with the *morcha* of the big cannons. These five cannons are meant for breaking the lower portion and the upper portion of the wall, Retī Burj (the river bank tower) and the gate on the right side of the Bengālī Tower. They would simultaneously fire three to four cannon balls each.

(4) The *morcha* with five small cannons under the command of a *sardār*: two cannons, one of them light will be used only for throwing shells at the time of invasion of the fort, and another for throwing cannon balls to break the upper portion of the Bengālī Tower. Another three cannons will be used to hit the lower and upper portion of the wall, the gate, and upper and lower part of the fort, and the gate on the right side of the Bengālī Tower.

Ensure that the firing is carefully targeted and is not incessant so as to prevent the wastage of cannon balls. Intermissions will ensure that the task is best executed. In order to clear the combat zone and make the fort wall clearly visible, destroy by burning the plants and the big peepal tree opposite the *morcha* with ten cannons. u.d.

Folio 63a. To Nawab Shuja-ud-Daula.

I received a letter from Nathaniel Middleton *ṣāḥib* saying that he has left Calcutta to join the army. He reached Murshidabad, from where he took a boat to Azimabad, and will come by road from there [Azimabad] to reach your court along with the *sawārī* of the *dāk*. I enclose a letter he had sent for you from Murshidabad. It will be kind of you to reply. 23 Ẕīqa'da, Saturday night, dispatched the same night.

Folio 63b. To Mir Muhammad Azim.

I received two letters of yours—one of 29th Shawwāl on the 12th of Ẕīqa'da and the other of 27th Shawwāl on the 21st of Ẕīqa'da. I learnt from these letters about the non-availability of the shawl (*rumal* shawl) and the availability of the double shawl (*fora* shawl) and the quilt (*razāi*). At the moment I do not need the shawl and the quilt but I want you to come here soon with the *'amārī* and the *ḥauda*. The embroiderer (*naqqāsh*) is a bastard and will be punished accordingly. The wine which is left with you should be sent sent soon so that it can be dispatched to Monsieur Gentil who is in Etawah with the army of the Nawab. I hear that the tent is ready; send it soon. 23 Ẕīqa'da, Saturday night, dispatched Saturday night.

Folio 64a. To Ganga Ram Bhawani Singh kumaidān.

I received your two letters (*'arẓī*). You had written earlier that you would reach here soon. From your letter today I undersatnd that you will take some time. I am also keen to meet you but I will not be staying here for long. Your brother Pitambar Singh *Ṣūbadār* had come here to meet me. 24 Ẕīqa'da, Sunday night.

Folio 64a. To I'jaz Raqam Khan.

I received your letter and learnt about the slackness in the preparation of the newspapers (*purzahā-i-akhbār*), the strict instructions regarding this from Mir Muhammad Ata Khan and about your subsequent attendance on Monsieur Gentil.

Ata Khan's instructions were precautionary to ensure that I receive the news [regularly], ignore them; those days I did not receive most of the newspapers. But now that you are with Monsieur Gentil, make it a point to record the daily news and hand them over to Monsieur Gentil so that they reach here without delay. 24 Ẕīqa'da, Sunday night, sent through Mayaram *harkāra*.

Foilo 64b. To Nawab Shuja-ud-Daula.

I had written to you earlier about the lack of war materials here and requested you for a catapult. This must have been brought to your notice. I have arranged the cannons as I thought proper and today, the 25th of Ẕīqa'da, the firing has commenced. As a result, a portion of the [fort] wall from above is broken. This wall, which is not so strong, would have been destroyed completely had my suggestion to use the big cannons been followed. Whatever has been achieved with fourteen cannons was possible with only two big cannons. I feel helpless and cannot confirm if the whole wall will fall.

It has been a month long seige; the people inside the fort have fixed twelve to thirteen cannons at different places and have thus strengthened their position to the extent that no one can raise their head because of the firing. However, with the grace of God and your high fortune, I will not spare any effort. 25 Ẕīqa'da, Monday night, sent with the *dāk.*

Folio 65b. To Najaf Khan.

Since I have a headache and am indisposed I am unable to come to the *morcha.* But I will be there in the night time. Please take care to prepare them [*morchas*] in such a manner that the firing does not give the opponents a chance to carry out the repairs. Distribute the cartridges to the *barqandāz* right now , and instruct them to fire continuously at the walls and the gates until the fort falls. Send me the detailed information. I hope that the two big cannons, for the upper side of the *damdama,* that you have asked for reach you early, because the two existing small ones at the *damdama* are ineffective and we cannot fight with these. Prepare also the scaling ladders and instal them ahead of the *morcha.* Treat this as urgent.

I am sending a pair of pistols as a gift, though not a very precious one. I will be happy if you accept them. 25 Ẕīqa'da, Monday night, sent with Muhammad Jafar *chūbdār.*

Folio 66a. To Nawab Shuja-ud-Daula.

Yesterday, the 27th of this month, I wrote to you the details of the *morcha.* Today, I reached there and started the bombardment which damaged the gate and the *retī* [river bank side] wall severely. The upper portion of the Bengālī tower drooped after being hit; the lower portion of the wall was also damaged and the cannon balls were embedded in it. Today, there was little counter-attack from the fort side. We intend to storm the fort tomorrow. I will let you know the details of what happens. 26 Ẕīqa'da, Tuesday night, with Mayaram *harkāra,* dispatched in the *dāk.*

Folio 66b. To Shuja-ud-Daula.

Yesterday, the 26th of Ẕīqa'da, I had informed you that we would storm the fort. But the attack could not be conducted today because, despite my strict instructions to Najaf Khan's men to be ready in the late hours of the night so that the raid could commence at the crack of dawn, they [the men] did not come out at the scheduled time when I reached the *morcha*.

I was informed by Najaf Khan that 700 people from inside the fort approached him yesterday night with the proposal that they would defect at night and hand over the gate of Shāh Burj to his people if he [Najaf Khan] sent them an agreement (*iqrārnāma*) with his seal stating that their arrears would be cleared and services maintained. It will be good if this is achieved, for many people will be saved from fighting and bloodshed. But this seems to be a ploy—due to this proposal Najaf Khan has relaxed [his efforts]. 27 Ẕīqa'da, Wednesday afternoon, with Mayaram *harkāra*, dispatched with the *dāk*.

Folio 67a. To Najaf Khan.

I have suggested to you several times that brave and strong people should be selected and prepared for storming the fort. But nothing has been done so far. The time is ripe for the attack and it will be detrimental for us to delay it. It is advisable to select appropriate people since at the time of battle panic among the worthless people unnerves the brave too. They [the selected people] should be present at the *morcha* in the late hours of the night and should not wait for the others to join them. However, it is not advisable for you to be there at the time of this attack. But Najaf Quli Khan's or some other knowledgeable and responsible persons' presence is necessary. The people for the attack should be selected right now from the retinue of Najaf Quli Khan or some other *risaldars*. The path from the *morcha* to the wall is very narrow, therefore they should all reach beneath the wall early in the morning and then reach the wall in single file. Since all of them cannot reach there at one time, it is advisable that they reach there in the darkness of the night. It is important that the *barqandaz* are ready around the wall of the fort so that anyone who looks out from inside the fort is hit. Each *barqandaz* should not have less than 100 cartridges. 27 Ẕīqa'da, Wednesday night.

Folio 68a. To Gora Mistri.

I received your letter of 9th Ẕīqa'da, stating the dates of the arrival and the departure of the *K͟hānsāmān*, on the 27th of the month. I have already responded to the other things you mentioned because you had referred to them earlier also. Act accordingly.

Two boats laden with my goods and those of Brooke *ṣāḥib* are reaching there; they are also bringing Bibi of Brooke sahib and his two children. Arrange for their accommodation, and take care to keep the goods safely. Arrange for the necessary expenses from the [nawab's] *sarkār.* Manik Ram's request regarding this matter will also reach the *sarkār.* 26 Ẕīqa'da, Wednesday night, dispatched with the *dāk.*

Folio 68b. To Nawab Shuja-ud-Daula.

I had earlier sent you the details which must have been brought to your notice. The situation here is as follows: Every day Najaf Khan intends to storm the fort, but till date—the 28th—nothing has been done due to lack of proper planning. I cannot do anything except advise and suggest the strategy. Neither Najaf Khan nor anyone of his people have followed my suggestions to recover the fort. I had insisted that the two big cannons of Sadabad be summoned for this purpose [recovery of fort], but they have not yet arrived. Najaf Khan's servants care little for his instructions. In his presence they agree to do whatever I suggest, but as I get away from the scene thousands of other people come up with thousands of suggestions. In such a situation of incessant queries I am helpless: the plan is ruined and they make Najaf Khan's head whirl.

Najaf Khan has faith in the negotiations [initiated] by the people inside the fort. He pays no heed to my suggestions for the better execution of the work. The lack of ammunition has further ruined the task. I have never heard about or seen this kind of misplanning (*bī tadbīrī*). I feel extremely concerned and am worried. May God save my honour. 28 Ẕīqa'da, Thursday night, dispatch in *dāk* with Mayaram *harkāra.*

Folio 69a. To Najaf Khan.

So many days have passed since I requested you for the Sadabad cannons with the assertion that [only] this will facilitate the task. But despite your repeated assurances to get them, they have not yet arrived. Think, whether this is your work or my work: everyday the preparation for the raid is made but nothing has been done so far. You are aware that when I reached the *morcha* today, even though two *gharīs* of the day had passed people of the *morcha* had not yet woken up. How can I do anything in such a situation?

I wish the report that there are 1000 people inside the *reti* wall and that our flag could be hoisted over this wall, and that thousands of our people raided the area and destroyed the people inside taking control of the fort gate, is correct. But I do not believe this. My guess is that there would not be more than fifty to hundred people inside.

If you can manage to forcefully wake the people do as follows: they should be ready by midnight; at the time of the early-morning prayer they should scale the wall and struggle to get [at least] a portion of the land inside the *retī*. It will be ideal if we get control of the big gate but if we capture even the small gate there is no harm. It is important that there should be a hundred or at least fifty people—experienced gentlemen figters, *najībs* and *ashrāf* inside the *retī* wall. Of these, ten to twelve should move further, one by one, to combat the people of the fort through the smaller gate. It is also important that the people who enter the *retī* wall should be fully equipped with ammunition, water and other necessities. After having attacked and broken the wall in the darkness of the night they will prepare the way from the *morcha* upto the *retī*.

Now I hear that the people inside the fort have again suggested a negotiated settlement. If they want negotiations why do they suggest it only in the evening? Why do they not [offer to] negotiate in the day time? It is evident that they are indulging in deception; they fear the night and therefore try to spend it under the pretext of negotiation. Therefore I suggest that unless the gate of the fort is in the control of your people and Dan Shah comes in person to meet you, you should not pay any attention to their excuses. All this is only deceit; you should also give them assurances but in reality do not deter from your task.

I had suggested to you earlier [the timing of the attack]. I repeat that the appropriate time for the raids will be when there are two *gharīs* left from the night. This is because the *najībs* obey orders throughout-day as well as night, but the non-*najībs* follow the orders only during the day. This is only to avoid embarrassment and ridicule from their peers. It is therefore important that the *sardār* who participates in the raids assures himself about the kind of people he is commanding and acts accordingly. The best time for the raid (*halla*) is only in the morning. 28 Ẕīqa'da.

Folio 71a. To Nawab Shuja-ud-Daula.

Today, the 29th of Ẕīqa'da, I reached the *morcha* late in the night [lit. when 4 *gharīs* were left from the night]. Najaf Khan was there. Yesterday one Zulfiqar Khan, who was earlier in the service of the Jats and had developed good relations with Sadaram, maternal uncle of Kehri Singh, and who is now in the company of Najaf Khan, had gone inside [the fort]. It was agreed that early next morning a confidant of his would come and meet Najaf Khan for negotiations, and that he would abide by whatever was agreed upon. For this reason the expedition to the fort was suspended.

This morning Sadaram reached the *morcha* and met Najaf Khan. Swearing by the Ganges and Ram he said that if his request for his own self and for Raja Kehri Singh is conceded to he would hand over the fort. Najaf Khan also took a pledge and said that he had been nice to whosoever came to him, and reassured him [Sadaram] that he would do whatever he could for him. It was then decided that he [Sadaram] would for the time being live in the residence of Zulfiqar Khan and correspond from there [with the people inside the fort]. Subsequently, he would hand over the control of the fort gate to Zulfiqar Khan. Sadaram is thus living with Zulfiqar Khan. Whenever he sends any letter inside, one of Najaf Khan's men accompanies it to ensure that no one makes preparation for the war or repairs the damaged wall inside the fort during the course of negotiations. In all probability a settlement would be arrived at by this evening or tomorrow morning. However, this is just a negotiation. Till the fort gate is not in the control of Najaf Khan's men I have no faith [in such a negotiation]. I will bring the details of the later developments to your notice. 29 Ẕīqa'da, Friday, two watches of the day have passed, dispatched.

Folio 72a. To Najaf Khan.

I heard that Sadaram wants the matter to be settled at the court of the [Mughal] Bādshāh. I do not think this is advisable. If he hands over one of the two gates—the Dehli gate and the Bukhara gate—that he has control over, preferably the Dehli gate, then there is no harm in delaying the settlement by five to six days, at the most ten days, but under no circumstances beyond this. Do not delay the matter if this [my proposal] is unacceptable to Sadaram. Tell him absolutely clearly that if the Dehli gate is handed over to our control then it is fine otherwise he can again go back to the fort. Do not listen to his implorations and make sure he is true to his protestations.

The Jats are all plunderers and cheats (*qaum-i-Jāt hama-hā g͟hanīm wa dag͟hā-bāz and*). Their words are nothing but a ploy. You should be extremely vigilant about this and should never be deceived by them. I briefed you about these things this morning; I again repeat that [you should] be very careful that no one from the opposition camp meets Sadaram and passes on any paper [message] to him, and that no note is passed on from his residence. Extreme care is absolutely necessary in this matter, and I insist so that your mission is fulfilled.

The letter you gave to me in the morning from a padre was from Pedrose De Silva. This is just for your information. 29 Ẕīqa'da, Friday night.

Folio 72b. To Bhawani Singh and Ganga Ram Kumaidān.

I received your letter in which you have expressed your desire to meet me. I am also keen to see you, but because of the war our meeting is delayed and we are helpless. [I feel that] since a time is fixed for all [kinds] of work, our meeting will also take place when the [scheduled] time comes. I will feel happy if you keep in touch and keep me informed of your welfare. 29 Ẕīqa'da, Friday night.

Folio 73a. To Shuja-ud-Daula.

I am honoured to receive two of your letters (*'ināyatnāmas*) simultaneously. You have advised [me] against precipitating the raid and the ensuing damage to the fort, and [you] want the matter to be settled amicably. I am in full agreement and feel that nothing should be attempted which yields no useful result.

At any rate, the proposal for the raid was made considering the fact that there is no adequate war material and the cannons are small in size. The fort could have been reduced and the way cleared with little effort, without the help of scaling ladders, if the big cannons and adequate equipment were available. But the fort wall is high and strong and the way to the *retī* wall [which is relatively vulnerable], is very narrow with deep ditches in between. In such circumstances I thought it appropriate to erect the *morcha* towards the Bengālī tower facing the vulnerable *retī* wall. Here there is a bridge over the ditch and the place below the wall is spacious. [I] also intend taking over a portion of the *retī* by *halla* or through raids and killings of the people. I thought that in the event of an invasion by our people, the beseiged would be forced to seek peace. Through all this, Oh Lord, my only purpose was to carry out the mission of the *sarkār*. I thought that in this way our task would be executed more successfully.

With the grace of God and your good fortune a situation for a negotiated settlement has emerged because of all these efforts. The portion of the *retī* which I had proposed to take over is now under the control of Najaf Khan's men. Two hundred to three hundred men have entered and the settlement of the dispute is no more complicated. I will write to you about whatever shape the matters take. 30 Ẕīqa'da, Saturday night.

Folio 74a. To Nawab Shuja-ud-Daula.

I have nurtured a sincere desire to do for you whatever work I can in a proper way . The Governor *ṣāḥib* while talking to you about me had said, Major Polier is my friend and is worthy of the work of the *sarkār*. He will execute in a proper way whichever service or work you order him to perform. At that time your excellency was gracious enough to accept me. When the necessity of this expedition arose I was present in your court and was looking forward to your command to perform [my duty] with sincerity and determination. After [staying for] a while in Etawah you ordered me to leave to recover the fort of Akbarabad.

In compliance with your orders I have been writing to you regularly about the developments here. My aim is to follow your commands. The lack of equipment notwithstanding, I made efforts for whatever was required: either a negotiated settlement or combat. Now that your Excellency desires to recapture the fort, the battle material is absolutely necessary. But it is difficult to procure it from Najaf Khan without your help.

I am determined not to disobey your orders even marginally and will do things much better than any one else. Considering the sincere friendship of the English people with you and my own absolute devotion to you, I hope that you will be fair to me. Do consider the favours I have received from you and all the expenses I have borne [for your sake] in the eight months that I have been in your service. Even if what I say is not very appropriate I think there is no harm in stating very clearly all that I need, to the person who is the centre of my hope and aspirations:

I have surrendered to you my own capital
You know best how to settle the account

1 Ẕīḥijja 1187, Sunday night, dispatched with Mir Muhammad Ata Khan.

Folio 75b. To Nawab Shuja-ud-Daula.

Along with my letter (*'arīẓa*) that I have sent, the statement of some important matters will be submitted to you orally by my confidant Mir Muhammad Husain Ata Khan. I am here to execute your command, and be in your service in all situations. He [Ata Khan] has been witness to the arrival of Dan Shah from the fort—he will apprise you of the details. 1 Ẕīḥijja, Sunday night, sent in the *dāk*.

Folio 75b. To Nadir Husain Khan.

I received your letter and am happy to hear that you have had the honour of receiving a shawl from the court, and that you are closely associated with the affairs of the court. I am thankful to God that the Nawab has been so kind to you and hope that his favours will increase with every day. I am keen to meet you and hope that you will keep in touch until we meet. 1 Ẕīḥijja, Sunday.

Folio 76a. To Nawab Shuja-ud-Daula.

I have sent you the report of the developments here until the 1st of Ẕīḥijja. Mir Muhammad Ata Khan will give you further details. Yesterday night Dan Shah met Najaf Khan and was with him for sometime, standing with folded hands, seeking forgiveness for his offences. Najaf Khan said that we have already forgiven him, whereupon Dan Shah requested for the conferment of the Raj upon Kehri Singh; permission to sell the grain to pay the arrears to the troopers, his own appointment and a number of other irrelevant and unacceptable demands. Najaf Khan said that he would accept his demands to the maximum reasonable extent only if he surrenders the Dehli gate to his people. He [Dan Shah] agreed that the following day, after he digs out the bones of Jawahar Singh interned inside the fort, [he] would hand over the Dehli gate and join him [Najaf Khan] with all his brothers and *sardārs*.

He then left and entered the tent which he had erected on the bank of the river adjacent to the *retī* [river bank] wall. Since the day Dan Shah came out of the fort and met Najaf Khan, he has not returned to the fort; and on his request Najaf Khan's men have been deputed to protect him. Today, the 3rd of Ẕīḥijja, one of Najaf Khan's men who had already entered the fort came out and reported that Dan Shah was engaged in digging out the bones of Jawahar Singh. I have just received the news that the *kotwāl* of the city is building a bridge over the moat leading to the fort gate. I will report the subsequent developments to you. 3 Ẕīḥijja, Tuesday, night.

Folio 77a. To Mir Muhammad Husain Ata Khan.

I am enclosing a letter (*'arīẓa*) with a report of the 2nd and 3rd of Ẕīḥijja. Do present it before the Nawab. I am also enclosing a copy of the same from which you will know the details. Let me also know what you have learnt about the developments there. The first day when Dan Shah came to meet Najaf Khan he was drunk and spoke very arrogantly. He is a mischievous and evil minded man, but is now willing to enter into negotiation.

Please write about the work I had assigned to you. Tonight the news came that Dan Shah along with his four *sardārs*—Sadaram, Bhao Singh and Umrao Singh, etc.—came to meet Najaf Khan. They were presented each with a horse, a shawl, and a roll of brocade. Subsequently, they went back to the fort. But Dan Shah till the time of writing this letter is with Najaf Khan. Seven hundred men from Najaf Khan's retinue are ready next to the fort gate waiting for Dan Shah to leave for his tent before they enter the fort. There is nothing more to write about. 3 Ẕīḥijja Tuesday, dispatched in the night.

Folio 77b. To Shuja-ud-Daula.

[Congratulation on the conquest of the fort of Akbarabad.] The fortune of your Excellency is the key to triumph, obliterating the difficulties from the path of all success [so that] whatever you intend materializes. This conquest also owes completely to your assistance. The army of your Excellency also reinforced by the presence of Najaf Khan who has worked with sincerity to achieve this success. With the grace of God and his help victory is now a reality, and the *morchas* of the crestfallen [the Jats] have been uprooted from inside the fort. About 1000 men from the retinue of Najaf Khan have entered the fort and the imperial standard has been installed. The enemies have been crushed and the atmosphere has been cleansed of the dirt of recalcitrance.

The wind of victory has begun to blow and the world is agog with the proclamations of greetings. Please accept my felicitations on this great victory, with the wish that you have many such victories and that this well-wisher can carry out satisfactorily whatever you command. I await further orders from you. 4 Ẕīḥijja, Wednesday night, dispatched with the *harkāra*.

Folio 78b. To Mir Muhammad Husain Ata Khan.

I have dispatched to the Nawab my *'arīẓa* containing my greetings on the conquest of the fort of Akbarabad. Do present it—a copy is also enclosed for your information. The arrogance of Dan Shah, at the initial stage of the negotiation, was because of drunkenness. Now, in all respects, he is in his senses. His people have left the fort and Dan Shah himself is with the army. Najaf Khan's people are inside the fort. With the grace of God all affairs are now settled. 4 Ẕīḥijja, Wednesday night, sent with Hira *harkāra*.

Folio 78b. 'Arzḍāsht to Shah Alam.

Salutations and compliments...With the grace of God and the fortune of his Highness, following the strategies which I chalked out, the inadequate war material notwithstanding, the fort of Akbarabad which is comparable in strength and height to the high mountains has been reduced. I am proud and thankful to God for this achievement, the announcement of which has travelled all around. The world has been saved from the oppression of the tyrants. May you achieve many similar victories. 5 Ẕīḥijja, Thursday, one watch of the day has passed. [Ẕīqa'da in the text has been wrongly written].

Folio 79b. To Maharaja Nawal Singh.

I received your letter and am delighted to know about your fine qualities from people here. You had written that I should act in accordance with the wishes of Mauji Ram—this is the time for appropriate action. Write to Mauji Ram to let me know your requirements. I will carry them [requests] out sincerely. 5 Ẕīḥijja, Thursday.

Folio 80a. 'Arẓdāsht to Shah Alam.

[Salutations and compliments] . . .Bhawani Singh and Ganga Ram *kumaidān*, old servants of the Company, came to meet me when I was in Akbarabad to assist in the work for the conquest of the fort. On enquiring about the *paltan* they said that nine *ṣubadārs* and two hundred troopers had deserted from one of the *paltans* which is now left with five hundred *sipāhīs* and one *ṣubadār*. On my wanting to know the reasons [for this desertion] they said that it happened because of the support they received from the *dārogha* of the *sarkār*. As a matter of fact none of the soldiers obey their orders. I feel concerned, because if this is the situation then what work can be expected of them?

In the light of the reputation of the English and my own achievements, I submit to you that these two *kumaidāns* are intelligent, experienced and well-versed in the English method of warfare, having been in the service of the Company for the last twenty years; also, they have never commited any offence. All soldiers were obedient at the time of their departure from Allahabad. But now a contrary situation prevails.

Since an experienced commander is sufficient and double command is not appropriate, the soldiers will serve the *sarkār* much better if the *paltan* [organization] is restored to its former stage.

Otherwise these useful people may be rendered worthless and ineffective.

In the interest of the state I request you to issue an order making the *dārogha* the sole authority for the emoluments and attendance of the soldiers, and the *kumaidān* having exclusive control over their appointments, dismissal and all other matters related to fighting. If a soldier disobeys them [*kumaidān*] he should be dismissed and they should get a worthy replacement. In this way things will be done properly, and in the event of any negligence they will be held accountable and punished. 7 Zīḥijja, Saturday.

Folio 81a. To Mir Saiyid Ali, kumaidān.

I have received a letter from the Nawab recalling me to the court along with all the people deputed with me for the expedition. Therefore [you should] cross the river early in the morning, stay for a day in Shahdara and proceed ahead the following day. Make arrangements for crossing the river without any delay. 8 Ẕīḥijja, Sunday night [wrongly written Shamba, Saturday].

Folio 81b. To Nawab Shuja-ud-Daula.

I received your letter (*'ināyatnāma*) on Sunday, the 8th night, recalling me along with all the *paltans* of the *sarkār.* I sent messages to Mir Saiyid Ali *kumaidān* to cross the river which he will do today, the 9th of the month. I will take leave of Najaf Khan tomorrow and camp at the tank (*tālāb*) of the Raja after crossing the river. I hope to earn the honour of reaching you very soon. 9 Ẕīḥijja, Monday, 2 watches have passed of the day.

Folio 82a. To Mir Muhammad Ata Husain Khan.

I am delighted to receive your letters. I have been recalled by the Nawab along with all the *paltans* of the *sarkār.* I will cross the river on the 10th and camp at the tank of the river. I am not sending a detailed reply to your letter since I will be reaching you soon. 9 Ẕīḥijja, Monday.

Folio 82a. To Bare Bābā and Chhote Bābā [the sons of Polier].

I am delighted to receive your letters and have noted your demands for pomegranate and other fruits, and for a roll (*thān*) of cloth. You must have received the two caps, made of the *tāsh,* which I had sent to you. Now I have dispatched *tāsh,* enough for two shirts, and fruits including pomegranate which were ready. If you require more *tāsh* I will give it to you on my arrival. Keep writing to me about your welfare. 9 Ẕīḥijja, Monday night.

Folio 82b. To Nawab Shuja-ud-Daula.

I left Akbarabad on the 10th of Ẕīḥijja after taking leave of Najaf Khan and arrived in Shikohabad on the 11th. Since Mir Saiyid Ali needed some more time to cross the river along with his cannons I left him behind in Firozabad. I hope to join the victorious army on Friday, the 17th, and earn enduring happiness. Mir Saiyid Ali *kumaidān* will join me a day after and earn the honour of touching your feet. 11 Ẕīḥijja, Wednesday night.

Folio 83a. To Dīwān Manik Ram.

The nine porters whom I had sent with the plants of cypress, plums etc. to Faizabad have returned and left for Akbarabad. Besides carrying the plants, they have other instructions from me as well. I am writing to you to give them whatever they ask for.

I came to know that the gardener who had gone to Faizabad with these plants is not giving the service bond because he says the work does not interest him. You should write to the *sarkār* to decline the gardener anything that he asks for, and refuse to accept him. 11 Ẕīḥijja, Wednesday night.

Folio 83b. To Najaf Khan.

Three days after taking leave of you, I arrived here in the camp of the Nawab on the 11th. Since I have very close and sincere relations [with you], words fail to express the magnitude with which I mentioned your excellent attainments to the Nawab. If you think it proper come and meet the Nawab here since he is kindly disposed towards you. In case you decide to come you should be here within ten days, because after this [period] the Nawab will set out towards the Ganges. This is for your information. 13 Ẕīḥijja, Friday night.

Folio 84a. To Saiyid Niyaz Ali Khan.

I am back in the Nawab's camp after the conquest of the Akbarabad fort. I have responded to the note, enclosed in the letter of Law *ṣāḥib* of Azimabad, for the request of Rs 10,000 towards payment of the elephants bought from Mir Sulaiman Khan. Najaf Khan's *tan<u>kh</u>wah* (*jāgīr*) had been paid in advance, upto Rajab 1188 in *hundi*, to be encashed at the shop of Ramchand Shah. But the *vakīl* refused payment without a letter (*shuqqa*) from Najaf Khan in the name of Bishwanath *vakīl* and a note under the seal of the *qāẓī*. I sent this information in my letter to you.

I have written to you in unequivocal terms about the matter. Do whatever you feel is appropriate. It is fine if you get the payment in cash from Najaf Khan; and if it is to be paid from the income of the next year you may secure a *shuqqa* of the kind I have mentioned under the seal of Najaf Khan and in the name of Bishwanath *vakīl*. Nothing can be achieved without this. 13 Ẕīḥijja, Friday night.

Folio 84b. To Mir Lutf Ali Khan.

Acquire four to five beautiful milch berberi goats, which give large quantities of milk, from Shahjahanabad where they are readily available and send them [to me]. The other matters will be clear to you from the letters of Niyaz Ali Khan. 14 Ẕīḥijja, Saturday morning.

Folio 84b. To Gora Mistri.

Dispatch along with the other things ten to fifteen *sers* of big and small bullets of the gun that are kept there. I need them here. 14 Ẕīḥijja.

Folio 84b. To Najaf Khan.

I am sending to you Yusuf Ali Khan who I know is sincere and good in fighting. I recommend him for the honour of being in your service. He will render good service whenever required. 15 Ẕīḥijja, Sunday.

Folio 85a To Gora Mistri.

I received your letter of 4 Ẕīḥijja on the 17th of the month. I also learnt of some details from Martin *ṣāḥib* and some other men. You had written that a turkey died because the climate did not suit it. It is true that the climate there is unsuitable for such birds, but if sufficient care is taken it is not so disastrous. Besides their routine bird feed, the turkeys should also be fed with wheat bran soaked in water; once in a week they should also be given onion pieces and dry garlic. They should be kept clean and their wings protected from water. Ask Lat *ṣāḥib* to arrange whatever you need for them.

One barrel of *madira* has reached there in Brooke's boat. Clean the bottles which have come along with this [*madira*] and fill them with the *madira*. I will write to you to send these when I require them.

Some other thing from here will reach there tomorrow or day after—keep it safely. 19 Ẕīḥijja, Thursday.

Folio 85b. To Gora Mistri.

Your letter of 15 Ẕīḥijja reached here on the 19th. I have written to Lloyd *ṣāḥib* about the salary of the gardeners—follow his advice. Ask the gardener from Akbarabad, who is indifferent to his work, as to why he accepted it in the first place and availed a month's salary in advance. Now that he is upto mischief and is negligent in his duty, beat him with a stick ten to twenty times and dismiss him. As for your salary, I will do something now that I am back from Akbarabad and am in the Nawab's camp. 19 Ẕīḥijja, Thursday night.

Folio 86a. To Shahbaz Beg Khan Musta'id Jang.

I rejoined the Nawab's army on the 13th after the conquest of the fort of Akbarabad. Since you have not written to me anything after your departure I am concerned about you. Write to me so that I feel at ease. In the meanwhile I received from your son in Azimabad five letters in your name and one for me. I have sent them [your letters] to you. I have nothing more to say. Keep me informed of your welfare. 19 Ẕīḥijja, Thursday night.

Folio 86b. To Ram Sundar Datt and Kali Prasad, gumāshtas.

I have heard that you receive something, out of greed and wickedness, from the dealers and merchants who arrive in Faizabad from different directions; and [you] allow them their business without any regard to the loss of revenue [that it entails] to the Nawab. This is improper and [amounts to] treachery. Give it up if you do not want to be punished. I am warning you that if I hear of this again your nose and ears will be severed. 19 Ẕīḥijja, Thursday night.

Folio 87a. To Ram Sundar Datt.

Gora Mistri had brought to your notice my desire, which I had written to him, for the payment of the gardeners from the *sarkār*. But even after seeing my letter you argued with Gora Mistri out of sheer mischief. This is not proper and you will be punished for your mischief and arrogance. 19 Ẕīqa'da, Thursday.

Folio 87a. To Khiradmand Khan Don Pedro.

I received your letter on the 19th. You have written that since it was not appropriate to write certain things in Persian you wrote in a European language (*ba-khaṯṯ-i-Firangī*) to Padre Wendel, and that he would write to me accordingly. I will try to do his work at my convenience whenever he writes to me. Keep me informed about your welfare until we meet. 20 Ẕīḥijja, Friday.

Folio 87b. To Ṣadr Islam Khan.

I have received your letter regarding the release of your *a'imma* and *jāgīr.* Earlier, despite Harper *ṣāḥib's* best efforts nothing could be done. Subsequently, when *Ṣāḥīb-i-Kalān* [Governor Mr. Hastings] was in Benares along with your son, Shaikh-ul-Islam Khan, he [Hastings] submitted your case to the Nawab. Before leaving he introduced your son to Muhammad Ilich Khan and entrusted the work to him. Muhammad Ilich Khan wanted your son, Shaikh-ul-Islam, to stay back for some time and pursue the matter; but he did not stay back. If he had done so the work would have been accomplished. In the event of failure the matter would have been again brought to the notice of *Ṣāḥīb-i-Kalān* [Mr. Hastings] who would then have again written about it to the Nawab. He [your son] ruined the case. You may also note that if your work could not be done at that time despite the recommendations of *Ṣāḥīb-i-Kalān* [Mr. Hastings] and Harper *ṣāḥīb* then how can I do it? 22 Ẕīḥijja 1187, Etawah.

Folio 88a. To Gora Mistri.

I received your letter of the 23rd regarding the five boxes of Brooke *ṣāḥib* and informed him as instructed by you. I have sent with the Telinga guards one cart, two camels laden with wares and some horses. Read the enclosed list when they arrive: understand [the instructions], receive them and keep them safely. Be vigilant about the ponies, the horses and the other animals, and as mentioned to you earlier, load the above mentioned camels with the goods and dispatch them to the Nawab's camp. Also send the two trays that are there for cooling the water and four pitchers of saltpetre [bought] from the bazaar. I am also sending a porter, send through him the ten bottles of wine which Mr. Store had brought from Azimabad and the hundred wax candles. 27 Ẕīḥijja, Tuesday night, handed over to Mir Muhammad Azim.

List of goods sent to Faizabad with Mir Muhammad Azim.

A. In the large carton *(pitāra)*

(1) *Gulbadan*—8 *thāns*

Qarmizī of 20 yards length—1 *thān*

Susanī of 12 yards length—1 *thān*
Gul-i-anār—1 *thān*
Sabz—1 *thān*
Khanjarī, red and green—1 *thān*
Khanjarī red—1 *thān*
Khanjarī lākhī—2 *thān*

(2) *Dārāi*:
Qarmizī—1 *thān*

(3) Brocade—4 *thāns*
ūdah—1 *thān*
Qarmizī—1 *thān*
Susanī—1 *thān*
sabz pistaī—1 *thān*

(4) *Nawābī sabz mothra dar*—two to three yards less than a *thān*

(5) Lucknow made shoes—1 pair

(6) Lucknow made—*Kardas* [small spear] and *dastakī* [gloves]—2 pairs

(7) Dabiya—1 packet (*potlī*)

(8) Seeds of *gulzār*—1 packet (*thailī*)

B. [In the] *takhta* [wooden plank box]

(1) Orange shawl—1 pair
(2) *Lakhī* shawl—1 pair
(3) *Lakhī* shawl with small floral designs—1 pair
(4) White shawl—1 pair
(5) Saffron shawl—1 pair
(6) Quilts—2 pieces
(7) *Fotah* of *Lakhī* shawl—1 piece
(8) *Razāī* of shawl white—1 piece
(9) *Jāmadār* of white shawl—2 *thāns*
(10) Almond colour shawl—1 *thān*
(11) Ladies (*mahramat*) shawl—1 *thān*

C. In the *boghband* [large cloth]

(1) Quiver and arrows—1 piece
(2) Black *sabīrī* quivver with arrows—1piece
(3) *Dupatta* and *peshwaz kārchūbī* and sarcacium—3 *thāns*
(4) *Asavarī*—3 *thāns*
(5) *Gulbadan*—wrapped in white cloth for the Baba (son)—2 *thāns*
(6) Small *basta* covered with *momjāma* for Scott *ṣāḥib*—1 piece

D. In the jute bag (*thaila-i tāt*)

(1) Chint—8 *thāns*
(2) Bed covers—2 pieces

(3) A small bag (*pitārī*) covered with white cloth containing toys for Baba (son)
(4) A box full of *kinārī*, *gota* and knives

E. *Sanduq* etc.
(1) 2 boxes of cloth
(2) Empty bottles—62
(3) *Murabba*— 2 jars
(4) White marble table—1
(5) Iron stove—1 piece
(6) Empty jars—2

F. Horses and other animals
(1) Horses—12
(2) Loaded camels—2
(3) Loaded cart—1
(4) Wild ass—1
(5) Lamb—1
(6) Deer calf—1
(7) Goats—15
(8) Kids—8
(9) Cage for *tītar* (black partridge)—2
(10) Cage for *chakor*—2
(11) Peacock—1

Folio 91a. To Gora Mistri.

You had written that on the 23rd of Z̠īḥijja you sent one bottle of cinnamon essence, four flint guns, two nozzles, three packs of arrow, one packet of tea (*chāh*), and a little bit of cabbage with the *harkāra*. I have not yet received [these things] but don't worry I will receive them. I wonder what the condition of the carriage will be, having covered so much distance. I will write to you when I receive them. I will ask for the cabbage when I return from here and camp in your vicinity. I had written to you earlier and am repeating that you should clean 100 to 150 bottles and send them to me after filling them with *madira*.

You have full authority to do whatever you like with the gardener. Earlier I had sent you *gulzār* seeds. Even though this is not the season for sowing them, there is no harm if you try. 28 Z̠īḥijja, Saturday.

Folio 91b. To Shaikh Hasan Riza.

I have received two of your letters regarding the non-payment of Hari

Singh's debt to you. I have tried whatever I could from here. Now I feel helpless. I will do whatever I can when I arrive in Faizabad. Keep in touch. 28 Ẕīḥijja 1187, night.

Folio 92a. To Maharaja Nawal Singh.

I am delighted to receive your letter with an *'arẓī* for the Nawab. Manik Ram also apprised me of your welfare. At the moment because of my travels I could neither present your *'arẓī* to the Nawab nor tell him anything about you. When he camps and is relaxed I will bring the case to his notice in an appropriate manner. I will write to you whatever transpires. I will also set right your case in consultation with Najaf Khan. You will know more from the letter of Manik Ram. Keep writing till we meet to embrace each other. 29 Ẕīḥijja 1197.

Folio 92b. To Mauji Ram gumāshta of Maharaja Nawal Singh.

I received your letter enclosed with the one from Maharaja Nawal Singh containing the *'arẓī* for the Nawab. These days we are not camping anywhere due to continual travels. I will present the Maharaja's *'arẓī* to the Nawab when we camp somewhere, and rest assured that [I] will let you know whatever transpires. I have sent my reply to the letter of Maharaja Nawal Singh. Hand it over to him. You will know further about it from Manik Ram. 29 Ẕīḥijja, Sunday night.

Folio 93a. To Mir Muhammad Azim.

The day following your departure the army of the Nawab set off towards Ram Ghat.Dispatch the following to me at the place which I will let you know in due course:

1. Six pairs of shoes, three pairs of which can be of the size you had got for me earlier. The remaining three pairs, for Mr Middleton, can be smaller by ½ finger. Send three to four pairs for me as well. Of these, two to three [pairs] should be slippers. Find out where we are camping before you dispatch them. 30 Ẕīḥijja, Monday 1187. Corresponding to the 15th Regnal year of Shah Alam.

Folio 95b. To Gora Mistri. *

I received your letter of the 23rd along with the goods on the 5th of Muḥarram. I am delighted to learn that you meet Lloyd *ṣāḥib* regularly and attend to your assigned work. Rest assured that I will make you

*[After completion of the Hijrī year the scribe leaves two folios blank and the manuscript then resumes on folio 95b.]

happy since your hard work has pleased me. Keep in touch with Lloyd and perform your duty regularly and sincerely. 5 Muḥarram, Saturday night, 1188.

Folio 96a. To Raso Sarkar.

On the 5th of Muḥarram your letter regarding the details of the betel nuts reached here. I am delighted to learn from Lloyd *ṣāḥib's*, letter about your sincerity and hard work. Attend to him and keep him informed of everything that you consider proper. You will be duly rewarded. 5 Muḥarram 1188, Saturday night.

Folio 96a. To Shiv Parsad, gumāshta.

I received your letter regarding the details of the sale of betel nut and the other matters. You had written that despite strict instructions from Lat *ṣāḥib* Ram Sundar Datt Sarkar is not giving the account. I have written to Lat *ṣāḥib* to enquire about it and do the needful. Either the money should be recovered from Sarkar [Ram Sundar Datt] or else he should face the consequences. I have written to Lat *ṣāḥib* to give you whatever you had received earlier. Attend to him regularly. 10 Muḥarram, Wednesday.

Folio 96b. To Manik Ram Ganguli.

The receipt of the *hundī* for Rs 900 which I sent to you through my Diwan Manik Ram and was to be encashed at [the shop of] Balram Majumdar is still awaited. Delay in such matters is not appropriate. Write to me whether you have received it or not. 10 Muḥarram, Wednesday.

Folio 96b. To Mir Muhammad Azim.

I have not received any letter from you since the day you left. Write to me so that I am at ease. Look around for about fourty to fifty ducklings and send twenty of them with porters, along with a reliable man, to Math [Master?] *ṣāḥib.* Send him also my greetings. Dispatch the remaining ducklings to Faizabad to be kept safely in my *havelī.* The *'amārī* that you have sent is very small: its roof and the planks used are thin, and the narrowness [of the space within] has made it inconvenient. The *ḥauda* which is being prepared should not be like this. It should be strong, spacious and convenient to ride.

The Nawab will leave for Farrukhabad in about twenty days. This is for your information. 11 Muḥarram, Thursday.

Folio 97a. To Gora Mistri.

I received two letters of 6 Muḥarram and 10 Muḥarram on the 12th and 15th respectively. You have written that the cabbage flower is very good and you intended to send it to me but refrained from doing so because you feared that it may get spoilt on the way. Do not sell the cabbage and keep it for the seeds. Send two hundred to three hundred wax candles which are required here everyday for lighting. It was fine that you sent the wine and the other things. I am aware about your fears of the fire because the wood that is heaped in front of the *ḥavelī* gate has not yet been removed. Bring it to the notice of Lat *ṣāḥib* who will summon the owner of this firewood and ask him to remove it. If it is not removed he [the owner] will be responsible in case of a fire. 15 Muḥarram, Monday.

Folio 97b. To Gora Mistri.

You would know the details from my replies sent to you earlier. This is to ask you to send me twelve bottles of pure vinegar and four bottles of (*wilāytī*) European gunpowder. Get the sheep and lamb of Monsieur Gentil which he has now given to me and keep them carefully. I have a big and long English gun there. Take it out, clean it and have it ready so that you can send it in time. 16 Muḥarram, Tuesday.

Folio 98a. To Bhim Singh ḥavaldār.

I received your letter (*'arẓī*) regarding your escorting eight boats laden with forty packets of shirts to Benares. Meet Math *ṣāḥib* and take the goods to Faizabad as per his instructions and hand them over to Lloyd *ṣāḥib*, my *karānī*. Take care that no loss is incured on the way. Lloyd *ṣāḥib* will relieve you after you hand them [the goods] over to him. 23 Muḥarram, Tuesday.

Folio 98b. To La'l Khan, domestic attendant (mu'tamad ul-khidmat).

I heard from other people that the junior Bībī is in distress and is six months into pregnancy. But you have not written anything about it. You should have informed me. If she is uncomfortable arrange separate accommodation for her. I am sending my servant (*mulāzim*), Kalb-i Ali, who will arrange for one or two *aṣīls* to live with her in the house of my *karānī* or in some other house.

Clean the house [where she moves] and see that the *aṣīls* attend on her day and night. Also entrust one of the *aṣīls* who is intelligent and reliable the monthly Rs 15 meant for the junior Bībī which I had sent and had hitherto been kept with the senior Bībī. Further, arrange from the house whatever clothes and other things are necessary for her. Take care of her and keep me informed about the daily developments. I was unhappy that you did not write to me about her distress. I warn you that if, God forbid, anything untoward happens you will be responsible. 27 Muḥarram, Sunday.

Folio 99a. To Mir Muhammad Azim.

I am pleased to receive two of your letters: one about your arrival in Faizabad and escorting the goods to Lloyd *ṣāḥib,* and the other of 21 Muḥarram about your arrival in Lucknow and the preparation of the things I had ordered. Since the mango season has arrived you should acquire two to three *mans* of pulpy raw mangoes (*ambia*) and get first rate pickle prepared with white vinegar and the following ingredients: dry garlic, ginger, nigella seeds (*kalaunjī*); annis seeds, etc. Use these ingredients generously so that the pickles in the vinegar get thoroughly tender. Keep it and send it at a proper time to my *ḥavelī* in Faizabad.

You have not written anything about the case of Bangar Mau that I had asked you about. Write about it quickly.

For the moment send five *sers* of good pickle, of whatever category you can arrange for my consumption. You have also not written anything about another *'amarī* that I had asked you to prepare. If it is ready send it so that I can use it for riding. Send the ten ducklings through Kalb-i Ali when he comes to you from Faizabad. 27 Muḥarram, Saturday.

Folio 100a. To Gora Mistri.

I have received two letters, one of the 11th and the other of the 15th, on the 18th and the 25th respectively. I have also received the detailed list that you have sent with the wife (Bībī) of Brooke *ṣāḥib.* There are ten candles short in the 140 to 150 wax candles that were required. This is for your information. I assure you that I am thinking of a way out for the [problem related to] unfairness (*bi i'tidalī-o- shor pushtī*) of the *kotwāl* of the bazaar, and will write to you. The *kotwāl* will be admonished. You continue doing your work with care and diligence (*lawāzim-i taqaiyud-o-khabar dārī*).

I had written to you earlier about the vinegar. I write again for the quick dispatch of twelve bottles of *wilāytī* vinegar, five bottles of gunpowder, and one to two packets of tea. It is fine if you have already sent it, but if not then send it soon.

As for the case of your salary, rest assured that if it is not paid by the *sarkār* I will pay you. I understand that you are under strain (*'usrat*) because of the arrears for the last three years. But don't loose heart (*iẓṭirāb*); it will soon be over. I am thinking of a way out (*tadbīr*). 27 Muḥarram, Saturday.

Folio 100b. To Baṛe Bābā and Chhote Bābā, the sons.

I am delighted to receive your letter. As for your mother's indisposition, summon a reliable physician (*ḥakīm*) and get his advice for her treatment so that she may recover soon. I will arrange for the *thān* of *tāsh* and the pair of pearl that you have mentioned when I reach Faizabad. Ask Lloyd *ṣāḥib* to buy you the dry fruits. 27 Muḥarram, Saturday.

Folio 101a. To Mir Muhammad Azim.

I had written to you to expedite the preparation and the dispatch of the elephant *ḥauda*. Get it ready and keep it with you to send it [later when I require it]. If it is possible to get the Bangar Mau case resolved as you had mentioned, then get it settled and write to me.

I had written to you earlier about the mango pickle. Get five *sers* more and send it to me soon. I am sending you a *ḥauda* with a chair fixed on it. I do not approve of the chair, but I have no objection if you find somebody who can prepare a better one than this. Otherwise, forget about it and keep it safely in your house. 1 Ṣafar 1188.

Folio 101a. To Gora Mistri.

I received your letter containing information about the turkey ducklings and the waterfowl chicks, and the possibility of getting their eggs roosted by Indian birds. Take care of these birds as per the advice of Store *ṣāḥib*. Continue to feed them, ie. the turkey, etc. with onion etc. I am seized with your matters as much as you are devotedly busy with my work.

You have written about the death of a turkey and some goats—this is inevitable. Since there is no escape from such eventualities you could have done nothing. Rest assured that something will be done about the *kotwāl*. As suggested by you I am sending the letter of Muhammad Bashir Khan, regarding the construction of the *bāradārī*, to Sayidi Alam. You will hear soon from Monsieur Gentil about the sheep and the lamb.

I am delighted to know that the *gulzār* seeds which were sent from Akbarabad and sown there have bloomed. Do whatever you feel appropriate—the garden and the *ḥavelī* are in your charge. As for the spoiling of the *wilāytī* watermelon seeds, one can't help [it]. The cucumber and the other vegetables from my garden which are of no use to me can be consumed by the people there. But keep their seeds safely in a bag.

Do not economize in the preparation of the barge for Martin *ṣāhib* and get an excellent one ready. Take out the girth and the breast harness of my saddle which is kept there, and send it to me through somebody. You had written to Manik Ram that you had sent cinnamon essence, but I have not received it. If you have not yet dispatched it then keep it there. The case of your emoluments has been approved and it will be finalized in a day or two. 8 Ṣafar, Wednesday.

Folio 102a. To La'l Khan.

I received your letter (*'arẓī*). You have written that the letter I sent you reached Bībī *ṣāḥib* and that you did not receive it. I presumed that the letter I sent to you through Kalb-i Ali would have reached you. Since it contained something necessary I enclose herewith another copy. You must act accordingly and never think of the quarrel of Bībī *ṣāḥib*. Keep me informed and do not neglect [your duty]. 8 Ṣafar, Wednesday.

Folio 102b. To the senior Bībī.*

I received your letter containing your apologies (*isti'ẕar*) for your acts which contravened the norms of amity and sincerity (*ā'īn-i ittifāq-o-ikhlāṣ*). I am relieved to know the reality. It was your responsibility to keep writing to me about the condition of the junior Bībī. But I am astonished that during the past six months you did not indicate to me any of her problems and did not take care of her while she was all along in distress. Your welfare is linked to hers. I therefore write to you to remind you that it is your responsibility to take care of her. Make sincere efforts to please her (*khāṭir pazūhī wa diljūī*). I will be delighted if she is comfortable and if I hear anything contrary to this I will keep her separately.

Since I love you I am happy that now you have made up [with her]. Rest assured that I am fond of you (*mutawajjih-i aḥwal-o-mustāq*) and forget the heart burn (*ghubār-i kadūrat-o-afkār*). 12 Ṣafar, Sunday.

*The name of the addressee is missing in the text. From the compliments at the beginning of the letter and the contents, however, it is clear who Polier is writing to.

Folio 103a. To La'l Khan.
Keep in abeyance my earlier order about arranging a separate accomodation for the Bībī. If she has no problem and is comfortable it is fine. But if there is any problem you should keep her separate, as per my earlier written instructions to you, and do not wait for any further orders. Arrange in such case a midwife, who is vigilant and takes proper care of her. Keep me informed of the daily developments. 12 Ṣafar, Sunday.

Folio 103b. To Mir Muhammad Azim.
I received your letter (*'arẓī*) regarding the Bangar Mau case, the dispatch of the pickles, the *kārchūbī* specimens, and other matters. Resolve the Bangar Mau case in the light of what I told you when you were leaving. It has been over two months since you wrote to me, and you have not done anything. Do not delay this matter further.

I did not like the *kārchūbī* specimen that you sent. There is no comparison between this and the one which was prepared in Akbarabad, being 10 times inferior to it. Give up the work for the moment and look around for some *thāns* of plain cloth. Send it whenever I need it.

I need the elephant *ḥauda* urgently. Dispatch it soon if it is ready. I have written to Jugal Kishore to pay you Rs 1000 for your expenses. I enclose herewith a copy of the letter [that I sent to Jugal Kishore]. One of the many jars of pickles that you had sent broke and the juice spilt over. I do not like the spiceless pickle of the gourd, it is fit for the poor people. You have not written anything about my earlier instruction to you regarding the preparation of spices for the pickle and the rose water. I have paid Rs 2 to the porter—include it in his account. Send one *man* of fine quality white sugar candy for my own use soon, and get ten *mans* of the same ready. 18 Ṣafar, Saturday.

Folio 104a. To Mir Muhammad Azim.
I received your letter. Send the *ḥauda*, if it is ready, along with the fans if they can be prepared soon. The three pairs of shoes that you sent are fine. Send the remaining pairs also when they are ready. You have written to Aqa Hasan regarding the Bangar Mau case; whenever you receive his reply send it to me. I noted the details of this town sent by you. Do not make haste, wait for some time and get the work done when you feel fit or else forget about it.

At the moment I do not need the brocade that you have written about. [Instead] get the silver vessels prepared. I had written to you and Jugal Kishore earlier about the payment for the expenses [incurred]. My letters must have reached. When you receive the multicoloured silk which was ordered from Akbarabad send it to me. Send [also] six *qanāts* of the same size and quality as those which Muhammad Sa'id Khan had prepared earlier and sent along with the tent: its [the *qanāt's*] outer part should be made of *patāpatī* and the lining should be of *chhatka.* Send whatever wine is left in the house to the camp. Since the rainy season is approaching, it is important that a few *thāns* of first quality water-proof sheets be prepared and sent. These are required for the *palkī* and other things. The news is that the next camp (*chhāonī*) will be in Basauli. Get the things ready and bring them there. 23 Ṣafar, Thursday.

[The following was written in the margins (*ḥāshiya*) of this letter].

It is strange that you have not written anything about Mirza Abdullah Beg *kumaidān,* and about the *barbarī* [wild] goats. You do not write [back] anything regarding the cases that I write to you about. This is not expected from an intelligent man like you. In future do reply to whatever matters I write to you about. Write about the goats.

Folio 105b. To La'l Khan.

I received your letter (*'arẓī*). It is fine that you have arranged separate accomodation for the junior Bībī in the house of my *karānī,* and that two *aṣīls—one* found there and the other brought by Kalb-i Ali—are with her. It is fine if the Bībī is happy but if she wishes to live together [with the senior Bībī] do accordingly. Do whatever is [best] for her comfort and happiness. If she lives separately, get Rs 15 from the *sarkār* for her food expenses and also the monthly wages of the *aṣīls.* Arrange clothes for her daily-use and when I reach there I will get [her] good clothes. In addition to the *aṣīls* if a midwife is needed then arrange for one as well. Keep her [Bībī's] happiness above every other thing. If the Mughlani *aṣīl,* brought by Kalb-i Ali, is clever, entrust her with the maintenance of the routine expenses. Take care that there is no unnecessary expense. 25 Ṣafar.

Folio 106a. To the senior Bībī.*

I received your letter. Whatever you have written about the separate accomodation of the junior Bībī, her happiness and comfort and your

* Here again the name of addressee is missing in the text.

unhappiness about it, and about her return to you from her separate accomodation is contrary to what I have heard.

You know from the beginning what my temperament is and that I do not tolerate (*rawādār*) anyone's discomfort. If she [junior Bībī] was not in trouble then why should I have arranged a separate accommodation for her. Now that you have approved of her living separately you should also show concern for her; and [needless to say] it will give me great pleasure when I hear about your love and concern for each other. 25 Ṣafar.

Folio 106b. To the mother of the senior Bībī.

I have heard that your daughter went to the house of the *karānī ṣāḥib,* and dragged the junior Bībī [to her own house] without any regard for her pregnancy. She said that she [junior Bībī] was her slave (*kanīz*) and that she [senior Bībī] would do whatever she liked. This was not in the fitness of things and I am extremely pained. It is strange that you did not stop your daughter from resorting to this offence even though it was committed in your presence; it appears that you connived [with her].

She calls her, 'her slave'. [Imagine] what honour will be left if I call your daughter her slave. It is loathsome for women to come out of their seclusion (*parda*), not to speak of running out from their own house to that of others and raising a commotion. Shame! This is far from decency.

It seems that you have not understood my nature. I swear that if there is any harm [done] to the junior Bībī or to her pregnancy I will finish both of you there and then and will never see your faces again. It is in your interest that as soon as you receive this letter you take her [junior Bībī] immediately to the place where she was. Otherwise in the event of any negligence, you will face the consequences. 29 Ṣafar, Wednesday.

Folio 107a. To La'l Khan.

I noted whatever you had written about the senior Bībī's visit to the junior Bībī, and the former's dragging of the latter to her house. I enclose herewith a letter that I have written to her mother. You are instructed to take the Bībī to her separate house and in the case of resistance or excuses from the senior Bībī write to me immediately, so that I can find a way out. 29 Ṣafar, Wednesday.

Folio 107b. To Mir Muhammad Azim.

I have written to Faizabad that they should send the *pattū*(?) velvet, and Dhaka cloth, etc. to you in Lucknow, so that you can take it further to Akbarabad. A letter from me will follow. Accordingly, hand over the goods to Najaf Khan and then come to me. These items have already been sold to Najaf Khan and I want a reasonable person to escort them. I am writing all this to you in advance so that you start preparations and there is no delay.

I had written to you earlier to send me the ducks which I have not yet received. Do not forget to send me whatever number—thirty, forty, fifty—you can get. 30 Ṣafar, Thursday night.

Folio 108a. To Gora Mistri.

The papers [*barāwurd*] of your salary upto the end of Muḥarram 1188 have been prepared. The order (*parwāna*) for the payment, in accordance to the *barāwurd*, is also ready: one in the name of Mir Sad-ud-Din and another in the name of Saiyidi Nasir. These are being sent after necessary corrections. The case of your salary has been fully settled. Do not worry [as] there will be no further delay.

Two to three letters containing the details about the developments there have reached me. I have noted from your first letter the details of the fire which had raged next to the *ḥavelī*, about your reaching there and extinguishing it and about the mischief of the *chelas* of the bazaar street. Indeed, you have done well and in future also you should be careful about such matters. I am preparing a plan to take over the bazaar. As for your request for a letter from Bashir Khan regarding the repair of the *bāradarī* of the *ḥavelī*, he [Bashir Khan] is at the moment in Pilibhit. There is therefore a delay in dispatching his letter to you. When he returns I will get a stern letter from him in the name of Saiyidi Alam.

In the second *'arẓī* you mention that you have sent the eight breast harnesses and the saddle parts along with the wine of Store *ṣāḥib*. But these have not yet reached here. I am relieved to note that the houses of *karānī* and *Bībī ṣāḥibs* are ready. Now attend to the construction of the concrete wall for my house. I also noted your dissatisfaction with the houses which were made according to Saiyidi Alam's plan. Whatever is ready is fine for the moment. We will think about it after the rainy season (*barsāt*). Take care that the roofs of the *ḥavelī* are not affected by the heavy rains.

I have also noted that the seeds of the *gul-i-ashrafī* in the garden have flowered. Be vigilant about the garden—it is in your charge and do whatever you think is best for it. Since I am at a distance and cannot send fruits for my son from here, [you] arrange them for him and get the expenses reimbursed from Lloyd *ṣāḥib.* Meet [also] Monsieur Gentil who is reaching Faizabad soon.

The ten poles which I had with me have been destroyed due to constant travels. Prepare two tent poles, stronger than the ones that I have at the moment, from the wooden logs that I had brought from Calcutta. In a day or two Store *ṣāḥib* will leave for Faizabad. Follow his advice. 1 Rabī' I, Friday, 1188.

Folio 109a. To Gora Mistri.
You have not informed me yet about the preparation of the organ. I wonder whether the watchmaker has done anything about it. Inform [me] also about the progress of the work of the painter. 2 Rabī' I, Saturday.

Folio 109b. To the painter of the sarkār.
For a long time I have no knowledge about the progress of your work: what you are doing and what you have done so far. When Store *ṣāḥib,* who is leaving for Faizabad returns, accompany him back here with your works and instruments. It is necessary for you to come here because the Nawab is camping here for about five to six months. Meet me so that I can get to know the progress of the work and assign you some other work. I had asked you earlier to prepare five to six portraits of the Nawab. If these are ready it is fine; if not, then prepare a specimen sketch with black ink and bring it along with you. 2 Rabī' I, Saturday.

Folio 109b. To Mir Muhammad Azim.
I had asked you earlier to get an Indian (Hindustanī) gun prepared. I do hope it is ready. Send it immediately along with three to four *sers* of dry tobacco. Second, two boxes belonging to Brooke *ṣāḥib,* one black and another red, had been sent to you earlier. Now he requires them. Send them soon. 3 Rabī' I, Sunday.

Folio 110a. To Gora Mistri.
Received your letter of 9 Ṣafar. I came to know that you had noticed a hole (*sūrā<u>kh</u>*) in the big *wilāyatī* gun which you had taken out. You wanted instructions from me for its repair. I do not know what kind of hole it is. Whatever happened has happened but it is necessary to

repair it immediately. See to it that such things do not happen in future, for the gun is a valuable gift (*bisyār tuḥfa*). 3 Rabī' I.

Folio 110b. To La'l Khan.

I am sending you three young women, two of them with their mothers and one of them without [her mother]. Since they are young I appoint Sa'id Begum to take them under her charge and look after their welfare. Arrange their accommodation separately, with one *shaṭranjī*, a small carpet and other spreads; have them clean themselves when they reach there and provide them with copper utensils.

Hand over to Sa'id Begum Rs 36 per month that has been fixed for their maintenance from the *sarkār*. If required we will consider about their clothes or else follow the instructions that I sent you. See to it strictly that their clothes are always clean and hair duly dressed and combed.

I have already written to you earlier about the junior Bībī being kept separately. Please do attend [to her] and take care if there is any problem. I have written to Sa'id Begum about the case. Hand over to her regularly a sum of Rs 15 per mensem for the routine expenses. Keep me informed. 7 Rabī' I,Thursday.

Folio 111a. To Mir Muhammad Azim.

I had written to you earlier to send the two boxes of Brooke *ṣāḥib*. He does not require them at the moment. Since the rainy season is approaching send the boxes and other goods of Brooke *ṣāḥib* to Faizabad. Also send the elephant *ḥauda* to Faizabad. 7 Rabī' I, Thursday.

Folio 111a. To Mir Muhammad Azim.

I had asked you earlier to send here the elephant *ḥauda*, the silver utensils, the Hindustanī gun, the pairs of shoes, the ducks, white sugar candy and other goods. If these are ready send them to Faizabad before you leave for Akbarabad. Keep the wine with you if it has not already been dispatched—nothing is required here at the moment. However, you should be ready. When you receive the goods from Faizabad, leave for Akbarabad without any delay along with these things.

As for your enquiry about the camping plan of the Nawab, I have now discovered that he will return to Faizabad after ten to twenty days. This is only for your information—keep it to yourself. 9 Rabī'I, Saturday.

Folio 111b. To Dīwān Manik Ram.

I have received your letter regarding the demand for a *hundī* of Rs 5000. You know that an agreement has been signed that on a sum of Rs two lac, twenty thousand will be paid and that I have now paid on Rs one lac, fifteen thousand—Rs 5000 in excess. You should understand the case properly and find out how much payment both in cash and kind Mr Young (?) has made. If he has paid to the effect of Rs 80,000, then this sum is [in actuality] equivalent to my Rs 40,000 because of the profound friendship that I have with the Nawab. 10 Rabī'I, Sunday.

Folio 112a. To Gora Mistri.

I had written to you earlier to send me some of the things from Faizabad. Since now I hear that the Nawab is returning to Faizabad and that the [journey] would commence in ten to fifteen days time, do not send anything here. You are hereby directed to prepare the *ḥavelī* and the houses in whatever manner you think appropriate. I am reaching there soon. 10 Rabī'I.

Folio 112b. To Gora Mistri.

I am enclosing a copy of the letter I wrote to you on the 10th of this month. You are instructed to collect [sufficient] firewood for three months consumption in the kitchen and chickens for daily use. Keep these things in a safe place so that they can be used in the rainy season. Acquire wooden planks and a rope , either by purchasing them or in whatever manner, for an Indian swing (*jhūlā*). Keep them ready. I will set it [swing] up when I come. Arrange the *sāyabāns* [parasols], screens, blinds and white ground spreads (*chāndnī*) immediately for the concrete *bāradarī* inside.

If Sayidi Alam arranges for these things then it is fine. Otherwise, the expenses for these will be borne from my *sarkār*. Do not cause any delay in this matter. I had sanctioned a sum for your maintenance since the case of your salary was pending. I had thought this would serve your purpose for the moment; but with the grace of God your work [regarding your salary] has now been done. 11 Rabī' I, Monday.

Folio 113a. To Mehrchand, the painter.

I had earlier summonned you to come here. But that is no logner necessary, so [you may] stay back. Add two to three more portraits to the five or six that I had written to you about and keep my order ready. I will inspect them at an appropriate time. 14 Rabī' I, Thursday.

Folio 113b. To the senior Bībī. *

I received your letter in which you have complained of not receiving my letters, and of your agreeing to the junior Bībī's separate accomodation. I never delay replying back to you and always write back immediately on receiving your letters. I was distressed to know that you had acted in a manner contrary to what I had written to you. However, now I am very happy to know that you have followed my advice. I understand your point that as the junior Bībī is young and pregnant she will be uncomfortable if left to live alone. Now that I think you have no ill feelings [towards her] you can take her to your place if she agrees [to go].

Also, Sa'id Begum along with three girls will be reaching there soon. I have told her that it is fine if the junior Bībī agrees to live with her, but nothing would be better than her joining you. Thus, I have asked the junior Bībī to live either with Sa'id Begum or with you. I am concerned about her comfort—this is for your information.

Rest assured that I am now very pleased with you. Take care of your health. I will be delighted to meet you and the sons very soon. 15 Rabī' I, Friday.

Folio 114a. To La'l Khan.

On the 15th I received a letter from the senior Bībī who says that she has agreed to the junior Bībī's separate accomodation. I appreciate this very much. But from her letter I understand that the junior Bībī, because of her youth, is scared to live alone. Since my purpose is her [junior Bībī's] comfort, ensure that if she prefers to stay with the senior Bībī she may be able to do so. It is also fine by me if she prefers to stay with Sa'id Begum who is reaching there. Thus in whichever of these places she wishes to stay it is fine by me. 15 Rabī' I, Friday.

Folio 114a. To Mehrchand, the painter.

I received your letter (*'arẓī*) and noted that you have nothing to do these days after finishing the five portraits and you are facing hardship because of the non-payment of your emoluments. I wrote a letter to you yesterday—the 13th—which you must have received by now.

I fail to understand why you are sitting idle. Prepare some more similar portraits if you have finished the ones you were engaged with so far. This [making potraits] is your work, and it is meaningless to sit

*The letter heading wrongly says that it is addressed to the son.

idle. Manik Ram has written to his *gumāshta* about your emoluments—you will receive the money and will not be in distress any more. 15 Rabī' I, Friday.

Folio 114b. To Mir Muhammad Azim.

I have not received your letter for a long time and am looking forward to hearing from you. I do hear regularly from Jugal Kishore and [therefore] I feel that you do not care to write to me. I do not know about the state of affairs there. I am surprised at your carelessness and neglect in sending letters to me. God protect the works [that I have put in your charge]; I do not know how they will be carried out. Write soon and let me know why you have not written for so long. 15 Rabī' I, Friday.

Folio 115a. To Gora Mistri.

I received your letter and noted that the watchmaker will prepare the organ only after the *ḥavelī* is ready. Get the *ḥavelī* ready soon. Keep the organ wrapped in double covers: one padded with cotton and the other of plain cloth. It should not only be protected from the dust but also from the [humid] air. This is a gift item. Be careful that no one touches it except the watchmaker who should be entrusted with the key.

The *wilāyatī* wooden logs that are there should be oiled intermittently, with a gap of three to four days, with sesame oil. Take care that they do not crack and get spoilt. I had written to you to send something with Store *ṣāḥib*—but that is no longer necessary. Tell the painter and the two carpenters to obtain their wages from my agent, Manik Ram, as I have written to him. I received a letter from Mehrchand, the painter, and have replied back to him.

Retain the good carpenters and artisans to do the job excellently. Prepare seven wooden cots (*chaukīs*), of which two should be strong and sent here. The repair of the boxes and the mirrors was fine. You had written that it is difficult to repair one of the boxes, which is full of goods, because its key is missing. All the keys are with Store ṣāḥib. Take it from him, and get the box repaired after emptying it.

If Saiyidi Alam does not attend to the tiles for the roof of the hen house and duck house then pay for the expenses from my *sarkār*. I have not yet received the breast harness and the girth of the saddle that you have [written having] sent with Mr Store. This is for your information. Repair the *wilāyatī* [European] gun properly and send it here. You had written that five *mans* of onions was produced in the garden and that you will send one *man* to me. It is fine if it reaches here. Keep the remaining onions safely for home consumption while I live there. You and Lloyd *ṣāḥib* share the fruits and the vegetables of the garden and send some to my sons.

I have noted that nine turkey chicks and fourteen chicks of waterfowl have hatched. Take care of them and the other birds and feed them properly. Dr Clue's agent has requested for an accommodation; arrange it either in the *ḥavelī* or in the *kothī* of Awadh—where ever you think proper. Gokulchand Mukerjea will reach there subsequently. Arrange a place in the *ḥavelī* for him as well.

Mir Muhammad Ata Husain Khan had sent a letter to his house on the 1st of this month by *dāk*. Find out from the *harkāra* of the *dāk* and take the letter to his [Ata Khan's] house. One more letter has been dispatched along with the packet (*chuktī*) of Lloyd *ṣāḥib*. Reply to all of them. 16 Rabī' I, Saturday.

Folio 116b. To Mir Muhammad Azim.

I had received your letter of 14 Ṣafar on the 22nd. Meanwhile, I received a second letter of 12 Rabī' I on the 19th of Rabī' I. There is a gap of one month between these two letters and in between I have sent you several letters: On 1 Ṣafar regarding the escorting of the goods to Akbarabad; On 3 Rabī' I asking for the Indian gun and Mr Brooke's box; On the 7th regarding stalling the dispatch of these items and sending them to Faizabad; On the 9th urging you to leave for Akbarabad and sending these goods to Faizabad; On the 15th regarding your dereliction [of duty], not sending letters and other important matters. I am writing to you yet another letter in addition to these. You have been inordinately late in not replying to any one of these letters.

I cannot be aware of the developments there if I receive your letters after a month or two. I had asked Jugal Kishor to pay you Rs 1000. He has written that he has given you the money, but even though one month has passed I have not yet received any acknowledgement [note] from you for this payment. I am dismayed. Now you write for further payment of Rs 600. I cannot understand the reason for your silence, more so because you do not even acknowledge [receipt of] my letters. [This is despite] my repeated instructions to you to respond to my letters the day you receive them.

What is this style of working? (*chi qism kār, kudām kār kardagī*) What do you have in mind that makes you consistently careless about writing to me? How can I be satisfied about the execution of works for which prompt communication is necessary (*kihar laḥẕa ittilā'i ū ẕarūr ast*). Write to me clearly if you are determined to be negligent in your duty so that I can give up hope of getting any further work done by you. I am tired. How long can I keep sending you stringent instructions? It is useless.

Keep with you the essence, the shield and the saddle that you have written about. I am reaching Lucknow in ten to twelve days and will [then] inspect these three items. I will buy them only if I approve of them.

Jugal Kishor manages to reply promptly to my letters and is regular with his correspondence, but it is strange that your letters never reach me even though you both live in the same city. There is nothing more to write about. 20 Rabī' I, Wednesday.

Folio 117b. To Mir Muhammad Azim.

I received your letter acknowledging the receipt of the *hundī* for Rs 1000 from Jugal Kishor, and the dispatch of the elephant *ḥauda*, three cartons of wine, one *man* sugar candy and three crates of pickle. I had asked you to prepare a *ḥauda* because the '*amārī* that you had sent earlier was small by two *girah* (about 4 inches) and was inconvenient to ride. The new *ḥauda* that has now arrived here is big by two *girah* and has an inconvenient wooden back support. Further, you have got it knitted with cane which is difficult to find everywhere. You should have used *nivār* which is easily obtainable. It is strange that you have not followed my advice.

I have noted the expense of Rs 1000: You have spent Rs 600 in the preparation of the silver vessels and Rs 200 for the pairs of shoes. I wonder on which silver vessel you have spent Rs 600, because this much money is not required for the *pāndān, gulāb pāsh* etc.—the two or three—necessary items [that I had asked for]. I am also amazed that you spent Rs 200 on the shoes.

I fail to understand your style of working. It was important that you should have informed me earlier about the price and the necessary equipment [needed] for whatever you were preparing. But you delayed your letters. Why did you not send by *dāk* a copy of what you had written so that I could know the state of affairs? I do not know how to comment on your carelessness. You allow [for] delay, negligence and indifference in every work. If this is the situation then I am afraid I will not send you on my work to Akbarabad.

I noted the case of the person whose property was confiscated by Makhu Khan *kotwāl* and in front of whose house he [the *kotwāl*] had posted his men. It was best to have acted on this matter covertly. Now you have brought it in public knowledge and I feel helpless to do anything. It is advisable that we forget about this.

I have counted sixty-three bottles of the wine sent by you. Your man who had brought the shoes suffered from stomach pain, and when he recovered after two days he left for your place. I do not know why he has not reached there yet.

I noted that you did not buy the goats from Abdullah Beg *kumaidān* because they were useless. This is an old case about which I had written to you long back and you delayed the reply. You are informing me about it now though you should have brought it to my notice there and then. Words fail to describe your dereliction in every matter.

As for the payment of Rs 500–600, I will find out the state of affairs when I reach Lucknow and do whatever I feel is appropriate. If you are leaving very soon with the goods for Akbarabad, ask a reliable person to display the orders that I had placed with you in front of me when I reach Lucknow. I will do whatever is appropriate after inspecting the goods. 21 Rabī' I, Thursday.

Folio 119b. To Mayachand Sāhū of Akbarabad.

I received your letter. You gave Rs 718 to Captain Martin when he was in Akbarabad. It is strange that despite my writing to you several times that Captain Martin was close to me and that you should fearlessly provide him whatever he desires, you caused him inconvenience. This is not in keeping with our friendship.

You have written that it will take a fortnight to prepare the gold thread work. [You] get it completed soon and send it to me at the earliest, for the rains have already commenced and it will be difficult to protect it [gold embroidery] from the downpour. It is alright if the preparation of the other items is delayed by a few more days. Get the *pāndān* ready and send it.

You had written that the Raja of Mainpuri had confiscated the goods. But this refers to the past. I have sent you the goods again and you should write to me their rate and the market [for their sale]. Chitrbhuj has arrived from Farrukhabad but has not yet presented the English account to me. I will take up the case of leave, as advised by you, after scrutinizing the account. In any case my aim is [to see] that your work is done well. 23 Rabī' I, Saturday.

Folio 120a. To Mir Sulaiman Khan.

I am delighted to receive your letter after having already received two other letters from you. Since all these three letters refer to the same issues I am replying to them together.

I am concerned about the payment of *tankhwāh* of Rs 10,100 pertaining to the price of the elephants. Because of our friendship I am keen on getting your work done even better than my own. I have thought about its payment in the following way: Najaf Khan has a *salyāna* [annual payment] from the Company from which he has allocated Rs 8000 in the name of Baḍe *Ṣāḥib* [Hastings?], to me. But the matter is still under consideration. Once it is settled I will write that your money be deducted from this account.

Second, Diwan Manik Ram had disposed off the fourty-four rolls of soiled cloth that you had given him for Rs 2560. Your money is here with me. According to the agreement you will be paid this amount when the money is realized there. However, write to me the amount [commission] that should be paid to Diwan Manik Ram. You should also write about the money I owe you. Do not worry as this will be sent to you soon.

You and Khwaja Pedrose did not write about the payment of any money to Monsieur Gentil. The Khwaja had, however, asked him [Gentil] to sell the elephants. If there is a copy of the [sale] document, send it. In case Najaf Khan pays for the elephants, the payment may be made from the same money.

My dear, Monsieur Gentil followed the instructions of Khwaja Pedrose and extended hospitality to his agent and confidant, Sharf-ud-Din Khan. The fact that his [Sharf-ud-Din's] name was associated with yours, he accommodated him in his own house and spent his [own] money on his hospitality for about a month. I have already sent you the bond (*tamassuk*) of Sharf-ud-Din Khan. Khwaja Pedrose's letter is in Faizabad and I will send it to you as soon as I get it here.

From the total debt, Rs 400 have been paid to Monsieur Gentil and the remaining Rs 600 are still due. Saiyid Niyaz Ali Khan and Saiyid Lutf Ali Khan have arrived in the camp from Shahjahanabad. This is for your information. 27 Rabī' I, Wednesday, *Chhāonī, pargana* Basauli.

Folio 121b. To Mir Muhammad Husain Ata Khan.

I received your letter and noted that you and Manik Ram had to stay back there and start a day later due to delay in the payment of the troopers and other important matters.

Please note that I will leave for Bareilly tomorrow and will stay there to meet Manik Ram who will join me. According to your instructions I have prepared and dispatched to you the letter, in English, for Mr Middleton. This pertains to the case of Tekchand Sahu. This is for your information. Aonla, 28 Rabī' I, Thursday.

Folio 122a. To Ghulam Hussain, havaldar.

I received your letter regarding the details of the following : Mir Naim Khan, an elephant, a palanquin, a chariot, two horses, four to five bullock carts, the arrival of the brother of Shah Madan and the payment of the money. Mir Naim Khan owes [to me] Rs 2500, it is fine if you can procure this amount from him in cash; otherwise obtain [from him] commodities in good condition [equivalent to this amount].

I left the camp and set out on 28 Rabī' I for Faizabad. You [should] reach there without delay after collecting the money. 30 Rabī' I, Saturday, Bareilly.

Folio 122b. To La'l Khan.

I received your letter and noted that you have arranged separate accommodation for the junior Bībī in the house of the *karānī sāhib,* adjacent to that of Sa'id Begum. The objective is to provide her a place where she is comfortable and happy. I have left the camp on 28 Rabī' I for Faizabad and will be reaching there soon. I do not think it is advisable for Bika *harkāra* to go inside the house. Discourage him from going in. 30 Rabī' I, Bareilly.

Folio 122b. To Mir Muhammad Azim.

I received your letter of 21 Rabī' I on the 27th, indicating your departure to Akbarabad with the goods. You wish to know [from me] who to handover the goods to in Akbarabad before leaving for this [my] place. Report at the *kothī* of Mayachand *sāhūkār* when you reach Akbarabad. Hand over the *pattū,* clothes, Dhaka textiles, etc. to Agha Sadiq, the *khānsāmān* of Najaf Khan, and come here after securing the receipt.

I do not require the silk, but if you need it you can bring it. Find out secretly and write to me if the fifteen *mans* of silk that I had sent to

Akbarabad, to the *kothī* of Mayachand Sahu, has been sold, and at what rate per *man*. Take care that nobody notices your inquisitiveness. If Mayachand has prepared any of my orders bring them with you. 30 Rabī' I, Saturday, Bareilly.

Folio 123b. To Mir Muhammad Azim.

I received your letter of 30 Rabī' I on 10 Rabi II regarding your taking the goods to Firozabad, the *kotwāl's* objection to taking them [goods] any further, your reporting to Agha Sadiq, and your request for a letter, apropos this, from Agra. Accordingly, I have written a letter to Najaf Quli Khan under my own seal and also a letter to Agha Sadiq. Collect these letters from Diwan Manik Ram and hand over the goods to Agha. Obtain receipts under the seal of Agha and get back here. 12 Rabī' II.

Folio 123b. To Mir Muhammad Azim.

I received your letter of 12 Rabī' II on the 17th and got to know the details. It is a strange letter because you have written about three different things in such a manner that no clear picture emerges.

You begin the letter with the statement about your entering Akbarabad with the goods; then you write about the confiscation of the goods by the *kotwāl* under the pretext of tolls; and then you indicate that you handed over the things to Chitrabhuj on the 12th and left for the camp of the Nawab. It is good that you have handed over the things to Chitrabhuj.

I had earlier written to Najaf Khan in response to your letter. But now that he has left for Shahjahanabad [Delhi] I have sent two letters to you—one under my own seal and another from Manik Ram to Agha Sadiq. As soon as the letters reach you, send your men to the Agha and hand over the goods to him through Mayachand and Chitrabhuj and obtain the receipts. Enquire, on the quiet, the rate of the silk and bring it with you. Get the things which I ordered from Chitrabhuj, inspect them and find out their quality. Also, check the *huqqa* which is being prepared there. 18 Rabī' II, Wednesday.

Folio 124b. To Muhammad Murid Khan.

I am sending you a gift—a very nice European (*wilāyatī*) casket which I hope you will accept as a souvenier from a friend. 22 Rabī' II, Friday, 1188.

Folio 125a. To Mir Muhammad Azim.

I received two of your letters—of 18 and 19 Rabī‘ II—on the 30th. I have not only written back to you but have also dispatched to you the letters [which you required] in the name of Agha Sadiq—one under my own seal and the other under that of Diwan Manik Ram. I am helpless if these letters did not reach you.

I noted that you are making repeated visits to Agha Sadiq with your plea [to allow transit of your goods] and that he is unrelenting and will not allow the goods to pass without the payment of the tolls (*maḥṣūl*). The letters in the name of the Agha, dispatched from here on 18 Rabī‘ II, must have reached him and he must have stopped interfering. However, as requested by you, another well-drafted letter is being dispatched for the Agha. Take this letter to him; if he accepts it well and good, otherwise bring it to the notice of Mayachand. Tell Mayachand to pay whatever *maḥṣūl* is due and get the goods released. This money will be listed in the account of Najaf Khan and I will incur no financial damages.

Understand all this and leave for this place after obtaining a receipt from the Agha. The Agha will be embarassed for what he has done. You had written earlier about your own financial stringency. Show this letter to Mayachand and Chitrabhuj and get Rs 50 to 100, whatever you require from them. Do not hesitate in matters of expenses. 2 Jumāda I, Wednesday.

Folio 125b. To Mir Waliullah Khan.

I received your letter in which you have written that I have not replied to two of your letters. I received your letter one on 18 Rabī‘ II and replied the same day. I am helpless if it has not reached you.

I am worried about the Nawab's health and pray to God that he recovers. I have sent two letters—on 17 Rabī‘ II and 3 Jumāda I—through the *dāk* to Hasan Riza Khan enquiring about the Nawab's health. Bring them [the letters] to the notice of the Nawab and obtain his replies.

When I left that place you took the responsibility of sending the daily news to me—in fact you stayed back for this reason. But I am dismayed that since then you have sent only two letters. Ensure that the daily news is recorded without fail and sent to me through the *dāk*. I will be very unhappy if there is delay in the dispatch of the daily news. I look forward anxiously to receiving the news.

The estimate for the salary of the English officers is ready. Get the orders for the payment and send it soon. 5 Jumāda I, Friday.

Folio 126b. To Mayachand sāhūkār.

I received your letter and noted that when you asked Mir Mansur for a *parwāna* to sell the cocoons and the silk he asked you to pay the taxes on the goods. Manik Ram is already there with a *dastak* and a letter, under the seal of Najaf Khan, regarding the waiver of the *maḥṣūl* on the goods sent to you as well as on the gold embroidery cloth and my other orders. It is strange that you are complaining despite [the receipt of] such a strong [worded] document. [All this] appears to be simply an excuse. Agha Sadiq and his deputy have no power to interfere in the transit [through the city] and sale of the things I want. If they dare do this they shall be accorded exemplary punishment.

On my way from Akbarabad you had promised to get my orders ready and dispatched soon. [But] this [the orders] is long overdue and I have not received anything[from you]. There cannot be any justification for the delay in getting ready such a small order. Clearly, then, you are issuing false statements (*nādrustī-ye sukhan-i īshān bazahūr paiwast*) which does not behove a *mahājan* (*ba'īd az shīwa-i mahājanī*). In the last six months you have sent me only the cushions, pillows and the *masnad*. Under such conditions how do I believe that you will carry out my other works.

[Anyway] forget about the past and dispatch expeditiously all the goods through the troops and the *ḥavaldār* who have reached there with the goods from Kanpur. It will not be nice if there is any negligence in this [work].

Forward the letter addressed to Najaf Khan through a messenger to Shahjahanabad and hand over the letter of Agha Sadiq to him along with the goods. Carry out all this [instructions] without delay. You will know the other details from the letter of Manik Ram. Friday, 5 Jumāda I.

Folio 127b. To Mir Waliullah Khan.

I received your letter along with the newsletters. I am worried to hear about the Nawab's indisposition and am praying for his early recovery, which will be a source of joy and relief to the people of [his] state. Send the good news of his recovery to me regularly as well as the details about the court. 12 Jumāda I, Friday.

Folio 127b. To Mir Waliullah Khan.

I received your letters of 9 and 10 Jumāda I on the 16th. I am worried about the Nawab's indisposition and am praying day and night for his recovery. I look forward to hearing the auspicious news of his return to full health.

In the meanwhile I received another letter from you on the 17th in which you mention the Nawab's order to prepare the salary estimates on the 13th. I will appreciate if you send these [estimates] to me along with the daily newsletters. 17 Jumāda I.

Folio 128a. To Lala Kashmiri Mal, sāhūkār.

Scott *ṣāḥib* has written to me that you would like to sell the 13 elephants, both male and female, which you possess. The price he has quoted for them appears high since the elephants are not of good size. Anyhow, it is difficult to know if the price is appropriate without inspecting them.

Whatever goods the Europeans send to me for sale I, as a matter of principle, charge 50 per cent of the profit as my share. If this is fine by you then you can send them [elephants] to me and I will dispose them off [in the same manner] as I handle the goods of other Europeans. Rest assured that I will care for them as I do for my own [things]. Mr Scott has written to me that you also have some muslin for sale. If you like you can send this as well. If these conditions are acceptable to you, I will send you the *dastak* of *rāhdārī* and the men to bring these things. 18 Jumāda I.

Folio 129a. To Mir Waliullah Khan.

I received your letter of 14 Jumāda I on the night of the 18th Thursday, and was happy to learn that the Nawab is recovering. May he return to full health soon. I am glad that the Nawab has deputed a contingent for the chastisement of the mischievous Rohillas who have advanced further, and that the battle is about to commence. Keep writing and continue to send the reports about the army and the Nawab's camp without fail.

I noted the dilly–dallying tactics of Hasan Riza Khan. Do acquire from him the salary [estimates] according to the agreement (*qarārdād*) and send them soon. 18 Jumāda I, Thursday.

Folio 129b. To Mir Waliullah Khan.

I received your letter and am happy to learn that the Nawab is in good spirits. Continue to keep me informed of the details in the same way.

You have written that the Nawab has issued orders for the [preparation of the] estimates of the salaries of the Europeans and the others [with them]. Obtain [also] the salary estimates of Nauruz Ali Beg and send it [to me]. 28 Jumāda I, Saturday night.

Folio 129b. To Mir Waliullah Khan.

I received two letters—one of the 16th and the other of the 17th on the 21st of Jumāda I. Continue to send the daily news of the camp in the same way. Also find out and write to me the news of Shahjahanabad [Delhi] so that I am informed about the developments there as well. 21 Jumāda I, Sunday.

Folio 130a. To the wife (Bībī) of Captain Kanvei.

I learnt from your letter that people from the vicinity throw stones at your residence in the night, and that these people have been apprehended and punished.

As a matter of fact nothing can be done in these matters. Write to me [for security men] if you consider it necessary and I will send some men for the protection of your house. If you wish to send a letter to Mr Kanvei send it to me and I will forward it to him from here. 21 Jumāda I.

Folio 130a. To Mir Sulaiman Khan.

I received your letter and came to know from Manik Ram and Niyaz Ali Khan about the case of payment for the clothes, etc. I need not emphasize that you are my close friend, but because I have been travelling constantly I could not help the delay in the payment of these sums. I have received an [authority letter] under the seal of Najaf Khan for Rs 80,000, his *tankhwāh* from the Company, the payment of which is due in the month of Rajab. Accordingly, I have written to the *Ṣāḥib-i Kalān* [Hastings] that when the order for the payment of the *tankhwāh* is issued he should inform you [so that you may get] the payment of the clothes and [also] the Rs 10,100 for the elephants. Be rest assured and keep informing me about your health and welfare. 24 Jumāda I, Wednesday.

Folio 131a. To Mir Waliullah Khan.

Your letter of 22 Jumāda I with the news of the camp reached here on the 29th. Continue to send letters like this. You have written of not having received my letters. The delay from my side is due to the fact that I do not hear from you. I write back to you the same day as I receive your letter. 29 Jumāda I.

Folio 131b. To Mir Waliullah Khan.

I received on 2 Jumāda II your letter of 25 Jumāda I. You have written about having sent the newsletter on the 24th. But I have not received any newsletter of that date. This is just for your information. You must, without fail, send me the daily newsletters. 2 Jumāda II.

Folio 131b. To Mayachand Sāhū.

Received your letter. You must have noticed that the people responsible for the mischief have been punished. In future whosoever dares to play pranks will face the consequences of their doings. I have sent a strongly worded letter regarding this to Mir Mansur. You should not worry about this. Send my orders soon through Tikaram *havaldār* and the troopers of the *sarkār.* I have written to the above-mentioned *ḥavaldār* that if there is any interference at the time of his departure or on the way he should ignore it. I will be extremely offended if there is any delay now [from your side] in sending the goods. 4 Jumāda II, Saturday.

Folio 132a. To Tikaram ḥavaldār, Akbarabad [Agra].

I had sent you word earlier about bringing the goods from there. It is fine if they are ready, otherwise stay with Mayachand Sāhū until they are ready. Inspect them according to the detailed list when they are prepared, and procure them after getting the seal of Mayachand. Bring them carefully with you. In case any one of the officials there interferes [for] *maḥṣūl,* ignore them. Instruct the soldiers to take proper care of the goods on the way. 4 Jumāda II, Saturday.

Folio 132b. To Mir Waliullah Khan.

I received your letter with news of the excessive rains and inundation, the Nawab's departure and his arrival at [a place] twenty *kos* from the camp of the doomed Rohillas and one *kos* from Amroha. You had written that you could not procure the *parwāna* for the *tankhwāh* of the Europeans (*firangīs*) due to the continuous travelling [of the Nawab] and that you will obtain it when he camps. I am sure that you will get it soon and send it to me. 6 Jumāda II.

Folio 132b. To Mir Waliullah Khan.

I received your letter with the information about the departure of the

Nawab from Amroha, his arrival in the garden of Chandpur, the departure of Kallu Khan towards Delhi (*Dār-ul-Khalīfa*), the rise in the prices of grains and the other details. Continue to write in the same manner.

You had written that the *parwānas* have not yet been prepared because of continuous travel. It is absolutely imperative to get them [prepared] and have them dispatched at an early date. Give it utmost priority. I have sent one *pattū*, as a reward for the news supplier (*khabardār*) that you had written about, along with two letters—one congratulating the Nawab on his recovery to health and the other about some other important matters. Do present to the Nawab the letter [addressed] for him, and obtain a reply. 9 Jumāda II, Thursday, night.

Folio 133a. To Mir Waliullah Khan.

I received two of your letters of 9 and 10 Jumāda regarding the news of the camp, your dispatch of my letter to the Nawab and your reasons for the delay in writing to me. I am surprised at the delay—do not let it happen again. Acquire the *parwāna* for the salaries of the Europeans and send it soon.

I noted that you mentioned to Ilich Khan about the letter to Chait Singh regarding the *tankhwāh* at Benares. He [Ilich Khan] promised to write to him, i.e. Chait Singh, the following day. It has since been ten to twelve days but I have not received that letter. Obtain it and dispatch it. 10 Jumāda II, Saturday.

Folio 133b. To Mir Sulaiman Khan.

I received your letter regarding the *tankhwāh* issue. The *parwāna*, under the seal of Najaf Khan, for the *tankhwāh* of Rs 80,000 has been sent to Mr Bilai. I have also written to him that your account (*ḥisāb*) should be cleared when the money for the *tankhwāh* is obtained from the *sarkār* and that you should be paid according to the details of my purchases from you. I am enclosing the English letter addressed to him, which I hope you will hand over personally to him.

I have also written about the payment of the elephants, i.e. Rs 10,100 *rakābī* which is equivalent to Rs 10,302 *chālān*. I regard your work as my own work. The delay in this matter was because I was with the army. I have great affection for you. Do keep me informed of your welfare.

According to the *tamassuk* of Sharf-ud-Din Khan, given to Monsieur Gentil, Rs 600 will be deducted from the price of the elephants, and another Rs 54 *batta* at the rate of 9 per cent. The remaining Rs 9648 will be paid to you. Further, I learnt from Diwan Manik Ram that you had expected to be paid 10 per cent on the sale. But the payment on this count will be of 5 per cent as this is the rule of my business. The details of the account, in Persian, are herewith enclosed for your perusal. 4 Rajab-ul-Murajjab, Sunday night.

Folio 135a. To Mayachand Sāhū.

Received your letter. The goods that you had sent were useless. I had thought that you are a clever person and to prepare such [useless] things is not becoming of a man of your intelligence and wisdom. Chitrabhuj had agreed to send the *pāndān* in two months time, but I have not received it even though six months have lapsed. He has also not sent the six *thāns* of sircussian clothes which he said were ready and about to be dispatched. This has caused me embarassment since I had ordered the *thāns* at the behest of the other Europeans. I wonder what kind of work he does and why he has not dispatched these things to me. Every thing that I had ordered for should now be dispatched forthwith.

I am dismayed that in every letter you write about the problems you face from the officials there. This is contradictory to what Najaf Khan writes. I fail to understand. At any rate, get all my orders ready soon and dispatch them to me. The *ḥuqqa* that you had sent is of no use and its functioning is disgusting. I am sending it back to you since I did not like it. You will know about the other things from the letter of Manik Ram. 8 Rajab-ul- Murajjab, Thursday.

Folio 136a. To Mir Waliullah Khan.

I have received five of your letters dated the 21st, 22nd, 23rd, 24th, and 25th. I noted Ilich Khan's observations on the *tankhwāh* matter—they are absolutely baseless. It is not proper to secure any change in the estimate that has been procured. Try to realize the actual salary and in future get the *tankhwāh* from some other place.

You have not written anything about the preparation of the estimates of the other *tankhwāhs*. You had written that you had sent them to me on the 12th and the 13th . But in the last one month and seven days I have not received anything. This is strange because I had left you behind there precisely for this. Do write the details about the estimates of the *tankhwāh* as well as the regular news of the camp. 38 Rajab, Friday.

Folio 136b. To Mir Sulaiman Khan.
I had written to Calcutta earlier about the Rs 80,000 *tankhwāh* of Najaf Khan and had also sent you a letter stating that the Rs 10,100 for the elephants and the other arrears that I owe you will be paid from this amount. I now discover that the issue has not yet been settled. In consideration of our friendship I now write to you to acquire the money for the elephants in whatever manner you feel appropriate, from my account in Calcutta. The remaining money that I owe you will be sent together with the interest later. Rest assured that I am fully concerned about the fact that the money has to be paid to you. 1 Sha'bān, Saturday.

Folio 137a. To Mir Waliullah Khan.
Received your letter of 26 Rajab on the 3rd of Sha'bān. I got to know from your newsletter that Faizullah Khan had an interview with the Nawab, was awarded a *khil'at*, bejewelled *sarpich* and a tray of clothes. Continue to send the daily news. 3 Sha'bān.

Folio 137a. To Mir Waliullah Khan.
I received on the 3rd of Sha'bān two of your letters dated 28 Rajab and 3 Sha'bān. You should continue to send the daily news to me so that I do not worry in anticipation. The change in *tankhwāh* is not proper without the order of the Nawab. However, since you insist and Diwan Manik Ram has also written about it, you may get a *parwāna* for Rs 20,000 ***sicca*** for any place in the *ṣūba* except Kora. Why have you not sent me the *parwāna* of the *tankhwāh* of my retainers? Procure it and send it forthwith. 3 Sha'bān.

Folio 137b. To Mir Waliullah Khan.
Received two of your letters of the 3rd and the 4th of Sha'bān on the 11th and got to know of the affairs. I am surprised to know from you as well as from Manik Ram that despite my writing to you several times on the *tankhwāh* matter you are still awaiting my instructions to get into action. I write again that in view of your and Manik Ram's insistence on the matter, you may acquire a *tankhwāh* of Rs 20,000 from any place in the *ṣūba*, except Kora, Gorakhpur and Khairabad, even though the substitution of the *tankhwāh-i*-Benares is not proper without the Nawab's order.

Why have you not acquired and dispatched the *parwāna* of the *tankhwāh* of Mr Sangster and the others which is ready? I repeat what

I have already said above that you [may] obtain the *parwāna* of the *tan<u>kh</u>wāh* from anywhere in the *ṣūba* and send it to me without any delay. You will know about the other matters from the letter of Manik Ram. 11 Sha'bān, Monday.

Folio 138a. To Mir Waliullah Khan.

I received two of your letters—one of the 5th and the other of the 6th of Sha'bān—on the 12th and the 13th respectively. Continue to write like this so that I do not have to wait.

You mention again that you will act in the *tan<u>kh</u>wāh* matter only after receiving my instructions. My dear, I have already written to you that in place of the *tan<u>kh</u>wāh* of Benares you [should] obtain a *parwāna* of Rs 20,000 *sikka-i-ḥālī tan<u>kh</u>wāh* from any other place in the province, except Kora, Gorakhpur and Khairabad, and inform me. Why have you not obtained the *parwāna* of *tan<u>kh</u>wāh* for Mr Sangster even though the *barāwurd* [estimate] of his emoluments is ready? I insist that you get it from any place in the province except the *maḥāls* [mentioned above]. You will know of the other details from the letter of Manik Ram. 13 Sha'bān.

Folio 139a. To Mir Waliullah Khan.

I received your letter of 11 Sha'bān on the 17th. You have written again about the *tan<u>kh</u>wāh* matter and the *parwāna* for the salary estimate of Mr Sangster which is ready. I write to you again that you should obtain the *parwāna* of *tan<u>kh</u>wāh* from any place in the province, except the *maḥāls* mentioned [Kora, Gorakhpur and Khairabad] and send it to me forthwith. You will know the other details from the letter of Manik Ram. 27 Sha'bān, Monday.

Folio 139a. To Mir Waliullah Khan.

I received three of your letters dated 12th, 15th and 17th of Sha'bān. Continue to write to me like this. I noted that the *parwānas* for *tan<u>kh</u>wāh* have been acquired for places in Bareilly and that you will send them to me soon. I have earlier written to you to get them ready according to my instructions and dispatch them soon. 22 Sha'bān, Saturday.

Folio 139b. To Mir Waliullah Khan.

Received two of your letters of the 24th and the 29th on the 21st and got to know of the details: the arrival and camping of the Nawab at a distance of three *kos* this side from Bareilly, and his departure for Faizabad covering seven *kos* a day.

You have written that you spoke to the *munshī* of the *sarkār* regarding the *parwāna* of the *tankhwāh* from Benares, and that he wanted the earlier *parwāna* and the *shuqqa* returned before he wrote another one. The *shuqqa* of the Nawab in the name of Chait Singh was sent to him but not a single penny from the *tankhwāh* money—as is obvious—has been received so far.

Convey this to the *munshī*, and negotiate [with him] to get the *parwāna* [for me] as well as the *parwāna* of the *tankhwāh* regarding the salary estimate of Mr Sangster. It is your duty to send me the news of the developments in the camp and not to keep me waiting. 29 Sha'bān, Saturday.

Folio 140a. To Bābā Antony.

Received your letter. I remember you and am waiting eagerly to meet you. I hope to reach there soon and have the pleasure of seeing you. I will bring the fruits with me. 5 Shawwāl, Friday, Lucknow.

Folio 140b. To La'l Khan.

Regarding your request for the clothes for inside [female apartments], I have instructed Manik Ram, who in turn has sent a letter to Ram Sundar Datt Sarkar. You [should] acquire whatever you need from him [*sarkār*] and get them made in your presence.

You must have received Rs 25 to meet the expenses for the mother's milk-weaning ceremony of the bābā. I have ordered for the payment of another Rs 25 since this money was not sufficient—in all [you now have] Rs 50. Receive this money and spend it on the ceremony. I have written to Captain [Martin] to provide my son with fruits when he comes and asks for them.

Ram Dayal *harkāra* will reach you with two Bībīs. Accommodate them with the junior Bībī and get whatever else is necessary—clothes, cots, utensils—from the *sarkār*. Arrange also some money for their monthly expenses. Take utmost care about this matter. 15 Ṣafar-ul-Muẓaffar 1189, from Mahdighat.

Folio 141a. To Antony Bābājān.

Received your letter on the 19th of Ṣafar with the information that the husband of your *dāya* wants her to leave but she has not yet left.

My dear son, I had earlier written about Rs 25 and now about Rs 50 to Ram Sundar Datt Sarkar and La'l Khan. I am sure La'l Khan must have obtained this sum from Ram Sundar Datt Sarkar and handed it over to you. You spend the money in whatever manner you feel appropriate. 19 Ṣafar, Wednesday, Mahdighat.

Folio 141b. To La'l Khan.

Since the treatment of the Ḥakīm Nawab did not suit my son, there is no harm in discontinuing it. I do not know why you did not follow Captain Martin's suggestion for [changing to] the treatment of Ḥakīm Mir Jan. I do not approve of your disobedience and as soon as you receive this *shuqqa* you must follow whatever he [Martin] says. Call Ḥakīm Mir Jan for a complete treatment [of my son]. I will be very unhappy and it will not be good for you if you deviate even a little from Mr Martin's suggestion. 23 Ṣafar, Mahdighat.

Folio 141b. To Bībī Jawahar.

I am delighted to receive your letter which arrived exactly when I was waiting for it. It is due to your love for me and your anxieties, as well as your loneliness which has made you averse to eating and suffer from insomnia. But for your fears of travelling this side—i.e. Bengal–Bihar—I would have brought you with me. However, I will soon be back and will be delighted to meet you. Do not loose heart and be careful about your regular food and timely sleep. Remain happy. 15 Rabī' I, Tuesday, Azimabad.

Folio 142a. To Bībī Jawahar.

I received your second letter in Azimabad and noted that you have given up food and sleep since the day we parted. As I wrote to you earlier, it is your love for me that has caused you so much anxiety. I am returning soon. You should take care of your food and sleep. Remain happy as your happiness will lead to my happiness (*K͟hushnūdī-ye ū har ā'īna mūjib-i riẓā-i k͟hāṭir-i īn jānib ast*). 18 Rabī' I, Tuesday.

Folio 142b. To Bībī Jawahar.

I am delighted to receive three of your letters. From the first I knew that you intended to visit and circumambulate the *dargāh*; and from the second that you were back home after receiving the blessings. I arrived safely in Calcutta on the 8th of Rabī' II, Wednesday. God willing I will soon return from here. Be happy and remain in touch. 11 Rabī' 2, Saturday, Calcutta.

Folio 142b. To Bībī Jawahar.

Received your letter of the 4th of Rabī' II on the 18th. You have complained about not receiving my letters. In this matter I feel helpless. I have written to you regularly, particularly in response to the letter which required an answer.

I heard that you have quarrelled with the junior Bībī. I did not like it. It is your responsibility to keep her pleased. Take care that her diet is nutritious and keep her happy, in the same way as you do to me, so that there is no apprehension on her part. [Similarly] it is also necessary for her to treat you like her mother, to keep you happy and to act on your advice. All this will make me happy. 19 Rabī' II, Sunday, Calcutta.

Folio 143a. To La'l Khan.

I received your letter and learnt of the painful incident of [the death of] the younger son. We are all helpless before the will of God and should remain composed.

I am glad to know of the elder son's good spirit and health and am delighted that you are so devotedly working for his happiness. 30 Rabī' II, Thursday, Calcutta.

Folio 143b. To Bībī Jawahar.

I was happy to receive two of your letters and to note that you are anxiously waiting for me. Your anxieties will be over soon. Keep in touch. 9 Jumāda I, Saturday.

Folio 143b. To La'l Khan.

I received your letter and was happy to know about the recovery of my son and the birth of a baby girl to the junior Bībī. Keep in touch. 24 Jumāda I.

Folio 143b. To Bībī Jawahar.

I got to know of the happiness of your heart from four of your letters. Patience begets relief even if the days of separation are unpleasant. Be patient [and] you will soon be happy. I am reaching very soon and will be delighted to meet you. Write to me regularly about your welfare. 24 Jumāda I.

Folio 144a. To Antony Bābājān, the son.

Received your letter on the 23rd of Jumāda I and am happy to know that you are fully recovered. I am reaching very soon and will be delighted to meet you. Do not worry, I will bring the pair of pearls that you have asked for with me. 24 Jumāda I.

Folio 144a. To Bībī Jawahar. *

I am happy to receive your letter. I have noted that you are waiting for me anxiously. I am reaching soon. Keep writing to me. 2 Jumāda II.

Folio 144b. To Bībī Jawahar.

Received on the 9th of Jumāda II your letter of the 25th of Jumāda I. If you wish to come here you may do so by boat along with the junior Bībī and some other people. It is fine if we cross on the way, otherwise you arrive here. However, stay back if you feel you will be happy there. I have written about this to Mr Martin. In case you decide [to make the journey] start forthwith. Get the necessary people but if some are not willing to come, leave them there in the *ḥavelī*. Get the money to meet the expenses for two to there months from Ram Sundar Datt, to whom I have already written. If you undertake the journey, take the route via Murshidabad since I am also taking the same route. 10 Jumāda II, Tuesday.

Folio 145a. To Bībī Jawahar.

Received your letter. You must have received my earlier [letter] asking you to come here. You should do whatever Captain Martin advises. If he agrees to your journey then set out in this direction. Take the route via Murshidabad since I will also do so [take the same route] when I depart. In which case we will meet on the way. [However], in case we do not [cross our ways] then you [should] come to this place. Keep up your spirits until we meet. 22 Jumāda II, Sunday.

Folio 145a. To Bībī Jawahar.

I received two of your letters on the 3rd and 8th of Rajab. I noted that Qadir Bakhsh is not well. Get him treated. As I wrote to you earlier, follow Mr Martin's advice for your journey for this place. Keep in touch. 8 Rajab.

Folio 145a. To Bībī Jawahar.

Received two of your letters on the 26th of Rajab. I had written long

*Name of the addressee is missing but the text clearly shows who it refers to.

time back about your coming here and had presumed that you must have left that place and would be nearing Calcutta. But I note from your letter that you have not yet left that place—this is strange. Meet Captain Martin even now and do whatever he suggests. 29 Rajab.

Folio 145b. To Bībī Jawahar.

I received your letter of 21 Rajab on the 9th of Sha'bān and learnt that the delay in your departure for this place was due to the non-receipt of money. I have therefore written to Ram Sundar Datt to give you the money for two months in advance. Obtain the money from him and leave with Captain Martin for this place. God willing we will meet on the way. 9 Sha'bān, Thursday, Calcutta.

Folio 146a. To Antony Bābājān.

I am delighted to receive your letter of the 12th of Sha'bān. I am unhappy to know that you keep inside [the house] all the time and do not come out even to stroll in the garden. I repeat what I had written to you earlier about going for horse riding or chariot rides after every two or three days. [You should] stroll in the *ḥavelī* courtyard and the garden, and meet Mr Lloyd and the other Europeans (*ṣāḥibs*). It is unhealthy to remain indoors. I will be extremely angry if I hear about this [your keeping indoors] again. 14 Shawwāl, Saturday.

Folio 146a. To Bībī Jawahar.

I was delighted to receive, on the 15th of Shawwāl, four of your letters on my arrival in Munger. I note that you have reached Azimabad and are waiting for me along with Captain Martin. [This is] fine. I will be reaching there in a week's time. 16 Shawwāl.

*Folio 146b. To Bībī Jawahar.**

You should leave back for Faizabad immediately. In case you want to travel by road take the chariot which is already there with you. But if you wish to travel by the river route [then] take the boat of Bakhshi (?) *ṣāḥib* together with my goods. 6 Ẕīqa'da.

Folio 146b. To Bībī Jawahar.

I waited for you until now but it is difficult to meet [you] since it is already too late. You set out for this place and stay here in my *ḥavelī*. I

*In this as well as in the following letters the names of the addressees are missing but the texts clearly show who the addressees are.

intend starting from here whenever it is appropriate. I will write to you when I reach there and then you act accordingly. [In the meanwhile] I have written to Ram Sundar Datt [to give you money] for your expenses. 6 Ẕīḥijja, Sunday, Faizabad.

Folio 146b. To Bībī Jawahar.

I am relieved to receive your letter. I have requisitioned for my [household] goods from Faizabad. You come along with them and the escorts. Your arrival will make me happy. 9 Muḥarram, 1190.

Folio 147a. To La'l Khan.

I have been asked to send to Mr Paktat (?) *ṣāḥib*, in Jangipur, a girl belonging to Imam Bakhsh. Assure her that she is being sent to his [Paktat's] brother. I have written to Manik Ram to arrange money for her clothes and travel expenses. Also arrange for two intelligent women to take care of her and send her, escorted by the *harkāra* who is being sent from here, to Jangipur by boat. Give her also whatever money for her expenses Manik Ram writes [about]. 24 Muḥarram, Sarai Peterganj.

Folio 147b. To La'l Khan.

Received your letter. It is good that you declined to send the girl for Perceret ṣāḥib because you had not received any instructions from me. I now write [to you] that one girl belonging to Imam Bakhsh, who is there, should be sent to Paktat (?) *ṣāḥib* in Jangipur. Assure her that Paktat (?) *ṣāḥib* will send her to his brother. She should not worry. I have written to Manik Ram for money from my *sarkār* for her expenses and her clothes—one *peshwāz* with *kotha,* six to seven *kurtas* [shirts], a few *odhnī dupattas,* two pairs of *gulbadan* trousers, and one shawl from the category of *doshāla tūsī.* Get also two sensible and reliable women to escort her safely in a boat. Dispatch along with them the expenses which Manik Ram will write to you about and the *harkāra* who is being sent from here. 11 Ṣafar, Monday.

Folio 147b. To La'l Khan.

Received your letter. You did not acknowledge the receipt of my earlier letter written in response to yours. Write in detail after every ten to fifteen days about the developments there. Ensure that the song and dance teachers are not indifferent to their duty, and write if there is any improvement in their training.

Bābājān's clothes are being prepared here and will be sent along with the *harkāra* when he leaves here. Take the money for the expenses incurred there from Mr Lloyd—I have written to him. Keep me informed about the welfare of the Bābā and about other things. 24 Ṣafar, Sunday.

Folio 147b. To the Bībī [junior].

I received your letter and learnt about the difficulties you had to go through because of the non-receipt of last month's emoluments. Earlier, I had written about this to Mr Lloyd and hope that before you receive the letter you would have obtained [money for] the expenses. In future you shall receive the expenses regularly every month. You will also get the clothes from him. Be vigilant regarding the training (*ta'līm*). I will send for you soon. 29 Ṣafar.

Folio 148a. To Bābājān.

I received your letter of 14 Rabī' I and noted that you have not received any news from me, and that you have also not received any clothes for [the people] inside.

I could not write to you all these days but I am well in all respects and am keen to meet you. I will send for you after the rainy season is over. I have written to Mr Lloyd about the clothes and he will send you whatever is necessary. 22 Rabī' I.

Folio 148a. To the junior Bībī.

I received your letter of 11 Rabī' I and noted that you require money for the birthday ceremony of the son and also to have another *daya* [foster-mother]. The earlier one was hired for Rs 10 per month and that the present one is not willing to accept Rs 8 per month.

I have written to Lal Khan and he will give you the money for the birthday expenses in due course. It is good that you have hired another *dāya*, give her Rs 10 per month, the amount that you paid the earlier one. Do not loose heart—I will ask for you all very soon. Keep in touch. 22 Rabī' I.

Folio 148b. To La'l Khan.

I received your letter and came to know that Mr Lloyd will arrange for clothes for the girl after he receives my letter. Dispatch the girl here as soon as these [clothes] are ready, and do not neglect the song and dance training. The emoluments for the singers (*qawwāls*) will reach along with those for the other people. There is no harm in hiring a physician (*ḥakīm*) if it is necessary. Write to me what his monthly payment will amount to. Be vigilant of the routine [affairs] of the house (*deorhī*) and inform me [of the developments] after every ten to twelve days.

The junior Bībī had written to me about the expenses for the birthday ceremony of the son. I have written to Mr Lloyd about it. On her request [you may] collect Rs twenty to twenty-five from him [Mr Lloyd] and hand it over to her. Insist upon the singers to work hard in the training so that I enjoy the fruits of their labour when they reach here. Manik Ram will send their earlier emoluments from Lucknow and in future they will obtain them from Mr Lloyd. 22 Rabī' I.

Folio 149a. To La'l Khan.

I received your letter of the 26th on the 12th of Jumāda I. Keep writing about the developments there in the same way. You have not written anything about the progress in the [training of] song and dance. Urge the trainers and the tutors to keep working hard. Since I have not seen the person whom you have hired I am not in a position to suggest his monthly salary from here. I have written to Mr Lloyd to observe him and fix his monthly payment at whatever he thinks is suitable. Be vigilant in taking care [for the maintenance] of the *deorhī*. 13 Jumāda I, Monday.

[A new preface figures (ff. 151b–154a) here for the second part of the volume I containing the letters drafted by Kishan Sahai for the year 1188. Translation of this preface has been given in the Introduction (p. 65–7). It appears that the letters in the earlier pages for the year 1188 and 1189 were drafted by some other *munshī* whose name unfortunately does not figure anywhere in the text. That these letters were not drafted by Kishan Sahai is supported both by their style as well as by the compliments used for the addresees.]

Folio 154a. To Saiyid Niyaz Ali Khan.

Earlier I had sent you a letter, along with a copy of *tankhwāh* [paper] for Rs 10,000, pertaining to the elephants of Mir Sulaiman Khan. This letter was returned from Azimabad and subsequently I sent it to Padre *Ṣāḥib* [Wendel] to hand it over to you. I know from a letter from the Padre that the person who was to take it to you had left for Shahjahanabad [Delhi] with Ilich Khan, leaving the letter behind in Akbarabad. I am sending a copy of that letter through the *harkāra*. I hope he will inform you of all the happenings here. You can then do whatever you like. 1 Muḥarram, 1188.

Folio 154b. To Saiyid Lutf Ali Khan.

I had written to you earlier about some milch berberi goats. Since this letter was in the same packet which contained the letter of Saiyid Niyaz Ali Khan and was left behind, I write to you again. Acquire genuine and beautiful berberi goats along with three to four pairs of high quality sable (*sumūr*). You will know of the other developments from the letter of Niyaz Ali Khan. 1 Muḥarram.

Folio 154b. To Saiyid Lutf Ali Khan.

I received your letter on the 3rd of Muḥarram in which you have complained about not receiving my reply to your earlier letter. As a matter of fact till date I have not received your letter. If there were one I would not have been late in my reply.

I am happy that you have acquired a pair of sable (*sumūr*). As for the *kurti*, it is fine even if they are expensive. Acquire them at whatever price they are available if they are of good quality and presentable. Do not buy any more sables (*sumūrs*) if good ones are not available there; these are sufficient. I had written to you earlier about the genuine milch berberi goats. Obtain four to five of them if they are available. As for the money of Mir Sulaiman Khan, I had earlier written to Saiyid Niyaz Ali Khan whatever I heard from Mr Law. I reiterated the same in the following letter. You will know the details from these letters. I am concerned about your welfare. Keep in touch. 3 Muḥarram, Thursday.

Folio 155a. To Shaikh Hasan Riza.

I received your letter in which you say that you will repay your debt by paying Rs 500 in cash and the rest in monthly instalments of Rs 100. This is fine by me. I did reply to your earlier letter which may be reaching you soon. 5 Muḥarram, Saturday.

Folio 155b. To Maharaja Nawal Singh.

I have replied to your letter earlier. I have also presented your case, as desired by you, to Najaf Khan. But there has been some delay in your work since he has left for Shahjahanabad. In view of our relations, I will ensure that your work is done appropriately as soon as he comes back. For your satisfaction I am enclosing a letter from Najaf Khan. I thought that for the moment it will not be proper to present your case to Shuja-ud-Daula. I will put it up to him later and send his response to you. 7 Muḥarram.

Folio 156a. To Mauji Ram.

From my letter written in response to that of Maharaja Nawal Singh you must have learnt of the developments here. At the moment I did not consider it appropriate to put up the case before Shuja-ud-Daula and there is [therefore] some delay. I will put it up soon and dispatch the details subsequently. You must have received Najaf Khan's letter which I have dispatched to you. He is in Shahjahanabad and the work will be done properly on his return. Keep in touch and inform me of the developments there. 7 Muḥarram, Sunday.

Folio 156b. To Najaf Quli Khan.

Najaf Khan has been nice enough to grant a village as *āltamghā* to Padre Wendel. I had obtained the *sanad* for it during my stay in Akbarabad but the deputy of Mir Mansur, the '*āmil,* is delaying its implementation. I am therefore writing to you to enable Padre ṣāḥib to take possession of the village and collect the revenue of the Rabī' *faṣl.* Najaf Khan has also written to you about this matter. 7 Muḥarram, Sunday.

Folio 156b. To Bishnath (Vishwanath), vakīl of Najaf Khan.

A sum of Rs 1633 due on Najaf Khan for which he has sent the *parwāna* under his small seal to you (*muhr-i-khurd*) is to be given to Mr Thomas Carnegi. Please hand over the money to him and obtain the letter of Najaf Khan which I have sent to him. Get it also signed by the ṣāḥib [Mr Carnegi] and obtain the receipt of payment. A proper handling of this work will ensure our friendship. 7 Muḥarram (?), Sunday, 1188.

Folio 157a. To Najaf Khan.

Manik Ram, who had taken leave from you at Kol, has arrived here and has given details of your welfare. Since I am your sincere friend, I pray for your speedy promotions and high positions. Please keep me informed about your health and welfare as it pleases my heart. I have recently received essence of cinnamon from Calcutta. Since this is genuine and of high quality I am sending 11 *tola* of it to you as a gift through the *harkāra.* 7 Muḥarram 1188, Monday(?).

Folio 157b. To Mir Sulaiman Khan.

The money, pertaining to the feed of the elephants, that you owe Monsieur Gentil, has now been assigned to me. It has now been settled that I will pay it off to him. If it pleases you, the arrangement is fine by me. The situation is as follows: Rs 400 out of the Rs 1000 has already been given to him. Rs 600 are still due. I will obtain a *tamassuk* [bond] from him when this remaining amount is paid and send it [*tamassuk*] to you after obtaining a receipt for it. Rest assured and take care of your health. 10 Muḥarram, 1188.

Folio 158a. To Raja Chait Singh.

I learnt from Manik Ram that your *vakīl*, Muhkam Singh, approached him with the suggestion that out of Rs 2500 that you were to pay to me as compensation for the goods stolen in your territory, Rs 500 be discounted. As a matter of fact payment of only Rs 2000 has been made. Perhaps your *vakīl* has got a wrong impression from the letter of my Diwan, Manik Ram, and thinks that we are greedy for a mere Rs 1000 or Rs 500. For goods worth lakhs of rupees a sum of Rs 1000 or Rs 500, whether paid or unpaid, has no value. However, it is strange that such an idea came from you. It will cause me no harm even if I, in consideration of our mutual relations, forego the entire amount. There is nothing more to write about. 12 Muḥarram, Friday 1188, morning.

Folio 158b. To Maharaja Nawal Singh.

I have sent to you two letters together with one from Najaf Khan. I enclose a letter for you from Shuja-ud-Daula which I received when I put up your case to him. Najaf Khan will soon be back from Shahjahanabad [Delhi] and then your work will be carried out to your satisfaction. 12 Muḥarram, Friday.

Folio 159a. To Najaf Khan.

I am delighted to receive your letter. I am your sincere friend and am happy to say that our friendship is increasing day by day and its results will soon be evident. I hope that you will finish your work at the Imperial court and come back, and that we will soon meet. I have collected the details of the money of the *tankhwāh* in Azimabad and have also written a letter to Mr Law. As soon as I receive his reply I will proceed to enquire further about it from the *Ṣāhib-i Kalān* [Hastings]. Having obtained his reply, I will write to you about the case. 12 Muḥarram 1188, Friday, night.

Folio 159b. To Ganga Ram kumaidān.

I have come to know that you wish to keep your relatives and retinue (*muta'alliqān*) in the *katra* and the *ḥavelī* of Devman which has been bought by Lala Nihalchand. Since Lala Nihalchand is my friend, I suggest that you should not create any problem for his *katra* and *ḥavelī*. Choose some other place for your residence and send a statement (*razīnāma*) to me through your *gumāshta*. 13 Muḥarram, Saturday. Dispatched through Mir Ata Husain Khan.

Folio 159b. To Saiyid Niyaz Ali Khan.

Your letter of 9 Muḥarram reached here on the 14th of Muḥarram. I have noted that Mir Sulaiman wants a letter from Najaf Khan regarding the case of the money for the elephants. This money is actually my money and you should do whatever makes you feel comfortable in this matter. Najaf Khan is expected to be back soon from the imperial court. If you are free you can come here and talk to him personally so that the matter is settled soon. Direct conversation resolves matters in a way in which correspondence can never do. I reiterate that the work of Mir *ṣāhib* [Mir Sulaiman] is [like] my own work. 14 Muḥarram, Sunday, 1188.

Folio 160a. To Mir Lutf Ali Khan.

Received your letter on 14 Muḥarram. I am happy to know that you are looking for the goats and have bought three pairs of sables (*sumūrs*). As soon as you acquire the goats send them and the pair of sable (*sumūr*) through my men. Keep me informed of your welfare until we meet. 14 Muḥarram, Sunday.

Folio 160a. To Ganga Ram kumaidān.

Dhotal Singh *jamā'adār* who is in my service has gone for some work to Shahjahanabad. If he approaches you for help then do as he desires. 14 Muḥarram, Sunday.

Folio 160b. To Saiyid Niyaz Ali Khan.

I received two letters from Mir Sulaiman for you. I have sent them to you and you will know the details from them. If Najaf Khan is coming back soon you may also accompany him so that the matter of *tankhwāh* is resolved in your presence. If his departure is delayed, acquire from him a *parwāna* for the *tankhwāh* for the coming year under the big seal and a letter under the small seal and bring them here with you.

Both the *parwāna* and the letter should be in the name of his *vakīl.* 21 Muḥarram, Sunday night.

Folio 160b. To Najaf Khan.

I am keen to meet you. May the blessing of the Emperor be with you and [may] you attain promotions and we meet soon. On the 26th, Friday, the army [of the Nawab] camped at Mahdighat and it is believed that it will soon cross the river. Please keep me informed of your health and welfare until we meet. 25 Muḥarram, Thursday.

Folio 161b. To Najaf Khan.

Earlier, during our stay in Akbarabad, I had submitted to you that Captain Martin, an English ṣāḥib from Calcutta, would come to measure and prepare the map of the fort which he would present to the *Ṣāḥib-i Kalan* [Warren Hastings]. In consideration of the trust that you have in the friendship of the English *ṣāḥibs,* you said that you are an ally (*mutawassil*) of the English and that you owe everything to them. Subsequently, I wrote to Captain Martin to reach Akbarabad and prepare the map and thereafter to go around in the district. Accordingly, he arrived there. However, I came to know that Najaf Quli Khan met him three days after his arrival and when Martin reached near the fort his [Najaf Quli's] men stopped him. They ordered him to go away and threatened to shoot him. This is strange. This uncivil behaviour was unexpected since you enjoy a relation of faith and confidence with the English.

I am your sincere friend and wish that your relations with the English grow further. You had said that the horsemen in the retinue of Captain Martin would be arranged from Kol. But this has also not been done. I am surprised that your orders have been disregarded, nay even contravened. I do not want such things to happen again. Please do consider this and write to Najaf Quli Khan to do whatever is good for the Government. 27 Muḥarram, Saturday.

Folio 162a. To Najaf Quli Khan.

Earlier during our stay in Akbarabad I had requested Najaf Khan that Captain Martin Bahadur, *sardār-i angrez,* would arrive in Akbarabad to measure land and prepare a map for the fort so as to present it to the *Ṣāḥib-i Kalan.* He [Najaf Khan] had said that he owes everything to the English people, that they could do whatever they liked, and that no prior permission was required. Such being the case I did not proceed with the matter any further.

However, now I hear that when Martin reached there you did not meet him for three days. When he wanted to enter the fort to draw the map your people resisted (*muzahim*) and threatened to shoot him if he proceeded ahead. In view of your close relations with the English it was expected that when you heard of the arrival of Mr Martin you would have gone ahead to welcome him. You should have seen to it that the works which he wanted to carry out were done without his uttering a single word about this.

I am surprised that now everything is to the contrary. This is not in keeping with the sincere relations which Najaf Khan has with the *sardār-i angrez.* I could not have imagined that something like this could have happened in your name. Further, no arrangement has been made for the horsemen and the two companies of the *sipāhīs,* to accompany Martin *ṣāḥib,* about which Najaf Khan had directed you. 27 Muḥarram, Saturday.

Folio 163a. To Najaf Khan.

I had written to you earlier about the arrival of Captain Martin in Akbarabad [Agra], the behaviour of Najaf Quli Khan, and the intervention of the people of Dauḍ Beg Khan, *qil'adār.*

Today again I received a letter from Martin in which he mentioned that on the very first day he arrived to draw the map, the people in the bastion began interrogating him and threatened to kill him if he did not leave. Martin therefore came back to the residence (*dera*). Later in the evening Martin sent a note to Najaf Quli Khan detailing the incident. He [Martin] said that if the events had his approval it was fine otherwise it should be enquired into. In response he [Najaf Quli Khan] sent a message to Martin *ṣāḥib* that the people in the fort had behaved improperly and that he should go to the fort the following day and prepare the map. He assured him that in future such acts would not be repeated.

Subsequently, Martin *ṣāḥib* rode to the fort but was again mistreated. The third time when he approached Najaf Quli Khan he asked his *chūbdār* and his own people to accompany the ṣāḥib. But then Daud Beg Khan began interrogating Martin and said that without an imperial order and instructions from Najaf Khan he would not allow anyone to draw a map of the fort. If you remember, before we parted in Akbarabad I had sought your permission for the purpose. If I had known that you were not in agreement with it I would have never come up with this proposition. It is indeed a matter of concern that an Englishman was insulted by these unworthy and non-descript people and the reputation of the English sullied.

Considering your undisputed relation with the highly dignified English people I, a sincere friend of yours, am not simply angry but will also advise you that in case [these] developments took place without your approval, you [should] dismiss Daud Beg Khan and the *faujdār* of Kol for their misbehaviour and their refusal to make arrangements for the arrival of Mr Martin. If they are not dismissed I will be constrained to write to the Governor in Calcutta. Further, when Mr Martin asked Najaf Quli Khan to allow him to proceed ahead and as instructed by Najaf Khan, supply him with people for his army, he adopted an evasive attitude. He agreed to make the arrangements but in reality not a single person was arranged to accompany him [Martin]. 29 Muḥarram, 1188.

Folio 164b. To Najaf Quli Khan.

Earlier I had reported to you about the treatment meted out to Mr Martin by the people at the fort. Today I came to know from a letter of Mr Martin that following a request from him you had arranged the *chūbdār* and some people to accompany him. But Daud Beg Khan again refused to allow him to prepare the map. He said that he would not permit anything like this without an imperial order or instruction from Najaf Khan. All this was according to the agreement which I had arrived at with Najaf Khan. I had asked him for a *parwāna* but he had said that since he owes everything to the English no *parwāna* was required. Further, if you had mentioned earlier that you have no control over the fort affairs I would not have written to you about it. I wrote to you because I thought that you had full control (*mu<u>kh</u>tiyār*) over the fort. 29 Muḥarram, 1188.

Folio 165a. To Gokulchand Sah.

I received your letter and noted what you had written about Jugal Kishor. He is always with me and does my work well. I am very happy with him and would agree to whichever way he executes the task assigned to him. For the moment the earlier *tamassuk* is cleared and the new *tamassuk* is being prepared. Rest assured that you will get it. Never consider Jugal Kishor in any way different from me. 1 Ṣafar, Wednesday.

Folio 165a. To I'jaz Raqam Khan.

I received your letter and got to know about the developments there.

There is nothing new to report from the Nawab's camp. We are hoping to achieve victory soon. You must keep sending the news of that area. It will make me happy. 8 Ṣafar.

Folio 165b. To Jugal Kishor.

I received your letter and learnt of your safe arrival in Lucknow, handing over of the goods to Mir Muhammad Azim and the dispatch of the carts (*chhakṛa*) to me. On 11 Ṣafar, Saturday, we scored victory over the mischievous Hafiz [Rahmat Khan]. He has been defeated by the brave soldiers and his head, severed from his body, rolled like a ball on the ground. We now feel relaxed. Free yourself from the celebrations and reach here soon. 12 Ṣafar, Sunday.

Folio 165b. To Najaf Khan.

In the morning of 11 Ṣafar, Saturday, Nawab Shuja-ud-Daula and General *Ṣāḥib Bahadur* [officer of the Company] set out to fight the accursed army of the enemies. Considering that the English people are brave and manly, General *ṣāḥib* entered the foray fighting against the foes both sides. The cannons began to throw fiery balls, as a result of which pools of blood gushed out from the wounds of the bodies of the brave people. The horsemen fell down in the field. The ill-starred opponents could not face the onslaught of the English. The rain of fires scattered their bodies like grains of dust. Thousands, nay countless fell dead on the ground; and many from the victorious army achieved martyrdom. Ultimately, a cannon ball pushed the insecure (*nāmaḥfūẓ*.) Hafiz [Rahmat Khan] to hell—his head severed from his body and bounced like a ball in the field. Subsequently, the remaining [Afghan] soldiers could not bear the pressure and ran away. With the grace of God and the high fortune of the Emperor the breeze of victory blew and the triumphant standards of the celebration trumpeted. The world was cleared from the dust of mischief and tumult. I hope that the Badshah has countless such victories. I have not heard about your welfare of late. I hope that you will keep me informed. 13 Ṣafar, Monday.

Folio 166b. To Najaf Khan.

I received your letter and am happy to note that you have reprimanded Najaf Quli Khan and Daud Beg Khan for their misbehaviour towards Martin and asked them to apologize to him, and that Martin *ṣāḥib* will soon send his letter (*rāẓīnāma*) to this effect to me. I believed that before Martin's departure from Akbarabad things would move the way you wanted. But till now he [Martin] has not written anything to me, nor has there been any apology from Najaf Quli Khan and Daud Beg Khan. However, in this matter Najaf Quli Khan is not at fault. In a situation in which one does not have the power to control [the subordinates] one is helpless. But the mischief and the contemptible manners of Daud Beg Khan are unimaginable.

You have written that at the time of our departure from Akbarabad there was no mention in our conversation about the drawing of the map. Perhaps you have forgotten about it. Please recollect that when I met you at the Muṣamman tower in the fort I mentioned about Martin's map making. You had given permission for it and admitted that the fort in your possession was because of the English people's [help] and thus there was no need to seek permission for it. Captain Martin was sent there for this very purpose. Otherwise I know that in no country can a person be sent to prepare the map of the fort without the permission of its master. I am also not the type of person who would send an Englishman to prepare the map of the fort without your permission.

Anyhow, we have to be careful in future. Further, I sent you the details of the development in this region out of my respect and love for you. But you do not write to me anything about the developments there nor about your plans. This is far from what our friendship demands. Since I am always concerned about the news of your welfare and the developments there, please keep me informed. 14 Ṣafar, Tuesday, 1188.

Folio 168a. To Najaf Khan.

Today, on 15 Ṣafar, I received a letter from Captain Martin. I knew that you had written about his case to Najaf Quli Khan. I had earlier written and again reiterate that there is no serious fault on the part of Najaf Quli Khan since he had no control over the situation there. He was helpless. But Daud Beg Khan did not leave any meanness undone. I have sincere relations with you and fear that such improper behaviour may impair them. I am surprised that you have allowed such an unworthy person to get close to you and to interfere in important matters. If you overlook his mischief, I will consider it an unfriendly [act]. I hope that I will be kept informed regularly of your welfare. 15 Ṣafar, Wednesday.

Folio 168b. To Najaf Quli Khan.

Received your letter. It is a matter of relief and happiness for me to know that you welcomed Captain Martin, treated him well, and had Daud Beg Kurji, who had interfered in his measurement work, reproved. Mr Martin has also written to me about your good behaviour towards him and also about the letter which Najaf Khan has written to you regarding this matter.

I am indeed very happy with you. You did not commit any fault or error. Your word went unheeded and Daud Beg, because of his mean and mischievous character, transgressed the limits in misbehaving with an English *sardār*. He committed a grave offence and for this he will soon be punished. I have written to Najaf Khan about your good behaviour with the Captain and about the mischief and baseness of Daud Beg. I believe that in view of our friendship, Najaf Khan will give him exemplary punishment. Keep writing about your welfare and the developments there. 17 Ṣafar, Friday.

Folio 169a. To Mayachand Sāhū, Akbarabad [Agra].

I have come to know that Captain Martin, in view of my sincere relations with you, approached you with a request of Rs 1000. But you declined to give him the money. This is surprising since Manik Ram has written to you several times about this matter and stated that you should arrange whatever Martin requires from there. I write to you again that there should not be any delay in the arrangement of the things for Martin *ṣāḥib.* I have not yet received any of the goods which I had ordered for, nor is there any news about them except the jewellery from Ram Singh *mināsāz* which reached here. Ensure that the agate (*sang-i-yashm*) betel box (*pāndān*) and its studded tray, and the gem-studded hookah is prepared soon. Show Martin *ṣāḥib* all the other things and when he sets in this direction hand over to him all my goods together with four pairs of *shaṭranjīs* which I had asked for earlier. 18 Ṣafar, Saturday.

Folio 169b. To Najaf Quli Khan.

Captain Martin has been staying in Akbarabad [Agra] for many days; you had promised to arrange people for his retinue but till now nothing has been done. Since you knew that the soldiers do not pay any heed to your orders why did you not tell him clearly on the very first day that the people would not be arranged. You preferred to postpone the matter. I am astonished and annoyed. If you had told him earlier he would have written to me, in which case I would have arranged the people from here. 18 Ṣafar.

Folio 170a. To Jugal Kishor.

Mir Muhammad Azim has written for some money to meet the expenses of my orders. If he approaches you, give him upto Rs 1000 without waiting for any instructions from me so that the goods are prepared early. If you are now free from the marriage celebrations come over here soon. I am also sending a copy of this letter through the *dāk.* 18 Ṣafar, Saturday.

Folio 170b. To Najaf Khan.

I received your letter in which you have mentioned about the crossing of the river by the Emperor, his return to the city because of indisposition, your taking leave from the Emperor to join the victorious army, and the arrival of the happy news of the victory. I am happy to receive your letters and know all this. Even if you could not participate in the actual battle you were, as desired by the Nawab, attending to important matters. You were also all the time concerned about the victory achieved.

Since you were busy these last two months in important matters you could not attend to my work. This has been my loss. Everything has been suspended. But with the grace of God I believe that the loss will soon be amended. I am keen to meet you and hope that till we meet you will keep in touch. 21 Ṣafar, Tuesday.

Folio 171a. To Najaf Khan.

I have received the happy news that the day after tomorrow you will proceed towards Bareilly, and that I will have the pleasure of meeting you on the 26th. I hope that until we meet I will have the privilege of receiving affectionate letters from you. 24 Ṣafar, Aonla.

Folio 172a. To Majd-ud-Daula Farzand Khan Bahadur Bahram Jang.

I am delighted to receive your letter. It will be my pleasure to be your friend even if we have not met earlier. I do not have to say anything in matters relating to the Emperor. But since Bhawani Singh and Ganga Ram *kumaidān* have written to me at your behest, I therefore write to you as follows: The rule in the East India Company (*Ẕābita-i Sākār-i Angrez*) is that the soldiers are expected to hand over their guns when they leave the old company (*paltan*) to join a new company. The *ṣūbedār* of the new company provides them with [new] guns. This rule is there to ensure that the movement of the soldiers does not effect the arsenal of the Company. I hope that you consider me your sincere friend and keep me informed. 29 Ṣafar, Wednesday.

Folio 172b. To Bhawani Singh and Ganga Ram kumaidān.
Your people gave me your letters which stated that you needed a *parwāna* and a *shuqqa* [letter] under the seal of Shuja-ud-Daula in the name of Haider Beg Khan, and a letter from me addressed to Majd-ud-Daula. I obtained the *shuqqa* from the Nawab and handed it over to Bakhshi Ram for you. Along with this is also a letter which I had written to Majd-ud-Daula. They will reach you. The *parwāna* of *nānkār* is also being prepared. After it is ready it will be sent through your people. 30 Ṣafar, Thursday.

Folio 172b. To Bhawani Singh and Ganga Ram kumaidān.
I received your letter seeking my help in the case of the former *qil'adār* of Akbarabad, Bhao Singh. I do not have time to do everyone's work and make recommendations to Najaf Khan for everyone. But since I consider you as one of my own (*az khwud*) your work will be done in whatever way possible. 30 Ṣafar, Thursday.

Folio 173a. To Jugal Kishor.
I had received your letter earlier. In the case of the leave of Shaikh Amin-ud-Din, as per your wish, I released him. But he himself told me that he would not like to leave because of the disturbances there. In such circumstances there is no use of your being confined to Lucknow because of the troubles. Come here without delay as soon as you receive this letter. I have many works for you here. 30 Ṣafar.

Folio 173b. To Khiradmand Khan Don Pedro.
I received your letter and noted your pleasure at the victory over the accursed Rohillas. I am happy to know that you are keen to meet me. I am also keen to meet you. 1 Rabī' I, Friday.

Folio 173b. To Majd-ud-Daula Farzand Khan.
I am happy to receive your letter. I was also pleased to hear about you from my old friend Niyaz Ali Khan. My primary task as also that of the English people, is to serve the Emperor and to satisfy the high

grandees. I hope that whenever you require your work will be done in keeping with the demands of the sincere friendship that we share with you. The rest will be clear from the writings of Niyaz Ali Khan. I hope that you will keep me informed of your welfare and the court news. 3 Rabī' I, Sunday.

Folio 174b. To Mir Lutf Ali.

I received your letter in which you write that you have been appointed by the Nawab in Bareilly and that you did not have [the time to come to this place]. I appreciate that you are acting according to the orders of the *sarkār*. Everything is destined to take place in its own time. I hope that when the time comes we will also meet. 5 Rabī' I, Tuesday.

Folio 174b. To Jugal Kishor.

I received your letter and noted that you have given Rs 1000 to Mir Muhammad Azim, and [you are undergoing] treatment for the relapse of the pain in your leg. It is good that you have given the money to the Mir since most of the work is being done through him. Get well soon. Get yourself properly treated and come over here soon. 5 Rabī' I, Tuesday.

Folio 175a. To Bhola Singh ṣūbadār in the retinue of Marsack ṣāḥib.

I have received your letter regarding the difficulties that you are encountering because of the shortage of money. I had written to Marsack *ṣāḥib* about a fortnight back to release all the troopers and horsemen that he has, since Shuja-ud-Daula wants them here. Therefore, as soon as you receive this letter, you also leave for this place along with the horsemen and the troopers. 12 Rabī' I, Tuesday.

Folio 175a. To Najaf Khan.

I am happy to know of your welfare from Manik Ram. There appears to be some discrepancy in the agreement that I had with you in person at the time of your departure. The negotiation had been about a *tankhwāh* of Rs two lac for which I wrote to the Governor *ṣāḥib*. Subsequently, in my presence Rs one lac was cleared. The Dīwān took me along on the understanding that [the remaining] Rs one lac would be given from another place. I did not agree to this since I had already written to the Governor *ṣāḥib* about Rs two lacs and did not want to write to him again. This by itself is a matter of concern.

But what is more disturbing is that contrary to all this understanding, you have finally written about the *tankhwāh* of Rs 80,000. It is evident that in this matter the main fault is that of the Diwan who accepted this amount. Otherwise it is difficult for me to believe that such a discrepancy would take place in the agreements of high nobles, in particular with sincere people like me who are still happy to be in your service. Anyhow, in view of our agreement for the *tankhwāh* of Rs one lac, the Rs 80,000 *tankhwāh* that you have sent is being returned.

I am shocked and venture to ask why you trusted Major Hang(?) who had never been your friend. For his sake you have completely neglected our old friendship. I need a clear answer from you. If I know what is in your heart it will not pain me even if it is against my interest. But if I do not know and if [your] actions are to the contrary, it will pain me.

The horse that you sent for me through Manik Ram cannot be used for riding. Despite a thorough search good horses are not available here. I therefore want you to send me one which is genuine, strong, of good height and beautiful. This horse is of no use. I have it with me as your *amānat* that will be returned to you. 12 Rabī' I, Tuesday.

Folio 176b. To Jugal Kishor.

Received your letter (*'arẓī*). Since you had sought to stay there for some time because of the illness of the people in the house, you should set out for this place as soon as they recover. I am happy to receive your letters regularly. But I have not received any letter from Mir Muhammad Azim since long. I do not know what keeps him so busy that he does not get time even to write a letter for me. If you meet Mir Azim urge him to write to me the details of the developments there. Ask him also to explain to me why he did not write, so that I know the exact state of affairs. 15 Rabi' I, Friday.

Folio 177a. To Mir Lutf Ali.

I am happy to receive your letter with the details of your dispatch: A jar of mango *murabba* and one basket of berry (*phalsa*). The *murabba* is very tasty and the *sharbat* [drink] of *phalsa* is soothing. May you remain prosperous. Keep me informed of the developments there. The specimen sugar candy that you have sent me is also available here in plenty. I have sent a camel with the *harkāra* along with Rs 20 to you. With this money, obtain saltpetre, to cool water, load them on this camel and send them here. I need it for the *ābdārkhāna* [water storing room]. 15 Rabi' I, Friday.

Folio 177b. To Ganga Bishan, gumāshta of Dr Clue ṣāhib.
I received your letter (*'arẓī*) in which you mention that you require money to buy the goods. What are the goods that you intend to buy and where do you need to go to obtain them? Write in detail how much [goods] you require.

I have also received the specimen of the clothes that you have sent. Keep whatever clothes are available in the *kothī*, and send them here later. I have written to Gora Mistri for your accommodation. He is incharge of matters relating to the *ḥavelī* and will arrange a place for you. I will also be there in a couple of months. When I reach there I will find out the details of your requirement. 16 Rabī' I, Saturday.

Folio 177b. To Maharaja Rana Chhatrapat Diler Jang.
I am happy to hear from Captain Martin about your fine qualities and your friendship for me. Nothing in this world is superior than the ties of friendship (*amr-i sharīftar az rawābit-i dostīhā nadīda and*). So do consider me equally eager [for your friendship]. I will be happy to receive your letters regularly. 16 Rabī' I, Saturday.

Folio 178a. To Bhawani Singh kumaidān.
A *shuqqa* of the Nawab in the name of Haider Beg Khan and a letter under my seal addressed to Majd-ud-Daula has been sent to you earlier through Bakshi Ram. Subsequently, an old *parwāna* which had earlier been issued in the name of Zorawar Singh, and in place of which you had wanted a new one, was sent. However, considering that the preparation of a new *parwāna* would take a long time, I had updated and corrected the earlier one in the name of Raja Perisal and sent it. I am sure that you must have received it. Earlier, I had written to you that the shirts (*kurtīs*) will be arranged. There has been some delay in this because of the non-availability of cloth. Now I am sending to you four and half English yards of red cloth, with seals of identification on both ends, for the *kurtīs*. Keep me informed regularly about the developments at the court and about your own welfare. 17 Rabī' I, Sunday.

Folio 178b. To Ganga Ram kumaidān.
I had told you earlier that you will be given *kurtīs*. But because of the

non-availability of cloth there has been some delay. Now I am sending you four and half yards of English cloth with seals on both ends for your *kurtīṣ*. Keep me informed of the developments at the court. 17 Rabī' I, Sunday.

Folio 179a. To Mir Lutf Ali.

Your letter together with your people and my own *harkāra,* and the saltpetre arrived here. I am pleased that despite the fact that you had written earlier about the non-availability of saltpetre in your city you did work hard to look around for it. The jar of pickles made in vinegar which you sent is delicious. Keep in touch and keep me informed about the conditions there. 21 Rabī' I, Thursday.

Folio 179b, To Shuja-ud-Daula.

I had written to you earlier about the case of Imam Bakhsh, a close attendant (*khawās*) of yours (*ḥuẓūr*), whose offence had been forgiven but who has yet to join the *chaukī.* An order had also been issued in this matter. But Hasan Riza Khan wanted a fresh order. I thought that at the time of seeking leave from you today I would procure the *parwāna.* But since I was in a hurry I could not do it. I have given him assurances several times. He [Imam Baksh] hopes that today the *parwāna* is issued to Hasan Riza Khan to the effect that Imam Bakhsh should join the *chaukī* routinely. 27 Rabī' I, Wednesday, *chhāonī* [camp] Basauli.

Folio 179b. To Najaf Khan.

You had earlier said that on your arrival in Akbarabad you would assign the responsibility of negotiation at the Nawab's court to Mir Muhammad Muin Khan. I believe that it is in recognition of his ability that you have chosen him for this task. Now that you are in Akbarabad keep your word. It will make me happy and ensure that the work is done properly. 27 Rabī' I, Wednesday, Basauli.

Folio 180a. To Najaf Khan.

I had asked Achal Singh, a *mahājan* in Akbarabad, to arrange the preparation of the *rath* [chariot], the embroidery works, and most of the other things. He handles the preparation of these things from his own house at the moment and will continue to do so in the future. Instruct your officials there not to create problems for him in the preparation of the goods as well as in matters related to the road tolls. This will enable the goods to reach me without any delay.

A certificate or *sanad* that I have ordered for Achal Singh for the preparation of these goods should be granted to him. Instruct Najaf Quli Khan to help him in his work. 27 Rabī' I, Basauli camp.

Folio 180b. To Najaf Quli Khan.

I have asked Achal Singh, the *mahājan* in Akbarabad, to arrange the preparation of the chariots, embroidery work and other things. He is preparing these things in his own house and will do the same in future also. It is therefore necessary that you instruct your officials not to interfere or create difficulties in the preparation of these things or in the collection of road tolls, so that the goods reach here without any disruption. Always help Achal Singh adequately. 27 Rabī' I, Wednesday, Basauli camp.

Folio 181a. To Najaf Quli Khan.

My goods, prepared through Mayachand Sāhū in Akbarabad, were dispatched to me earlier. Apparently, your people stopped them. I fail to understand that this happened despite the fact that you are there and notwithstanding an earlier *parwāna* from Najaf Khan regarding the non-interference in the flow of my goods from Mayachand Sāhū. It is necessary that you instruct your people to refrain from creating problems in the flow of goods sent or required by me. You should depute troopers to escort these goods safely to me. In view of my friendship with Najaf Khan, it is surprising that there are problems in [the transit of] my goods.

I hope that in the future you will prepare and send the *rāhdārī* immediately for whatever goods are sent there from my side and whatever the Sāhū tells you about. Your people are again creating a problem in the sale of the silk and the other goods which are there in Akbarabad in the *kothī* of Mayachand. Issue strict instructions [to your people] to refrain from interfering and give *parwānas* to the *beopārīs* as well. 27 Rabī' I, Wednesday, Basauli camp.

Folio 181a. To Nawab Shuja-ud-Daula.

You had given orders for the *tankhwāh* of the troopers of the Company. But Rai Tibrchand says that he has no money, and that it [*tankhwāh*] will be paid from whichever place you instruct. Since I have to depart I hope that you will issue orders for the early payment of the [*tankhwāh*] of the soldiers. I also hope that I will be provided with two elephants at the earliest—one for my own use (*sawārī*) and the other for the *sawārī* of Martin *ṣaḥib.* In the event of one being tired on the way the other will be used. 27 Rabī' I, Wednesday, Basauli camp.

Folio 182a. To Najaf Khan.

Received two of your letters: one pertaining to the *tankhwāh* of Rs 80,000 and the second regarding the *tankhwāh* of Rs 10,100 relating to Mir Sulaiman Khan. You say that since you have intimated the Governor, Hastings *ṣāḥib,* of the *tankhwāh* amount it will not be possible to enhance the amount so as to bridge the discrepancy between the present amount and that stated earlier in the letter. Otherwise there would have been no problem in increasing the amount by Rs 10,000 to 20,000.

My dear (*mushfiq-i man*), according to the agreement which we had arrived at, and in keeping with our sincere friendship and your pleasure, which I always seek, I am sending the same money, i.e. Rs 80,000 to Calcutta.

You write that you looked around for a good horse but could not find one. Look for one again when you reach Shahjahanabad [Delhi]. I would not have bothered you had such a horse been available here. Now that you have reached Shahjahanabad and the horse dealers visit your court I give you the trouble of procuring and sending me a genuine, beautiful big sized horse for riding. Let me know its price and I will send you [the money].

It had been stipulated that the clothes which you had bought from me would be sent to Akbarabad and handed over to Aga Sadiq *khānsāmān.* Following your order I had sent these goods through Mir Muhammad Azim to Akbarabad. I now learn from the Mir's letter that when these goods arrived in Firozabad the *kotwāl* confiscated them on the plea of non-payment of road toll. It is strange that your own people are creating problems for your goods. I wrote about this to Najaf Quli Khan as well. If the goods by any chance get soiled because of the rains I will not be responsible for it.

I left the camp and am in Faizabad in connection with some necessary work and look forward to receiving your letter here till we meet. 12 Rabī' II, Thursday.

Folio 183a. To Najaf Quli Khan.

I learnt from Manik Ram that the clothes, *pattu,* Dhakai etc. which Najaf Khan had bought were to be dispatched to Akbarabad. I therefore sent them with Mir Muhammad Azim. I gather now from the Mir's letter that when the goods arrived there the *kotwāl* of *sāirs* confiscated them, refused to release them and demanded *maḥṣūl.* Thereupon, the Mir went to Agha Sadiq and appraised him of the details. But the Aga paid no heed to his entreaties.

This is strange since the goods were bought by the Nawab and sent on his instructions. I believe that Najaf Khan must have reported this to you and Agha Sadiq. As soon as you receive this letter you should send your men and release the goods. Hand them over to the Agha, obtain a receipt under his seal and give it to Mir Muhammad Azim without any delay. This is the rainy season; if the downpour ruins the goods I will not be responsible because they have entered your jurisdiction and your people have confiscated them. Forward to Najaf Khan a letter that I enclose for him, get his reply and send it to me. 12 Rabī' II, Thursday.

Folio 184a. To Najaf Quli Khan.

I have written to you the details earlier. Now two cart loads—one loaded with five boxes of books and wine for Padre *ṣāḥib,* and the other with clothes which include those left here for Najaf Khan—have left Kanhpur. They are being sent to Agra through Amanullah *harkāra,* Tukait *ḥavaldār* and five troopers, together with the *parwāna* of *rāhdārī* under the seal of Shuja-ud-Daula. Prepare a *dastak* of *rāhdārī* for their passage between Firozabad and Akbarabad and send it through Mayachand Sāhū. This will strengthen our friendship. 13 Rabī' II, Friday.

Folio 184b. To Shuja-ud-Daula.

Since you were unwell when I was leaving I am worried and look forward to hearing about your health and welfare. I always wish for your good health and hope that you will favour me with your reply containing news about your health and the developments there, as well as the works and services that I should do. 17 Rabī' II, Tuesday.

Folio 184b. Addresee's name missing.

I received your letter with the news of the camp. It is important that you keep sending me daily reports in this manner regularly. You say that the estimate (*barāwurd*) of the Englishmen has been prepared and handed over to Mirza Hasan Riza Khan, and that a copy of this has been sent [to me] which I should see soon. But Manik Ram informs me that the estimate (*barāwurd*) is of an amount less than that ordered by the Nawab. It is important that you compare the amount entered in the *barāwurd* with that listed in the order and arrange the *barāwurd* accordingly. 18 Rabī' II, Wednesday.

Folio 185a. To Agha Sadiq Khan.

It had been agreed in the presence of Manik Ram that the goods which Najaf Khan had brought from me would be taken to Akbarabad and handed over to you. Subsequently, they were to be given to Mir Muhammad Azim. In the meanwhile, I learnt that the *kotwāl* of Firozabad confiscated them on the pretext of non-payment of tolls. It is very likely that Najaf Khan must have written to you about this. I have also written to him as well as to Najaf Quli Khan.

I am a friend of Najaf Khan and it is not appropriate that there should have been any problem [in the passage of the goods]. It is strange that you obstructed the flow of goods and Mir Muhammad Azim's appeals to you about the same produced no effect. Instead there was demand for more tariff. These are the *sarkār's* goods and since both you and I serve the *sarkār* you should send your people to procure these goods and get them under your control. Hand over a receipt to the Mir, and send the goods to me without further delay so that the Mir can attend to other works.

In accordance with Najaf Khan's instructions, more goods to you follow. They may take some time [to reach] because of the rains. This is for your information. Further, now that I have dispatched the goods to you I am absolved of all responsibility. God forbid if there is any loss because of the weather you will be held responsible. 18 Rabī' II, Wednesday, Faizabad.

Folio 186a. To Maharaja Chhatr Singh.

I received your letter and was happy to read about the sincere friendship that you have with me. Believe me, my heart is with you. Keep in touch. 25 Rabī' II.

Folio 186a. To Najaf Khan.

I had sent you a number of letters regarding the goods that you had bought from me: their dispatch, as per the agreement with Mir Muhammad Azim, to Akbarabad for Agha Sadiq; the fact that the *kotwāl* confiscated them; about Mir Muhammad Azim approaching Agha Sadiq for assistance and the latters apathy to his petition. I had also sent you another letter regarding the embroidery works and other orders of mine being prepared here by Achal Singh *mahājan*, and [informed you] that my *harkāra* will be permanently posted with Achal Singh. I had requested you to write to your officials to refrain from creating any problem in my works. I had also written about this to Najaf Quli Khan. I believe that these letters must have been brought to your notice even though I have not received any reply from you. However, [I know] you have issued two *parwānas*—one under my seal and the second under the small seal of Manik Ram—to the effect that no one should interfere in the sale and purchase of the goods belonging to Major Polier. At the time of the clearance of the *tankhwāh*, another *parwāna* was issued in the name of Agha Muhammad Sadiq to the effect that whatever goods I sent through Mayachand Sāhū and Mir Muhammad Azim should be purchased when they reach there and a receipt under seal be given. Nobody should create any difficulty in the payment of tolls, etc. I also know that along with this *parwāna* you also ordered that a letter from Manik Ram in the name of Mir Muhammad Azim regarding the dispatch of goods to Agha Sadiq could be procured.

However, nothing has been done so far. On the 30th of Rabī' II, I received another letter from the Mir—dated 19 Rabī'—stating that the goods are still in confiscation and that Agha Sadiq insists on releasing them only after payment of *maḥṣūl* or *ẓāmin* [security]. Mayachand and Chitrabhuj, the *mahājans*, offered to be the *ẓāmins*, but the Agha declined to accept them.

Further, *shaṭranjīs* and many other goods ordered by me have also been detained by the Agha. It is unimaginable that your servants not only defy your instructions, they act contrary to them. I fail to comprehend how this can happen without your consent.

I am approaching you again solely because of our friendship. Otherwise who can dare to do anything against the interest of the English people—your protestations of close friendship with them notwithstanding. If you had abandoned all this [friendship] from your heart then such pettiness would be understandable. This is the time to test [our friendship]. Let bygones be bygones. In future if the correspondence [between us] discontinues, it will be because of the fault of your people. Please make sure that the people who are in your service do not go against your wish [in day to day matters]; only then can it be ensured that they do not act against the interests of the state. Just consider the labour put into escorting the goods to you. And in this there was no personal interest involved—except considerations of friendship. Above all, nothing belongs to either of us—but the reputation of the English is the link between us. In such a case such treatment was not appropriate. 2 Jumāda I, Tuesday.

Folio 188a. To Agha Sadiq

According to the agreement, the goods which Najaf Khan had bought from me were to be sent to you. Mir Muhammad Azim was therefore deputed to take them to you now. From a letter of the Mir I came to know that the *kotwāl* of Firozabad confiscated the goods on the pretext of non-payment of tolls. You did not pay any heed to the Mir's petition about the same. Instead the demand for *maḥṣūl* was enhanced.

On the 18th of Rabī' II, I wrote to you that since the goods belonged to Najaf Khan there should not have been any interference [in their passage]; and that you should collect them from the Mir and Mayachand and give them a receipt for the same. I now know from another letter of the Mir that nothing has been done so far, and the insistance is for either the payment of the *maḥṣūl* or *ẓāmin* [security]. Ironically, when Mayachand and Chitrabhuj stood security they were not accepted.

It is strange that you declined to recognize your own master's goods. You had no concern for the fact that this is the rainy season and the goods might get ruined. I do not know why you are so adamant. It seems that it could be with the connivance of the Nawab, otherwise there is no reason for this stubborness despite [my] repeated pleas.

The goods that are ready there—*shatranjis,* etc.—are now being dispatched to me. Instruct your people not to interfere in their passage. But I will not be surprised [if they do interfere] because they did so in the case of the goods of your own master. Mayachand Sāhū has a *dastak* for the uninterrupted passage of my goods. You can ask him to produce the same. Refrain from any mischief and cause no harm to my goods, else you will face the consequences. If your master overlooks your mischievous activities I alone am sufficient for [dealing with] your people. 2 Jumāda I, Wednesday.

Folio 189a. To Shuja-ud-Daula.

I have not had the privilege of receiving any news since I left your court. I remember you day and night and look forward to hearing from you. I am particularly worried since you were not well when I left. I had sent to you my letter (*'arīẓa*) earlier with prayers for your health.

But I have not been fortunate to receive your reply. I hope that I will be honoured with your letter (*'ināyatnāma*). 3 Jumāda I.

Folio 189b. To Nawab Shuja-ud-Daula.

I am concerned about your health since the day I left your court, particularly because three of my letters to you still remain unanswered. I pray to God for your recovery and good health. I hope that I will be honoured with a letter (*nawāzish-nāma*) from you.

Even though at the moment I am more concerned about your health, yet you know that when something happens the English people do not like to feel neglected. I am therefore constrained to submit that the Rs 20,000 which you had ordered as *tankhwāh* on Raja Chait Singh, the zamindar of Benares, were given by me to Mr Scott there and then. Subsequently, a special *shuqqa* was issued by you on the request of Manik Ram because the Raja had made an excuse for the payment of the 11th instalment. I sent this *shuqqa* [to Benares] even though I knew that this will not make any difference. Now the pretext is one of the letters of Muhammad Ilich Khan. I am sure that unless this letter is received the money will not be paid. I fear that the *ṣāḥib* [Mr Scott], might suspect [my intention]. Before that happens I request you to ensure that a letter under the seal of Muhammad Ilich Khan for the payment of the money be issued in the name of the Raja immediately. With the grace of your favours I will be saved from any accusation of discrepancy in my words. I hope that until I have the honour of meeting you I will be privileged to receive your letters containing the good news of your health and success. 12 Jumāda I, Friday,1188.

Folio 191a. To Raja Hindupat.

I have come to know of the fine qualities of your personality and am therefore keen to open correspondence with you. This is how the foundations of mutual affection and regard are cemented. I have a little work relating to your area—you will know its details from the letter of my *mutaṣaddī*. I hope that you will keep in touch. 14 Jumāda II, Sunday.

Folio 191b. To Najaf Khan.

You must have taken action on the several letters that I sent you regarding some important works. But till date I have not had the pleasure of receiving your reply. I take this contrary to your kind deportment. I hope that till we meet I will have the privilege of hearing from you regularly. 17 Jumāda I, Wednesday.

Folio 192a. To Shuja-ud-Daula.

I have written to you regularly since the day I arrived in Faizabad and pray for your health. I am surprised and astonished that I have not received a single letter from you. I fail to find any reason for this since I have not neglected the requirements of the service. I hope that in the future I will receive your *'ināyatnāma* with the good news of your health. This will give me pleasure. 24 Jumāda I, Wednesday.

Folio 192b. To Nawab Shuja-ud-Daula.

Earlier I had sent you several letters in succession but have not received any reply so far. I have so far been steadfast in my services to you. Hence I am surprised at not hearing from you. I am worried and pray for your good health.

Further, nothing has been realized so far regarding the sum of Rs 20,000 *tankhwāh* assigned to me at Allahabad. My people, who went there to collect the money wrote to me that the Naib, Kirpa Dayal, has died. His son was approached by my people, but to no avail. I therefore request you to send a *parwāna,* in whichever way you feel appropriate, to Allahabad.

Not a single penny has been received yet from another *tankhwāh* at Benares. Raja Chait Singh insists for a letter from Ilich Khan. I had written to you about this earlier but have not heard from you. The realization from there also is thus postponed: I have earned a bad name among my own people (*abnā-i jins*) since I had assigned the *tankhwāh* from both places to Mr Scott and there has been a discrepancy. I hope that you will issue strict orders and ensure that Muhammad Ilich Khan's letter is issued in the name of the Raja so that the money is realized. 27 Jumāda I, Saturday.

Folio 193b. To Mirza Ismail Beg, Allahabad.

I received your letter (*'arẓī*) with the detailed report about the developments there. I noted the misbehaviour of Raja Kirpa Dayal, the state of affairs regarding the revenue of *pargana* Chail which is in your *ta'ahhud,* and the painful fact that you were imprisoned.

Even though it is not customary for us to interfere in the financial and civil matters, and as a matter of fact we never intervene in such things, yet, in view of your difficulties I cannot help but think of a way out. Unfortunately, these days the Nawab is in your area, he left Basauli for an expedition. I am thus helpless. If the Nawab were here I would have approached him with your problem and made all possible efforts to find a solution. Rest assured that I will not spare any effort to do your work when the Nawab is here. Keep writing to me until we meet. 29 Jumāda I.

Folio 194a. To Sadanand, Akbarabad.

I received your letter (*'arẓī*) and noted the fine qualities of Raja Chhatar Singh that you mention, your request for a letter, and the suggestion that I should start a correspondence with him to establish our friendship.

Since I am already in correspondence with the Raja I do not think it is necessary to write to him again. I am happy to learn of your trustworthiness from Mir Muhammad Azim. I would therefore love to have you correspond with me regularly until we meet. Write to me whatever you feel appropriate without hesitation and I will do accordingly. 29 Jumāda I.

Folio 194b. To Hasan Ali Beg Khan.

I am delighted to receive your letter. I noted that my *mutaṣaddī*, Ratanchand, who will be reaching here will request for a *dastak* for the passage of two boats from Faizabad to Allahabad. Following his request and your letter [recommendation] I acquired the *dastak* and have sent it to you. This will reach you soon. Keep writing. 29 Jumāda I.

Folio 194b. To Najaf Khan.

I received your letter which acknowledges the receipt of my letter [to you] regarding the case of interference in the passage of my goods. I noted that Sadiq Beg met you. God is witness to the degree of friendship that I have towards you and words fail to express the extent of my sincerity. I am therefore surprised that you did not even care to write to me a few words about your health.

Further, my people write to me that now one Mir Mansur is creating problems [in the preparation and the passage] of the goods I had ordered. He is not allowing them to move out. He is creating obstruction in the sale of the silk goods that I have there, the plea being that the *dastak* for their sale was issued in the name of Daud Beg Khan. Since now he has replaced him, [Daud Beg Khan] the goods will be released only if he receives a letter [in his name]. How much can I write everyday for every case. These people do not refrain from mischief. They want to impair the bonds of our friendship. These matters are disturbing even if they do not affect our relations. Please be firm and ensure that things are done properly.

Sadiq Beg, who is now with you, must have cooked up a story against me. This man is mischievous. It is necessary that such people should be reprimanded so as to set an example for others, and also to prevent them from taking recourse to such abominable activities in future.

Further, the day I met you in Akbarabad [Agra] we also talked about Madec. I hope you remember what I told you about him. Now I learn that you have developed a relation with him and have also obtained a *jāgīr* for him. This is contrary to what we discussed the other day. Since I am your friend I should warn you that if *Ṣaḥib-i Kalān* hears about it he will be very unhappy. I hope that you will keep writing to me about the developments there until we meet. 4 Jumāda II.

Folio 196a. To Mir Mansur, Akbarabad.

I have come to know from the *harkāras* that you are obstructing the sale and movements of my goods. I do not know what you consider yourself, and from where you have got the power to indulge in such mischievous activities. You commit such offences knowing well of my friendship with Najaf Khan. God willing, in due time you will be punished in such a way that it will be a lesson for others. Even now, if you are concerned about your welfare, allow my *harkāras* to escort my goods from there without any further delay and hesitation. You can ask your people to accompany them [*harkāras*] upto the borders.

As soon as you receive this letter send for the *dallāls* and *beopārīs* and instruct them to sell my goods, which at present are with Mayachand Sāhū, immediately. The *dastak* is with Mayachand Sāhū. I hope you will not have any objection to it and will not ask for any *maḥṣūl.* This is to warn you. 4 Jumāda, Saturday.

Folio 197a. To Shuja-ud-Daula.

I have sent you five letters in succession since I arrived in Faizabad and I am still waiting for a reply. I know that my letters have been brought to your notice. I am concerned at not receiving any response from you since I have never neglected your services. I do not know what is the reason.

Raja Chait Singh declined to release the *tankhwāh* sum of Rs 20,000 on the pretext that he has not yet received the letter of Muhammad

Ilich Khan. The problems in matters already decided by you is due to the machinations of the officials. Raja Kripa Dayal, who has been delaying the *tankhwāh* of Allahabad, has now expired. His son is unwilling to consider the matter without a *parwāna* from you. As a result the collection of money from both the places is postponed. This has caused me embarassement among my own people because I had assigned the money from both the places to Mr Scott. I made repeated requests to you but of no avail. I am surprised that I have not received any response from you. I am your well-wisher. If you want me to suffer I am helpless. 9 Jumāda II, Thursday night.

Folio 197b . To Shuja-ud-Daula.

[Congratulates him on his recovery in hyperbolic, verbose style with artistic phraseology and usage of ornate Persian metaphors: frequently used metaphors being those of spring, singing nightingale and intoxicating wine, and then comes to the following *mudda'ā*]

I am grateful to God that He has given you health and you are again fully recovered. Your good health has spread happiness everywhere. Praises are being showered on you everywhere and there is general jubiliation. 9 Jumāda, Thursday night.

Folio 198b. To Shuja-ud-Daula.

This is to submit that I have sent you seven letters earlier: on Rabī' II, 3 Jumāda I, 12, 24, 27 Jumāda I, and two letters on 9 Jumāda II. I am still awaiting your reply. But till date, i.e. 17 Jumāda II, I have not received any reply to these letters. I am surprised at having to stay here without your kind favours since I have never been negligent in my duty towards you. Despite giving it an intense thought I am unable to resolve this problem.

I have also submitted to you the exact situation of my *tankhwāh.* To this also I have not received any response from you. Since this is necessary I again report to you that Raja Kirpa Dayal, who was delaying the payment of the *tankhwāh,* has died and not a single penny has been received from him. Your *parwāna* is awaited. The *tankhwāh* from Benares is also in the doldrums on the pretext of the non-receipt of a letter from Ilich Khan. I have not received a single penny from there as well. Instead I have discovered that Ilich Khan has written to Chait Singh that I should not get a single penny without his letter.

I fail to understand that while you favour me with a salary, your people create obstructions. I am extremely embarassed because I had sub-assigned the amount from both the places to Mr Scott. God knows that I have no other support except your excellency and favours which I consider a great fortune for myself. But I am helpless because I have not received any letter from you and am therefore sending my request and petition through Mr Middleton. I hope that I will receive your letter. I am enclosing a copy of a letter of 9 Jumāda II. 17 Jumāda II, Friday night.

Folio 199b. To Gokulchand Sah.

I received your letter and noted the case of Jugal Kishor. He is sincerely engaged in my business and does my work devotedly. I am not neglectful of people who do my work earnestly and am concerned about their promotions in all respects. Be rest assured and keep in touch. 24 Jumada II, night.

Folio 199b. To Mir Muslih, resident of qaṣba Jais.

I received your letter and noted that you were pained to part company with me, that you left for the Deccan and have now returned to your hometown, Jais. I am happy that you are back again. Since we are known to each other and are in correspondence since long we should keep in touch until we meet. 25 Jumāda II, Saturday.

Folio 200a. To Rai Jaspat Rai, nāib of ṣūba Allahabad.

It is four to five months since Rs 20,000 were assigned to me and a *parwāna* [issued about it] to Raja Kripa Dayal by the Nawab. Since it was written that the money would be paid within a month I sub-assigned the *tankhwāh* to Mr Scott. But the deceased Raja delayed the payment, and when my men reached to collect the money he had died. At that time you promised my people and wrote to my Diwan, Manik Ram, that the money would be paid immediately if you received a new *parwāna*. It has been ages since you received the [second] desired *parwāna* from the *huzūr*. But the payment is still pending.

I fail to understand why after the Nawab assigns the *tankhwāh* your kindness delays its payment. I therefore write to you to arrange the payment as soon as you receive the letter and inform me. Any further delay will not be good. I do not entertain any unpleasantness in my relations. This is just for your information. Manik Ram will appraise you of the other details. 4 Rajab night, sent through Manik Ram.

Folio 200b. To Raja Hindupat.

I received your letter at an opportune time and am very happy since the contents reinforce our relationship. I noted that I will know the details from the letter of my *mutaṣaddī*. Now my *mutaṣaddī* has also written to Ramchand Dichhit [Dixit] and has come out with some more new details. Dichhit will also write to you about it. So keep me informed about your health. 5 Rajab.

Folio 201a. To Najaf Khan.

I received your letter informing me about the arrival of my goods in Agra, the handing over of them to Agha Sadiq, and your instructions for non-interference in their movements. I have full faith in your friendship and believe that no negligence was done on your part and that it was the officials who commited excesses. It was fine if they by any chance wanted the tariffs to be paid. But what I fail to understand is that they acted against your advice. It will be appreciated if you issue instructions as soon as you receive my letters.

Only a part of the things which were with Mayachand Sāhū were received, and the receipt of the goods which Agha Sadiq had given is yet to arrive here. Further, the sale of the goods which Manik Ram had sent to Mayachand has been postponed because of the interference of your officials. I do not know who will be responsible if any damage accrues to these goods. I have written to you only out of my sincerity. I look forward to hearing from you. 8 Rajab.

Folio 202a. To Najaf Khan, about the case of Muhammadi Khan.

You may recall that I had recommended to you the case of Muhammadi Khan: about his rehabilitation in Badshahpur and its fort on a long-term basis (*istimrār*). You were good enough to promise that when you reached Delhi this matter would be sorted out. I had also asked Mirza Abdullah Beg to remind you of this case.

However, I learnt that Muhammadi Khan is still in trouble. I have full faith in your promise [that you will keep to your word]. Since this is a trivial matter I would have not given you any trouble. But since I understand that the poor fellow is unsettled and deserves to be rehabilitated I recommend his case to you. I am surprised that Mirza Abdullah Beg who had taken the responsibility of reminding you has forgotten about it. Otherwise the matter would not have been neglected.

I request you to give Muhammadi Khan's case attention so that he can achieve his objective and be in your service. I am writing to you again so that my word does not go unheeded. Amongst our people [the English] not keeping one's word is considered bad. 8 Rajab, Thursday.

Folio 203a. To Mirza Abdullah Beg kumaidān.

I received your letter and noted that Muhammadi Khan's work is still to be done. I enclose a copy of the letter which I have written again to the Nawab in this case. I hope you receive it in time and can take it to him so that I receive a timely response.

As for the clothes and the European articles that you have enquired about, I do not know which clothes you refer to, nor do I know where the European articles are. But I have received one packet of cinnamon and one packet of *mulethi* from Mr Scott which, because of the negligence of the people here, is still lying in this place. I am sending it to you to Lucknow. You can get them from your house whenever you require. Always keep in touch. 8 Rajab, Thursday.

Folio 203b. To Mir Muhammad Muin Khan.

I am happy to receive your letter and sorry to hear that you did not receive my reply. I reply promptly whenever I receive your letter. I hope you are happy wherever you are. My happiness is in your happiness.

Rest assured that Najaf Khan will not ignore your services. I will write to you subsequently about the verbal message that I received, regarding the horses and the oxen, through the person who came from Jainagar. 8 Rajab, Thursday.

Folio 204a. To Muhammadi Khan zamindar of Badshahpur.

I received your letter (*'arẓī*) and got to know the details. In accordance to your request I have written to Najaf Khan, a copy [of the letter] of which is enclosed in the letter of Mirza Abdullah Beg. I have also written to him to investigate into the matter and get the work done. I firmly hope that by now Najaf Khan would have attended to your problem and resolved it. You will know the rest from the letter of Manik Ram. 8 Rajab, Thursday.

Folio 204a. To Rana Chhatar Singh Sawai.

I am glad to receive your letter. I am delighted to receive the three *chikaras* and am happy to learn that you would like to know if I require some more [*chikaras*]. I do not need any more. Obviously our relations are not based on these things. I hope that in consideration of our friendship you will send me details about the developments there; also let me know what I can do for you. 21 Rajab, Wednesday.

Folio 204b. To Rai Jaspat Rai, naib of ṣūba Allahabad.

From your letter to Mr Scott I came to know of the situation. I think that your request for a receipt is just an excuse. The receipt is [normally] given only after receiving the money. Manik Ram has repeatedly written to you about it. From his letter it is clear that you are resorting to delay tactics in the payment of the money. This is not good. When the Nawab had assigned me a *tankhwāh* you had promised to make the payment within a month. Now it is already four months, you should not forget that you will have to pay the interest (*sūd*) for this delay. I will not forgo even a single penny of the interest.

I am not suffering [any hardship] because of this [non-payment]. But I could not keep the word which I had given to the officials to whom I had sub-assigned [the *tankhwāh*]. It is therefore important that you pay the money of the *tankhwāh*, along with the interest, to Mr Scott. Dispatch it to him and obtain a receipt under his seal. Send a copy of it to me. This is in your interest as well. You will know the other details from the letter of Manik Ram. 29 Rajab.

Folio 205a. To Gokulchand Saha, Benares.

Manik Ram must have written to you about the sample of the *tāsh*. Send, along with your letter, first quality specimen, both of small and large size, to Mr Math (?) from where they will be sent to me. Write the price of each one of them separately. Send them without further delay. 30 Rajab, Friday.

Folio 205b. To Najaf Khan.

I have not heard from you since long. I am worried because you know that I am so fond of you. It was in consideration of our sincere friendship that the case of the payment of the *tankhwāh* of Bengal has been entrusted to you. About Rs 50,000 has already been paid and the acknowledgement received. But I am now worried about the remaining amount. I consider the matter, whether it relates to you or to me, as the same. It appears that to obtain the payment of Rs 80,000 from Calcutta is difficult. I am therefore writing to you about it.

Generally, the English officers do not create problems for those who are sincere, but are unsparing with their opponents and culprits. The problems in the payment of your *tankhwāh* from the Company are alarming. I think in reality the case is different.

I urgently require money in Calcutta these days. I therefore request you to approach the Governor [Hastings] to issue the orders for the payment. I have two considerations why I urge upon you to do so: To create conditions for the promotion of your friendship with the English *ṣāḥibs*, and [of course] the payment without any hassels to me. In case you feel that the payment in Calcutta will be difficult, I hope that you will be good enough to arrange Rs 50,000 immediately. I am here to be in your service in whichever manner you desire. This is just for your information. A reliable person should soon meet you to collect the payment.

As for the dispatch of the steel and the iron, I have asked Manik Ram to acquire them. The bullock carts are ready. This is for your information. He will do whatever you write. Please write immediately. 1st Sha'bān, Saturday.

Folio 207a. To Gokulchand Saha, Benares.

I had written to you earlier to send the specimens of the *tāsh* varieties available in Benares to Mr Math and to write to me the price of each variety separately. Now Mr Lacos is reaching Benares. So instead of Mr Math you may hand over fourteen *thāns* of *tāsh* of different varieties and the two pairs of *khil'at* of your choice to Mr Lacos. Note down their prices in my account. 2 Sha'bān, Sunday, night. (Reply received on 23 Sha'bān.)

Folio 207a. To Jaspat Rai, nāib of ṣūba Allahabad.

I have learnt that Karim Quli Khan, son of Munir-ud-Daula, has captured seven elephants belonging to me and wants to send them to some other place via Delhi and Bundelkhand. I am writing to you to get back the elephants from him [Karim Quli Khan] or from his people, and prohibit them from proceeding ahead without my *parwāna*.

Inform me so that I can send my own people to bring them here. I have ordered these elephants for the Nawab *ṣāḥib*. If they are allowed to go ahead the Nawab will be angry. Do not let them take these elephants. However, if they are really coming towards Faizabad then send them here accompanied by your people. 9 Sha'bān. (Reply received on the 20.)

Folio 207b. To Raja Chait Singh.

I have come to know that Karim Quli Khan has captured seven elephants belonging to me and wants to send them to some other place via Delhi and Bundelkhand. These elephants have reached Benares. I therefore write to you to capture [the elephants] and get them under your control. Do not allow them to proceed ahead without your *parwāna.* The elephants are meant for the Nawab, and if they are allowed to go ahead the Nawab will be angry. Do not let go of them [even] if they say they are taking them to the army of the Nawab. If they are going towards Faizabad [then] send them with your men. 9 Sha'bān. (Reply received on 22 Sha'bān.)

Folio 208a. To Haider Beg Khan, faujdār of Kora.

I have come to know that Karim Quli Khan has captured seven elephants and wants to send them [somewhere] via Delhi and Bundelkhand. I therefore write to you to capture these elephants which have passed through Kora. Do not let them go ahead without my *parwāna.* Inform me so that I can send my men. I have ordered these elephants for the Nawab ṣāḥib. Do not let them go even if they say that they are taking them to the army of the Nawab. If they are going towards Faizabad then send them to me. 9 Sha'bān. (Reply received on the 28 Sha'bān.)

Folio 208b. To Hasan Ali Beg Khan, qil'adār of Allahabad.

I have come to know that Karim Quli Khan has captured seven elephants and wants to send them somewhere via Delhi and Bundelkhand. If these elephants pass through Allahabad capture them and do not let them proceed without my *parwāna.* Inform me soon so that I can send my people. I have ordered these elephants for the Nawab. If they go away unchecked the Nawab will be angry. In case these men say that they are taking them to the army of the Nawab do not let them proceed. But if they are on their way towards Faizabad then send them to me with your men. 9 Sha'bān. (Reply received on the 24th.)

Folio 209a. To Kashmirimal Sahu, Benares.

I received your letter and noted that the elephants have been sold. If you intended to sell them you should have written to me earlier. It is ungentlemanly and inappropriate that you reply to me after a month. 9 Sha'bān, Sunday.

Folio 209a. To Ramchand Sah, Benares.

I have come to know that these days you are in Benares. However, I am surprised that you did not inform me of your arrival in Benares.

Seven of my elephants, which were on their way from Sylhet, have by mistake been handed over to Karim Quli Khan, the son of Imad-ud-Daula. Since these elephants had been ordered by me for the Nawab, I wrote to Azimabad on hearing this news. I said that these elephants should be acquired from Karim Quli Khan when he arrived there.

However, Karim Quli Khan bypassed Azimabad and took another route, and having reached Benares now intends to go somewhere. I have written about them [elephants] to Raja Chait Singh. I write to you also to investigate into the matter and send your own people to capture the elephants from Karim Quli Khan and his people. Do not let them go ahead without my written orders.

In case these elephants are going to Faizabad, ask Chait Singh to send them accompanied by strong men. But do not allow them to proceed if they are going to some other place. I am sending the *filbān* [elephant-rider] accompanied by a *harkāra.* Six of these elephants are male and one is a female elephant. This is just for your information. You will know of the other details from the letter of Jugal Kishor. Keep in touch until we meet. 10 Sha'bān, Monday. (Reply received on the 23rd of Sha'bān.)

Folio 210a. To Nawab Shuja-ud-Daula.

I have written to you seven to eight letters (*'arīẓas*) to you which must have been brought to your notice. But I have not been honoured by your reply to any of them. Eventually, I sent an *'arīẓa* containing all the details through Mr Middleton which he brought to your notice, and to which I did receive a reply. It has been two months since you ordered [the release of payment] but I am still waiting. This [attitude] towards a simple man whose sincerity is beyond doubt is unexpected of your kind and merciful Excellency.

If, God forbid, by any chance you are angry with me over something I will still feel privileged to receive a two sentence letter from you. I hope to know where I have erred so that I can make amends for it. This humble servant is here because of your grace and generosity. If there is any lapse in your graciousness it would impair the position and strength of this humble servant. 14 Sha'bān, Shab-i-bar'-āt. (Reply received on the 6th of Ramẓān.)

Folio 210b. To Haidar Beg Khan, faujdār of Kora.

I had written to you earlier about the elephants that were coming with Karim Quli Khan. The matter has now been resolved. It is therfore advised that you do not interfere in the matter of Karim Quli Khan. In future keep in touch. 21 Sha'bān, Friday. (10 Ramẓān, reply received.)

Folio 211a. To Raja Chait Singh, Benares.

I had earlier written to you about the elephants coming with Karim Quli Khan. Now the matter has been resolved amicably. I write to you so that you do not stop these elephants from going ahead. I am always a sincere friend of yours. Keep in touch. 21 Sha'bān, Friday.

Folio 211b. To Raja Jaspat Rai, nāib of ṣūba Allahabad.

I had written to you earlier to capture the elephants coming with Karim Quli Khan. Now the matter is resolved. I write to you to let these elephants pass through. I am your friend. Keep in touch. 21 Sha'bān, Friday.

Folio 211b. To Ramchand Saha, Benares.

I received your letter of 18 Sha'bān regarding the elephants on the 23rd of this month. I noted that the elephants that were with Karim Quli Khan did not belong to me. He had bought them from someone else. In this case you should refrain from any further interference in this matter. I have also written to Chait Singh about this.

As for the five elephants of Mir Sulaiman Khan, please note that there is no difference between me and him. But eight elephants which belong to me—seven male and one female—have arrived in Azimabad [Patna] and will be proceeding to [reach] me. When they reach Benares ask Raja Chait Singh to accompany them. Keep me informed about your welfare. 23 Sha'bān, Monday.

Folio 212a. To Gokulchand Saha, Benares.

I received your letter and noted that twelve *thāns* of *tāsh* of your choice, priced at Rs 1041 and 2 annas, and one *jor khil'at* costing Rs 551 and 8 annas has been handed over to Mr Lacos. I have also received the list. Well done. As instructed by you, I have deposited the money into your account. 23 Sha'bān, Monday.

Folio 213a. To Nawab Shuja-ud-Daula.

I received your letter. As for the relationship between the English and your Excellency—this is a fact, and your kindness and generosity to me is well-known. I am living in this country because of you. Only God knows that this humble servant is never oblivious of paying his service and wishing well for your power.

I was concerned and worried even if the delay in your letters was because of your indisposition and preoccupation in the affairs of the state. I am now happy to hear about your welfare. I never consider myself away from your august audience (*ḥuẓūr*). Now that the shadow of your fortune and victories is reflecting this side, I hope I will be privileged to have an audience with you. 6 Ramẓān (Reply received on 6 Ramẓān?).

Folio 213b. To Najaf Khan.
Kishan Sahai, who is a clever and useful *mutaṣaddī*, is looking for a job. He is reaching there with my letter of recommendation. I have experienced his ability and it will give me pleasure if he gets your due care and consideration. 6 Ramẓān.

Folio 214a. To Nawab Shuja-ud-Daula.
I had replied to your letter earlier. This must have been brought to your notice. Since I owe my strength to your boundless grace and munificence, I wish day and night to endow my eyes with your beauty and graciousness.

I came to know from Ikhtar-ud-Daula Salarjang, who is leaving to meet you, that because of your indisposition you will stay in Lucknow for some time. Since I am your faithful servant and always pray for your welfare I am also arriving in Lucknow very soon to have the fortune of an audience with you. 8 Ramẓān, Sunday.

Folio 214a. To Mirza Ismail Beg, resident of Allahabad.
I received your letter (*'arẓī*) regarding the arrival of Captain Brooke's goods in Allahabad escorted by a *harkāra.* I am redirecting the letters along with the *harkāra* to Lucknow. This is because the Nawab is there [Lucknow] and I will take some time to arrive there. You will receive my reply from there [Lucknow]. 9 Ramẓān, Monday.

Folio 214b. To Khiradmand Khan Don Pedro.
Received your letter and noted with pleasure that you have been directed by the Nawab to arrive in the camp and are keen to meet me. Since I am equally enthusiastic to see you and there is a chance to do

so, I write to invite you to come over to my place. Consider it as your house and have meals with me. 16 Ramzān, Monday.

Folio 215a. To Najaf Khan.

I am pleased to receive your letter just at a time when I was concerned about your welfare. You write about the annual payment (*wajh-i salyāna*) which the Company has assigned to you. You have received this payment and will continue to get it without delay. My dear (*mushfiq*), it is my desire to see that you receive the annual payment as always.

You have written that it is not possible that you will side with the Company's opponents, and that whatever you did was due to practical exigencies of the time; also, that this has been brought to the notice of the English in Calcutta as well as their agents in your territory; [finally] that you have not acted on anything without bringing it to the notice [of the English].

I have full faith in your wisdom and intelligence and believe that you would not take action without informing the English. But since I am your sincere friend and always seek your success and promotion it just occurred to me that I write to you what I did. Now that I know, I am sure that things will be carried out appropriately thus reinforcing our relationship.

As for the payment you owe me in Calcutta, I had written to you earlier as a precautionary measure that I have once again come to know that due to certain reasons the payment may be delayed. Since I require money for some work there I request you to be kind enough to dispatch some money through some person, in which case your payment can be made here. I am sending people to you for this purpose. Since I need the money urgently I hope that you will think of its payment at an early date. It is not befitting our friendship that I keep writing to you about it.

About the steel (*ispāt*) and iron which you mention, I would like to report that the Nawab is in Lucknow and [since] I am also there, there has been a delay. I hope that it will reach you soon.

I had written to you earlier about the *āltamghā* of Padre *ṣāḥib*. Despite the *sanad* there is a dispute about it. It is said that this place is the seat of governor (?) (*ḥākim nashīn*) where the *kachehrī* is held. Since you had written earlier that the Padre *ṣāḥib* will be given the *sanad* I had accepted it as your pleasure. But there is still some problem.

Now I have come to know that this place has been given to Samru.

The substitute you had suggested for the Padre has not yet been given. Perhaps his grant has also been suspended. This is strange. I am writing this for your information. 17 Ramẓān, night.

Folio 216b. To Rao Gangaram and Rao Bhawani Singh kumaidān.

I received your letter and was pleased to know that you have been given titles and *manṣabs* from the imperial court. I had earlier sent for both of you, through your *vakīl*, Bakshi Ram, nine *gaz* red cloth for your *kurtīs*, a *shuqqa* for the Nawab, and a letter to Majd-ud-Daula. I have not received your acknowledgement for long. I do not know the reason for this delay. I therefore write to you to acknowledge it and keep me informed of the developments at the imperial court. 29 Ramẓān, Sunday night.

Folio 217a. To Mir Sulaiman Khan.

I received your letter along with your acknowledgement and a note about receiving a letter as well as one from Balai (?) *ṣāḥib.* Your money is like my money. Whenever your money is received, it will be deposited in your account.

I am concerned about your Rs 10,100 regarding the price of the elephants and I am trying my best for its immediate payment.

There has been a discount over the *chalanī* as the current account here is modelled after the Murshidabadi. And you know there has been discount (*batta*) over this. But it does not mean your loss. The fact is that there is a *batta* over the *chalanī* in Murshidabad and your account is there. We all know what the amount of *batta* is for the Murshidabadi years. Thus there is no discrepancy in the accounts and there will not be a loss of a single penny for you. You will also receive the interest.

The delay in the loan of money was because I was in Faizabad and the Nawab was in Lucknow. I have therefore not yet received the money. The Nawab was also not well and hence has not been investing. Now that the Nawab and I are both in Lucknow the payment will be made. Be rest assured and keep in touch. 5 Shawwāl, Friday, Lucknow.

Folio 218a. To Majd-ud-Daula Farzand Khan.

I received your letter. Ever since Niyaz Ali Khan told me about your fine qualities my heart has been restless for your friendship. I have been keen to develop relations with you which by the grace of God are growing.

The case of Saiyid Ali Khan that you have written about will be dealt with according to the instructions of Niyaz Ali Khan. You will know the rest from his letter. I hope I will be kept informed of his welfare. 17 Shawwāl, Wednesday. (Written in reply to his letter.)

Folio 219a. To Muhammad Riza Pirzada, resident of Benares.

I received your letter and noted that you came with the treasury and then took leave to return to Benares without meeting me. Since all matters are destined to take place in their own time we will meet *inshā-Allāh.* But it is necessary that you keep in touch. 19 Shawwāl, Friday.

Folio 219a. To Najaf Khan.

I received your letter and noted that according to you the annual payment (*wajh-i salyāna*) assigned by the Company is never delayed. With the grace of God it has always been paid in time and now if there is a delay of a day or two it is fine.

My dear, I always want that the payment to you should be regular. But I wrote out of my sincerity, because you also know that the payment of *salyāna* is nowhere in sight. You had written that there might be some delay, but it has now been ten months and the paymemt you owe me is still nowhere in sight. You know that I have waited all along in consideration of our friendship. But I do not know how long I will have to wait. Further, I had taken money from some Europeans on the promise that it would be repaid from the *tankhwāh* of Calcutta. They are disappointed and are insisting on its [re] payment. But you write to me to wait. This is not befitting of our friendship. I therefore urge you that if you really want to maintain our friendship send the entire sum through a *harkāra.* Arrange people to accompany it. But if, as is the practice of other people, you want me to repeatedly ask for it then I am helpless. Many things can be done if I receive the money, but if I lose, it will be my loss. You may make the payment in whichever manner you please.

Five papers relating to the titles of the English are enclosed herewith. I hope you will get the signature of the Emperor and hand over the memoranda (*yād-dāsht*) with the silver seals. 28 Shawwāl, Sunday, 2 *gharīs* of day past.

Folio 220b. To Nawab Shuja-ud-Daula.

Earlier, a *parwāna* for the payment of the emoluments of Mirza Hasan

Riza Khan had been issued in Lucknow. The follow-up has also been issued. But the payment is being delayed. Emoluments for eight to nine months are due to the troopers and they have been reduced to destitution. It is therefore requested that the officials be instructed to pay the emoluments according to the *barāwurd* so that the poor soldiers get their due and pray for the stability of your power. 28 Shawwāl.

Folio 220b. To Raja Chait Singh, Benares.

I received your letter and appreciate your anxiety. I never delay replying to the letters I receive. I am your well-wisher. Keep in touch until we meet. It will be my pleasure. 20 Ẕīqa'da, Monday.

Folio 221a. To Sawai Maharaja Guman Singh Bahadur Dilawar Jang.

I am delighted to receive your letter. Words fail to express my concern for you and my pride in having built a friendly relationship with you. It is clear to the intelligent that there is nothing better in this material world than friendship and love.

Niyaz Ali Khan had written about your high culture and etiquettes. I hope that we correspond with each other and you will keep me informed about you health. 20 Ẕīqa'da, Monday.

Folio 221b. To Murid Khan.

I received your letter and am yet to recover from the shock. Today is the third day [since the death of the Nawab]. I will write to you when I regain my senses. 25 Ẕīqa'da (written in reply).

Folio 222b. To Majd-ud-Daula Farzand Khan.

On the 23rd of Ẕīqa'da, Friday night, the Nawab expired. This was cause for gloom all over the world. At the moment with the grace of God Asaf-ud-Daula has succeeded his deceased father.

As your sincere friend I desire that there should be a cordial relationship between you and Nawab Asaf-ud-Daula. Thus, even though you had not asked for it, I have sent you a letter from the Nawab. I hope you will send me an appropriate reply since I consider you my friend. It is in the interest of all of us that both of you should have good relations. You will know the other details from the letter of Niyaz Ali Khan. 27 Ẕīqa'da, Monday, dispatched in the morning.

Folio 222b. To Najaf Khan.

I had written to you repeatedly about the money that you owe me. You had replied that in case there was no payment of *tankhwāh* from Calcutta you would send me the money. I had written to you about this earlier also.

You know it well that the matters of the world depend on money and the money you owe me is long overdue. In such a situation I cannot carry on with my business. If there was any hope for the payment of the *tankhwāh* in Calcutta I would not have insisted on the payment. It is impossible to do anything without the money. I therefore suggest that in consideration of our friendship you clear the debt along with the interest accrued on it so far. Ensure that there is no further delay. I would consider this as a favour. 27 Ẕīqa'da, Monday, sent with a *harkāra* in the morning.

Folio 223a. To Mir Sulaiman Khan.

I received your letter together with one in English regarding the payment of the money which had earlier been made to you.

I can understand that your debtors must have been worried because of the delay. But I assure you that the delay by this sincere friend of yours in the dispatch of the money has been for reasons beyond my control. With the grace of God I will now send you the money within a period of twenty days.

I have written to you about the discount over the *chalanī* and I hope it is clear to you. You have also written that I write another letter to the Governor in Council regarding the payment so that you can meet him in person and get the money. My dear, I know it well that the payment of this sum is now impossible. There is no use in sending another letter. Please keep in touch. 28 Ẕīqa'da, Tuesday.

Folio 223b. To Najaf Khan.

I received your letter on 12 Ẕīḥijja and noted the appropriate strategies and their implementation: maintaining of a relationship with the Company; dispatch of the imperial *shuqqa* to reprove Nawab Asaf-ud-Daula; and the dispatch of the *tabarruks*.

I had a very sincere and cordial relationship with the deceased Nawab and share an even better relationship with the present Nawab. I feel that those who were close to the late Nawab should consider the present one as his legitimate successor. They should do their best in his interest. This is particularly true of you because you had such a close relationship with Nawab Shuja-ud-Daula. I request you to ensure that all matters related to this Nawab are carried out well at the imperial court. This will be good for you now as well as in the life hereafter. 13 Ẕīḥijja.

Folio 224b. To Nur Ali, gumāshta of Colonel Muir.

I had sent a letter earlier through the *harkāra.* I believe you have received it but you have not yet come here. You are now instructed not to come [here] since we have departed from here and will be travelling for some time. If you like you may continue to acquire the clothes there and write to me whatever you obtain. However, in case you do not like them, write to me the details of whatever you have bought and spent. Keep all the clothes with you. Write to me and I will send the boat from here along with the soldiers and the *dastak* of *rāhdārī* so that these could be taken to the boatman. 15 Ẕīḥijja, Thursday, Begumganj.

Folio 225a. To Nawab Iftikhar ud-Daula Mirza Ali Khan.

It is beyond the power of my pen to write to you the affection and sincerity I have for you. I am always eager to know about your welfare. I therefore implore to you that until we meet you write to me about your welfare. 17 Ẕīḥijja, Daryabad.

Folio 225b. To Nur Ali, gumāshta of Dr Clugh.

I received your letter (*'arẓī*). You write that you have arrived here in Faizabad but because of the non-availability of *sawārī* [carriage] it is difficult for you to come here. It is not imperative for you to be here. But it is necessary that you write to me about the sum of Rs 12,500 belonging to Colonel Muir: how much of it you have spent and what is the amount left with you. Also, how much is still due to different people. Subsequently, after two to three days I will send a *dastak* of *rāhdārī* to Captain Martin. I will also write to him about the payment of the soldiers. Manik Ram has already written to him about his *gumāshta* in Faizabad and for arranging the boat. Take change of the things when my letter, *dastak* for *rāhdārī* and plea about the soldiers reaches Captain Martin. 19 Ẕīḥijja, Pratapganj.

Folio 226a. To Nur Ali, gumāshta of Dr Clugh.

I received your letter. The *dastak,* as requested by you, has been sent to Captain Martin. Collect the *dastak* and the *sipāhīs,* from him and take them to Manjhi. Also collect the boat from the agent of Manik Ram in Faizabad. Write about the copy of the invoice, in the current currency, for the cloth and send it to me so that I get to know. 24 Ẕīḥijja.

Folio 226b. To Najaf Khan.

I am happy to receive your letter. It does not behove of our friendship that you take fifteen days to reply. If your reply takes fifteen days in important and necessary matters I wonder what the case will be in other instances.

I need money urgently and have written to you about this time and again. I hope that on receiving this letter you will immediately make the effort to dispatch the *hundī* to me. I am writing to you repeatedly for such a small matter.

Keeping in view our sincere relationship, send me the *hundī* in reply to this letter. I do not need to write to you again. In any case the persistent demand for money is not something very pleasant (*bataqāẓa-i shadīd ḥusūl-i zar-i dostdār luṭf nadārad*). 25 Ẕīḥijja, Lucknow.

Folio 227a. To Sri Sawai Maharaja Guman Singh.

I am extremely pleased to receive your letter and my fondness for you has increased. I hope that with each passing day it enhances—this will be my pleasure. Niyaz Ali Khan and Muhammad Taqi will give you the report about the developments here. We must keep in touch until we meet. 3 Muḥarram, 1189.

Folio 228a. To Mihrban Khan, an official of Nawab Muzaffar Jang of Farrukhabad.

I wish you well in matters of health. I note that you have been given the *khil'at* of regular service by Nawab Asaf-ud-Daula. You must be thankful for it and act according to my instructions.

I am sending you two packets wrapped in a sealed paper. One of the packets (*dibya*) has thirty-six tablets. The second has thirty-six smaller packets (*puryas*) within it. You should take one tablet before going to bed. Early in the morning take one *purya*, which contains *chūb-i chīnī* [China root] and *mulethī* [liquor], boil them in half *ser* water. Cool the water after half of it has evaporated and drink it two to three times a day. Take these medicines for thirty-six days.

God willing, you will see the difference in a period of twenty days. You will recover fully after thirty-six days. But remember that the more particular you are about diet restrictions, the better it is for you. Protect yourself from the cold but keep doing all your work as this is good for your body. Second, add less of *garam masāla* and fat in your diet and refrain from sour, gastronomic and rich food. Use only hot water for bathing and never have a cold water bath. You should also abstain from copulation. You should recover after thirty-six days and then do whatever you like.

Folio 228b. A note in the cover of the letter to Mihrban Khan.

A *shuqqa* from the Nawab Asaf-ud-Daula, regarding Rs 4 lacs due to the late Nawab [Shuja-ud-Daula], will be reaching Nawab Muzaffar Jung. Obtain the money from him and send it. 3 Muḥarram.

Folio 229a. To Majd-ud-Daula Farzand Khan.

I received your letter. I have been a devoted servant of the Emperor for the last fourteen years and have prayed day and night for the stability of the Empire. I have therefore brought your letter to the notice of Nawab Asaf-ud-Daula. I wish that your efforts result in the strengthening of your relations with the Nawab. I have also obtained a letter (*'arẓdāsht*) from the Nawab for the Emperor and one for you.

I believe that since I am your and the imperial court's sincere well-wisher and always appreciative of your efforts, the prospects of the fulfilment of the task will increase. These matters are important and it will be impolite and undiplomatic to divulge them to any other person. Take all possible caution regarding this. You will know the rest from the letter of Niyaz Ali Khan and [you] act accordingly. 3 Muḥarram, 1189.

Folio 229b. 'Arẓdāsht to the Emperor.

The slave Major Polier who has the honour of kissing the threshold of your service is present with his *'arẓdāsht*. It is submitted that I have been your sincere and devoted well-wisher for the last fourteen years and have been endowed with your boundless graces. I have always desired that the affairs of the state get strengthened with every passing day. In view of this I have brought to the notice of Asaf-ud-Daula the letter which Majd-ud-Daula had sent through Niyaz Ali. I have explained everything to him. God willing, he will do whatever is best for the empire, and you will also keep the interest of his government and the welfare of the people in mind. Things will be done as you wish. But until the ground work is done you should not divulge them to anyone—except Majd-ud- Daula—so that things remain in control. 3 Muḥarram.

Folio 230b. To Mir Muhammad Muin Khan.

I received your letter and noted the problems that you are encountering because of the non-payment of the *tankhwāh*, and the fact that you are planning to come here.

If there is some gain in continuing there in your job and if you can maintain yourself it is fine, otherwise there is no point in staying there. God is everyone's provider. If you are planning to come here, do so by all means. I will make all possible efforts to carry out your work. 3 Muḥarram, 1189.

Folio 231a. To Majd-ud Daula Farzand Khan.

I received your letter along with the *shuqqas* from the Emperor. This increases love [between us]. Since you wanted Asaf-ud-Daula to depart, I have requested him to leave Faizabad and we have reached Mahdighat and are camping on the banks of the Ganges. We will be here for sometime because of Muḥarram. Whatever is required will be done later.

I am very happy to know from your letter that the Emperor is favourably disposed towards me. I am also devoted to him and hope to receive more of his favours. I have the desire to kiss the threshold of his court and have audience with him. Words fail to express my emotions for him. 7 Muḥarram, 1189.

Folio 232a. A note in the cover of the same letter.

You had asked for the perfumes but since I am in the army I do not have anything with me. I have written [about them] to Faizabad where these things are kept. I have also asked for them from Azimabad where many such things are housed. You will know the rest from the letter of Niyaz Ali Khan. 7 Muḥarram.

Folio 232a. Second note in the same letter.

I have brought to the notice of the Nawab your letter and the copies of the *shuqqas* from the Emperor. The Nawab is extremely pleased with your excellent services. I have acquired a letter from the Nawab with your seal and am sending it to you. 7 Muḥarram.

Folio 232b. To Najaf Khan.

I received your letter and noted that you have arrived near Akbarabad [Agra] and will send the money soon. I do not know how the dispatch of money depends on your arrival in Akbarabad. You have the power to send the money from anywhere. It is strange that despite the protestations of our sincerity the money has not yet been received. I have written to you several times but the payment is being delayed. I need the money urgently and as soon as you receive this news dispatch it. Many works are dependent on that money and I do not have to remind you about that.

I note that you are getting the memoranda of titles for the English people prepared. I will appreciate if you send these at an early date. 8 Muḥarram.

Folio 233b. To Nur Ali, gumāshta of Colonel Muir.
I received your letter. It is not clear if you also enclosed the list of clothes.

I had written to you earlier to dispatch to me the full accounts of the Rs 12,500 that you had taken from Colonel Muir: How much you have spent? How much is due? etc. But you have not written anything about it. You also write that Colonel Muir has written to you to collect a sum of Rs 5000 from me. This is fine. But the condition is that you should not permit any negligence in the purchase of clothes. There should not be any loss. Write to me and I will send you the *hundī* immediately. 8 Muḥarram.

Folio 234a. To Mirza Ali Khan.
I received your letter and noted your keeness to meet me. I am equally eager to see you. I implore you to keep in touch and maintain our sincere and cordial relations. We must keep in touch until we meet. 8 Muḥarram, 1189.

Folio 234b. To Mihrban Khan.
I received your letter. I have obtained the *shuqqa* and sent whatever was appropriate to Hoshmand Ali Khan. Convey this to Hoshmand Ali Khan so that he can tell the Nawab accordingly and things are sorted out as per your desire. 8 Muḥarram.

Folio 234b. Daud Beg Khan 'Īsā'ī (Christian).
I received your letter along with four baskets [bahangī] of oranges which are very tasty. I note that you have not received any news from me and that Padre *ṣāḥib* is coming here. I did not have time to write letters. You have also not written for quite some time and therefore I have also been quite negligent. When Padre ṣāḥib arrives here I will write to you the details. 8 Muḥarram.

Folio 235a. To Mir Sulaiman Khan.

I have obtained a *parwāna* for the payment of Rs 17,000. Of these Rs 10,000 are for the clothes I owe to you and Rs 7000 are for the elephants which the Nawab has bought from you. The *parwāna* is in the name of Basti Ram, *faujdār* of Awadh. I have sent Shaikh Baha-ud-Din with this *parwāna* to collect the money. My *harkāras* are also accompanying him. Rest assured that the money along with the interest will reach you. Keep me informed of your welfare until we meet. 9 Muḥarram, Sunday.

Folio 235b. To Muhammad Murid Khan.

I received your letter and noted with delight that you have taken the trouble of meeting my son. You should not remind me about your *jāgīr.* My dear, these matters do not get resolved by reminders. I remember everything and also how to resolve it. But the resolution of everthing is pre-destined. When the time comes it will be done. 10 Muḥarram, Monday, '*ashra* of the 2 *imāms.*

Folio 236a. To Mehrchand (the painter).

I am sending you sixty-eight paintings. Do as I instruct you. On twenty-three of these is embossed my signature and seal. Complete these with your own hand and keep them safely. Forty-three others have the letter *muṣawwir-i-duwwum* [second painter]. Get them completed by Dulichand. Keep the two on which I have written *nākāra* [useless] separately. Get them ready at an early date. If at the moment you are doing some other paintings attend to them when you get free. Write to me which paintings you are working on and how much work the *naqqāsh* [decorator] has done. Keep these paintings safely and write back in detail. Twenty-three of these sixty-eight paintings with my seal to be done by Mehrchand; fourty-three bearing the word *muṣawwir-i-duwwum* [second painter] to be done by Dulichand; two with the word *nākāra* are useless. 10 Muḥarram, Monday.

Folio 236b. To Raja Nawal Singh.

I received your letter. You have written that during my stay in Akbarabad [Agra] I could have tried to do something regarding your work. But things could not be done because of the mischief of some unfaithful people. Infact, I did my best to get your work done and had expected that things would be accomplished but you were indifferent. I was therefore helpless. Now that you have written again and have also come to know of the situation from Don Pedro, I hope that there will be no negligence in achieving your purpose. You will know the details from the letter of Don Pedro. 11 Muḥarram.

Folio 237a. To Khiradmand Khan Don Pedro.
I have received a letter from Nawal Singh. It says that I should ask you to write to him a letter on the lines that we had agreed upon. 11 Muḥarram.

Folio 237a. To Nawab Amir-ud-Daula Farzand Khan Bahadur Muzaffar Jang.
I received your letter and noted that Mihrban Khan has reached there with the papers (*kharīṭas*) of Colonel Muir and the Nawab, and that contrary to your expectations, the Nawab's letter, on his [Mihrban Khan's] intervention, is regarding the dispatch of Rs 2,40,000 which Hushmand Ali Khan arrived there to collect.

My dear, when Mihrban Khan took leave from the Nawab and left with the full authority (*mukhtiyār-ye-kār*) [for Farrukhabad] there was no mention of any particular amount. But after his arrival there, on the plea of some people the amount was fixed according to the writing of Mihrban Khan. Since Colonel *ṣāḥib* and I are your sincere friends we did our best and requested the Nawab to consider it. It was after our efforts that the Nawab agreed to accept the payment in instalments over two months. Later, when he realized that you have written to me regarding this, he further considered my request and agreed for the payment in four months time. I hope that now you will keep your word and make the payments because the matter involves the English people as well.

Muhammad Beg Khan will apprise you further about the matter. Hushmand Ali Khan will soon be removed. 13 Muḥarram.

Folio 238a. To son, the fortunate ṣāḥibzāda.
My dear son, I received your letter just when I was looking forward to seeing you. You write that you have not been well and that now you are better with the grace of God and the treatment of the Ḥakīm *ṣāḥib.* I am happy that you have recovered from your illness. Take care of your health and follow the advice of Ḥakīm *ṣāḥib.* Do not be careless.

I have sent Rs 25 through Manik Ram to Ram Sundar Datt for the celebration of the milk giving-up ceremony. Take this money from him and spend it on the celebration. Secondly, Manik Ram has sent

Rs 150 to Ram Sundar Datt Sarkar. Of this sum Rs 25 will be for the celebration and Rs 125 for buying a horse for Mir Buddhan. 17 Muḥarram.

Folio 238b. To Mir Buddhan.

My dear son, I received your letter and am happy to know that you are taking good care of your health. I also noted that the horse is available there and that you will buy it if I send you the money. Diwan Manik Ram is thus sending Rs 125 to Ram Sundar Datt Sarkar for the purpose. Look around for a good horse and buy it. Write to me about your welfare.

Manik Ram has sent Rs 150 to Sarkar. Take this money and spend it as I write. 17 Muḥarram.

Folio 239a. To the son.

My dear son, I received your letter and am happy to know of your welfare. I noted that you are not well and are remembering me. I reciprocate [your feelings] and remember you every night and day. I hope that by the grace of God I will meet you very soon.

I am sending a basket of pomegranate: twenty of them are *bīdāna* and ten are *dānedār*. I am sending these through the people of Mir Buddhan. Further, make it a point to go for horse riding twice [a day]. Also stroll in the garden and refrain from taking heavy, hot and gastronomic foods. Such food [items] have a bad effect. Do as the *ḥakīm* advises and take maximum possible care of your health.

I have sent the reply of the letter that I had received earlier yesterday itself–the 18th of Muḥarram. Manik Ram will send Rs 150 for the celebration of the milk-leaving ceremony and the other expenses. 19 Muḥarram.

Folio 239b. To Mir Buddhan.

My dear, I received your letter. I had written to you earlier on the 18th in response to your letter. You will receive [this letter] soon. I write again that since you require money to buy the horse, Manik Ram will send it to Ram Sundar Datt for this purpose. 19 Muḥarram.

Folio 239b. To Aqa Ali Khan.

I am fine and happy to receive your letter. I hope that you will keep in touch with me in the same way. 20 Muḥarram.

Folio 240a. To Mir Sulaiman Khan.
I received your letter. I had written to you earlier on the 9th of Muḥarram. I am sure you have received it and learnt of the situation here.

I have obtained a *parwāna,* in the name of the *faujdār* of Awadh, of Rs 17,000. Of this amount, Rs 10,000 are for the clothes which are with me, and Rs 7,000 is the price of the two elephants which the Nawab brought from you. I have handed over the *parwāna* to Shaikh Baha-ud-Din and sent him there to collect the money. I hear that the money has been received and will reach you soon. Rest assured that I am your sincere friend and need your consideration. You will know the rest from the letter of Niyaz Ali Khan.

Following the death of the Nawab there has been some delay in sending you the money. [But] now you will not have this problem. I wanted to send you the money through *hundī.* But Niyaz Ali Khan told me that you need the money to pay Lutf Ali Khan for the clothes, etc. As soon as Shaikh Baha-ud-Din comes back, the money will be paid in full with the interest. 20 Muḥarram, Mahdighat.

Folio 241a. To Raja Lalit Sah, zamindar of Srinagar (Garhwal).
I have come to know of the fine qualities of your Excellency. Nothing is dearer than friendship and I am writing to you as a mark of my sincere overtures. In keeping with the norms of friendship and customs of this world, I am sending you five *thāns* of Chinese cloth and some medicines to enhance your vigour and vitality (*muqa'vī-o-mubahhī*). Also enclosed is the gift of some essence of *darchīnī* which is not available in your territory.

Raja Ratan Singh will tell you the details about the medicine—these are incomparable for the purpose of vitality (*quwwat-i- bāh*). I require somethings here and I have given Ratan Singh the list for these [items]. I hope you will instruct your officials to arrange these as he wishes. I will perceive this as a caring gesture which will strengthen our relationship. Please do not hesitate to write to me whatever you require from this area. I will be happy if you keep me informed of your welfare.

I have also given Rs 6000 at the moment to Ratan Singh to buy something there. If this money is sufficient then its fine. But if more money is required then please arrange it and send reliable people with Ratan Singh so that I can send back your [additional contribution] through them.

1. Musk deer
2. Sheep for making fur
3. Sura cow
4. Some [hill] gift birds.
5. Two slave boys 8–9 years old
6. Ten slave girls 11–12 years old.

23 Muḥarram 1189.

Folio 242a. To Farzand Khan Muzaffar Jang.

Received your letter. Rupees one lac and six thousand have been fixed as *tankhwāh* from your territory and I have sent Manik Ram and Husain Ata to you who will tell you things I can't write about.

You must be aware that I had made efforts to remove Hushmand Ali Khan who had been misled by some people. I have already dispatched the *shuqqa* of the Nawab with Muhammad Beg Khan. You must have received it. You should respect our sincerity and not be lax in the payment of the money at an early date. This will be good for you. The *qaulnāma* that you had sent me earlier has been brought to my notice and to that of Colonel *ṣāḥib.* 23 Muḥarram.

Folio 242b. To Saiyid Murtaza Khan.

Received your letter. I have noted that you want that if Saiyid Ali Khan has not left he should be sent to you.

My dear, I had intended to send him to Delhi but he will have to now stay here for five to six days for his own work. He will leave as soon as he is free. 23 Muḥarram, Sunday, Mahdighat.

Folio 243a. To Mihrban Khan.

In every case your suggestions have been acted upon. In addition, the order for the removal of Hushmand Khan has also been sent. Now Manik Ram and Husain Ata Khan have been sent. You should collect and hand over the money to Manik Ram without any further delay. Manik Ram should leave and not stay there beyond five days for everything here depends upon him. If, God forbid, anything is done contrary to what I am writing it will not be good for you. 24 Muḥarram, Monday, Mahdighat, sent with Dīwānjio to Farrukhabad.

Folio 243b. To Mir Muhammad Husain Ata Khan.

I received a letter from Najaf Khan [who is in] Delhi. It is clear from this letter that he is still unwilling to send me the money. You know about the letter that I had sent him earlier—I am sending it [to you] through a *harkāra.* Read the letter and send its reply to me. I will send it to Najaf Khan through Niyaz Ali Khan. 24 Muḥarram, written in the night, sent in the morning from Mahdighat to Farrukhabad.

Folio 244a. To Diwan Manik Ram.

I received your letter and noted that you will be reaching Farrukhabad in two days time. At the time of your departure I had insisted that you reach Farrukhabad in a day's time and not halt on the way. I am surprised that you are contravening my orders.

Enquire about the developments in Farrukhabad when you reach there and write to me. I know from the enclosed letter of Mihrban Khan that Muhammad Beg Khan had been sent twice but both times he came back empty handed. I will not do anything unless he reaches Farrukhabad. Investigate into the matter and write to me. I am extremely angry over the way Mihrban Khan has done the work. 25 Muḥarram, Tuesday, Mahdighat.

Folio 244a. To Mir Muhammad Husain Ata Khan.

Find out the situation on your arrival at Farrukhabad and write to me the details. I am not going to do anything here. The letter which Mihrban Khan had written to Manik Ram has now reached me. It is strange that despite all my efforts, in accordance with his suggestions, he writes that nothing has been done so far and that Muhammad Beg Khan came back empty handed. I am totaly disgusted. Now that you have reached there write to me so that I can do something to make up for the loss. 25 Muḥarram, Tuesday, Mahdighat.

*Folio 244b. To the wife.**

I received your letter and noted that you are in difficulty because you are not getting your routine monthly allowance for your additional expenses.

I do not understand why you are complaining because you are receiving a sum of Rs 16 fixed for you. Money for the clothes will also be arranged. I have written to La'l Khan about your complaint of not receiving milk. I have given him strict instructions to supply you the milk regularly. Fruits are also being sent to you as soon as someone goes that side.

*For this letter as well as for the following one the text does not mention the names of the addressees.

I do not know what is the state [of preparation] of dance and music there these days. What are the kind of songs and dance being taught? This is your responsibility and you should take care of this and write. 25 Muḥarram.

Folio 245a. To La'l Khan.

I received your letter (*'arẓī*) and noted your demand for clothes for the female apartments (*andrūn*). Write to me the details of whatever you want so that the arrangement is made accordingly.

I learnt from the letter of Sa'id Begum that the milk is not being arranged for the female apartments. Despite an abundance of milk there why is it so? You must see to it that it is made available to everybody for the purpose of drinking as well as for food preparation. I should not receive complaints any more.

Lastly, you have not written anything about the practice of song and dance [being done] by the singers: how much have they already done and how much of it remains. It is your responsibility to see to that they do their work. 25 Muḥarram.

Folio 245b. To Khiradmand Khan Don Pedro.

Received your letter. You have asked about the price of the dictionary [lit. book which I have sent to you] for English–Persian translation. I had bought this book from an Englishman (*ṣāḥib*) and sent it to you when I discovered that you require it. The word price does not exist in the world of friendship. It will be my pleasure if you like it. 26 Muḥarram.

Folio 246a. To Diwan Manik Ram.

I received your letter today, the 25th of Muḥarram, and noted its contents: your meeting with Nawab Muzaffar Jang, the postponement of the queries regarding the payment, the difficulties of the soldiers there because of the non-payment of the *tan<u>kh</u>wāh* of Cholier, and the requirement of the *shuqqa* from the Nawab regarding this matter.

My dear, I am not concerned with the problems of each and every case. How can I make any effort for the cases of others when my own money assigned on Nawab Muzaffar Jang [in his territory] has not yet been paid. I have done so much for Mihrban Khan but I am now angry with him. The money has now been fixed at 1,60,000 and no work has been done.

I have also told you about the four blinds (*chiqs*) the size of which you know. Send these soon. 27 Muḥarram, Thursday, Mahdighat.

Folio 246b. To Mir Muhammad Husain Ata Khan.

I received Manik Ram's letter regarding his meeting with Nawab Muzaffar Jang and the postponement of the matter regarding the *tankhwāh* of Cholier. My dear, is it necessary that for everybody's case I have to approach the Nawab *ṣāḥib*? My own *tankhwāh* has been fixed in Farrukhabad on Nawab Muzaffar Jang. As for the payment of this money, this is still the first day. Why should I do things for others? I have done so much for Mihrban Khan but he has not done anything for me. I am very angry. 27 Muḥarram, Thursday, Mahdighat.

Folio 246b. To Mir Muhammad Husain Ata Khan.

I received a number of letters from you concerning the details of your journey and meeting with Muzaffar Jang. But it has been four to five days since you left for Farrukhabad and the third day since you met the Nawab and you have not written anything regarding the payment of money. I am concerned. Please write to me the situation. 28 Muḥarram, Friday, Mahdighat.

Folio 247a. To Diwan Manik Ram.

I received several letters from you regarding your meeting with Muzaffar Jung. It has been four to five days since you arrived there [Farrukhabad] and met the Nawab but you have not written to me anything about the payment. I am worried. Find out the exact situation and write to me.

In the meantime I have received *dārchīnī* and *monga.* Write to me if you want these things so that I can send them to you. 25 Muḥarram, Mahdighat.

Folio 247b. To Jugal Kishor.

I received your letter and noted that you had earlier sent me two letters to which you say I have not replied. My dear, the delay can be because of the negligence of the *munshī.* Besides, I did not write because I did not think that a prompt response was necessary. You also write that you have a sincere relationship with me and do not harbour any avarice. I had never alleged any such thing. Keep writing to me and do as I instruct. Do not let useless ideas enter your heart. I have sent you for my work—be rest assured and do it. Keep sending me the exact news of the developments there. 28 Muḥarram, Mahdighat.

Folio 248a. To Manik Ram.

I received two of your letters dated the 27th and the 28th today—the 29th. My dear, I know that whatever is transpiring there is contrary to reality and there is no truth in it. I am extremely disgusted. There is no reasonable settlement about the payment that is due on Nawab Muzaffar Jang for me, as also of the money pertaining to Mihrban Khan. Every thing has been postponed and you still bring up useless matters relating to others about which I do not even wish to hear.

I hear that Mihrban Khan, using my name and that of Colonel *ṣāḥib*, is perpetrating atrocities there. Why is he abusing our names and bringing us disrepute for his own interest. I am distressed at this foolishness. It is now best that you come here so that I know the details of the situation from you. Leave Mir Husain Ata Khan behind on the condition that he will do something reasonable to carry out the task. But if that is not possible then there is no point in leaving him there. In case you fear neither of you will achieve anything, it is best that you all come here. But in case you fear that nothing can be achieved inspite of all our efforts, none of my people there should know [of my apprehended failure]. I will return my papers to the Nawab after you come back.

When Muhammad Beg, the *vakīl* of Mihrban Khan, had come here he had said that there was an album of paintings which he had forgotten to bring. When he came from there the second time he said that he had given most of the paintings for repair and would send them soon. Now I discover from your letter that apart from some unimpressive paintings there was neither any album nor any significant painting there in Farrukhabad. As the proverbial saying goes one can evaluate the quality of a thing from just a small sample of it (*musht-i namūna az-kharwāre*). It is now absolutely clear that everything there including the money and the words of people there are false. 1 Ṣafar-ul-Muẓaffar.

Folio 249a. To Mir Muhammad Husain Ata Khan.

I received your letters of the 27th and the 28th. My dear, I had known it for certain that all this is to mislead. There is no sincerity and truth in any negotiation and I am extremely disgusted. Nothing has been settled about the payment of my *tankhwāh* due from Nawab Muzaffar Jang, or even the payment of the *tankhwāh* of Mihrban Khan. I only hear of this or that dispute and my own case is brushed aside. I have also heard that Mihrban Khan is misusing my name and that of the

Colonel, and has been committing excesses on the people there. What is this? Why is he maligning the name of the Europeans (*angrez*)? I am distressed at this canard. You can stay there for sometime if there is any chance of achieving this task [i.e.settlement of pay]. But send Manik Ram here so that I know the details from him. But if there is no hope then there is no use of your people staying there any longer. See to it that when you leave none of my people stay there any longer. I will return the papers of my salary to you on my return. 1 Ṣafar ul-Muẓaffar, Mahdighat.

Folio 249b. To Mir Muhammad Husain Ata Khan.
Received your letter of the 29th of Muḥarram today on the 1st of Ṣafar. I noted whatever you have written about the activities of Jugal Kishor. I am happy about your style of functioning, your shrewdness and your cautiousness. In this matter also do whatever you feel is appropriate and reasonable. I have also written a letter to Jugal Kishor which is enclosed in this letter. Forward this to him if you feel it is appropriate.

Folio 250a. To Jugal Kishor.
Many of the works here are pending. You should therefore come over here along with Manik Ram. 1 Ṣafar, Sunday, Mahdighat.

Folio 250b. To Manik Ram.
I am yet to receive the blinds about which I had written to you about a month back. I am astonished that you are taking so much time for this ordinary work. Send three to four blinds without any further delay. There is a lot of problem here because of the flies. 1 Ṣafar, Sunday, Mahdighat.

Folio 250b. To Manik Ram.
I received your letter of 1 Ṣafar. I consider you one of my dependables and have full faith in your concern for my work. I am confident that whatever you propose for the completion of my work would be acceptable. Do whatever you think is best.

I have sent you four garlands with 404 pieces of *monga* [coral] in response to your earlier request for specimens of the same. If you require more I will send it to you.

I note that the album of paintings has been sent to Delhi for repairs. Thus they have not arrived here. I have repeatedly written to you about the blinds which you have still not sent. I urge upon you to send them soon. 3 Ṣafar, Tuesday, three *kos* away from Mahdighat on the banks of the Ganges.

Folio 251a. To Mir Muhammad Husain Ata Khan.

I received your letter of 1 Ṣafar today on Tuesday the 3rd. I noted your effort and hard work for my work there. I have full faith in you and write to you to do whatever is good for me. You have full authority there (*mukhtār-i-mutlaq*). Do whatever you feel is appropriate for the time. It is not necessary for you to write to me. I know that you are sincerely devoted to my work. 3 Ṣafar, Tuesday, the day of departure three *kos* from Mahdighat on the Ganges.

Folio 251b. To Manik Ram.

I had written earlier to Jugal Kishor and then three or four times to you [about the blinds]. Why have you not sent them yet? Is it because of their unavailability that despite strict instructions you are unable to send them. I am distressed. There is so much delay and negligence for such a trivial matter. You did not even bother to reply to me. The moment you receive this letter dispatch four to five blinds. 4 Ṣafar, Wednesday, the *ghat* facing Kannauj.

Folio 251b. To Majd-ud-Daula Farzand Khan Bahadur Bahram Jang.

I received your letter. Only God knows the extent of my friendship and sincerity towards you. I do not have words to express it [sincerity] and hope that it will increase every day and that we will meet soon.

I am an old and sincere devotee (*'ubūdiyat-i qadīm*) of the Emperor and eager to strengthen the edifice of the state in a manner that his dictate is followed and the world is graced with his justice and favours. I brought your letter to the notice of the Nawab. With the grace of God he is ready to serve the state and augment his [Emperor's] power. He also appreciates your sincerity. The negotiation regarding things related to him is entrusted to you and no one is allowed to interfere. Try to achieve the aim of the Nawab devotedly. Anything can be achieved [if we work] in collaboration with each other. If we work in tandem with each other we can restore the power of the state.

I have obtained and dispatched to you an *'arẓdāsht,* addressed to the Emperor, from the Nawab and a cordial letter in your name. Murtaza Khan has gone to Faizabad for some work. He will be sent to the court when he comes back. Niyaz Ali Khan is also reaching you.

The Emperor's mind will be known when they reach there. Consider me your sincere friend and keep in touch. Get a reply for my '*arẓdāsht* from the Emperor. 5 Ṣafar, Thursday, on the bank of the Ganges, six miles before Kannauj on the way to Delhi.

Folio 253a. 'Arẓdāsht to the Emperor.

With due respect and all sincerity, this servant desires to be of service for the purpose of strengthening the edifice of the state and extending your bounties and justice to the entire universe.

I have brought Majd-ud-Daula's letter to the notice of Nawab Asaf-ud-Daula. God willing, he will always try to please you as he is firm in his resolve to serve you. Since this will result in the good of the state it is hoped that he who is a *k͟hānazād** is honoured with your favours. 5 Ṣafar, Thursday, on the bank of the Ganges, six miles from Kannauj.

Folio 254a. To the son.

My dear son I am very happy to receive your letter. I note that you have received the pomegranates that I had sent to you earlier. More will be sent subsequently—rest assured and be happy. You write that you have received Rs 25 to meet the expenses for the giving up of the milk-drinking ceremony, but that there is no money left to tip the foster *āyah.* You have asked for some more money. My dear son, manage everything [all expenses] within this budget. When I reach there and see you I will make her [*āyah*] happy with gifts of cash and clothes. 2 Ṣafar, Saturday.

Folio 254b. To the son. **

My dear son, I received your letter and noted that you have received Rs 150 which includes the price of the horse. Look around for a nice horse, buy it and inform me. Keep in touch. 7 Ṣafar, Saturday, same place.

Folio 254b. To Sawai Maharaja Ghuman Singh.

I am happy to receive two of your letters. You write that I should know the degree of your sincerity from Niyaz Ali Khan and Shaikh Muhammad Taqi. My dear, I am already convinced about your friendship from the letter and it is not dependant on their statements.

*Lit. born in the house, for generations in service. Here Polier used this expression to emphasize his close links with the Mughals.

**The text does not mention the name of the addressee.

I am busy here doing whatever is good for you. But it is important that I should know what you want. Keep in touch. 11 Ṣafar.

Folio 255a. To Najaf Khan.

I received your letter (*mihrbānī nāma*) together with the papers with signatures of the Emperor and ten seals [in connection with the titles of the English officials], big and small. You write that when you arrive in Akbarabad you will arrange the money that you owe me. My dear, it is not difficult for you to arrange this small amount of money. I have written to you several times and you have resorted to cooking up excuses. This was not expected of you. Pursuance is not advisable in money matters and I have tried in my own way—keeping in mind our friendship—the best possible means. But I do not think you wish to be friends. I fail to figure out the difference between Akbarabad and Shahjahanabad in this case. If you [really] want to pay then you can do it from whichever place you like. Your order is operative from anywhere and a small note with your signature will suffice for the payment to be made in Akbarabad. Your arrival in the city is not necessary. If your authority is such that you can only pay when you reach Akbarabad [personally], then I am afraid the payment will never be made. I know that each time I write [to you] it is about money—so a similar [letter] is being sent through a *harkāra*. Arrange the money with interest and send the *hundī* so that our fiendship remains firm. 11 Ṣafar, sent through a *harkāra* who had come from Najaf Khan in the night time.

Folio 256a. To Nawab Amir-ud-Daula Farzand Khan Muzaffar Jang.

I received your letter and noted that your income is less than your expenditure and that there are disputes regarding money matters. I had already heard about your problems from Manik Ram and Mir Muhammad Husain Ata Khan. I feel worried because these are matteres of concern for you. But as you know all matters are pre-destined in terms of time. I am sure that when the [right] time comes God will help you and the problem will be solved. As your sincere friend I am writing whatever is good for you. I suggest that you come here and meet the Nawab. I am sure that once you meet him the matter will be resolved amicably. 13 Ṣafar, Friday.

Folio 256b. To Mehrchand, the painter.

Received your letter and noted that you have received the sixty-eight paintings that I had sent you earlier. I am now sending ninety-six more paintings. Forty-two of them are of the first order (*awwal*) and forty-one of the second category (*duwum*) while thirteen are useless (*nakara*). The grading has been indicated at the back of each painting. Keep the useless ones separately and complete the remaining eighty-three paintings as follows: Call the binder (*ṣaḥḥāf*) and ask him to prepare three albums for them according to their different size—big, medium and small. In the first place an excellent artistic touch should be given to the parchment paper on the paste board (*pushta-i wasliha*). Then note down the name of the person at the back of each portrait on a separate piece of paper, to be [finally] written on the paste-board. Take care that in the process of the preparation of the paste-board the identities [of these portraits] are not lost.

There is no need for separate paste-boards for those paintings which are sketched in black and white. Keep them safely and when I reach there I will fix these black and white paintings on the reverse side (*pusht*) of the other paintings. Get the paste-boards for the first and the second categories of the paintings that I had sent you earlier prepared in the same manner as for these eighty-three paintings, bound in three—big, medium and small—size albums. Take maximum possible care. 14 Ṣafar, Saturday.

Folio 257b. To Mehrchand (the painter).

I hope you have followed the instructions regarding the ninety-six paintings that I sent to you yesterday, the 14th of Ṣafar. I repeat that get the paste-boards prepared by the binder according to the size of the paintings and that these boards should be three sizes: big, medium and small to suit the three different size albums. The decorator should decorate these boards, repair (*marammat*) and give touches in such a manner that after they are bound each one fully adjusts with the original and does not appear to be prepared separately [from the paintings] (*barang-o- ṭirāz aṣlī hamrang gardad wa sākhtagīha ma'lūm nashawad*). When I reach there I will inspect them. Do this in a manner that brings delight to me and you are rewarded. Take care that nobody has access to them. Keep them safe from dust and flies. 15 Ṣafar.

Folio 258a. To the mother of the Nawab Muzaffar Jang.

I always desire that the works of both Asaf-ud-Daula and Muzaffar Jang are done appropriately and I keep striving for this. The case of the former's claim over the latter has been brought here to the notice of the Nawab [Asaf-ud-Daula]. But everything now depends on Muzaffar Jang's arrival here and his meeting with Asaf-ud-Daula. He should come here and meet the Nawab soon. This will cement the bond of friendship between the two and everything will then be done satisfactorily. 18 Ṣafar, around Mahdighat, Thursday.

Folio 258b. To Shaista Khan. Afghan.

I received your letter and noted the case of your *jāgīr* which is in the control of Murtaza Khan. I will report the matter to Nawab Muzafar Jang who is expected to be here within two or three days. I have kept the two baskets of almonds and pistas and am sending back the garlands of pearl. 20 Ṣafar, near Mahdighat.

Folio 258b. To Majd-ud-Daula Farzand Khan.

Since your friendship with Nawab Asaf-ud-Daula is established, consider me [also] as your true friend. There is no difference any longer between you and me. I am sure that all my matters assigned to you will be carried out satisfactorily. It is inevitable that I leave for Calcutta. I will join the Nawab's camp in about two months time.

I am leaving all my goods and people here with Manik Ram and Mir Muhammad Husain Ata Khan who will act in consultation with Murtaza Khan. Please do whatever you consider proper regarding the matters of Nawab Asaf-ud-Daula. They will present the matter to the Nawab and write back to you.

The Nawab as well as Saiyid Murtaza Khan had appointed Niyaz Ali Khan to report to you the details of the matter here. [You] take these details as though you are being reported about them directly by me. Write to me whatever else you require. The things you have ordered have now arrived from Faizabad and will be sent to you by Niyaz Ali Khan. Opium has been sent for from Azimabad. If it arrives here before he leaves it will be sent, otherwise it will be sent later. 21 Ṣafar, Tuesday, in the camp of the Nawab, written in the afternoon, dispatched in the night.

Folio 260a. To Sawai Maharaja Guman Singh.

I received your letter. As I am your sincere friend I consider your work as my own. There will be no negligence in it. I am leaving for Calcutta for some urgent work and have assigned your work to Manik Ram, Niyaz Ali and Mir Muhammad Husain Ata Khan who are all here to look after my business (*kār-o-bār*). I will also be back in a period of two months. God willing whatever is best for you will be done. You will know the rest from the letter of Shaikh Muhammad Taqi. 24 Ṣafar, Tuesday, the camp of the Nawab.

Folio 260a. To Najaf Khan.

I had to leave for Calcutta on the 24th of Ṣafar for some important [work]. I left behind Manik Ram and Mir Muhammad Husain Ata Khan to take care of my work in the Nawab's camp. I hope to be free from my work in Calcutta and be back in two months time.

I have sent Niyaz Ali Khan to you to collect my money. You have already postponed its payment for long. I hope that now as soon as you receive this letter you will arrange for the payment so that our relations continue to remain cordial. I do not want our relations to be strained on [account of]this petty matter. 24 Ṣafar, Tuesday, the camp of the Nawab.

Folio 261a. To Manik Ram.

I am redirecting to you a cartload of dry fruits, etc which has arrived from Faizabad. Also enclosed are three other boxes, eight cartons and one roll of Chinese cloth. Hand over one big box of dry fruits to Colenel Gils. The other two boxes and the roll of Chinese cloth, which is wrapped in jute, belong to us. Keep them safely for sale. Seven of the eight cartons are empty. One of them contains the *zīn* [saddle] and a copper kettle for boiling water. These are to be handed over to Mr Bristow.

I am also sending the letter of *munshī* Chaman Lal that I received along with the elephants, through the *harkāra.* Hand over the letter to him; clear the account of the elephants and send it to me. There are no troops here to dispatch to you. Acquire them from the [contingent] of Mr Danes(?) and keep them with you. Tip the *harkāra* as per custom. Investigate about the disappearance of one of my European (*wilāyatī*) cat from the camp. Locate it and dispatch it to me. 25 Ṣafar, Wednesday, Takia.

Folio 261b. To Nawab Asaf-ud-Daula.

I have left Takia and reached Mohan where Shah Mir Khan came to meet me. I hope you remember that I had mentioned him to you before I took your leave. He is a friend of mine and an old servant of the court. I hope that he will receive your favours. He will carry out whatever is assigned to him to the best of his ability. 26 Ṣafar, Mohan.

Folio 262a. To Manik Ram and Mir Muhammad Husain Ata Khan.

Shah Mir Khan met me on my way to Calcutta and has left for the court. I have spoken about him to the Nawab and have also written a letter to him. You are instructed to consider Shah Mir's work as my own and get it accomplished. This will give me pleasure. 26 Ṣafar, Mohan.

Folio 262a. To Saiyid Murtaza Khan.

Shah Mir Khan is close to you and I therefore hope that in view of your relations with him you will make efforts to get his work done. He is also an old friend of mine. He will meet you with the hope of getting his job done. I will be grateful to you. 26 Ṣafar, Mohan.

Folio 262b. To Manik Ram.

I am sending to you two packets of opium which arrived from Azimabad on my request. Do whatever you feel is appropriate. Send me soon the two tray covers that Dr Thomas will give you. 26 Ṣafar, Mohan.

Folio 263a. To Manik Ram and Mir Muhammad Husain Ata Khan.

A *dastak* is required by Shaikh Baha-ud-Din to carry the goods of Mir Sulaiman Khan. Obtain a *dastak*—under the seal of the Nawab—for him so that he may take the goods safely. 4 Rabīʻ I, Faizabad.

Folio 263a. To Nawab Asaf-ud-Daula.

I am now in Faizabad having travelled for six days after I took leave of you. I will stay here for three to four days for some important work. I will take the boat and proceed ahead by 5 Rabīʻ I, and continue to be in your service on reaching my destination. I will keep you informed. God willing, I will be back soon and have the honour of an audience with you. 5 Rabīʻ I, Saturday.

Folio 263b. To Manik Ram and Mir Muhammad Husain Ata Khan.

I had written to you earlier to reward Fath Khan after he cures the female elephant. I repeat that now that she has recovered you should reward him with whatever you feel is appropriate. 5 Rabīʻ I, Saturday.

Folio 264a. To Manik Ram and Mir Muhammad Husain Ata Khan (letter 1).

I received your letter today, the 4th Rabīʻ I. It has been eleven days since I left the camp and in this period I have received only one letter of yours. I had expected to hear from you regularly since I was not very far from you. I do not mind delays in communication if we are at long distance.

You will receive my letter in *angrezī* about the soldiers of Mr Danes (?). Please also note that from now on whenever you write to me you should specify the number of the letter on top. Number also the subsequent letters and continue numbering in this manner so that I know what I receive and what is lost.

I had taken 1 *man* of *bhīliya* tobacco from Makkhu Khan. I have forgotten the price he quoted. Pay him Rs 20–30 at the current price. Write in detail about the money which I had received from Nawab Muzaffar Jang and make all efforts to get it. I need it urgently here for various expenditures.

I have sent to you Fath Khan—the elephant-man—with five elephants. Give Mr Bristow two female elephants for riding. Sell the remaining three elephants—one of which belongs to Mr Middleton and two of which were earlier sick—along with the five others which are with you, a total of eight elephants, at a reasonable price. Further, sixteen more elephants have arrived in Benares and they will reach Faizabad in two to three days time. These will also be sent to you. Captain Martin will write to you about them. Sell these so that the sick ones are also disposed of along with the good ones. Sell them fast so as to prevent any loss. From the consignment of glasses, iron goods, clothes etc. that I had recently sold to the Nawab make a separate inventory for Mr Martin's goods and those of Mr Lat [from whom they had been procured]. Get the payment of Mr Martin's goods from the *maḥāls* in the neighbourhood of Faizabad and inform him. Procure the order of payment for my goods from areas which you think are safe, and try to get the collection at an early date.

The preparation of houses on the other side of the *ḥavelī* is still incomplete. That is fine, but see to it that the apartments (*makān*) meant for me are completed soon. Get the money for their completion from the *sarkār.* [of the Nawab]. The total expenditure should be presented to the Nawab and not included in my account.

I learn that Rs 18,000, the salary of Saiyidi Nasir, has been received. Hand over whatever you receive from my *tankhwāh* in Farrukhabad to

Mr Bristow. Also deliver to him whatever money is received from Mr Middleton as well as the money left from the *tankhwāh* of Saiyidi Nasir. Despite my telling you that you should hold back three per cent of the money obtained in selling my goods and five per cent from the other goods so as to pay the *mutaṣaddīs* and utilize in the *sarkār's* expenditure, you have again included the expenditure of the establishment and the *mutaṣaddīs* in my account.

Send Rs 100 through Ram Sundar Datt Sarkar to *ḥakīm* Nawab who is treating my son. I am not familiar with the customs of this country, so pay him commensurate with my position and that of the *ḥakīm ṣāḥib.* Direct Ram Sundar to pay Rs 50 to Mir Buddhan until he receives his monthly salary from the *sarkār.* See to it that in future the money for Mir Buddhan is received from the *sarkār* every month. Depute Mir Buddhan in the retinue of Mirza Ali Khan so that he gets the monthly payment from him.

Hand over Rs 3500, Captain Brooke's salary for seven months, to Mr Lloyd. When you receive the remaining salary I will write to you how to spend it. I had loaned Rs 176 to Yusuf Ali; deduct this amount from his salary when it is received. Make efforts [to obtain] his salary at an early date.

The work on the decorated headgear being prepared through Gokulchand jeweller (*jauhri*) is complete. But two *Panna* stones are required for the pendants. Buy them there and send them to me. Send to [masters] Math *ṣāḥib* Rs 1000 i.e one-third of the Rs 3000 received for the *kurtis* regularly. This will be part of the account of Mr. Bligh. The money should be sent to Benares through *hundīs* so that no loss is incurred by Math *ṣāḥib.*

Earlier I had written to you that five elephants had been sent through Fath Khan, the elephant-man. But I have come to know since that one elephant is ill and have therefore instructed that only four of them should be sent to you. The other instructions regarding them remain the same.

I had written to you earlier that Rs 3500 from the salary of Mr Brooke should be handed over to Mr Lloyd. Note that when the remaining part of Brooke's salary is received, then Rs 1000 should be given to Astrasan (?) Brooke and Rs 1000 to Mr Sangster. Thus it is necessary to send in the *hundī* of Rs 5500: Rs 3500 for Mr Lloyd and Rs 1000 each for these two gentlemen. Keep the remaining money with yourself safely. Subsequently, do as I write to you.

You had asked for some papers. I would have sent them but they are not in the boat. However, do not let the work remain pending because of their non-receipt. You know the place, do whatever is economical and sell the things. I received the two tray covers which you sent me. Prepare a list of all the goods—with details of weight and number of items—that I have for sale both in the camp as well as in Faizabad or even here. Write to me also in detail about the money that people owe me. In short, write all the details related to the money and the goods. I will keep your letter as a kind of proof (*dastāwez*).

Write also about the things which relate to the Nawab. I do not know if the money due from the court of the late Nawab has yet been received.

I have sent Munawwar Khan there with a company. Of the *asharfis* that I have brought from the court I discover that I will incur a loss because of the current rate here. I have suffered a loss of Rs 1500. I have also sent to you six chandeliers and eight glass candlestands. Hand them over to Niyaz Ali Khan so that he can take them to Delhi.

Send the emoluments of Gora Mistri and the people in the *ḥavelī* to Captain Martin so that he can pay them there. 5 Rabīʿ I, Saturday, Faizabad, day of departure.

Shuqqa enclosed in the cover of letter no. 1.The gift that you had spoken to me about and which was to arrive from Farrukhabad in fifteen days time has not yet been received here. It has now since been one month. I will be very happy if you try to get it soon.

Folio 268a. (Letter 2) To Manik Ram and Mir Muhammad Husain Ata Khan.

I received your letter of 1 Rabīʿ I on 5 Rabīʿ I. I am happy to know that the agreement (*qaulnāma*) for Nawab Muzaffar Jang has been finally confirmed and his objective achieved. It is now absolutely necessary for you to plan for the collection of the *tankhwāh* [from his territory]. Get the payment at the earliest.

Send the two-month account that you write about to Ram Sundar Datt. He will bring it to the notice of Mr Lloyd who will carry out all the work properly without causing difficulty to any one. Take whatever action is necessary regarding the letter of Raja Guman Singh. 5 Rabīʿ I, Saturday, at the time of departure from Faizabad.

Folio 268b. (Letter 3) To Manik Ram and Mir Muhammad Husain Ata Khan.

You had written earlier about the papers and the things sent to you during my journey. I have now discovered them and sent them to Mr Lloyd who will redirect them to you. Arrange their sale at an appropriate price when you receive them.

Second, I had written to you earlier about the sixteen elephants which had arrived from Benares. Of these, eight female elephants, one adult and one calf, i.e. a total of ten elephants belong to me. The remaining six belong to the other *ṣāḥibs*. Buy these elephants at a reasonable price and then sell all of them—including mine. But ensure that no loss is incurred in the sale. All these elephants are in good condition. But some of the seven elephants, about which I had written to you earlier, are in bad shape. Do whatever you think is best and economical for my establishment.

Third, I had written to you earlier that Rs 18,000 from the salary of Saiyidi Nasir be handed over to Mr Bristow. Now this money should be given to Bakhshi Peppan *ṣāḥib* and a receipt obtained from him. The remaining money may be passed on to Mr Bristow. I have written about this to Bakhshi Peppan *ṣāḥib*.

Fourth, assure Emmanuel *firangi*, who is escorting the sixteen elephants, that when he reaches there safely with all the elephants in good condition, he will be suitably rewarded. I will take care of him.

Fifth, I have received from Dr Hunter an account of the price of seven elephants which had reached there earlier. I have dispatched this account to Mr Lloyd who will redirect it to you. I do not think the account is correct. Compare it with the *dārogha* and the *harkāra*, find out the expense involved in the escort and send the exact account to Dr Hunter. If there are still dues on me and if the *dārogha* there is not in a position to make the payments then the matter will be settled with Dr Hunter in Azimabad.

Sixth, I repeat that prepare a detailed account of whatever money people owe me and send it to me so that I know how much money is to be collected [and from whom]. Do not show any negligence in this matter. There should not be an error of even a single penny [in your account].

Seventh, of the sixteen elephants one is young. Hold back this or some other big elephant which is good for riding so that I can sell it at a good price whenever I like.

Eighth, I left Faizabad on 6 Rabī‘ I. When I reached Azimabad on the 14th of this month I received a letter regarding the commotion in the Najib *paltan* on the issue of their emoluments, and a request for a letter to Asaf-ud-Daula for their payment. I have accordingly enclosed with this letter a letter for the Nawab *ṣāḥib.* I am also attaching a copy of it. Present it to the Nawab *ṣāḥib* and obtain his reply to this letter as well as to the one I wrote earlier and send them to me.

Ninth, send the detailed draft for works related to the Nawab's, court to me so that I can prepare the letters accordingly.

Tenth, I had written to you earlier about receiving orders for the payment of the arrears of the monthly emoluments of Mr Lacos. I had also said that the estimate of his salary should be included in those for the *paltan* of Chevalier *ṣāḥib.* You have not yet written anything about it. Write in detail and note that Mr Lacos took leave from the deceased Nawab and now he is back.

Eleven, I learn from your letter that Mir Muhammad Husain Ata Khan has been deputed by the Nawab to go to Farrukhabad to collect the money. Nothing can be done since this was inevitable. But I want both of you to remain together so as to carry out my work there. In the event of his departure [to Farrukhabad] attend to the work there more vigilantly. 15 Rabī' I, Tuesday, Azimabad.

Folio 270b. To Nawab Asaf-ud-Daula.

I have been thinking about you and remembering your favours from the day I took leave of you and left for this place. The desire to serve you is reinforced. God willing I will be safely back and have the honour of an audience with you. May God give you success.

I left Faizabad on 6 Rabī' I and travelled by boat for nine days, reaching here on the 14th. Since the boats have to be changed, I am staying here for two or three days after which I will resume [the journey] for my destination. I have not yet received your reply to the letter (*'arīẓa*) I sent you before my departure for Faizabad. I hope that I will be favoured by your reply.

I also submit to you to order that the estimates of the salaries of the English officials, which have now been signed, be forwarded to the artillery [department]. As for my salary, it seems improper to request for it since I am indebted to you. At any rate, considering your favours to me, I have asked Manik Ram and Mir Muhammad Husain Ata Khan to approach you with the request of payment of my emoluments as well as that of others. I hope that you will issue orders accordingly.

I did not consider it necessary to bring along Mirza Yusuf Ali. He has therefore been left behind in Faizabad to look after my work there. I hope that you will issue orders for his salary as well. 15 Rabī' I, Tuesday, Azimabad, Dutch (Wollandez) *kothī.*

Folio 270b. To Najaf Khan.

I am delighted to receive your letter. In view of our friendship, from the day I left I have been thinking of meeting you again. God willing, I will soon be free from my work here and return to have the pleasure of seeing you. The things you had ordered for in your letter have been acquired. I consider your work as my own and do my best to carry it out. 15 Rabī' I, Tuesday, Azimabad.

Folio 272a. (Letter 4) To Manik Ram and Mir Muhammad Husain Ata Khan.

I received on the 17th in Azimabad two of your letters of 7 Rabī' I, along with the *shuqqa* from the royal court and the letter from Majd-ud-Daula, as well as a letter from Niyaz Ali Khan. I came to know the details of the developments there. You have written that Mir Muhammad Husain Ata Khan has been deputed to proceed to Farrukhabad along with Nawab Muzaffar Jang to collect the money.

As for the request for the company of troopers, before my departure for Faizabad I had deputed Munawwar Khan on the company. Ask Mir Muhammad Husain Ata Khan to take this company along.

Regarding the payment of the salary of Mr Lacos, whatever is collected is to be handed over to Mr Martin. I had instructed you earlier on this matter. Act accordingly.

I note that the departure of Nawab Muzaffar Jang has been delayed because of some problems with European officials regarding the support to Beni Ram. My dear, I could write to these officials but the case of Nawab Muzaffar Jang has been finalized directly with Nawab Asaf-ud-Daula. I do not think that you or he require any one's help. You have full powers there to do the needful.

I noted that you have obtained assurances for the early payment of my money [but] make plans for its early realization.

As for the elephants, there is no harm as long as four or five are concerned; but make sure that there is no problem in the future.

You will receive a precious stone from Mr Martin; hand it to the engraver according to the instructions enclosed with the paper. If you receive letters addressed to me which you feel need to be replied, prepare a draft of the reply and send it. I will reply [accordingly]. 18 Rabī' I, Friday. After having departed from Azimabad.

Shuqqa enclosed with this letter.

The Nawab has fixed Rs 3000 per month for me. Most of the other European officials get the same salary. You are expected to do something for the raise—in whatever manner you think appropriate—since this amount is not commensurate with my position. 18 Rabīʿ I.

Folio 273a. To Munawwar Khan, ṣūbadar.

In order to carry out the work of the company in Farrukhabad, Mir Muhammad Husain Ata Khan needs troopers. You are therefore deputed with him. Act as per his instructions. 18 Rabīʿ I, Friday.

Folio 273b. (Letter 5) To Manik Ram and Mir Muhammad Husain Ata Khan.

It is the eighth day since I left Azimabad. But the wind is against the current and we thus covered the distance [only] upto Pehti Bhetti. The delay is because of the adverse wind direction.

Arrange the preparation of a Hindustanī *k͟hilʿat* similar to the one I sent for Bararad *ṣāḥib*, also one Irani dress made of bright coloured *kimk͟hwāb* (brocade) akin to the one I had got made for myself earlier; and socks and a gold thread cap (*kulāh*). The price of the Hindustani *k͟hilʿat* along with the turban and the accessories should be around Rs 500 to 550. It should be of Mr Lloyd's size; the length should be two *girah* less than that of Mr Lloyd's size but in width it should be of the same size. Get these ready and keep them with you. I will inspect them when I come and tell you what is to be done.

If *rūmāl-i-shawl* [handkerchief] are available procure four or five white ones and keep them with you.

If you have not yet sold the jewel for the turban and the pearl necklace which I had given you before I left, keep them with you. But it is fine if they are sold.

If you find good Indian guns purchase two to three for me and keep them.

If Padre Wendel *ṣāḥib* needs money and asks you for it you can give him upto Rs 1000 in cash. If he requests for money at the time of departure to Akbarabad, pay him in *hundī.*

Prepare the accounts upto the day of my departure and hand it to Mr Lloyd so that he can pass them on to me. Follow my instructions regarding the other matters; write to me so that I know the progress of the work there.

I have written to you earlier about the gift from Farrukhabad. I again remind you [about the same]. I was told in the camp that it will arrive in ten to twelve days. I have not heard anything about it yet, even though it has been a month since I left the army and its camp. I wonder what the reason [for the delay] is. Write to me soon.

Six months ago I had ordered two *thāns* of silver coloured Benarsi *tāsh*, with flower motifs, and had given you a specimen as well. You have neither sent it nor responded. Send it quickly.

I have repeatedly asked you to procure and send to Calcutta Tanda cloth worth Rs10,000–12,000. There has been no investigation regarding this [on your part]. You should collect the necessary information before my return. I will inspect the same and buy it when I reach there. But remember that the cloth should be of big width and the price should be between Rs four to five per *thān*.

You have not written anything about the developments there. Write to me without delay about Najaf Khan, Elich Khan, the imperial court and the Nawab's camp.

If you feel that Niyaz Ali Khan will take some time to leave for Shahjahanabad then send him to Farrukhabad for the collection of my money. Since Shahjahanabad is close to Farrukhabad he can go there whenever he desires. 25 Rabī' I, Friday, place Pahti Bheti and Ganga Prashad.

Folio 275b. To Mir Muhammad Husain Ata Khan.

I have written to Niyaz Ali Khan that if his departure for Shahjahanabad is delayed for the moment he should go and collect my money from Farrukhabad. He may leave for Shahjahanabad from there at an appropriate time. I do not want you to be separated from Manik Ram even for a moment. You should be there to carry out my work. A lot of money needs to be collected from different people there. I am very concerned and anxious because no account has been prepared yet. Since you are an intelligent and mature person it is important for you to stay there. Send the progress of the work there secretly to Dr Thomas who will pass it on to me. If Niyaz Ali Khan has to leave for Shahjahanabad then do whatever is appropriate for the collection of money from Farrukhabad. 25 Rabī' I, Ganga Prashad station (*manzil*).

Folio 276a. To Niyaz Ali Khan.

I received your letter and noted that your departure for Shahjahanabad has been delayed. I had thought that your going there would help expedite my work. But there is no harm if for the moment this is not possible. Go there whenever it is appropriate. But if there is too much delay then please leave for Farrukhabad and from there you can proceed to Shahjahanabad. Enclosed is a letter in the name of Mir Muhammad Husain Ata Khan. Hand it over to him secretly so that he can act accordingly. Keep me informed. 25 Rabī' I, Friday, Ganga Prashad *manzil.*

Folio 276a. (Letter 6) To Manik Ram and Mir Muhammad Husain Ata Khan (from Calcutta).

I received two of your letters earlier—one of the 3rd Rabī' I on the 14th and the second of 7th Rabī' I on the 17th. I sent my reply on the 18th—the day of my departure from there. I reached Calcutta on Wednesday, the 8th of Rabī' II. Till date, i.e. 11th of this month, I have not heard from you. It has been a month and a few days since I received your last letter. I am both surprised and unhappy at this negligence in sending letters. How will I know the progress of the work there if you do not write to me. I have repeatedly written to you to send letters to Captain Martin or, in his absence from Faizabad, to Dr Thomas and Dr Fulman [both of] whom you know well. They will send the letters from there to me.

Second, Nawab Asaf-ud-Daula has written to Najaf Khan regarding the case of my money. But you have not written to me whether Najaf Khan has replied or not. Write in detail about this.

Third, Nawab Asaf-ud-Daula had agreed to give Rs 5000 to Rafi-ud-Daula at the time of arrival of Murtaza Khan. This agreement was made in my presence. But I forgot to present this matter [to the Nawab] at the time of my departure. Bring this to the notice of the Nawab. Take the money if he agrees to pay; otherwise, whatever the Nawab wishes will be for the better. 11 Rabī' II, Saturday.

Folio 277a. To Mir Yusuf Ali.

I received two of your letters and came to know about my sons' welfare. Continue to take care of them in the same way. Be vigilant about their treatment and dietry restrictions and keep me informed about their health. I have already written about the case of your payment to Nawab Asaf-ud-Daula, Manik Ram and Mir Muhammad Husain Ata Khan. 11 Rabī', Saturday, Calcutta.

Folio 277b. (Letter 7) To Manik Ram and Mir Muhammad Husain Ata Khan.

Today, the 14th of Rabī' II, is the seventh day since I arrived here in Calcutta. But ever since I left Azimabad I have not received any letter from you, though I have been writing to you regularly. I have also sent you from Calcutta on the 11th Rabī' II two copies of the previous letters. I am surprised that you have not received them yet. If you fear that the letters are lost in the way then send them to Captain Martin. Or else to Dr Thomas or Dr Fullman. They will redirect them to me. Second, I had told Ram Sundar Datt Sarkar that he should give Rs 50 per month to Mir Buddhan until the time he [Buddhan] begins to receive his emoluments from the *sarkār*. You also write to him. Also make arrangements for his deputation in the retinue of Mirza Ali Khan so that his salary is paid along with [the salary of Mirza Ali Khan]. I have written about this to you earlier as well.

Third, there is a lot of negligence in communication. I am completely in the dark and know nothing of the progress [of my work]. This is bad. I do not know what is the reason for this. I am concerned. In future be careful and keep writing so that I do not have to wait. 15 Rabī' II, Wednesday, Calcutta.

Folio 278b. To Nawab Asaf-ud-Daula.

I arrived in Calcutta safely on 8 Rabī' II. Earlier on my way I had sent you three letters. One month and twenty-three days have passed since the day of my departure, but I am yet to be honoured with your letter. I am concerned. I have been waiting day and night for your letter. I heard many things on my arrival here. But unless I receive your letter I will not know your mind and will be unable to act accordingly. May God enhance your position. 19 Rabī' II, Sunday.

Folio 279a. (Letter 8) To Manik Ram.

I am very angry with you because despite my writing to you several letters on important matters, ever since I left Azimabad you have not replied till date, i.e. 18th of Rabī' II. I do not know whether you have prepared the account of the expenditure. I have not received a single piece of relevant paper from Captain Martin. I do not understand this dereliction [of duty]. Such dereliction has beset you within a few days [of my departure] I will be very angry if you continue this way.

Acquire a *parwāna* for *tankhwāh* against the goods which Mr Martin had given to Nawab Asaf-ud-Daula and send it to him. I have written to you earlier also about this.

I have learnt that a boat full of books and other papers and a *wilāyatī* chariot with musical instruments for me have gone astray towards Chunar. They were on their way from Calcutta to Faizabad. As soon as you receive this letter, send a *harkāra* to bring this boat from there to Faizabad. Unload it and keep the things in my place. 19 Rabī‘ II, Sunday, Chitpur garden, Calcutta.

Folio 279b. To Mir Muhammad Husain Ata Khan.

I entrusted to you everything (*mukhtār*) related to my work there since I regard you as an experienced, clever and intelligent person. It is strange that despite being my sole spokesman there you have not accomplished any of my work. You have not said anything regarding the cases about which I wrote to you repeatedly. I have given you strict instructions for the maintenance of accounts but have not received any reply [from you].

You are an intelligent person and should know that I trust you completely. But if you do not communicate with me on the issue of my work there and neglect the work, then how will I manage. Also, how will I know what is good or bad? I am worried and anxious and feel lost. Take care of each and every matter and write to me directly. I trust your capacity [to get things done]. I have sent copies of my previous letters to you for which I have not received any reply. 19 Rabī‘ II, Sunday, Chitpur garden, Calcutta.

Folio 280a. To Ram Sundar Datt Sarkar.

I have come to know of your carelessness in maintaining my accounts and also of your delay of three to four days in reporting to Captain Martin. It is not in your interest to be negligent. Believe me, I will settle things and fix you. Complete the accounts and get it recorded with Mr Perceret. Also attend to Captain Martin regularly. This is best for you.

I have learnt that a boat full of books and other items, as well as a chariot (*wilāytī*) with a musical instrument for me have gone astray towards Chunargarh while on its way from Calcutta to Faizabad. As soon as you receive this letter you are requested to send a *harkāra* and get the boat unloaded and keep the goods in my place. 19 Rabī‘ II, Sunday, Chitpur garden, Calcutta.

Folio 280b. To Mirza Yusuf Ali.

I received your letter and am happy to know about the health of my elder son. I also note that my younger son is indisposed and is being treated by the *ḥakīm ṣāḥib*. You want my permission for consulting another *ḥakīm* for my son's illness.

I am so far away that I have no idea about the condition of bābā. Also, how will I know of another *ḥakīm* [sitting] here. Do whatever you and Captain Martin think is proper.

I have already written about your salary to Manik Ram and Mir Husain Ata Khan—be rest assured. 19 Rabī' II, Sunday, Chitpur garden.

Folio 281a. (Letter 9) To Manik Ram.

I received your letter of 1 Rabī' II on the 22nd of this month. Since you replied to my previous letter from Faizabad it is fine. But I am still surprised that you have ignored my queries about the cases I had mentioned. Also, your response to two or three other things is scanty and provides me with no information.

I have instructed you earlier also to number each letter: as 1, 2, 3 so that I know which letter you received and which one went undelivered. I do not know why you have not followed the instructions. This extent of negligence and carelessness is far from the path of faithful service. So far nothing has been done as per my verbal and written instructions. In this period I received only one letter. I instruct you again that copies of all letters that you send to me, with dates and names of people you have entrusted them to, should be dispatched separately. This will enable me to keep track of the number of letters you have sent to me.

Second, you write about the case of a Khan of Farrukhabad, the details of which could not be submitted. I cannot figure out which case you are referring to. I disapprove of this style of insinuation. It is important that you write in detail and legibly.

Third, you should send your letters to Martin or Thomas or whosoever you know [amongst the Europeans] so that they reach me safely.

Fourth, I have written to you several times about the elephants. It is all right if you have acted accordingly. Otherwise it seems useless to write further on this matter.

Fifth, I had written to you earlier about the money that Najaf Khan owes me. You have not written whether the Nawab has replied.

Sixth, you had written that your nephew, Gopi Mohan, will meet me in Calcutta. I have now been in Calcutta for 15–16 days but your nephew has not yet contacted me. What is the matter?

Seventh, the copies of the previous letters have been sent to you in the cover of the letter which I sent you on 19 Rabī' II. A copy of the letter of 19 Rabī' II is enclosed herewith.

Ninth, when I arrived in Calcutta Mr Richie demanded Rs 350 from me for the watch. But I recollect that when you had settled the account of Mr Richie in Faizabad you had paid him this money. Write to me whether you have given him the money or not. 22 Rabī' II, Wednesday, night, Calcutta.

Folio 282b. To Mirza Yusuf Ali.

I received your letter and was shocked to learn about the sad demise of my younger son. Since we are all helpless and have to abide by the will of God we can only be patient. Please take utmost care of the elder son. I had earlier written about the fee (*tawāzū*) of Ḥakīm Nawab to Manik Ram. Now that the elder son is fully recovered, ask Manik Ram to send whatever is appropriate to the *ḥakīm.* But if Manik Ram has already sent the fee to *ḥakīm ṣāḥib* then it is fine.

As for your complaint about my not replying to your letter, I must inform you that I have sent you two to three letters and am surprised that they have not reached you.

Be careful about the copying of the *Āīn-i-Akbarī* because it has not been ready for quite some time. Please hurry up in completing the copy. I note that Nawab Asaf-ud-Daula has returned. Keep writing to me regularly. 25 Rabī' II, Saturday, 16th Regnal Year, Calcutta.

Folio 283a. (Letter 10) To Manik Ram.

I have written to you about [preparing] the account for the expenditure. I do not know how many times I will have to write to you [about this]. I fail to understand what you are doing sitting there that you did not get time to prepare it even in two months period. Such negligence is not proper in money matters. Prepare the account upto the date I left Faizabad. Ram Sundar Datt will hand it over to Perceret *ṣāḥib* and I will get to know the exact situation.

Second, you have not yet acquired the *parwāna* against the goods [that I had given to Nawab Asaf-ud-Daula]. A *parwāna* is needed for the salary of the agent handling these goods. Why has there been a delay in this matter? Get the *parwāna* for a good area and inform me. Also get a *parwāna* for the goods of Mr Martin and send it to him.

Third, it has been two months since I left the Nawab's camp and as yet I do not know about the progress of money collection from Farrukhabad. There was a promise of payment in four months time. Now two months have already passed. I do not know how much money has come and what is left. Find out the details and write.

Fourth, you are instructed to send Lutf Ali Khan and Shaikh Baha-ud-Din immediately as Mir Sulaiman Khan wants them back. 22 Rabī' II, Monday, 16 Regnal year.

Folio 283b. To Mir Muhammad Husain Ata Khan.

I believe that you have received my letter with a copy of the letter to Manik Ram. Now that I have written an *'arīẓa* to Nawab Asaf-ud-Daula and yet another letter to Manik Ram, I am enclosing their copies so that you may get to know their contents. Since you have left for Farrukhabad to collect the money, I am sure the work will be done excellently. Keep writing to me the progress of the situation. 22 Rabī' II, 16th regnal year.

Folio 284a. To Nawab Asaf-ud-Daula.

After my arrival here I sent you a letter which must have been brought to your notice. It is two months since I took leave of you, but I have not yet received any letter (*nawāzishnāma*) from you. I am concerned. I hope that until I have the honour of meeting you I will be graced with a letter from you. This will be a source of strength to me.

Second, Mir Sulaiman Khan met me here. He is keen to meet you and I have assured him of your kindness. He wants to have an audience with you after the rainy season. He will feel honoured and enter the court in a relaxed way if a *shuqqa* is issued in his name. 27 Rabī' II, Monday 1189, Calcutta.

Folio 284b. (Letter 11) To Manik Ram.

It has been one month since I arrived here and, except for one letter, I have not heard a single word from you. You know that when I do not receive your letters I have no idea of the developments there. What is the reason [of your not writing]? I receive everyone else's letters except yours. I again instruct you to write to me, but [it seems] in vain. The tip of my pen has dried writing to you.

I have earlier written to you to make, according to your estimate the payment of arrears to Mr Jarri. I told you this three to four months back. I am sure that you have made the payment to Mr Jarri and obtained the letters of clearance of his debt from him. Get two such clearance letters and send one of them to me. 30 Rabī' II, Thursday, Calcutta.

Folio 285a. To Aqa Ali Khan.

I am happy to receive your letter. I noted that you have not received the opium and that you have gone back only to place your order again. I have written to you earlier also that if for the moment you require a small amount [of opium] you may obtain it from Manik Ram. I will get the remaining opium for you later when you come here. With the grace of God I have acquired one *man* of pure opium which I will bring with me. You can then collect from me whatever quantity you require. The *chhatar* (?) also will reach you. Keep in touch. 30 Rabī' II, Thursday, written in reply.

Folio 285b. To Mir Waliullah Khan.

I received your letter and noted that Manik Ram and Muhammad Husain Ata Khan have gone to Faizabad. I do not know what has happened to my people that they do not write to me about the progress of my work there. I have received only two to three letters from them during these months. I can not even mention this matter, I am tired of writing to them. I received letters neither from Manik Ram nor from Mir Muhammad Husain Ata Khan. I do not know anything about that place. It will be nice if you send me the report so that I know of the developments over there. 1 Jumāda I, Tuesday, Calcutta.

Folio 286a. To Mir Sa'id-ud-Din Ahmad.

I received your letter and learnt about the arrival of Mir Muhammad Husain Ata Khan in Farrukhabad. I am surprised that I have not received any letter from him informing me about the developments there. Keep in touch so that I know [the details]. 4 Jumāda I, Tuesday.

Folio 286a. To Murid Khan.

I was happy to receive your letter (*mihrbānīnāma*). Since a letter is almost like meeting, and because you are my friend I do hope that you will keep me informed of your welfare. 5 Jumāda I, Wednesday, Calcutta.

Folio 286b. To Mir Lutf Ali.

I received your letter regarding your deputation and return to Faizabad. You sent me the details in consideration of our friendship and I am very happy. I am concerned about your welfare. Keep in touch. 5 Jumāda I, Wednesday.

Folio 286b. To Mehrchand, the painter.

I have learnt from Mr Martin's letter that you are preparing a painting of the dance. I instruct you to suspend this work for the moment. Instead prepare a half-size portrait of Didar Bakhsh(?) (*shabīh-i nīm qad Dīdar Bakhsh*). After you have finished this, prepare a draft (*musawwada*) of the painting of the dance (*warqa-i taṣwīr-i raqṣ*). I will see the draft when I come back and then you can finalize it as per my instructions. 9 Jumāda, I, Saturday, Calcutta.

Folio 287a. To Mirza Yusuf Ali.

I received your letter and noted that Mr Martin has suggested a powder medicine (*sufūf*) for my son. But the ladies inside (*az-andrūn*) do not approve of it. It is strange that the instruction of Mr Martin is not being carried out. I am furious. Whatever medicine or suggestion (*tadbīr-o-tadāvī*) comes from Mr Martin will be good and useful and you should see to it that he takes the medicine and treatment (*mu'ālaja*) suggested by Mr Martin in your presence. Keep me informed about the welfare and health of my son. 9 Jumāda I, Calcutta, written in reply.

Folio 287a. To Mir Jumla Ubaidullah Khan Bahadur Tar Khan.

I received your letter. I will bring to the notice of *Ṣāhib-i Kalān* [Governor General] the case of your appointment to the office of the *qazi* and *muhtasib* of Bengal province. I will make all possible efforts [in this direction]. But it will help if you enclose in your letter (*fard-i sawāl*) the *sanad* of appointment or a copy of the same. This is needed. I will keep you posted of the developments. 9 Jumāda I, Saturday, Calcutta.

Folio 287b. To Iftikhar-ud-Daula, Amir-ul-Mulk Mirza Ali Khan, Bahadur Dilawar Jang.

In keeping with your order for the banana plants I have dispatched 200 plants of *champā*—the best variety of bananas by boat. I have also instructed the gardener to take the maximum care in taking them to you. They are likely to reach you soon. I hope that you will keep in touch. 9 Jumāda I, Calcutta.

Folio 288a. (Letter 12) To Manik Ram and Mir Muhammad Husain Ata Khan.

I received your letter of 4 Jumāda I on the 19th. You say that only two to three letters of mine reached there. My dear, until this date i.e. the 19th of Jumāda, I had sent you twelve letters in addition to two to three copies of this letter. I do not know why they have not reached you. I had written to you earlier that you should write the number of my letter to which you are responding at the top of your letter, which should also be numbered. But you never followed this instruction. How will I know which letter you received and which you did not? In such circumstances my writing to you regularly becomes useless. Your negligence in such a minor matter makes me feel very helpless. I do not know for how long I need to instruct you.

You have written that you will carry out in full the instructions on matters I write to you about. I will appreciate if you make efforts for the speedy collection of money.

You write that Rs 3000 from the *tankhwāh* of Farrukhabad has been received. But you are silent about the remaining amount. The payment of the full sum had been promised but only Rs 3000 has been received in this period. Why this delay? Make all possible effort to get the full payment. I need money here to meet many expenses.

I noted what you have written about the *kurtīs* and other expenses; and also that you will send whatever money is received by *hundīs.* Do not send the money by *hundī.*

Buy the big *asharfīs* of Farrukhabad at appropriate and reasonable prices and send them to Dr Thomas who will then dispatch them to me. There is nothing but loss in *hundī,* whereas in this arrangement there will be no loss.

I am happy to learn that the gift from Farrukhabad is on the way to Lucknow. Be careful and in this matter do not even trust your own people. Write to me if she is alone or is being accompanied by her mother or by some other woman.

I hope to leave this place in about fifteen to twenty days time. Continue to attend to my business there with efficiency and responsibility.

It is good that you have handed over Rs 20,000 of the *tankhwāh* of Bakhshi Peppan to Mr Bristow. Mr Bristow has also written to me about this.

I noted that you have reached Lucknow and will send the required papers after completing the accounts.

I also noted that Niyaz Ali Khan has left for the royal court and also learnt to the news of Najaf Khan. But Niyaz Ali Khan has not yet written anything from there. Write to him that he must give me the report of the developments there. 24 Jumāda I, Sunday, Calcutta, the *kothī* of Rabī Sen *ṣāḥib.*

Folio 289b. To Murid Khan.

I was delighted to receive your letter on the 19th of Jumāda 1. I am also happy to note your desire to meet me. I too am keen to meet you. God willing, very soon I will reach there and our desire of meeting each other will be fulfilled. As for your order for *tānkhan* [horses], one *tānkhan* is being sent to an Englishman (*ṣāḥib*) from Rangpur to Mirzapur. I will write to him to escort it to you. I hope that you will keep in touch. 24 Jumāda I.

Folio 290a. To Aqa Ali Khan.

I received your letter on the 23rd of Jumāda I and noted that you have not received the opium. I have written to you earlier and I repeat that when I return I will bring with me a lot of opium from Azimabad. After I reach there you can take whatever you want. For the time being take whatever is necessary from Manik Ram. I will write to him and he will send it to you. 24 Jumāda I.

Folio 290a. To Mir Buddhan.

My dear son, I am delighted to receive your letter and know of your welfare. Earlier, in response to your letter I wrote to Manik Ram about your monthly emoluments. I believe that this will be done according to my instructions. Rest assured and keep in touch. 21 Jumāda I.

Folio 290b. To Ram Sundar Datt Sarkar.

I received your letter and am happy to note that on the receipt of my letter you had sent the *harkāra* to accompany the boat, containing the books and papers, and the *rath* with the European musical organ, which had gone astray near Chunargarh. Write to me when the *harkāra* comes back. I have also noted that you have prepared the account for two months and reported it to Mr Perceret and Mr Latt; you have the account of Mr Latt upto January; that you report to Mr Martin day and night; and keep the account of my establishment up to date.

Store my goods properly when the boat reaches there and keep them safe from rodents, etc. Take care of the watch and get it repaired by Gora Mistri. 24 Jumāda I.

Folio 291a. (Letter 13) To Manik Ram.

I received your letter of 9 Jumāda I on the 25th and learnt that you have sent the letter by the Benares *dāk*. Who had asked you to do this? If you wrote regularly then send me the copies [of these letters]. I repeat that each of your letter should be numbered. You should specify the date and the number of the letter to which you are responding. In future follow my instructions and send the letters through Dr Thomas and Captain Martin.

I noted what you had written earlier about the arrears of money and the goods. You have full powers there to do whatever you think is good for me.

You write that you have paid the *mahājans* of Akbarabad out of the money you received from Farrukhabad; that you have obtained a clearance letter (*fārigh-khaṭṭī*) from them; and that you will dispatch the remaining money by *hundī*. Buy big *asharfis* at Farrukhabad at a reasonable price with whatever money there is. Send these to Dr Thomas and he will pass them on to me. Do this at your earliest since I need the money here for many things. Never send money by *hundī* as this involves a loss. Do not insist on the money which Najaf Khan owes me. His monthly salary is prepared here and I can get the money from here as well. 25 Jumāda I, Monday, Calcutta.

Folio 292a. To Mirza Yusuf Ali.

I received your letter of 9 Jumāda I and noted the contents. Keep writing the same way. 25 Jumāda I.

Folio 292a. To Mir Muhammad Husain Ata Khan.

I received on the 27th two of your letters—one of 12 Jumāda I and the second of the 15th. I now have all the details of the developments there.

I noted that you have received and sent to Manik Ram Rs 40,000 from the *naẕrāna* and Rs 50,000 of the Rs 1,06,000 *tankhwāh.* I have received Rs 3000 by *hundī* here. Manik Ram has not given me any information on the collection of the *naẕrāna.* Give him a receipt for the Rs 3000 which I have received, find out the balance money, and after ascertaining that, send the remaining amount to Dr Thomas. Consider him (Thomas) like me.

I have sent a letter regarding your case to Nawab Asaf-ud-Daula. When you have collected the entire money in Farrukhabad, [you] arrive at the court and present this letter to him [Nawab]. You have full authority to attend to my work there. Keep me informed. I do not have any other trustworthy person like you to look after my affairs there. I entrust all these things to you; you will be accountable.

I noted what you have written about the order of the payment of

Rs 400 from Shah Sidq Ali. I have also received a letter from him. As I told you earlier, since the entire money has been received, the realization charges (*zar-i degi*) due to the Shah should reach him soon. I should not be accused of double speaking.

Earlier I had learnt that the gift from Farrukhabad is eleven to twelve years old. Now I gather from your letter that she is eight to nine years old. Write to me clarifying whether she is the same gift you had mentioned earlier or someone different.

I received a letter from Munawwar Khan about the payment of *tan<u>kh</u>wāh*. Do something about this and instruct Manik Ram.

Manik Ram had written to me earlier that four elephants had been sold to Murtaza Khan *risāldār* at a good price. Now he writes that some of these have been sold and some from the earlier lot have been gifted away (*taṣadduq*). I do not know the exact situation. Find out and write to me.

You write that you have written to me on three to four occasions. However, besides these two letters received on the 27 Jumāda, I have not received any other letter from you independently. The letters I received came along with those of Manik Ram. Send your letters through Dr Thomas.

I noted that you want me to write to Manik Ram to report to you all minor and major matters. I have done so. Enquire about your papers from him.

I learnt from the letter of Mirza Yusuf Ali that Ḥakīm Nawab has as yet not received any money I had sent for him. Find out what his proper fee should be and collect it from Manik Ram for payment to the *ḥakīm*. You should not worry about the money due from Najaf Khan. His monthly emoluments are paid from here. If I do not receive anything from there, I will then collect it here.

As regards my talks with the English officials and my plan to return, the fact is that I have got the papers brought from Nawab Asaf-ud-Daula ratified and sent them back to him. I do not consider it appropriate to write the details here. These will be made available at the proper time. I am returning soon. Continue to look after my work and accounts there—you are the over-all incharge (*mu<u>kh</u>tār*).

I had written earlier that a third part of the *tan<u>kh</u>wāh* for the *kurtīs* should be handed over to Mr Math (?). But now [you are instructed to] send the entire amount to Dr Thomas. Dr Thomas will send to me whatever he thinks is appropriate. The collection of the money is your responsibility. This is a big sum about which you are aware, along with the amount for which Manik Ram is responsible. Attend to my affairs properly.

I hear that Manik Ram has not done anything about the monthly payment of the *munshī* and his son for which he had the Nawab's approval. Ensure that the work of my friends, whether present there or on journey, is accomplished. For the moment, get the *munshī* and his son paid.

I have written about your case to Dr Thomas. He is like my brother and friend. Tell him whatever is necessary about your case and birth. You can obtain from me whatever you require.

Arrange to send me safely one sword (*shamsher*), one decorated European *katār* and three European enamelled (*mīnākārī*) tray covers.

When you speak to Manik Ram you should not talk about the things I have mentioned to you. But do discuss these things with him in a manner that he should feel ashamed and be alarmed. After having made your assessment, write to me about everything. 2 Jumāda II, Sunday, Calcutta.

Folio 295a. (Letter 14) To Manik Ram.

I received two letters of yours—one of 14 Jumāda I on the 27th, and the other of the 15th on the 29th. I have also received *hundī* of Rs 30,000 along with its duplicate copy (*peth*) in English that you had given to Dr Thomas. This is good. You should send whatever money you possess, and whatever you acquire, in future to Dr Thomas.

You have not responded to my queries about the cases that I have written about. Also, regarding many things you merely write that you will respond the following day. Why do you postpone things to the next day? Write clearly about whatever is to be done [in the matters I enquire about].

I had earlier written to you that you along with Mir Muhammad Husain Ata Khan [should] look after all my business there. I repeat that in all matters you should seek his advice and keep him informed. Prepare the account and send a copy of it to him. He is an experienced and wise man. You do not need others to inform you about a man's wisdom. This becomes obvious at the correct time.

You had written that the Farrukhabad gift is eleven to twelve years old. But now I gather that she is eight or nine years old. Is it the same gift that you had mentioned earlier or is it a different one?

Shah Sidq Ali had written to me about his realization charges. I have already told you about its payment. I repeat that as soon as you receive this letter you should hand over the sum to him. Do not be negligent.

I have also received a letter from Munawwar Khan *ṣūbadār*. You are instructed to arrange payment of his *tankhwāh* without delay.

You had written that four elephants had been sold at a good price to Murtaza Khan *risāldār*. Now you say that some of these animals had been sold whereas some were gifted away. Why are you making contradictory statements?

The monthly emoluments of the *munshī* and his son, fixed by Nawab Asaf-ud-Daula, have not been paid yet. It is strange that you are indifferent to the person who is regularly attending to my work. Arrange for his payment soon and look after the interest of my servants.

Stall the payment of one-third of the money, received for the *kurtīs*, to Mr Math. [Instead] send all the money to Dr Thomas.

I have sent my reply to Nawab Asaf-ud-Daula's letters. Bring it to his notice and get his reply.

Send the gift from Farrukhabad, with care and safety, to Faizabad. Hand her over to La'l Khan who is a dependable person. Ask him to keep her safely and not entrust her to other people. Write to me if she is accompanied by her mother or any other person.

Send me with utmost care one sword, one decorated European *katār* and three European *mīnākārī* tray covers. But send them in the name of Monteki (?) *ṣāḥib* so that if I am not here it may be received by him. 2 Jumāda II, Monday.

Folio 297a. To Nawab Asaf-ud-Daula.

I am honoured to receive your letter (*'ināyatnāma*). I note that you want me to come back soon having completed the matters that you had entrusted me with. I have brought the things to the notice of *Ṣāḥib-i Kalān* and got them cleared. But it is not proper to write about them. When I meet you I will tell you the details. Since your letter did not have much details I followed what you had instructed me at the time of your departure. I did things as I thought appropriate. Words fail to express the degree of my desire to have audience with you. I will be there soon and have the honour of meeting you. I hope to grow in your favours and remain honoured by receiving your letters. 2 Jumāda II, Calcutta, in the cover of letter to Manik Ram.

Folio 297b. To Nawab Asaf-ud-Daula.

As previously decided, Mir Muhammad Husain Ata Khan and Manik

Ram together are looking after my work. This has already been submitted to you. I have sent Ata Khan to Farrukhabad to collect my *tankhwāh* from there. With your grace he has performed his work well. I request you to issue an order for his regular attendance in your court since he is a man of wisdom and experience and I am fully satisfied with his work. He looks after all my work in collaboration with Manik Ram. I hope you will accept whatever he reports [about my affairs]. I am keen to return and meet you soon. 2 Jumāda II, Calcutta, enclosed with the letter for Mir Muhammad Husain Ata Khan.

Folio 298a. To Shah Sidq Ali.

I received your letter regarding the receipt of Rs 40,000 of the *nazrāna* and Rs 50,000 from the *tankhwāh* of Rs 1,06,000 and about your realization fee. I have already written to you about the realization charges and it is not sure whether I will send you a new *parwāna* for the purpose. I am writing again to Ata Khan and Manik Ram. I am sure they will soon arrange the payment. 2 Jumāda II, Calcutta.

Folio 298a. To Murid Khan.

I am happy to receive your letter. I had received a letter from you earlier as well for which a reply has been sent. I hope you have received it. I hope that we will meet soon. In the meanwhile I hope we remain in touch. 2 Jumāda II, Sunday.

Folio 298b. To Mirza Yusuf Ali.

I received your letter of 14 Jumāda I. I had earlier written to Manik Ram about the *tawāẓu*' (fee) to Ḥakīm Nawab. It appears from your letter that this has not been carried out. I write to you that this must reach him at the earliest. 2 Jumāda II.

Folio 298b. To Munawwar Khan ṣūbadār

I received your letter. Rest assured that I have instructed Mir Muhammad Husain Ata Khan and Manik Ram to arrange for the payment of the *tankhwāh*. Attend to the work assigned to you and do not worry. You will be paid soon. 2 Jumāda II.

Folio 299a. To Mir Shah Ali.

I received your letter. I hope that you will continue to send me the news of the camp and the area regularly. 2 Jumāda II.

Folio 299a. To Mir Lutf Ali.
I am happy to receive your letter. God willing, I will bring the two pistols that you ask for when I return. Keep writing regularly. 2 Jumāda II.

Folio 299a. (Letter 15, in reply to letter 10) To Manik Ram
Received your letter of 21st Jumāda I with the papers relating to the *tankhwāh* and the news about the elephants. I have already sent the reply to the two letters that you sent to me earlier along with the *peth* and *parpeth* [duplicate copy] *hundī* of Rs 30,000. You will receive these soon. Despite my repeated instructions you have still not numbered your letters.

I write to you again to separate the goods of Mr Martin and Mr Lloyd and send the *parwāna* of payment to Mr Martin. You should immediately act upon whichever case I write about. I should not have to repeat my instructions. But my repeated instructions are in vain as they do not seem to have any impact on you.

You have mentioned the *tankhwāh* of Rs 40,000 to Zalim Singh and Prashad Singh and that of Rs 15,000 to Nauroz Ali Beg. Make arrangements for payment to them soon. You mention that after the clearance of dues against the *tankhwāh* of Farrukhabad some other minor payments due from the Nawab could also be fixed from Farrukhabad. I do not agree with this suggestion. You know that for this *tankhwāh* Mir Muhammad Husain Ata Khan had to visit Farrukhabad and I felt very helpless. I do not want him to be away from his work even for a moment, and wish that you should attend to my business in consultation with him. [I] have written to him that as soon as the dues are cleared he should hasten back to the camp and join you. Send a copy of this letter to him. I disapprove of anything being done without his consultation. No laxity should be shown in this matter.

You write that five of the sixteen elephants which reached there from Benares have been sold in Faizabad by Ram Sundar Datt. I am not satisfied with this transaction. You should get all the elephants back in the camp and get them sold in your presence. Along with them sell two other elephants belonging to Dr Hunter. Write also at what price Ram Sundar Datt has sold the five elephants.

I had earlier suggested that one-third of the money for the *kurtis* be sent to Mr Math (?) But now you [should] hand over the entire amount to Dr Thomas. You have written that you have sent Rs 30,000 of the Rs 50,000 *tankhwāh* from Farrukhabad by *hundī* and the remaining Rs 20,000 has been used for the expenses there. I fail to figure out the expenditures there for which you need so much money including sums from other places as well as that of the *nazrāna.* I had earlier written to you to send every penny to Dr Thomas. Write to me in detail the reason for these expenses.

I note that you have dispatched money to Mr Lloyd, Mr Strachan (?) and Mr Sangster (?)

I saw the receipts of the money you have spent. You say that you have asked Ram Sundar Datt to prepare the detailed account of the cash and goods. I fail to comprehend this, for Ram Sundar Datt says that the papers are with you, wheras you say something else. In such circumstances I do not know what kind of papers will be prepared. At any rate prepare the complete set of papers. I will remain dissatisfied until I receive them.

I note the increase in the expenditure of my establishment.

Mirza Ata Ali Khan had written for the banana plants. I have dispatched 200 champā brand plants—the best banana saplings—by boat on the 21st of Rabī‘ II.

I will look for the *ābgīna* bricks in accordance with the Nawab's order. I will send them if they are available here.

I note that you have written about the *tankhwāh* of Monsieur Lacos and the papers for the estimate of Mr Perceret's emoluments.

I note that you have now received everything, including the cash and the goods, according to the account of Mihrban Khan. You stayed in Farrukhabad for many days and sent me several letters from there as well as from Lucknow but never mentioned this case. Now that you mention [this case] I am in the dark about the timing of your receipt of this [goods]. What goods? How many? And how much money? Why did you not write to me earlier.

I note Nawab Asaf-ud-Daula's instructions to you to ask me to complete his work and return soon. I have done everything and I shall report on it when I return. It is inappropriate to write about the matter.

I note that you have been favoured by the Nawab with a *jāgīr.* This is good for a person who has been earnestly and devotedly performing my work. I am delighted to learn that good things are happening to him. I have written to you to bring to the notice of the Nawab the details of the money that has been spent on the repair of the *ḥavelī,* and to obtain permission for its payment. It was important for you to have thought about this first and then of your interest. Well, it is good that you have done your work first—I am very happy.

I have paid Rs 3000 to Mir Sulaiman Khan—record this in his account.

I had asked you to give Rs 1200 to Mr Store. I wonder if you have paid him this amount. Do not hesitate to give Mr Perceret whatever he desires. 4 Jumāda II, Calcutta.

Folio 302b. To Mir Muhammad Husain Ata Khan.

I received a letter from Manik Ram dated 21 Jumāda I on the 3 Jumāda II. I enclose herewith a copy of my reply. In case he does not tell you about my letter you may get to know about the situation from this copy. I have also mentioned two–three other things about which you should know. You should return back to the camp and attend to my work there—I do not trust anyone else. 4 Jumāda II.

Folio 303a. To Ram Sundar Datt Sarkar.

Manik Ram writes that the papers regarding the details of the cash and goods relating to my establishment cannot be prepared unless he examines them. I had written to Manik Ram earlier about their preparation. He wrote back saying that without inspecting all the [relevant] papers he was unable to prepare the account. He said he would write to you about this. If it is ready it may be brought to the notice of the Nawab. [However], I gather from the letter of Mr Perceret that you have not yet cleared the account of his *'amārī*. It seems that you have been negligent in preparing the ralevant papers of this account and I disapprove of it. Send it immediately otherwise you will be in trouble. 4 Jumāda II.

Folio 303a. To Majd-ud-Daula Farzand Khan.

I received your letter and noted that you are looking forward to meeting me. I too am keen to meet you. God willing, our wishes will be fulfilled. I am happy to see your sincerity for Nawab Asaf-ud-Daula. The Nawab reciprocates this and is keen to be of service to ensure the stability of the empire. I am sure that with the grace of God our objective will be achieved and the work of the state carried on excellently. The enemies will be subdued to offer their allegiance to the court. I pray that you continue to receive the favours of the Emperor and be a source of fortune for us. In keeping with my faithful obedience to the Emperor I am keen to have the honour of being of any service to him. I hope to receive your letters regularly. I am grateful for the kind favours you have bestowed upon me. It is so nice of you to have prepared the memoranda for my *manṣab* and title.

You were nice enough to write about the money I owe Najaf Khan. But do not worry about it.

You say that I should persuade the English officials to maintain their friendship with Nawab Asaf-ud-Daula. Sir, (*mushfiqr-i man*) I am doing what is necessary to the best of my ability.

I will speak to the English officers and leaders here about the treasury of Bengal. I will spare no possible effort in this matter. I will write to you in detail when I come back.

As for the list of items that you have included in your letter, I will, God willing, bring whatever is available here. 9 Jumāda II, Monday, Calcutta. Sent in the cover of the letter to Manik Ram.

Folio 304b. (Letter 16, in reply to letter 11) To Manik Ram.

I received your letter of 22 Jumāda I and its copy written on the 24th today, the 7th of Jumāda. You say that ever since you received my letter with instructions to write regularly you have sent letters through Dr Thomas, and also that you were anxious on not receiving my letters. I reply as soon as I receive your letter. If you do not write then the question of my receiving it does not arise. Do not make excuses. I have written to you 15–16 times which is evident from the number on the top of my letter. But you have failed to carry out even a single instruction of mine.

I note that you have instructed Ram Sundar Datt to send me a copy of the receipt regarding the clearance of the debt of Mr Jarri (?)

I have repeatedly written to you not to be concerned about the money Najaf Khan owes me. His annual payment estimate is made here also and I will take care of it [here].

You write that Emanuel (?) *firangī* sold four elephants at cheap rates and then left. Earlier you had written that the elephants had been sold by Ram Sundar Datt but now you say Emanuel [has sold them]. [Anyway], the elephants reached there three months back but you are providing information about them now. What kind of work is this? I do not like lies and excuses. I do not trust Ram Sundar Datt's ability to sell. Let me know the amount of money he has as a result of this sale of elephants. I had written to you earlier to take the elephants and sell them after grooming them. On whose order did Ram Sundar Datt sell them?

You write that the *peshkash*, *nazr* and *niyāz* that you have presented to the Nawab were all to facilitate the work of my *jāgīr*. Since I am aware of all the developments and the efforts you make for me I am sure that you must have done it considering this work as your own. This is required of service (*bandagī*). But, in the case of nothing being achieved it becomes evident that the endeavour is for the purpose of doing your own work. This is against the rule of *bandagī*.

You write that because of the '*āmīls*' dismissal and the non-collection, the *tankhwāh* against the goods of Mr Martin and Mr Lloyd has not been paid. You also write that you have presented many gifts to the Nawab and won many favours. It is strange that despite all these favours on matters for which so much sycophancy was necessary you have not been able to achieve even this. I wonder if you can do the other things.

You want to know if it is appropriate to include the accounts of Mr Perceret, etc. in those of the people working in the arsenal. Forget about doing anything in this matter.

Majd-ud-Daula has written to me that you will write to me about all that he has done. But you have not said anything on the matter. You have neither forwarded to me the letter of Niyaz Ali, nor have you written a single word about the court. I have no explanation for this failure. 9 Jumāda II, Monday, Calcutta.

Folio 306a. To Mir Muhammad Husain Ata Khan.

I received a letter from Manik Ram dated 22 Jumāda I on the 7th of Jumāda II. I am writing to you since some of the things that he writes about need to be brought to your notice. I am also enclosing a copy of the letter that you sent to him so that you know the state of affairs. Please note that you have to find out and report to me if Manik Ram is carrying out my instructions. I send you a copy of whatever I write to Manik Ram. 9 Jumāda II, Monday.

Folio 306b. To Mir Muhammad Husain Ata Khan.

I received yesterday evening—9 Jumāda II—a letter for you with the signature of Manik Ram. I wonder why this letter has come to me. On opening the letter I was surprised to find that despite receiving so much money he is requesting you for more. I do not know what has happened to all this money—Rs 14,000 of the *nazrāna*, Rs 15,000 from the Farrukhabad *tankhwāh* of Rs 1,06,000—which you had collected and which had reached him. In addition, he has Rs 8000 from the sale of elephants in Faizabad, together with the different sums from different places. He has sent a total of Rs 30,000 by *hundī* to me. The Rs 18,000 for small expenses which was to be given to Mr Peppan *ṣāḥib* has not reached him yet. Besides this, there is no expenditure there. In these circumstances I cannot figure out this demand for more money. I am therefore sending this letter back to you. Take care of the situation there and keep a watch over the entries of Manik Ram in the account. It will be good if you go to Lucknow for a few days and write to me after finding out everything. You are the only dependable person. I had sent to you another letter of Manik Ram as well. A copy of my reply to him will reach you soon. I write to you again to send whatever money you receive to Dr Thomas. 10 Jumāda II, Tuesday.

Folio 307b. To Mirza Yusuf Ali.

I am happy to receive your letter and get the good news of the full recovery of my son (*ghusl-i-ṣiḥat*). You write that Manik Ram has written to you to meet him regarding the payment. I have also written to him. 10 Jumāda II, Tuesday.

Folio 308a. To Ram Sundar Datt Sarkar.

I had asked you to give Rs 1200 to Mr Store. I learn that so far it has not been paid. Hand over the money to Mr Store as soon as you receive this letter. Give money for two to three months' expenses to Bībī Jawahar and the junior Bībī if at the time of their departure to this place they ask you for it. 10 Jumāda II, Tuesday.

Folio 308a. To Mir Muhammad Husain Ata Khan.

I received your letter of 19 Jumāda I, together with copies of your earlier letters on 11 Jumāda II. I note the mischief of Mihrban Khan, the queries of Rajab Ali and the difficulty in the collection of *tankhwāh*, as well as the other developments there. Your letters take time to reach here. It is necessary that you keep writing regularly. Also, for important letters you should have a special messenger to deliver them to Dr Thomas. Take care that the letters do not reach somewhere else. Those received by Dr Thomas are certainly forwarded to me.

You write that Mr Convie (?) at the behest of Mihrban Khan has asked you not to interfere in the collection of money for me. I have assigned him no other work except the collection of my *tankhwāh*. Do not allow him to interfere in any other work. If you can collect the *tankhwāh* without much trouble it is fine. But if Mihrban Khan and the other *'āmils* create some problems then do not indulge in any dispute with anybody. Try and avoid any antagonism over the collection.

Earlier I had recommended your case to Nawab Asaf-ud-Daula. A copy of my letter to the Nawab may have reached you. I am also now writing to Nawab Muzafar Jang and the copy of that letter is enclosed. I am reaching soon and will get the things you have ordered. I have not heard from Niyaz Ali Khan for quite some time. Find out his welfare and write to me about it. 12 Jumāda II, Thursday, written in reply.

Folio 308b. To Nawab Amin-ud-Daula Farzand Khan Muzaffar Jang.

I have accumulated many treasures of your sincerity from the time we became friends. But a sincere friendship demands loyalty both in each other's presence as well as in absence. It is surprising that our sincerity notwithstanding, I have not yet been paid the money of my *tankhwāh*. The promised days have also passed off. This does not behove our friendship. I request you to see to it that the payment is made soon. I will soon leave this place and be available in all candor for whatever service you require. 12 Jumāda II.

Folio 309a. (Letter 17 in reply to letter 12) To Manik Ram

I received your letter of 28 Jumāda I on Thursday 12 Jumāda II, together with the papers of the sale of elephants, a copy of the *qaulnāma* of Nawab Muzaffar Jang and the receipt from Mr Richie. I had earlier received the *hundī* from Dr Thomas and the letters from Nawab Asaf-ud-Daula addressed to me and to Mir Sulaiman Khan, as well as the letters of Maj-ud-Daula and Najaf Khan. I had replied to them. Contrary to the earlier experiences, I am now receiving your letters on time. Keep writing regularly.

I am happy that you have made so much effort in selling the elephants. Whatever you are doing for the good of my business brings pleasure to my heart. It will also profit you.

I note what you say about Rs 42,000. Do something for its early payment.

I also noted that Nawab Asaf-ud-Daula has ordered for *kurtīs* of thirty-two *paltans*. They will be dispatched when they are ready

You write that you have brought the case of Rs 5000 for Rafi-ud-Daula to the notice of the Nawab but you have not received his response. Do not mention this case to him any more as he does not agree on it.

I will do something about the case of Murid Khan when I reach there. As per your demand, young, well-built and flawless elephants will be sent to you. I do not deal with the dispatch of *tānkhan* horses. But if someone wants them as a gift it can be arranged.

I note the report about the province of Awadh and the court. I also noted what you have to say about Niyaz Ali Khan and Ilich Khan. I have not heard from Niyaz Ali Khan since long. Write to me what the reason is.

I noted that you are of the opinion that when the money from the Farrukhabad *tankhwāh* is collected Major Hang will be paid his due.

You have received a lot of money: Rs 12,000 from the sale of elephants, the *nazrāna* and the Farrukhabad *tankhwāh*, along with the income from different places. Out of all this money you have dispatched to me only Rs 30,000 in *hundī.* I do not know where you spent the money and why [for the works assigned to you there].

I also note what you write about Mihrban Khan and Shah Sidq Ali and have inspected the copy of the *qaulnāma*.

You say that I should come back after completing the works assigned to me by the Nawab. I have already written to you about this.

At the end of Rajab, after a period of one and a half months, a ship will leave for Mecca from Calcutta. The ship owner is known to me and is my friend. Tell the Nawab that if anyone wishes to visit Mecca for *ṭawāf* he can come here. He will have a comfortable journey. Find out if anybody is there and write to me soon.

I will take time to write to you about the permission you seek to buy the six elephants from Captain Alier (?) for Rs 2000.

Your nephew, Gopi Mohun, keeps meeting me. Rest assured that there will never be any negligence on my part to do the needful for him.

I note that the wound that had appeared on the Nawab's back is healing. May God give him quick relief. 14 Jumāda II, Sunday.

Folio 311a. To Mir Muhammad Husain Ata Khan.

I received a letter from Manik Ram dated 28 Jumāda I on 12 Jumāda II. I enclose its copy to you since it is necessary for you to know what he has written. Earlier I had sent a copy of my reply to your letter. Give attention to my work there and keep me informed. 14 Jumāda II.

Folio 311b. To Sri Sawai Maharaja Guman Singh.

I am happy to receive your letter. Words fail to express the degree of my friendship. It is befitting our friendship that you keep me informed regularly. 14 Jumāda II, sent in the cover of the letter for Manik Ram.

Folio 311b. To Mir Muhammad Husain Ata Khan.
I received your letter of 27 Jumāda I on the 16th of Jumāda II. I had received several of your letters and replied to all of them. I hope you received the replies.

You write that as per the instructions of Manik Ram you have sent to me all the money you had by *hundī*. I have written to you earlier also and repeat that as and when you collect the Rs 5000–Rs 6000 you should send it to Dr Thomas. Do not ever send even a single penny to Manik Ram.

It will be kind of you if you reached Lucknow and looked after my work there and kept me posted of the developments. I trust only you.

It has been five months since Ratan Singh *munshī* left [for the court of] Raja Lalit Sah, zamindar of Srinagar, to bring back presents from there. He had promised to be back in three months time. I do not know if he is back. Find out and write to me. 16 Jumāda II, Monday.

Folio 312b. (Letter 18, in reply to letter 13) To Manik Ram.
I received your letter of 6 Jumāda II on the 21st. You say that you have sent me your letters regularly through Dr Thomas but you have not received any reply from me. I always reply as soon as I receive your letters.

I noted whatever you have said about the collection of money from Farrukhabad. I repeat that you [must] act according to my instructions. I noted that Nauruz Ali Khan's son and some other persons have been appointed in the *maḥāls*. Make efforts to obtain the orders for their *tanḵhwāh* without any delay.

I also noted the news of the court that you sent.

Regarding the Nawab's order of *kurtis* for the soldiere, I shall send them to you subsequently.

Do not mention to anybody the case of the debt of Najaf Khan.

I will send the letter that you ask for in the case of the *tanḵhwāh* to the Nawab. The copy will reach you soon. Get a reply from the Nawab.

You write that Rs 18,000 are to be paid to Major Hang, and you are not receiving the money from anywhere, and that this is a cause of concern for you. Rs 56,000 from the *tanḵhwāh*, of which Rs 6000 were sent to you by Mir Muhammad Husain Ata Khan, and Rs 40,000 of *naẕrāna* have already been received [by you] from Farrukhabad. In addition, there has also been income from the sale of elephants in Faizabad. I have received Rs 30,000 from you in *hundī*. I do not know where the remaining money is being spent. Why don't you write to me the details of the expenditure.

I have noted the news about Ilich Khan and Niyaz Ali Khan.

I appreciate the fact that the goods have been off-loaded from the boat and put on to the carts for [onward journey] Faizabad.

I [also] noted that you have written to Ram Sundar Datt to give Rs 200 in cash and a pair of *doshāla* to Ḥakīm Nawab. 22 Jumāda II.

Folio 313b. To Nawab Asaf-ud-Daula.

I had written to you earlier giving you the details of the affairs that I have dealt with. I am sure Manik Ram has presented those letters to you. I am keen to be in your service. I will be back soon and have the honour of an audience with you.

I am already fortunate to be endowed with your favours and do not feel the need to submit to you my desires, but in consideration of the kindness I have received from you, I submit that the papers of *tankhwāh* for the people and the goods, etc. will be presented to you by Manik Ram and Mir Muhammad Husain Ata Khan. I hope that you will issue *parwānas* for the payment from good areas. Keep writing. 22 Jumāda II, Sunday, sent in the cover of letter for Manik Ram.

Folio 314a. To Mir Muhammad Husain Ata Khan.

If you are free from the work there then it is fine. But even if you are not free, come to Lucknow for a few days and investigate into the account in which Manik Ram has spent so much money : Rs 56,000, plus Rs 4000 from the *nazrāna*, plus the money of the goods sold, plus money from the sale of elephants and the money obtained from different places—in all exceeding Rs 1 lac. Of this amount, I have only received Rs 30,000. Perhaps Manik Ram has loaned the money to somebody.

Also find out what Jugal Kishor is doing and whether he is coordinating his activity with Manik Ram. In other words, report to me about all the developments there. You know all about the payment that was to be made to different people. 22 Jumāda II, Sunday.

Folio 315a. To Mir Waliullah Khan.

I received your letter and noted that Manik Ram made special efforts to sell the elephants. It is necessary that you keep me similarly informed about the court news as well. 22 Jumāda II.

Folio 315a. To Ram Sundar Datt Sarkar.

I received your letter of 21 Jumāda II on the 8th of Rajab. I noted that you have handed over the account to Mr Perceret, and that clothes are required inside the *ḥavelī*. Arrange to take whatever clothes are required to the *deorhī* for around Rs 50. For the junior Bībī arrange whatever you feel is appropriate. 8 Rajab.

Folio 315a. To Anthony Bābājān.

My dear son, I received your letter of 10 Jumāda II on the 28th and noted that clothes are required inside. I have written about this to Ram Sundar Datt. My dear son, it is necessary that you go for horse riding and for strolls in the garden to enjoy the greenery and the beautiful flowers. You should visit Captain Martin two to three times a day without fail. Sit with him for sometime and introduce yourself to whoever comes there so that you get used to interacting with people. It is not proper to stay indoors for long. This is a must. I have also received two letters from Mir Buddhan. 8 Rajab.

Folio 315b. To Mir Sulaiman Khan.

I am happy to receive your letter. You want to know my travel plans a week or ten days in advance. When I decide to leave for Faizabad I will let you know ten days in advance. Rest assured that we will travel together.

Second, write to me if you bought pistols or any other goods from any merchant (*saudāgar*) here and did not pay him. I can make the payment [from my account]. The *saudāgar* is demanding the money. 10 Rajab, Tuesday.

Folio 316a. (Letter 19, in reply to letter 14) To Manik Ram.

I received your letter of 22 Jumāda II, along with three letters from Nawab Asaf-ud-Daula, one from Murid Khan and a letter from you addressed to Mir Sulaiman Khan. I have repeatedly asked you to send letters after a gap of three to four days. This letter of yours reached here after seventeen to eighteen days. What is the reason for this carelessness? In this letter you have not written about the news of Shahjahanabad.

You write that you have bought 6037 *Farrukhabadī asharfis* for Rs 10,000 and that you have sent them to Dr Thomas. What is this? Why only [for] Rs 10,000? You have so much money: Rs 40,000 *nazrāna,* Rs 56,000 *tankhwāh,* and other small incomes. From this you have sent me only Rs 30,000. Why have you sent only Rs 10,000 to Dr *ṣāḥib.* Send him the entire money.

I have noted that you have presented my letter to the Nawab,earned me a favour, and that the Nawab has given you a palanquin. I also note what you write about the dispatch of the sword, dagger and tray covers.

As for the money which Najaf Khan owes me, keep the account ready and send it when I ask for it.

I noted what you write about the *tankhwāh* and about the realization charges of Shah Sidq Ali.

I also noted that the *tankhwāh* of Munawwar Khan *ṣūbadār* has been fixed from Farrukhabad.

Took note of the fact that Salar Jung and Mirza Ali Khan want me to send the banana plants. Since I heard from Mirza Ali Khan I sent these to him. But Salar Jung had not mentioned anything about the plants to me. I will send them to him now that you write about it.

You write that you will make maximum effort to obtain *parwānas* for payment against the goods for Captain Martin and Mr Lloyd.To say something and to actually do it are different. At any rate try to get the *parwānas* soon.

You write that ever since Mir Muhammad Husain Ata Khan left you feel at a loss because you both did things together. Urgent matters are being left unattended. For the moment you attend to these. You can inform him later.

I took note of what you had written about the elephants earlier. I had written to you about them.

You write that the details of the income and the expenditure will be sent by Ram Sundar Datt. These are based on the papers prepared in English. My dear, you have Rs 56,000 from Farrukhabad, Rs 40,000 from *nazrāna,* money from the sale of elephants and money from some other places. You sent only Rs 30,000 to me, and Rs 10,000 were sent to Farrukhabad. Now you write that the papers will be sent in English. This work does not require so much effort. Write to me clearly.

I note that you have written to Ram Sundar Datt to prepare the papers.

I have noted the expenditure incurred in the preparation of the *ḥavelī.* I also note that you have entered the Rs 3000 payment made to Mir Sulaiman Khan into his account and that you will send Rs 1200 to Mr Store.

You write that the girl from Farrukhabad has been kept in a rented *ḥavelī* in Lucknow. I had earlier asked you to send her to Faizabad safely but you have not done so. You have not written about it. Write to me all the details.

I will bring with me the pistols, etc. that you had ordered for the courtiers of the Nawab.

I want to inform you that I have not done any work for the last fifteen days because I have been indisposed. 10 Rajab, Tuesday.

Folio 318a. To Mir Muhammad Husain Ata Khan.

I received your letter of 12 Jumāda II on 5 Rajab. You say that because of your illness you were not in a position to write to me. I hope you recover soon. We are helpless if any work is delayed because of illness. I received today, the 10th of Rajab, a letter from Manik Ram. I have sent a copy for your information. Keep in touch. 10 Rajab, Tuesday.

Folio 318b. (Letter 20) To Manik Ram.

I have repeatedly asked you to get the *tankhwāh* of the *firangis* and the *sipāhīs* fixed. But you have not done anything about it. As a result, the *sipāhīs* have raised a commotion in front of my havelī. I do not know why they have not yet received the payment when all the other soldiers of the Nawab's establishment are receiving their salary. Are they [the *sipāhīs* and the *firangīs*] not in the service of the Nawab that their payment has been delayed? You say that because of the Nawab's kindness towards us you have presented various things to him. What kindness? Despite the Nawab's kindness and your attending to him, the payment of the soldiers is still pending; so is my salary. I am sure that none of my work is being carried out there. It is confirmed that you are working towards the completion of your own work. Your work is always in shape, but my work is invariably left incomplete, and you always have the excuses of the *'āmil's* dismissals, etc.

Anyhow, let bygones be bygones. Now arrange for their payment at the earliest. Send Captain Martin whatever he requires soon. The *parwāna* of *tankhwāh* against his goods has not yet been prepared. Get it all done. Mr Perceret and Mr Lloyd will be the attorneys of my work when Captain Martin is away. It is therefore necessary for you to follow my instructions. 16 Rajab, Monday.

Folio 319a. To Ram Sundar Datt Sarkar
I had received your letter and replied to you. I write that the attorneys of my work in the absence of Captain Martin will be Mr Perceret and Mr Lloyd. Attend to them night and day and do all the work on their advice. 16 Rajab, Monday.

Folio 319b. To Mir Muhammad Husain Ata Khan
I have neither received your letter nor heard from Manik Ram for the last so many days. Keep writing to me regularly. This way I am kept well informed. I hear that the payment to the troopers and soldiers has not yet been made. I have sent strict instructions to Manik Ram. I am writing to him again with a copy enclosed to you. 16 Rajab.

Folio 320a. (Letter 21) To Manik Ram.
From Nawab Asaf-ud-Daula's letter, and from your letter of 22 Jumāda II which I received on the 10th, I gather that you have told the Nawab that I have completed his work here and am reaching back soon. This much enthusiasm in reporting matters to the Nawab was improper. You should have first properly enquired [my programme]. I have completed whatever was possible for me to do here. I have translated (*tarjema karda*) into English the papers that I had brought from the Nawab, submitted them to the Governor-General and explained to him the situation. But, strangely enough, the Nawab secretly [without informing me] took action on his own accord. While this is fine, [now] I am helpless. Who can act contrary to him when he has taken the matter in his own hands. Anyhow, now that this has happened, you should present the matter in a way that the Nawab is not offended, and feels that I did whatever was assigned to me to the best of my ability.

Once again you have not written anything about the court and the situation in Shahjahanabad. Neither Niyyaz Ali Khan nor you wrote anything to me. Write in detail where he is and what he is doing. 17 Rajab, Tuesday.

Folio 320b. To Mir Muhammad Husain Ata Khan.
I am concerned these days at receiving your letters intermittently. Send your letters to Dr Thomas so that they reach me here without delay. The copy of a letter I sent to Manik Ram is enclosed. Keep in touch, 17 Rajab, Tuesday.

Folio 321a. (Letter 22, in reply to Letter 16 and 17) To Manik Ram.

I received your letter of 3 Rajab on the 19th. I have also received the Nawab's letter in response to mine. You have written that the *asharfis* of Rs 10,000 have been sent to Dr Thomas and that you will send the remaining money also. But it will not be possible to make payment at the court of the Nawab for another two months. My dear , you have already received more than rupees one lac: Rs 40,000 as the *nazrāna,* Rs 56,000 as *tankhwāh,* and the rest as payment from other places. You have sent me only Rs 30,000 and the balance is still due. I do not know where it has gone.

You are complaining about the delayed payment from Farrukhabad. Why don't you write to me clearly and in detail what has become of the other money. I think it is enough if Mir Muhammad Husain Ata Khan goes to Farrukhabad for the collection of my money [because] if you also leave, my work at the court will be stalled. Ata Khan has already finalized the transaction and, as per the agreement, the money will be received in the promised period. If you also go there you too will receive the promise of payment. Therefore it is purposeless for you to go to Farrukhabad.

I noted that apropos the *tankhwāh* of Mr Perceret you have obtained the Nawab's signature on the papers for the period terminating on Jumāda I. I have also noted the points regarding the papers for the payment of Mir Buddhan, the *munshī* and his son, and also the memorandum of the *tankhwāh* of Mirza Yusuf Ali.

I have made a note of what you write about the dispatch of the sword, the dagger and the tray cover and that you have submitted the satin cloth belonging to Captain Martin, along with my clothes to the establishment of the Nawab. Write to me what price has been fixed for them [clothes]. Also settle the bill for the remaining clothes.

I have noted the problems being created by the *'amils* in the payment against the goods of Captain Martin and Mr Lloyd. What is this? Despite so much effort the money is being received now. There is no point in making excuses. I know that you have no concern other than that of your own work.

You want me to pay Rs 2000 to Gopi Mohan. For the moment I have to meet many expenses, therefore I will pay him later.

As for the gifts, I shall bring them later. I have obtained the specimen of the cloth you need. I will look around for it and bring it along if you require it.

You complain that I did not write to you about the summoning of the junior Bībī. I did not feel it necessary to write to you, and wrote instead to Ram Sundar Datt because you live in Lucknow and the junior Bībī is in Faizabad. There was no ill-intention—the programme was made in haste.

I have sent the reply to the letter of Mir Sulaiman Khan.

I have noted what you have said about Muhammad Ilich Khan and about Niyaz Ali Khan having reached Kanauj. Write the other details about him soon.

I am delighted to hear about the healing of the Nawab's wound. Keep sending me the news of the court.

Regarding your request for *kurtīs,* I feel that only eighteen days are left for Dussehra and it is, as you know, difficult to send them across at such short notice. But I will bring with me whatever [orders] are ready. Besides, you know that a large sum is required for getting *kurtīs* ready for thirty-two *paltans.* How can I manage with only Rs 30,000 that you have sent. I have to take care of other things as well.

I will acquire the *tānkhan* [horses] if I get them anywhere.

I have written to you earlier, and I again repeat, that it is useless to fix the salary of the troopers at Farrukhabad. There is no *jāidād* left there and the money which Muzaffar Jang owes me has already been assigned. It is therefore necessary that you get the *parwāna* for this *tankhwāh* in a routine way from the treasury. Otherwise you can get it made in the name of Qutb Jafar who should go to Faizabad to collect the money.

On the Nawab's request I had ordered the preparation of a boat in Faizabad. I know that it is now ready. Inform the Nawab about the same. If he acquires it then its fine; otherwise, keep it with you until I return.

I received on the 20th your second letter of 7 Rajab along with the letters of Niyaz Ali Khan and Najaf Khan. I have written to you a hundred times about the payment against the goods of Captain Martin and Mr Lloyd. This is important. Get the *parwāna* of *tankhwāh* from wherever it is easy to obtain the money and dispatch it to them. They will arrange for the collection. As for your desire to go to Farrukhabad, please do not go there. I will be very angry if you go.

You write that you mentioned the *kurtīs* on the orders of the Nawab. The fact is that you have not received any money from the Nawab nor did you send me any money for the work. Also, it has been about two years and I am yet to receive the payment for the *kurtīs.* The Governor-General says that we cannot arrange for the new *kurtīs* because the payment for the previous consignment has not yet been received. Obtain the Nawab's order for the payment of the *kurtīs* from Farrukhabad and inform me. 21 Rajab.

Folio 324a. To Mir Muhammad Husain Ata Khan.

I received your letter of 30 Jumāda II on the 19th. Continue with the routine [arrangement] in the manner I suggested: whatever money you receive should go to Dr Thomas, and not a single penny to anybody else. Take note of this and consider this letter as a document for this purpose. Show it to any one who asks for money.

I have repeatedly written to Manik Ram about the payment to the troopers. For the moment, to alleviate their difficulty, you can arrange for the money from my account. Dr Thomas has also written that we should think about the payment of the soldiers. I am also coming back soon. The salary of Mir Shah Ali and the other *harkāras* should also be paid from my money. Keep in touch. 23 Rajab, Monday.

Folio 324b. To Niyaz Ali Khan.

Received your letter on the 20th. I was very worried since I had not heard from you for the last five months. I appreciate your efforts to carry out the Nawab's work. You have earned the Nawab's and my admiration.

I note your news about the money that Najaf Khan owes me, and also that you have managed to obtain from him an order for the payment of Rs 37,000 of that money in the name of Bhawani Singh zamindar. Well done. As a matter of fact, we all know what Najaf Khan is like. I will try and get the payment of the money from the Company. Keep in touch. Send your letters through Dr Thomas. 23 Rajab.

Folio 325a. To Mirza Abdullah Beg kumaidān.

Received your letter. I am happy that you met the Nawab and have been awarded a *khil'at* and also that the account for the payment of *sarishta* has been settled. You are fortunate that God has created conditions for establishing contact with the Nawab with regard to your *naukarī*. Rest assured that I am also reaching there soon. Keep in touch until we meet. 23 Rajab.

Folio 325b. (Letter 23, in reply to letter 18) To Manik Ram.
The *Ṣāḥib-i Kalān* is happy to know that Mir Sulaiman Khan has been invited by the Nawab. He [*Ṣāḥib-i Kalān*] admires his experience, sobriety, and his style of work. He adds that it is good that the Nawab wishes to be in touch with such people. He has also written to the Nawab about the case of Sulaiman Khan and asked me also to write. He will leave [for Lucknow] within a day or two. Attend to his work since he will reach before me.

Send all the money that you receive for me to Dr Thomas. Attend to my business, in consultation with Mir Muhammad Husain Ata Khan, until I am back.

I received your letter of 10 Rajab along with the letter of the Nawab, ordering you to leave for Farrukhabad on the 26th for the collection of money. Even though it was not necessary for you to go, there is no harm in reaching there since the Nawab wants you. My pleasure is in [doing] whatever the Nawab desires. Do what is best for my work in consultation with Ata Khan. But do try and get free at the earliest and return to the court to expedite the payment of the *tankhwāh* which is still due.

I received the letter of Lalit Singh, the zamindar of Srinagar, together with your letter. Ratan Singh, who had gone there to bring the presents, sends the account of an expenditure of Rs 772. Of this amount, he says he has given Rs 500 to the Raja. However, the Raja is silent about the receipt of the money. Ratan Singh wants some more money. I am therefore sending you a copy of the details of things there. Act appropriately.

The Raja writes that he has sent four *kajkahs* [hooks and beams used in animal driven carts] and four musks. As per the letter of Azmatdeep, one pheasant is also included. But you write that there are two pheasants and four musks. Find out the exact details. If there is delay in acquiring the presents that I had asked for, then write to Ratan Singh that there is no need for him to stay there any longer. He should come back. 28 Rajab.

Folio 326b. To Mir Muhammad Husain Ata Khan.
I have received a letter from Manik Ram. He writes that the Nawab

has asked him to go to Farrukhabad. I told him several times not to go there but it appears that he has not received these letters. Come back to the court whenever you are free from the work in Farrukhabad and manage my work there which remains unattended [in your absence]. As I have written to you earlier, all the money received should be sent to Dr Thomas. 28 Rajab.

Folio 327a. To Nawab Asaf-ud-Daula.

I received your letter apropos your order to Manik Ram to proceed to Farrukhabad to arrange for the payment of the money. As I wish to serve you to the best of my capacity, it is indeed my good fortune that my servant has been so chosen by your Excellency.

I also received your letter summoning Mir Sulaiman Khan. The Governor-General was happy and has informed Sulaiman Khan that he is being summoned in appreciation of his good qualities. He shall proceed for Lucknow soon. The Governor-General was kind enough to issue letters under his seal and wished that I should also write a letter. Sulaiman Khan was close to the late Nawab Shuja-ud-Daula who was also very kind to him. He is now planning to leave tomorrow or the day after so as to visit you and hopes for your favours. I too am keen to meet you. But some matters here have delayed my departure. 28 Rajab.

Folio 328a. To Niyaz Ali Khan.

I had earlier replied to your letter. Since Manik Ram has left for Farrukhabad you must take utmost care of my work there. I enclose herewith copies of my replies to the letters of Manik Ram and Ata Khan. They should have left for Farrukhabad. Bring the letter meant for Farrukhabad to the notice of the Nawab. Write to me regularly. 28 Rajab.

Folio 328a. To Mir Buddhan.

I received your letter. My dear son, there is no use in staying in Faizabad. You [should] join Manik Ram in the camp. It will be easier for him to arrange the payment of *tankhwāh* and your deputation if you are there [in the camp]. I have repeatedly informed him of this. You should join him without delay. 29 Rajab.

Folio 328b. To Mir Muhammad Husain Ata Khan.

Since Manik Ram has left for Farrukhabad, send whatever money is received to Dr Thomas. I have repeatedly written to you about this. Since the work relating to the court is still unfinished, come back to Lucknow when your work there is over. Try and collect all the money that people there owe me. Keep in touch and send me an account of the income and expenses there regularly. Also, find out how much money has been received ever since I left, in which account, and from which area. In addition, [write] whether payment has been received from the people about whom I had mentioned earlier. Finally, how much money is due to be collected? In sum, find out the total amount of money [collected].

Mr Bristow has forwarded to me Jugal Kishore's paper relating to the expenses of Manik Ram. I am enclosing it here so that you can find out the details there. Take care that Manik Ram does not know that you are making investigations on this score. All the work must be done in consultation with each other without causing any one offence. Dispatch whatever money you collect for me to Dr Thomas. You should also meet him and brief him about what is necessary. You may also ask him for whatever you require. I have written to him regarding this. My departure in that direction [Faizabad or Lucknow] has been delayed because of my illness. God willing, I will also set out in a week or ten days after the departure of Mir Sulaiman Khan. 30 Rajab, Tuesday.

Folio 329b. (Letter 24) To Manik Ram.

As soon as you are free from the work in Farrukhabad, you should rush back to the court to complete, in consultation with Mir Muhammad Husain Ata Khan, the unfinished works.Collect all my money due from various places and send it to Dr Thomas. I have written to you earlier also to write in detail about all the money collected.

Mir Sulaiman has left for the court as per the orders. Since he is reaching there a few days before I arrive, attend to his work. There is no difference between me and Sulaiman Khan. Whatever you do [for him] will bring happiness to me. My departure from this place is delayed because of my illness. I will leave in a week or ten days time after the departure of Mir Sulaiman. 30 Rajab.

Folio 330a. To Mir Muhammad Husain Ata Khan.

I received two of your letters dated 7th and 12th of Rajab along with a letter of Nawab Muzaffar Jang on the 30th. I noted your response to the letters of Manik Ram. We all know that he is a liar and misleads and cooks up excuses. It was for this purpose that I sent you copies of his letters. I knew [all this] very well. I am aware of your excellent qualities, integrity and honesty. You need not write to me about these things. I am sure that your efforts to carry out my work will be successful. Rush back to Lucknow and collect all the money due to me. Attend to my work along with Manik Ram and keep me regularly informed.

You have written that Rs 16,000 from the remaining amount of the *tankhwāhdārs* has been received, and that of the Rs 2618 you have sent Rs 1000, on the suggestion of Manik Ram, to Gul Muhammad *saudāgar*. Also, that Rs 15,000 has been dispatched by *hundī* to Dr Thomas. Dr Thomas had written to me earlier about the receipt of the *hundī*. I am happy. Forward similarly any other money that is received. I noted the money that you have paid to Gul Muhammad *saudāgar* and the balance amount to be paid. Do whatever you feel is appropriate.

You write that all the money on the account of *tankhwāh*—a total of Rs 42,000—except Rs 36,000 in the account of *khānsāmān* and Rs 6000 from the account of Muhammad Ali Beg, has been received. Good. All this is a result of your efforts. But you should also think about the early collection of the remaining amount as we have more important work ahead. Attend to it when you are free from [collection work].

Regarding the salary of the troopers of the Company, you say that Nawab Muzaffar Jang has written to the Nawab that he is ready to pay Rs 623 towards four months emoluments. You have sought my permission for giving Rs 25,000. Do whatever is best to clear the matter of payment of salary to the troopers. 1 Sha'bān, al mu'aẓẓam, Calcutta.

Folio 331b. To Niyaz Ali Khan.

Mir Sulaiman Khan will arrive in Faizabad within four to five days, and on the 9th of Sha'bān—after nine days—I too will depart from here. You should also leave for Azimabad on the receipt of this letter. This will enable me to update myself on the affairs of the court, the courtiers and the advisers of the Nawab. Since I plan to stay for some time in Azimabad, you should request the Nawab to order the *dārogha* of *dāk* not to dispatch my letters directly to Faizabad. He should direct the *dāk* officials of Azimabad to expedite the dispatch and delivery of my letters. 1 Sha'bān.

Folio 332a. To Mir Muhammad Husain Ata Khan.

I received your letter of 15 Rajab along with the letter of *khānsāmān* as well as a copy of Mihrban Khan's letter to you. I noted that you have obtained the *khil'at* for the appointment of *khānsāmān* and sent it to him. You have also acquired an agreement for the payment of my money. You also report that Mihrban Khan will repay the Rs 6000 due from him in ten days time. Of these ten days four days have already passed and the rest of the money will be received in four to five days. I am satisfied with the way you are doing your work. I am no longer worried about the money and am sure that you will receive it. I also noted that you arranged everything for the settlement of the *tankhwāh* but just when the money was to be received, Manik Ram arrived and wanted to take all the credit. Do not worry. I believe in your sincere efforts and the impression of your hard work and sincerity will always remain in my heart. I know you very well. So you should not worry about what other people say.

I have written to Niyaz Ali Khan that subsequent to Mir Sulaiman's departure from here, I too will set out. He should leave for Azimabad on receipt of my letter so that I am informed of the latest by him. This is just for your information. I am arriving soon. Attend to my work with sincerity. Send the money to Dr Thomas. 6 Sha'bān, Monday.

Folio 332b. To Mir Sulaiman Khan.

I am happy to receive your letter along with two jars of *murabba* and *achār*, two letters with the *dastak* of *rāhdārī*, an album of the pictures and a copy of *Gulistān*. I relished the *murraba* and the *achār*, and enjoyed reading the book and going through the album.

Regarding your request for letters for Mr Math and Dr Thomas, fifty bottles of wine, half *ser* of *julāba julāb* [purgative] and two *ser* of gun powder to be sent with your people, [please note] that if I have time I will send you the *julāba julāb*, otherwise I will bring the *julāba* and a lot of *madira* with me.

As advised by you, I will write about the case of Agha Ahmad Beg and Muhammad Waris to the official in Sylhet. I will dispatch it through the internal correspondence [network].

Collect the money that you have paid to my *munshī* from Manik Ram and inform me. You write that there are other good pictures in Murshidabad. I would like to have a look at them on my arrival there. Write to me your Murshidabad address so that on my arrival there I can send my people [to bring these pictures]. 7 Sha'bān, Tuesday.

Folio 333b. To Mir Muhammad Husain Ata Khan.

I received your letter of 18 Rajab along with two other letters of 25 and 26 Jumāda II on the 9th of Sha'bān. I cannot fathom the reason for the late arrival of my letters. I noted that Beni Ram has been killed, and that Manik Ram is there. I hope that through your sincere efforts the collection of money will be completed. I am leaving soon for Azimabad. I have summoned Niyaz Ali Khan there so as to enquire about some cases before I leave for the court. I will report to you on the developments. Send whatever money you have collected to Dr Thomas. Attend to my work diligently. There should be no one else between you and Dr Thomas. 9 Sha'bān, Thursday.

Folio 334a. (Letter 25) To Manik Ram.

I had written to you earlier to arrange for the payment of salaries to the Company troopers and the people employed in my establishment so as to avoid any trouble. I wonder why you are neglecting this work. The payment to the troopers is not being made the way it was done so far. Why have they raised a commotion at the gate [of my *ḥavelī*]? If you cannot do even this much work what else can you do? Arrange for their payment without any delay. Of the large sum that you collected, you sent only Rs 30,000 to me and Rs 10,000 to Dr Thomas. I do not know what happened to the balance. Even my servants are not being paid and are facing difficulty. I am very unhappy and you will suffer the consequences. 9 Sha'bān, Thursday.

Folio 334a. To Ram Sundar Datt Sarkar.

I have repeatedly written to you that since Bībī Jawahar has been asked to come here, you should hand over to her two months advance payment for travel expenses to enable her to arrive here soon. I now know that you have not yet paid her. This has delayed her departure. Do I have to write to you for such a minor thing? At any rate, before you reply to this letter hand over the money to the Bībī and to Didar Bakhsh so that they can set off soon. 9 Sha'bān, Thursday, Calcutta.

Folio 334b. To Mir Sulaiman Khan.

I received your letter along with the one addressed to Shah Sidq Ali. In response to your query regarding my plans, I wish to state that I too have arranged the boat, etc. Since you are leaving on the 17th, I will also commence [my journey] two to three days after your departure. There would be no further delay in my departure. The *Ṣāḥib-i Kalān* [Governor-General] has written to the Company about Najaf Khan's case. A response approving his proposal has now been received. But the payment is dependant on the Counsel's decision which will be decided soon. In case of its non-payment this year, it will certainly be done the following year.

I had asked you in my earlier letter to send me your Murshidabad address so as to enable me to send my men to you. Despite my writing to you the address has not yet been sent. Send it soon. It seems you do not want me to visit Murshidabad. 13 Sha'bān, Monday.

Folio 335a. (Letter 26) To Manik Ram.

I had earlier written to Niyaz Ali Khan to arrive in Azimabad. I believe that as per my instructions he will reach there. I leave for Azimabad on the 22nd or the 23rd. Only the arrangement of the boats for the riverine route and the loading of goods needs to be done. This will be completed in two to three days. I have written to you repeatedly about the payment to the troopers and the people in my employment. They should be paid the same amount and in the same manner as has been done so far. I gather that so far no payment has been made to them. Why is it that despite my repeated instructions you pay no attention. You should understand that this will cause you a lot of embarassment. You have so much money with you and yet you claim that you are financially unable to pay their salary. Make the payments soon and inform me. Do everything in consultation with Mir Muhammad Husain Ata Khan. There should be no deviation from this.

Bring the two pairs of good horses stationed in Faizabad for the *wilāyatī* chariot (*rath)* and keep them there. 19 Sha'bān, Sunday.

Folio 335b. To Mir Muhammad Husain Ata Khan.

Your letter of 18 Rajab, was received on 18 Sha'bān. I am a bit worried because during this entire month I have not received any letter from you. I had earlier written to Niyaz Ali Khan asking him to visit Azimabad when I am there so that I get news of the court from him. Convey to him my programme if you see him. In case you do not meet him then write to me about the situation there. I have decided to depart from here. I am looking for a [proper] boat and conveyance arrangement, and waiting for the loading of the boat. This should be over in three to four days. God willing, I will leave this place by the 23rd. You attend to my work there. I am arriving soon. 19 Sha'bān, Sunday.

Folio 336b. To Mir Muhammad Husain Ata Khan.
I received your letter of 6 Sha'bān on the 22nd. I had written to you earlier to free yourself from the work at Farrukhabad and arrive at the camp to attend to my work. I hope you have acted accordingly. My departure is being delayed due to the loading of the goods on the boat. I had written to Niyaz Ali Khan to come and meet me in Azimabad. If you see him convey to him any important information which I should know. In this way I can update myself of the developments there. 23 Sha'bān, Thursday.

Folio 336b. (Letter 27 in reply to Letter 19) To Manik Ram.
I received your letter, dated 26 Rajab, containing the news about your work in Farrukhabad regarding the money collection and other news on the 22nd of Sha'bān. Relieve yourself soon [fromthe work] and rush back to the camp along with Mir Muhammad Husain Ata Khan so as to attend to my work there. I am also starting from here in a day or two when the loading of the boat will be complete. 23 Sha'bān, Thursday, Calcutta.

Folio 337a. To Mir Muhammad Husain Ata Khan.
I received your letter of 3 Sha'bān on the 26th. I repeat that you should relieve yourself of the work in Farrukhabad and reach Lucknow. Dispatch to me a report of the situation there through Dr Thomas. I am also leaving in two to three days. Everything has been completed there. God willing I will arrive in Azimabad soon. As I wrote to you earlier, you should send your letters through the *harkāra* to Dr Thomas. Send the details of the camp to me as soon as you reach there. 26 Sha'bān, Sunday.

Folio 337b. To Mir Muhammad Husain Ata Khan.
I had written to Niyaz Ali Khan to come and meet me so that I

could keep myself abreast of the affairs of the Lucknow court as well as that of Shahjahanabad. Meanwhile, I heard from Niyaz Ali that he left for Shahjahanabad at the behest of the Nawab. Since it is necessary for me to update myself of the developments there [in Lucknow] you are instructed to visit Azimabad once I arrive there so that I get to know the details from you. In case you cannot make it, then it is imperative for you to send me the details of this court as well as of the royal court. Find out all the details and write to me. It is necessary that you come over and meet me, even if it is only for two days. I will start the journey tomorrow, the 5th of Ramẓān. All the arrangements—loading of boats, etc—have been completed. I have also acquired most of the things that you had asked for. You will receive these when we meet. 3 Ramẓān-al-mubārak, Calcutta.

Folio 338a. (Letter 28) To Manik Ram.

I had written earlier to Niyaz Ali Khan to come and meet me so as to convey the news of the court and of Shahjahanabad. Meanwhile, I received his letter of 2 Ramẓān stating that he has been asked to leave for Shahjahanabad [Delhi] at the behest of the Nawab. Since it is imperative for me to be familar with the developments there and in the imperial court [Shahjahanabad], you are instructed to obtain the same and report to me. Write to me also about the developments at Farrukhabad since you have been there as well.

The arrangement of the boats and the goods is over. God willing, I will commence my journey tomorrow, the 5th of Ramẓān. Continue to attend to my work in all sincerity. This will be to your advantage. 3 Ramẓān, al mubārak, Saturday.

Folio 338b. To Mir Muhammad Husain Ata Khan.

I received your letter of 12 Sha'bān on the 4th of Rajab. Earlier, on the 3rd of Ramẓān, I had written to you and I write again that Niyaz Ali left for Delhi at the behest of the Nawab. I had wanted him to visit me in Azimabad. Thus the news that I had expected from him did not arrive.

Today, the 5th of Ramẓān, I have commenced my journey from here. I will be reaching there soon. Relieve yourself from the money collection, etc. and reach Lucknow so as to collect the news of the latest developments at the court. Come over to Azimabad for two days so that I can have the news from you. See to it that no news is left [unconveyed]. Manik Ram had given the Nawab the impression that I have completed his [Nawab's] work. But the reality is that I only translated into English the paper he had given me and presented it to the *Ṣāḥib-i Kalān*. I also orally explained the situation to him. But the Nawab settled the matter on his own in a manner he thought most appropriate. I was helpless in such a situation. Who else could have done anything? It was not proper of Manik Ram to show haste and give the Nawab an [erroneous] impression without consulting me. It is necessary that you clarify this matter with the Nawab when you reach the camp. Do come over to Azimabad for two days during my stay there. 5 Ramẓān al-mubārak, Monday, Calcutta.

Folio 339b. To Mir Muhammad Husain Ata Khan.

I have replied to your letter of 12 Sha'bān. It has been one month and a few days since I heared from you. I am completely in the dark about the developments there. You had written to me that on your arrival in Lucknow you will write to me all the details. I hear that you are now in Lucknow. But you have still not written to me.

I left Calcutta on the 7th of Ramẓān and entered Murshidabad on the 21st. I will start from here soon. You are instructed to visit me in Azimabad [Patna] for two days. In case this is difficult then send me a detailed report of the developments at the courts of both the Nawab as well as the Emperor. It is important for you to come. I take it that you will come saddled with the detailed news. I have taken along with me most of the things that you had ordered. I will give them to you when I reach [Azimabad]. I will also send a letter to the Nawab when I reach there. For the moment—until I reach Azimabad—write to me the news there. 21 Ramẓān, Wednesday.

Folio 340a. (Letter 29) To Manik Ram.

I had received earlier a letter from you dated 6th Sha'bān. I have not received any letter since then and have no news about the conditions there. It has been a month since you arrived in Lucknow. Despite the fact that you are close to Dr Thomas there has been much delay in the dispatch of letters. How will I know of the developments there if you do not write to me. It is important that there is no negligence in the writing and the dispatch of news.

I left Calcutta on the 7th, entered Murshidabad on the 21st, and am now proceeding ahead. Attend to my work there and continue to dispatch the details of the development at the courts of both the

Nawab as well as the Emperor. I will write to the Nawab from Azimabad. 21 Ramẓān, Wednesday.

Folio 340b. To Khwaja Pedrose.

I had intended speaking to you before my departure but it slipped out of my mind. As per the orders of the *Ṣāḥib-i Kalān* [Governor-General] I had handed over the paper for the Rs 80,000 *tankhwāh* of Najaf Khan *ṣāḥib* to Montague *ṣāḥib*. I had asked him to pass on to you Rs 10,000 pertaining to Mir Sulaiman Khan once he received the money of the *tankhwāh*. Now I have also written to Mr Montague about it. Find out about the matter. As soon as the money is received, meet him and collect [your dues]. Once the money is received, hand over to him the receipt stating that you have received from Mr Montague Rs 10,000 pertaining to Mir Sulaiman Khan. 21 Ramẓān, Wednesday, Murshidabad.

Folio 341a. To Gokulchand Mukherje, in Calcutta.

On my arrival in Jangipur from Muradbagh I discovered that Piru has left for Murshidabad. He has absconded without my permission. Enquire from his house about his whereabouts and arrest him if he is there. In case he is not there, he is then likely to be in Berhampur or Qasimbazar in Murshidabad. He may have got some employment there. Look for him and [retrieve] my money with which he has absconded. Also obtain from him Rs 10 of which he fraudulantly took Rs 5 from Raso Sarkar and Rs 5 from Chintamani *Kahār*. 25 Ramẓān, Sunday, Jangipur, the silk *kothī*.

Folio 341b. To Mir Muhammad Husain Ata Khan

I received your letter of 29 Sha'bān on the night of 3 Shawwāl on my way near Sakri, four to five *kos* beyond Rajmahal. I noted your comments on Jugal Kishore. I had sent you his note only for your information. I am aware of his fraudulence and deceit. It was unnecessary for you to mention his case.

I am surprised to note that your letter of 29 Sha'bān came along with a 16 Ramẓān letter of Dr Thomas. Why did you dispatch this letter sixteen or seventeen days after you wrote it. From Dr Thomas' letter I gather that you met him and informed him about my instruction to you to visit Azimabad; your inability to do so without the Nawab's permission; and your request to me to obtain this [permission] from the Nawab. He also writes that you have again returned to Faizabad. I am surprised at this. It is strange that you do not mention these things in your own letter. You do mention that the delay in writing to me was because of your departure to Lucknow from Farrukhabad. It would have been nice if you even alluded to the receipt of my letter. During the months of Sha'bān and Ramẓān I sent you nine letters: on the 1st, 6th, 9th, 19th, 23rd, and 26th of Sha'bān; and on the 3rd, 5th and 21st of Ramẓān from Murshidabad. I had mentioned about my departure from Calcutta in two of my letters. I have not received replies to any of my letters. Anyway, in future have some consideration for our friendship. I have crossed two *kos* from Sakri today the 4th of Shawwāl. God willing, I will reach soon. 4 Shawwāl, Wednesday, Gangaprashad, situated between Sakri and Teliagarhi.

Folio 342b. To Manik Ram.

I received your letter of 29 Sha'bān on the 3rd of Shawwāl on my way near Sakri. I noted, among other things, that you have received Rs 20,000 from the *tankhwāh* of Farrukhabad and a *tamassuk* of Rs 16,000 for the remaining money under the seal of Nawab Muzaffar Jang. The bond is accompanied with a promise to be paid in three months time. I wonder why there was delay in dispatching a letter written on the 19th which I received on the 16th of Ramẓān. I sent to you four letters from Murshidabad: on the 19th and 23rd of Sha'bān and on the 21st of Ramẓān. I am astonished that you did not respond to either of these.

At the moment I have proceeded two *kos* ahead of Sakri and, God willing, will reach there soon. You must make all efforts to attend to my work and collection of the money. Do not delay the dispatch of letters containing news of the Nawab and the Emperor's court. 4 Shawwāl, Wednesday, Gangaprashad.

Folio 343a. To Niyaz Ali Khan

I received your letter of 15 Sha'bān on the 3rd of Shawwāl on my way near Sakri. I am happy to know that you have been awarded a *khil'at* and jewels by the Nawab and have been ordered to attend the royal court. All these favours are timely and befit your status. I am confidant that you will show due consideration to our friendship and take care of my work earnestly.

I came to know from Manik Ram's letter about the sad demise of Lutf Ali Khan. This world is transitory and everyone has to pass off. There is no other way; therefore one has to console oneself and concede to the will of God. Keep in touch and continue to inform me about the developments at the imperial court. 4 Shawwāl, Wednesday, Gangaprashad.

Folio 343b. To Manik Ram.

It has been half a month or even more since you returned from Farrukhabad. It is surprising that you are nowhere close to Dr Thomas or Mr Martin, and have not sent me a single letter. You are an intelligent person and [I am sure] realize that it is part of your duty as my employee to inform me about all the details and carry out my work in a proper manner. But you have not made any genuine effort in this direction.

Mir Muhammad Husain Ata Khan writes that a monthly expenditure of Rs 8000 is needed there, and that you have made it clear that in case I do not reach there you will be unable to carry out the work. I am astonished at your estimate of the expenses. Well, you should write to me why you need Rs 8000. You are also instructed to meet Mr Lloyd and Mr Perceret. On their advice you can curtail the unnecessary expenses on the mule and the bullocks and on additional people, like *chābuk sawār*, Shah Ali and the *harkāra*.

I had repeatedly written to you about Mir Buddhan's deputation. But you have done nothing about it and have paid him every month from my establishment. If you had deputed him in one or the other of the retinues then his payment could have been drawn from the *sarkār* and not from my establishment. [Anyhow] let bygones be bygones. Now suspend his payment as well as that of all the others who should be paid from the *sarkār* of the Nawab.

As for the *deorhī*, retain whatever the two English officials advise and suspend the rest. It will be unacceptable to me if you spend money on items other than what they suggest. You will be held accountable for it.

You have not prepared the account for four to five months even though the rule is that it should be done within five to six days of the following month. It is imperative that you prepare all the papers with the details of the expenditure incurred and send it to me. It is the requirement of the service that you consider yourself the servant (*naukar*) and myself the master (*khudāwand*) in the conduct of work assigned to you. All the matters need to be carried out with honesty and in a proper manner. Keep me informed about everything. You have not done any of the work assigned to you.

One of the boats in Faizabad has been bought by the Nawab. I had earlier asked you to inform the Nawab about this but you did not write anything about it. You are aware that I have spent money getting it painted and varnished so as to present it to the Nawab. Ask the Nawab that if he wants the boat he should send some people with the *dastak* and some *dandiyān* [ropemen] to carry it to the court [Lucknow]. But it is fine if he orders it to be kept in Faizabad. It is not necessary to spend Rs 150 on its maintenance.

Apparently Ratan Singh *munshī* who had gone to get the presents from the Raja of Srinagar, and about whom I had intimated you, has returned. But you have not written anything about it. 15 Shawwāl, Friday, Munger.

Folio 345a. To Mirza Abdullah Beg kumaidān.

I received your letter and was happy to know that your work has somewhat been done and that you are now in Farrukhabad on the advice of John Bristow. Rest assured that things will be done to your satisfaction.

You write that I must have learnt about the misappropriation [of money] by Manik Ram from the letters of the European officials. You add that you have done a summary investigation of the matter and discovered that apart from the *sarkār* money, about Rs half lakh in cash, jewels, clothes and horses of Farrukhabad have also been misappropriated by him. You seek permission to investigate the matter further and send me a report. Many people have informed me about this but the details are yet to be established. It will be good if you enquire into the matter and report to me. This will reinforce the value of your friendship. I am arriving there soon. Keep in touch. 16 Sahwwāl, Sunday.

Folio 346a. To Mir Muhammad Husain Ata Khan.

I had received your letter of 29th on the 3rd of Shawwāl and had replied to it. Now I have received here in Munger, on the evening of 15th Shawwāl, another letter dated 6th of Ramẕān. You write that since for the purpose of practical expediency you collaborate with Manik Ram, it was not proper to write to me all the details. This is fine. But write to me regularly about the other matters. I have decided to send my *munshī* there on my arrival in Azimabad. Tell him everything when he arrives. In this way I will get to know the details from him. For the moment write to me about the developments there without delay. 16 Shawwāl, Sunday near Surajgarh.

Folio 346b. To Mir Sulaiman Khan.

When I met you in Jangipur you had mentioned that we will meet again in Rajmahal. Accordingly, I reached there. But I was told that you had left the place two days back. Thus my desire to meet you remained in my heart. Anyhow, the purpose was to know about your welfare. God willing, we will meet soon if we remain well.

I gather from the letter of Manik Ram that Lutf Ali Khan has expired. I am extremely sad to hear this news. I am sure you too will console yourself by the fact that this world is transitory. I enclose herewith a letter from Niyaz Ali Khan which is addressed to you. I hope that before we meet I will receive a letter from you. I will be happy even if you write two lines. 16 Shawwāl, Sunday.

Folio 347a. To Manik Ram.

I entered Azimabad on the 22nd of Shawwāl. Two boats of Mr Martin and two others for me—full of goods—have already been dispatched from here. Obtain and send to me soon the *dastak* and *rāhdārī* for all the four boats before they reach Durighat so that there is no interferance [in their passage]. This is a must. According to the orders of the Nawab, I have sent about thirty-three *mans* and ten *sers* of glass [glazer] tiles (*khishthā-i shīsha*) by the same boat. Hand these over to the Nawab and keep the other goods with you in whichever way you think best. 24 Shawwāl, Azimabad.

Folio 347a. To Mir Muhammad Husain Ata Khan.

I received your letter of 7 Shawwāl on the 22nd and noted the details about the affairs you write to me about. I have entered Azimabad and will dispatch the *munshī* in four to five days. You will know from him what I have in mind. Keep writing about the other matters. 24 Shawwāl, Azimabad.

Folio 347b. To Manik Ram.

I have sent the *munshī* to Faizabad. Since I need to consult you on some matters you are instructed to reach Faizabad before my arrival there. 6 Ẕīqa'da, Saturday.

Folio 347b. To Mir Muhammad Husain Ata Khan.

I received your letter of 17 Shawwāl on the 5th of Ẕīqa'da. I had sent the *munshī* on the 6th of Ẕīqa'da and he will be reaching there soon. You are therefore instructed to stay on in Faizabad until his arrival. You will know from the *munshī* what is in my heart. 6 Z̲īqa'da, Saturday.

Folio 348a. To Nawab Asaf-ud-Daula.

With the grace of God I reached Faizabad on the 24th of Z̲īqa'da. I am very keen to meet you and wish to rush to your court to fulfil this desire. But I have to wind up some matters here: the boats laden with goods are yet to arrive, and I am fatigued and indisposed following the long journey. I will have to stay back to receive the goods and to recover from my travel fatigue. Subsequently, I shall have the honour of presenting myself to you.

In the meanwhile, Mir Muhammed Husain Ata Khan had intended leaving for the court. But I will bring him along with me since I had asked him to stay here until my arrival. I hope that until I have the honour of attending your court I will receive a letter from you with the good news of your health. May God enhance your power and fortune. 25 Z̲īqa'da, Thursday.

Folio 348b. To Nawab Mukhtar-ud-Daula Bahadur.

I reached Faizabad on 24 Z̲īqa'da and am extremely impatient to meet you. But since some of my works are still incomplete—the boats with the goods are due to arrive, and I am feeling tired after the journey—I will stay here for some time. I will come over and meet you as soon as I recover from the fatigue and receive the goods. I hope that until I reach there I will be fortunate to have the news of your well-being. 25 Z̲īqa'da, Thursday.

Folio 349a. To Raja Chait Singh.

It has been one month since the four boats—two laden with my goods and two with the goods of Mr Martin—left Azimabad for Faizabad. I gather that they have crossed the territory of the English *ṣāḥibs* without any problem. But they have been captured (*qurq*) in *ghāt* Maner from where your jurisdiction (*'amal*) begins. I am surprised that despite our old and sincere friendship, an offence which was not committed even by the officials of the English Company has been perpetrated by your people. I fail to comprehend this. However, a *harkāra* is being sent to you. Courtesy demands that you hand over to him a letter (*chitthī*) of non-interference. You can also send one of your men with him so that nobody holds back the goods on the way. 25 Z̲īqa'da, Thursday.

Folio 349a. To Manik Ram.

I reached Faizabad on the 24th of Ẕīqa'da. But, for the last three to four months I have had no idea of your work or your whereabouts—whether you have been in the camp or in Faizabad. I have not received any letter from you at all. The arrangement for many of the matters here depends on your arrival. Please come over to Faizabad soon. I had earlier sent a letter through the *munshī* inviting you here. This has apparently been delivered to you by the *harkāra.* I repeat the invitation. Present to the Nawab the letter that I have sent for him, and obtain his reply. I had asked you earlier to send the Farrukhabad girl to Faizabad. But since she has not yet arrived here I wonder where you have kept her. 25 Ẕīqa'da, Thursday.

Folio 349b. To Mir Sulaiman Khan.

I received your letter along with one from Niyaz Ali Khan. I arrived here in Faizabad on Wednesday, the 24th. Since you had left Azimabad before I did, I thought you would arrive here prior to me. I look forward to meeting you. 29 Ẕīqa'da, Sunday.

Folio 350a. To Jagannath, the deputy of Mir Waliullah Khan.

From the 1st of Rabī' I, the Nawab had issued [the order] about the *tan<u>kh</u>wāh* of Mir Muhammad Husain Ata Khan, his elder brother and his nephew in the name of Mirza Ali Khan. The Mirza had subsequently written about the *tan<u>kh</u>wāh* to Mir Waliullah Khan. Since Mir Waliullah is presently with the army camp and you represent him in the *pargana,* you are asked to clear the dues regarding the *tan<u>kh</u>wāh* of Ata Khan and hand over the money to his people. Consider this as instructions from Mir Waliullah Khan himself. Mir Waliullah Khan is also an associate of the *sarkār.* Mir Muhammad Husain Ata Khan has come to me. He is in difficulty because he has not received his salary for ages.

Manik Ram, who is the *mutaṣaddī* of the *sarkār,* is familiar with this. In the case of an excuse that no instructions on the matter have been received from Mir Waliullah Khan, keep the money from 1 Rabī' I, 1189 for upto 10 months, i.e. until the end of Ẕīḥijja as *amānat* at the rate of Rs 600 per month. On receiving the instructions from Mir Waliullah, the money should be passed on to his [Ata Khan] people. See to it that in future their salary arrives regularly every month. For the moment, the arrears of their salary should be kept as *amānat* and not handed over to anybody. It is best for you to follow my instructions, for eventually Mir Waliullah will communicate to you the same. 11 Ẕīḥijja 1189, Thursday, Faizabad.

Folio 350b. To Makkhu Khan, kotwāl of Lucknow.

I have received a *shuqqa* from the Nawab summoning me to the court soon. I have decided to reach the camp via *dāk*. I want you to direct the *kahhārs* [mail-and load-bearers] of the *dāk* to prepare for my journey in a manner that there are four *kahārs* and one *mash'alchī* [torch-bearer] at every eight *kos*. In order to enable me to reach the court at the earliest, this arrangement should be made from Lucknow upto the camp. I will be happy if this is arranged soon. 5 Ẕīḥijja, Faizabad.

Folio 351a. Diwan Manik Ram.

I am enclosing my reply to the two *shuqqas* that I received from the Nawab, one after another. I had earlier asked you to come here. But now, in accordance with the Nawab's dictate, you continue to stay there. I am also planning to come over. I enclose a copy of my letter to the Nawab. 5 Ẕīḥijja.

Folio 351a. To Nawab Asaf-ud-Daula.

I received two *shuqqas* from you: one with your orders to arrive at the court of your Excellency and the other stating that you are aware that I have left the service of the Company and wish to meet you. But since you do not appreciate that people remain at your court without the consent of the English officers, you feel that it is in my interest if I return to my country (*mulk-i khwud*).

As a matter of fact, I have given up the *naukarī* of the Company on my own and I have every intention of returning to my country. But I entered Faizabad because people in your country owe me huge sums of money and I wish to clear my account. I intend to attend the camp soon in order to clear my accounts. After all this work [is over] I will depart for my country. 5 Ẕīḥijja, Faizabad.

Folio 351b. To Nawab Asaf-ud-Daula.

I feel encouraged and happy at receiving your letter. Words fail to express my gratitude for your favours to me. I had been in the good books of the late Nawab as well, and feel that it is because of his favours to me that you too are kind towards me. May God enhance your power and status with each passing day. I am keen to have the honour of an audience with you. It is my pleasure to hear that you have asked Manik Ram to attend your court regularly, and that you want me to visit you at the earliest. I am certainly going to be there very soon to have the honour of being in your audience. Mir Muhammad Ata Khan, who is with me at the moment, will also reach your court soon. 5 Ẕīḥijja.

Folio 352b. To Manik Ram.

On 4 Ẕīḥijja, after I reached here, I received five of your letters: two dated 2nd and 3rd of Ẕīqa'da, two of the 29th and one along with the letter from the Nawab. These had instructions for me to reach there soon since you have been detained there. I am happy that the Nawab has kept you there as a matter of favour. With you present there I have no need to worry about my affairs at the court. I will join you soon. Meet me one station in advance before I reach the camp. We will present ourselves at the camp together. 5 Ẕīqa'da, Faizabad.

Folio 353a. To Manik Ram.

I have left Faizabad and am proceeding towards Kohad via Manikpur. I have taken along whatever goods I considered necessary and have sent back the remaining ones. Since you are incharge of my work, you are instructed to send on my arrival in Kohad the goods that I have sent back along with the other goods. See to it that no inconvenience is caused to me by their non-arrival because I am not keeping well. I will stay there for a few days for treatment. The goods should reach me in this period. It will be better if you could come for two to three days and meet me. I have to apprise you of many important matters. Send also a *hundī* of Rs 2000 to Rs 3000 for the necessary expenses.

I had instructed Ram Sundar Datt to pay the salary to my servants upto the month of January. I have learnt that nothing has been paid so far. Arrange for the payment. 11 Ẕīḥijja.

Folio 353a. To Sri Maharaja Guman Singh Bahadur Dilawar Jang.

I have arrived here on my way to Akbarabad for some important work. I am happy to discover that this place is in your territory. As an old friend of yours, I request you to arrange for some escorts for my travel to Akbarabad via Kohad. I place this request since I left in haste and my retinue includes only some domestic servants.

I hope that you will arrange the people soon. 14 Ẕīḥijja, Monday, Resan.

Folio 353b. To Maharaja Guman Singh.

I am very happy to receive your letter informing me that you have sent reliable *harkāras* and that upto the village Matonda, which is in your jurisdiction, I will travel without any difficulty; and there [Matonda] I will meet your confidant who will arrange the *badarqa* [armed retinue] to escort me safely to my destination. As per your instructions I will reach *mauẓa'* Matonda accompanied by the *harkāra* tomorrow and will stay there until I meet your confidant. Please note that I am not well. I will consult a physician after reaching Agra. It will therefore be nice if your people reach here at the earliest. I hope that you will keep in touch until we meet. 16 Ẕīḥijja, Wednesday, Khanda.

Folio 354a. To Perceret ṣāḥib.

I had earlier intended to proceed to Akbarabad via Kohad. But since this is a longer route, I will now go straight to Akbarabad. I hope to reach there safely very soon. There is no need for any worry. Send me the palanquin, the *'amārī* and the tea box soon. If the boat from Azimabad arrives from Faizabad then send also a couple of suitcases full of summer clothes, writing materials and the boxes of medicines through the bearers of the palanquin.

I have arrived today, the 21st of Ẕīḥijja, in Atari which is situated at a distance of five to six stations from Akbarabad. However, I have not yet received your *harkāra*. I will write to you when I reach Akbarabad. Keep all the goods ready for dispatch. Send also a few candlesticks, candlestands, chandeliers, crates of wine and some Chinaware. 21 Ẕīḥijja, Atari.

Folio 354b. To Manik Ram.

I am sure you have received the letter I sent to you earlier through Karam Ali. I had said that I am proceeding [to Akbarabad] via Kohad and that I will wait there for the goods to arrive. In the meanwhile, I discovered that this route is longer and thus decided to halt at Ferozabad to receive the goods. As soon as you get this letter you should send the goods to Faizabad. You should also, along with Niyaz Ali Khan, come and meet me, after which you can return. Niyaz Ali Khan may accompany me to Delhi if he desires, otherwise he can also return to join the Nawab's camp. A lot of work is dependent on your arrival here. I will not accept your excuse of not getting the Nawab's permission for this visit. Also bring a *hundī* of Rs 10,000 for my expenses here.

John Bristow has two elephants which you should collect from him. I have already written to him about them. If, by any chance, it is not possible for you to do so, then get atleast one. I need an elephant here urgently. Also get urgently from Faizabad the planquin, *'amārī*, writing material and whatever else I ordered from Mr Perceret. If the boat from Azimabad has arrived in Faizabad, prepare a list of all the goods according to Mr Perceret's instructions and do whatever he wants. Send also one-fourth *ser* each of hot spices like *darchīnī* [cinnamon], *chhotī elāichī* [cardamon], *jāifal*, [mace] and *laung* [cloves]. Also, if the Indian chef and bread-maker (*bāwarchī-ye Hindustānī wa nān-puz*) has reached, send him here quickly. Also bring five or six *mash'alchīs* (lamp-holders) with you. As soon as you receive the letters for Perceret and Ram Sunder Datt forward the same to them through the *dāk*. 21 Ẕīḥijja.

Folio 355b. To Perceret ṣāḥib.

I will be arriving in Firozabad soon. I had written to you earlier that I have not been well ever since I left Faizabad. I feel slightly relieved now and treatment is not necessary.

The two elephants are with John Bristow. If it is not too inconvenient for you, collect them from him and send them here. Send atleast one of them through Manik Ram. I had written to Manik Ram to come here and see me. I know that he is making excuses and does not want to come here. Try to make him understand and see reason. He must come here soon with a *hundī*. 21 Ẕīḥijja, Atari.

Folio 355b. To Niyaz Ali Khan.

I will be arriving in Firozabad soon and will wait there for the goods. It is absolutely necessary for you to meet me. The moment you receive this letter, seek leave from the Nawab and rush to Ferozabad. Your friendship is of utmost importance [to me]. It will be better if you accompany me upto Shahjahanabad since your presence there is required for my work. Alternatively, you can go back from here to the Nawab's camp. 21 Ẕīḥijja.

Folio 356a. To Ram Sunder Datt.

You should send me the relevant papers about the emoluments of the servants since I do not know what the position is on that front. [The papers should include] the details of the months upto which they have been paid, the names of the people to whom payment has been made, and clarifications about the balance of payments, with details about the people who need to be paid and the amounts due to them. Send the *pālkī*, *'amārī* and whatever other goods Mr Perceret needs. Keep the porters and the escorts ready so that there is no delay. Send also one *man* of white sugar candy, and high quality *misrī* of Kalpi; keep some additional white sugar candy also ready to be dispatched subsequently. Also send the Indian cook and the baker along with these goods. 21 Ẕīḥijja.

Folio 356b. To Muhammad Ilich Khan.

I have arrived now in the territory of Najaf Khan. Since I left in haste, I have now only a few attendants. I am at the moment waiting in Firozabad to receive the goods from Faizabad. I will then proceed towards Akbarabad. [I have come to know that] these days Najaf Khan is busy with the expedition to subjugate the Deeg fort. I am enclosing a letter for him and hope that you will forward it to him in the *dāk*. I look forward to receiving your reply. 26, Ẕīḥijja, Saturday, Harnoth.

Folio 356b. To Maharaja Guman Singh

I am happy to receive your letter through Ḥakīm Mir Ali Khan. I understand that he has communicated to me verbally whatever you have in mind. It will be my privilege to do for you whatever is in my capacity. Rest assured that whenever the time comes I will do [whatever I can] for you. Keep writing to me. The three *harkāras* whom you had sent to accompany me are now going back from here, i.e. Firozabad. 28 Ẕīḥijja, Monday.

Folio 357a. To Nawab Najaf Khan.

On my arrival in your country, I gathered that you are busy with an expedition to conquer the Deeg fort, the centre of the rebels. May you conquer it speedily. I have always wished you an exalted position. I am here with a few attendants and will stop in Akbarabad and wait for the goods to arrive. I will subsequently leave for Delhi. I request you to depute some of your people to escort me to Delhi. I will be grateful to you. 26, Ẕīḥijja, Saturday, Harnoth.

Folio 357b. To Manik Ram.

I arrived in Firozabad today, i.e. Sunday, 27 Ẕīḥijja, and received your letter informing me of all the details. It is strange that you have not yet reached here since I had written to you earlier that I will wait here for you and the goods. This is vey bad. I repeatedly wrote to you that I am staying in Firozabad and that you should send your people there so that I may get to know the details. The distance [between Faizabad and the place where you are staying is not much that it should cause this delay. You must reach here soon and return after meeting me. Bring with you twenty-five young and strong Mewatis for the *chaukī* and the *pahra.* I have not yet received Niyaz Ali Khan's reply. 27 Ẕīḥijja, Sunday, Firozabad.

Folio 358a. 'Arẓdāsht to the Emperor.

I have been honoured with a special *shuqqa* from you which I received together with the letter of Nawab Majd-ud-Daula. It has been my long standing desire to be in your service and to do something to set right the management of the Empire (*intiẕām-i-mahām-i-sālṭanat*) and reinforce the law and order (*insidād-i-qawānīn-i-mamlikat*). I have given up the Company job and have arrived in Akbarabad with the intention to come to the court and meet you. I hope that I will soon be honoured by meeting you and by being ordered to be in your service forever. 7 Muḥarram, Tuesday, Akbarabad.

Folio 358b. To Majd-ud-Daula Farzand Khan Bahram Jang.

I have resigned from Company service and am now here in Akbarabad. I am planning to proceed towards the court at Delhi to manage, along with you, the affairs of the Empire. I am writing this just for your information. I am sure that you will bring this to the notice of the Emperor. 7 Muḥarram, Tuesday, Akbarabad.

Folio 359a. To Majd-ud-Daula Farzand Khan.

On my arrival in Firozabad I received four letters from you and one special letter (*shuqqa*)from the Emperor through Manik Ram. I also was honoured to receive some *pashmīna* which you had been so nice to send to me. I am now proceeding towards Delhi to meet you and to have the honour of an audience with the Emperor. When we meet we will act as per your advice and do whatever we feel is appropriate. 7 Muḥarram, 1190, Akbarabad.

Folio 359b. To Manik Ram.

After crossing the river, when I arrived in Akbarabad enroute to Ferozabad, I came to know that the road to Delhi was blocked because of robbers. I have therefore recrossed the river to take the route via Kol [Aligarh]. You may retain the *harkāra* sent to you and dispatch him later with the *pālkī, 'amārī* and other goods that you receive from Faizabad. You may instruct the *hārkara* that when he arrives in Shikohabad he should take the goods safely via Kol and Sikandra and deliver them to me in Delhi. I have written about the other matters to Mr Perceret and Mr Lloyd. Direct Ram Sundar Datt to act on their (*ṣāḥibs*) advice and to prepare these goods soon and send them to me. 7 Muḥarram.

Folio 359b. To Ram Sundar Datt.

I received your letter and came to know of details. Meet Mr Perceret and Mr Lloyd and act as per their advice. You also come along with the goods and meet me. 9 Muḥarram 1190.

Folio 360a. To Manik Ram.

I received the twenty *ser* rice sent by you. Forward to Dr Thomas the letter I had earlier sent for him. My dear, you are my associate and well-wisher. [You should] understand that it is in your interest to see that my work is executed well. I had earlier written to you to send the *pālkī, 'amārī* and other goods. I write to you again for their speedy dispatch. You should also come here after you have sent these items. 9 Muḥarram 1190.

Folio 360a. To Manik Ram.

The relatives of Mushtaq Khan Afghan Durrani, who is in my retinue, are stationed in Ghatampur about six *kos* from Kora. Send a *harkāra* to escort them over to you along with the people who are bringing the *pālkī, 'amārī* and the other goods. 9 Muḥarram 1190.

Folio 360b. To Mir Sulaiman Khan.

I received your letter and was very happy to know that you are visiting the Nawab's camp. May God help you in resolving the issue of your payments. I will feel as relieved as you. You have written that I did not send you the details. Believe me, if I had met you I would have explained to you every thing. I have already come to know from Manik Ram about the price of the elephants that you have quoted.

He [Manik Ram] says that the money has already been deposited with the *sarkār*. It is advisable that you take him along with you and clear the account. I have already written to Mr Bristow that as soon as the payment of the *tankhwāh* is received from the *sarkār* you will be paid for the elephants. You will get to know the details from Manik Ram. I hope that you will keep me informed about your health. 18 Muḥarram 1190.

Folio 360b. To Manik Ram.

I received your letter of 16 Muḥarram along with the letter of Faiyaz Ali Khan. I am happy to know about the developments. It has been a month since I wrote to Ram Sunder Datt to send the palanquins, *'amārī*, along with the baker and chef, but till date there is no news whether these have been dispatched. It appears from your letter also that you too are oblivious [of the developments]. But it is necessary that these items, including the tea chest and chef, etc. are sent through you when you arrive here via the Nawab's camp. You can load the other goods on bullock-carts and send them by some other route. There is no harm if the arrival of these items is delayed by a day or two. But the chef, etc. should reach here fast. They should take the shorter route so that there is no undue delay.

You also write that you are planning to proceed soon. I am leaving tomorrow, i.e. the 20th of Muḥarram and proceeding ahead. Dispatch the remaining items and come immediately.

You also write that you have handed over most of the bond paper (*tamassuk*) to John Bristow. Procure the other papers and hand them over to him along with the papers of accounts relating to the finances. This will make me happy.

You write that you obtained the *dastak* for two boats to proceed in the direction of Calcutta. Do not dispatch these boats now . When I reach Delhi and recover from my present illeness I will write to you about the dispatch of these boats. I am surprised that despite my writing repeatedly to Ram Sunder Datt nothing has been done so far regarding this matter. I have written to Mr Store and to the doctor to get leave for you to come here. It is in your interest that you do my work with your heart in it.

Along with the *'amārī*, etc. send also the *pashmīna*, etc. and the other things which you received from Nawab Majd-ud-Daula. Keep writing to me about the developments there at the address of Nawab Majd-ud-Daula. I will get these letters from there. 9 Muḥarram, Sunday, Kol.

Folio 361b. To Majd-ud-Daula.

I am proceeding towards Delhi on a fast elephant and have arrived here in the *qaṣba* of Kol. I have waited here for seven days for my own elephants and *pālkī* to arrive. But there is no news [of them]as yet. I am now anxious to proceed from here. God willing, I will cross the stations without any break and will have the honour of presenting myself at the court. 19 Muḥarram, Sunday, *qaṣba* Kol.

Folio 362a. To Faiyaz Ali Khan

I recieved your letter enclosed in the envelope of Manik Ram. I am happy to know that you have sought the Nawab's permission to come here. After waiting for the goods and all of you at Kol, I proceeded ahead on the 20th. I will be leaving from here also shortly for Delhi to get an audience with the Emperor and meet Majd-ud-Daula. 19 Muḥarram, Sunday, Kol.

Folio 362b. Majd-ud-Daula Farzand Khan.

I am honoured to have received the *shuqqa* from the Emperor. I feel privileged to hear that I should consider your exalted house as my own, and that without waiting any further for my goods to arrive here I should rush to him [the Emperor]. This is what I expect from sincere friends like you and I pray that our relationship is cemented further and that I am of some service to the Emperor. Accordingly, I have now left Kol and entered Sikandra on Wednesday, the 22nd. Tomorrow, i.e. Thursday, I will proceed from here and reach Surajpur where I shall look forward to receiving your letters. I hope that you will fix up an appointment for me with the Emperor and make appropriate arrangements for my accommodation and other things. I shall be reaching soon. 22 Muḥarram, Wednesday, Sikandra.

Folio 363a. To Nawab Asaf-ud-Daula Yahya Khan Bahadur Hizbar Jang.

I am honoured to have received your letter. I have always had regard for you and have ever been your well-wisher. I shall serve you to the best of my capabilities. I believe that I will be paid my arrears of payments due on the *sarkār* (Lucknow). The details of the earlier and present dues and arrears will be brought to your notice for clearance by Manik Ram. I have written about this to John Bristow who will also present the same to you. 22 Muḥarram.

Folio 363b. To Majd-ud-Daula Farzand Khan.

I received your reply to my letter along with the *harkāra.* You have written that after I reach Sikandra I should write to you about the [proposed] date of my entry in the city of Delhi as well as the date of audience [with the Emperor].

Fix whichever date and time you feel is appropriate. I will follow your instructions. Today is the 23rd and I have entered Surajpur. Tomorrow I hope to reach Patparganj which is at a distance of three *kos* from the city. Therefore, whichever day or time you suggest for the meeting will be all right by me. Since I have not yet received my own things, I will expect you to arrange for a *palki* for my *sawārī.* I am happy to know that you have arranged the *ḥavelī* of late Nawab Safdar Jang for me. 23 Muḥarram, Thursday, Surajpur.

Folio 364a. To Mehrchand, the painter.

I left Faizabad but did not hear about the completion of any one of the paintings that you and your assistants have been preparing and about which you have been keeping me informed. Rest assured and keep yourself engaged in the preparation of these paintings. Write to me whenever any of these are ready. Also inform Mr Lloyd [who is staying there]. Send me the painting 'Dīdā̃r Bakhsh' whenever it is ready. 24 Muḥarram, Patparganj.

Folio 364a. To Manik Ram.

Your letter with the *harkāra* arrived here after much delay. The change in route made the *harkāras* first go to Akbarabad and then to Delhi from where they came here to me.

The two bags of pistachio, and one *gurguṛī nīmcha* [hubble bubble and pipe], both decorated with gold threads, and the three pieces of musks that you sent have also arrived. I have also noted your meeting with the Nawab and the latter's queries about your welfare.

My dear, there is no news of the dispatch of the *pālki, 'amārī,* etc. that I had asked for. Inform me as soon as you receive them so that I can send some people to escort them here safely. I am surprised that despite my reminders to Mr Perceret and Mr Lloyd nothing has been done in this matter. I wonder if they have received my letter. I left for Delhi because I did not think it proper for me to proceed to Deeg. Today, the 24th of Muḥarram, I have arrived in Patparganj, three *kos* away. God willing, tomorrow I will have an audience with the Emperor and will stay at the *ḥavelī* of Safdar Jung.

You should prepare all the papers relating to the arrears of Najaf Khan in Persian. It is necessary that we charge him an interest [on this amount] as it has already been two years since he promised payment. Calculate the principal amount and the interest and send it soon.

I had decided that the girl of Imam Baksh be sent to Pektat *ṣāḥib* at Jangipur. Arrange for her one *peshwāz*, six to seven *kurtās*, a few *dupattas* with *gota* and two *pāijāmas* of *gulbadan* and the expenses for her travel. Also get two women to take care of her and be her escorts. Send the girl along with all these things with the *harkāra*.

Dispatch the girls and boys who have arrived there from Srinagar along with the goods. I also have one pair of *tūsī* shawls there in Faizabad. Give these to the *chhokrī* [girl]. Write to me the details about the monthly emoluments of the attendants who have come here with me. Write how much of their emoluments are due from the *sarkār*. I have sent the *harkāras* Dhan Singh and Rai Shambhu to escort the *chhokrī*. I have given them Rs 6 here. Pay them their emoluments for two months and send them here. 24 Muḥarram 1190, Patparganj.

Folio 365a. To Raja Dayaram.

I am happy to receive your letter. I am looking forward very keenly to meet the Nawab. I plan to cross the river tomorrow before sunrise, meet the Nawab and have an audience with the Emperor. You stay there with the Nawab and do not take the trouble of crossing the river. 25 Muḥarram, Patparganj.

Folio 365b. To Manik Ram.

On 24 Muḥarram, I camped adjacent to Patparganj. The same day Raja Dayaram came to see me on behalf of Nawab Majd-ud-Daula. I subsequently received the Nawab's letter stating that the astrologers had fixed Sunday, the 26th, for audience with the Emperor.

Yesterday i.e. the 25th afternoon, Raja Dayaram came here again and informed me that the imperial army had suffered defeat in a battle against Zabita Khan in Saharanpur in which the Nawab's younger brother, Abul Qasim Khan, was slain. It was therefore not appropriate to stay here any longer. The Nawab wanted me to cross the river and camp in the garden of Bahadur Ali Khan situated on the edge of the city. I would occupy the *ḥavelī* of Nawab Safdar Jung the following day.

Things followed accordingly. On the morning of the 26th, the Nawab came to meet me in the garden and we rode towards the court together. I offered thirty-six *asharfis* as *nazr* to the Emperor and to the princes. The Emperor honoured me with a *khil'at* of seven pieces and fixed the turban jewels and ornaments with his own hand. He thus elevated me to the sky. A pearl necklace was also put around my neck and I was presented with a sword, an elephant and a horse. Again, in the evening I received special food from the royal table (*ulūsh-khāṣṣa*). In sum, I have received abundant honours and affections from the Nawab. But the Nawab was extremely sad because of the death of his brother, Abul Qasim Khan. These are the developments here upto now. I will write to you later [about] whatever happens. 27 Muḥarram, Monday, *ḥavelī* Safdar Jang.

Folio 366a. To Manik Ram.

Earler I wrote to you the details of the events taking place here. I am sure you must have received my letter. Now the situation is as follows: The Imperial army was defeated at the hands of Zabita Khan, who has the support of the Sikhs, and fled. But Gangaram Kumaidan with his people stayed put in the fortress (*garhī*) of Amirpur. He will continue to be there if he receives reinforcements. But [at the moment] no such reinforcements are in sight from the Emperor. However, negotiations are on with the Sikhs, the supporters of Zabita Khan. Let us see what happens.

I have not received a single letter from you since I entered Delhi. I am, therefore, completely in the dark about the news from there. There is also no news about the palanquin, the *'amarī* and the other goods which I required. Please write to me if they have been dispatched from Faizabad. If they have been sent what is their current position. I have also not received any reply to my letter from Mr Lloyd. Write to me if you have received the goods. I can then send the escorts to cart them here.

You should also write to me about the developments in the Nawab's camp. I await [your letters]. Earlier I had received two bottles of tea and two packets of medicines through the *harkāra*. It is not necessary that you send the letter through the *harkāra*. You can address it to Nawab Abd-ul-Ahad Khan and dispatch it in the mail. I will receive [these letters]. 30 Muḥarram 1190, Thursday, Delhi, *ḥavelī* Safdar Jang.

Folio 367a. To Nawab Asaf-ud-Daula.

Congratualtion- - - - - Compliments on the event of Nawab Asaf-ud-Daula being invited to receive the office of the *wizārat* and the *khil'at.* Greeting, prayers and good wishes for further honours and promotions. 5 Ṣafar, Tuesday.

Folio 367a. To Nawab Asaf-ud-Daula.

Compliments- - - - -. Even if I am far away from you I do not wish to be deprived of the services and good wishes that I should offer to you. Ever since I had audience with the Emperor and met Nawab Majd-ud-Daula, I have thought of your welfare and have spoken very highly of you. The Nawab, who himself is your well-wisher, in response to my presenting the case of your *wizārat,* said that it does not depend upon the presentation of any gifts. [He said] that you may gift whatever you like, and that he has already sent you a *shuqqa* from the Badshah with titles of *Wazīr-ul-mamālik* on the 29th of Muḥarram.

Congratulations! You have also made a request to the Emperor for the *wizārat* and said that if it is given to you, you will receive it in person. The *shuqqa* is in response to that letter requesting you to come over. The Emperor pledges in the name of Quran and God that if you come here he will offer you with the *khil'at* of *wizārat.* The Nawab, i.e. Majd-ud-Daula is your well-wisher and the *khil'at,* the *qalamdān* and the *chārqab* are ready.

The matter of *peshkash* is left to you. However, there is no doubt that here at the imperial court there are heavy expenses. I have come to know that the expenditure is three times more than the income. Despite all this, Majd-ud-Daula has procured the *wizārat* for you, and the Emperor is willing to bear with the [financial] difficulties for the sake of your happiness.

Thus the only thing that I have to submit to you is that it is necessary for you to punish the enemies of the Emperor. As a matter of fact they are your enemies as well. 5 Ṣafar, Tuesday, Shahjahanabad.

Folio 368a. To Diwan Manik Ram.

Two letters of yours, one of 27 Muḥarram, sent through the *harkāra,* with details about the tea and tea kettle, and another of 29

Muḥarram sent through the regular *dak* reached here on 3 and 4 Ṣafar. I have communicated Mukhtar ud-Daula's message to Majd-ud-Daula. Both Majd-ud-Daula and the Emperor are kind to him. A special letter with an order of conferment of the *wizārat* upon the Nawab (Asaf-ud-Daula) has already, been dispatched. The *Khil'at* is also ready. I have given the relevant details in my letter for the Nawab, a copy of which is also enclosed herewith for you. I will send you further details later. 5 Ṣafar, Tuesday.

Folio 368b. To Diwan Manik Ram.

You write in your letter of 27 Muḥarram that there has not been any negligence on your part in acquiring the palanquin and *'amārī* from Faizabad. But [strangely enough] Ram Sundar Datt writes that he has despatched these from there only now. I fail to understand the reason for the delay. Is it because of the expenses involved? At any rate, inform me as soon as you receive them in Lucknow. I will then send my own men to bring them over here. Send them with the army of the Nawab, if there is any plan to march towards Delhi.

It is good that you have handed over the bonds to John Bristow. Give him also the bond for Rs 12,000 that Ghulam Murtaza Khan had obtained from Rao Raj Gopal. You better hand over to him all papers including the bonds and the salary estimates. Meanwhile, I am writing to Dr Thomas to contact Bristow to suggest him a way out for an early payment of my salary. Bristow it appears has pressed upon Mahbub Ali Khan and other officials the urgency of the matter, as Thomas writes to me. Thomas also mentions a European coach (*rath*) amongst the gifts given to the Nawab. If the Nawab really wants it, it is fine, but if he has not expressed any desire for it, then you should manage to get it back. Apparently Bristow needs one. Do whatever Dr Thomas suggests. I am writing to him also.

During the last ten or twelve days after my arrival in Delhi I have received only two letters from you. Make it a habit to send a letter every second day, even if there is nothing [significant] to write about.

I have noted that Faiyaz Ali Khan and Niyaz Ali Khan are to come over here in search of employment at the court. I will help them as you recommend. I have also noted that Mr Lloyd has disposed off the pair of small mirrors for Rs 400, that Mirza Ali Khan has offered Rs 2000 for the big mirror and that you have conveyed to Ram Sundar Datt the necessary conditions regarding this. Come over here along with the army of the Nawab. I need your advice in a number of matters.

As for Rs 2000 that you have sent to Faizabad, I think it is too small a sum for the expenses there. You know that I owe three to four months emoluments to my people there. Remove the useless Ram Sundar Datt and write to Dr Thomas to send to Mr Lloyd whatever money is needed for expenses for my household there. But for the payment of the arrears you must arrange the money.

I am told that the Farrukhabad girl is not willing to come over here. Ram Sundar Datt must have also written to you about this. Send for her and settle this matter soon without any further delay according to the decision we took when we met in Firozabad.

I am fine here, endowed with the kindness of the Emperor and Majd-ud-Daula. I need a Bengālī here to take care of my work at the court. Find out about one and send him to me. I have noted what you have written about Ram Ratan, the *chūbdār*. Write also about the emoluments of the elephant rider whom you have sent. This place is full of Kashmīrīs. However, to me there is no distinction between a Bengālī and a Kashmīrī. Look for someone capable of managing my work here efficiently. 5 Ṣafar, Tuesday.

Folio 370a. To Asaf-ud-Daula.

I am always your well-wisher and pray for the grant of your *wizārat*, promotions and honour. I am always looking for an opportunity to recommend your case. I have presented the case of your *wizārat* and the required *peshkash* to Nawab Majd-ud-Daula in an appropriate manner. The Nawab is equally keen that you receive this [*wizārat*]. As for the *peshkash,* he feels you have full authority [to decide]. A *shuqqa* from the Bādshāh has been sent to you along with the titles of *Wazīr-ul-mamālik.*

You had written to the Emperor that if he agrees to honour you with the *wizārat* you will come here. A *shuqqa* has been sent inviting you here. The Emperor promises to grant you the *k͟hil'at.* Nawab Majd-ud-Daula is your well-wisher.

The *qalamdān* is ready. Despite the heavy expenses incurred at the court, the amount of *peshkash* has been left on you to decide. Such being the case, it is your duty to come here,present yourself to the Emperor and chastize his enemies who at the moment do not seem to have much strength. If they acquire strength and establish themselves firmly, it will be difficult, nay impossible, to liquidate them. I have written to you whatever I thought was good for you. 5 Ṣafar, Tuesday, Shahjahanabad.

Folio 371a. To Manik Ram.

The situation is as follows: The Emperor had sent a special *shuqqa* to Asaf-ud-Daula with the title of *Wazīr-ul-mumālīk*. I believe you must have received that. The *khil'at* and the *qalamdān* of *wizārat* is ready here. Majd-ud-Daula is busy doing Asaf-ud-Daula's work sincerely. The Emperor has also been very kind. Since the expenses at the imperial court are exorbitant and the enemies from all around have raised *fitna* [disturbance], it is imperative for Asaf-ud-Daula to arrive here and suggest [ways] to liquidate the enemy forces. Otherwise, they will grow in strength, mobilize more people and it will then be difficult to handle them. Also, if the Marathas move in this direction, they [enemies] will be subjugated by them. It is therefore necessary to think of a plan before such an eventuality [occurs].

Bring all this to the notice of Nawab Asaf-ud-Daula. It is in his interest that somehow or the other the work of the Emperor is accomplished. Yesterday I had sent a letter with similar contents. His [Asaf-ud-Daula's] arrival here is very advisable. Today, I came to know in the court that if he moves ahead and arrives in Anupshahr, the Emperor himself would proceed from here to welcome him. 5 Ṣafar Tuesday.

Folio 371b. To Mir Muhammad Husain Ata Khan.

It has been two months since I left Faizabad. I am concerned at not having received any letter from you. I do not know how you are or what you are doing these days. Our relationship entails that you keep in touch so that I am assured [of your relations]. Send your letter to Dr Thomas and from there it will be passed on to me. At present I am in Delhi living in the *havelī* of late Nawab Safdar Jang. I am honoured to be in the service of the Emperor. 5 Ṣafar, Tuesday.

Folio 371b. To Manik Ram.

First, I gather that the relatives of the Farrukhabad girl, who is in Faizabad, are not willing to let her come here. I had written to you from Calcutta to keep her in my *ḥavelī*. If she had been looked after properly and lived in my *ḥavelī* this problem would not have arisen. I do not know if you have done anything in this matter. A large sum of money has been spent but the problem is still unresolved.

Punish anyone, other than her father or mother, who commits any offence. Large amounts have been spent on her monthly expenses. You had written earlier that you had acquired the deed (*rāẓīnāma*) with the seal of the *qāẓī* from her father. If this is the case and her father is willing then why are the others interfering. It is fine if her mother or any other female family member wishes to accompany her. I will do the best that I can for her. But resolve the problem soon and dispatch her quickly. Send also with her two other slaves—one girl and the other a boy—from Srinagar. Consider this matter urgent. As for the *almās gulābī*, bring this with you when you come over here.

The jewels are very expensive but we hope that we might soon procure them at a reasonable price. I have therefore written to Dr Thomas to dispatch a *hundī* so that I may purchase them here and also have some money for other expenses. When the money from Murtaza Khan is received, he will send a *hundī* for that as well. One incurs a loss in the dispatch of *asharfīs*. But there is no such loss in sending *hundīs*. I have written about this to Dr Thomas. You should send along with the *hundīs* the girl and the boy slaves from Srinagar. It is difficult to cart the two hundred *man* glass that is there to this place because of the disturbance enroute. You may therefore deposit this glass with Nawab Asaf-ud-Daula.

I came to know through a letter from Faizabad that salaries for four to five months are due to my people there. This is causing them immense inconvenience. I am surprised that you knew about this and yet did not act. Clear their dues upto the month of March. It is Mr Lloyd's duty to pay their emoluments and he shall do so in future. But it is useless to retain Ram Sundar Datt there any longer. He should be dismissed from there. I had earlier written to you to come along with my goods.

The musical organ which has been given to Nawab Asaf-ud-Daula, along with the other things, requires careful maintenance. Find out from the Nawab where he wants the instrument to be kept. Subsequently, write to Mr Lloyd to instruct Gora Mistri to accompany the organ to its destination. Also, tell him how to play it and give tips about its maintenance as he knows it very well. If some other person tampers with it, it will get spoilt. Tell the Nawab that he should make only one person incharge of it. In this way Gora Mistri will teach [the said] person the rules for its maintenance.

Regarding musical instrument expert and mechanics (*nairang, tandal and khalāṣi*) who have also been gifted to the Nawab, tell him that they should also be placed under the supervision of only one person. The deputed person should pay them their monthly emoluments regularly, which should be a little more than what they had received from me becuase they are knowledgeable persons. This [musical instrument] is a precious and rare gift in India, which in the hands of inexperienced people will go waste. It is therefore necessary to be considerate to those who maintain it and run [it efficiently]. These men should be well looked after.

Your *harkāra* is innocent. I had asked him to stay for sometime here . Instead, he has taken two to three letters for the *dāk* and now he has taken leave from me. 5 Ṣafar.

Folio 373a. To Muhammad Murid Khan.

I arrived in Delhi and am in the service of the Emperor. I am also keen to meet you. We are here to meet each other. But everything is destined to take place in its own time God willing we will meet sometime. Keep in touch. 6 Ṣafar, Wednesday.

Folio 373b. To Najaf Khan.

In consideration of our friendship I sent a letter to you through Ilich Khan from Firozabad and waited for a few days there and later at Akbarabad for your reply. It is a month now but I have not received any reply. I am very anxious to know about your welfare and health. Since [receiving] a letter is almost like meeting you, I hope that you will keep writing to me two sentences about your health. I am concerned about you. My heart is heavy since I have not met you for long. 7 Ṣafar, Thursday.

Folio 373b. To Mehrchand, the artist.

You should reach here along with two other painters and one *naqqāsh* [decorator] who should be a good person, skillful and keen to accompany you. If the *naqqāsh* is not willing, then let him go. We have a good *naqqāsh* here. Ask Mr Lloyd to arrange a cart for the goods and some transport for you. Leave Faizabad and join Manik Ram in the Nawab's camp. He will hand over to you two slaves, a girl and a boy. Bring them safely to Farrukhabad and then proceed to Khalilganj near Jalesar where I have my *jāgīr*. From there my people will escort you to Delhi. Rest assured that in all cases I will be considerate towards you. The climate here is good. My house is of the kind I wanted. A good accommodation has been arranged for you as well. Come soon. 7 Rabī' I (7 Ṣafar).

Folio 374a. To Asaf-ud-Daula.

I have always been in your service and continue to remain so. I have sent you two to three letters which you must have received. In future also I will keep sending you letters expressing my fidelity and loyalty. You had said that you have already dispatched Niyaz Ali Khan to the court and that I should act according to his advice. I am always present in your service and I will do as he advises. 8 Ṣafar.

Folio 374b. To Manik Ram.

I received your letter of 3 Ṣafar on the 7th through the *dāk* of Nawab Abd-ul-Ahad. I have written to you in detail about the developments here. I hope you have received the letter.

I notice that you have sent a *parwāna* to Mr Bristow about the *pālkī*, *'amārī* and tea box, etc. and also about the two elephants together with the elephant-keeper. I am not aware of the route they will take. Fifteen Mewatis and two *harkāras* have also been sent from Kol to escort these. Since the road from Kol to Delhi is disturbed I hope that they take a detour from there. It is not advisable to get the goods through this highway. The route via Ferozabad and Sadabad through which Niyaz Ali Khan is coming is free from trouble. There is no danger if the goods are sent through this route.

I have written repeatedly to Mr. Bristow about the payments. I am writing to him again. You may meet and consult Mr Bristow, Dr Thomas and Mr Store on this matter. You should meet them daily and consult them so that the matter gets resolved.

I had written to you earlier about the *shuqqa* from the Emperor to Asaf-ud-Daula. I have noted your advice about the *ḥavelī* of Safdar Jang and that I should relinquish it and take some other house. I had made no specifications in my request for accommodation. Majd-ud-Daula arranged this *ḥavelī* for me because it was close to his own *ḥavelī*. He accordingly got it repaired. It was in this context that I had to accept it. As a matter of fact, I do not like this place and am looking for something better. I will shift in a day or two. It is good that you informed me. Niyaz Ali Khan reached here safely and is staying along with Latafat Ali Khan in the *ḥavelī* of the late

Itimad-ud-Daula. He met me and I came to know from him about the developments there. I appreciate your advice that I should consult Majd-ud-Daula and bring to the notice of the Emperor the case of Najaf Khan. But have you received any message from Najaf Khan regarding this? I would prepare a report (*dastāwez*) on the case if I received any communication from him. It is not appropriate to open the case in the absence of the *dastāwez*. Things are not in good shape here. You would have realized it if you were here. From the news and from a meeting I had the day before yesterday with Majd-ud-Daula, I learnt that he wants a reconciliation with Najaf Khan. I supported his idea and said that this was the best solution.

I will appreciate if you come and see me for a day or two in case the army of Nawab Asaf-ud-Daula moves towards Delhi. For the moment the main task is to think of a plan to obtain money from Najaf Khan, prepare the papers and hand them over to Mr Bristow. Also acquire the receipts for the goods handed over to Asaf-ud-Daula. I am anxious to resolve all these matters. I will be relieved when all this is accomplished. Yesterday morning I sent a letter for you through the *harkāra*. It is absolutely necessary for you to get the money back from Najaf Khan. Write to me about whichever way you think is appropriate. The purpose is to get the money. This is the most important work at the moment.

I noted what you wrote to me through Dr Thomas. I am also worried and concerned. But I am a stranger here—unfamiliar with the place. I have sent a letter to Najaf Khan as per your instructions, a copy of which has been sent to you. From this you will learn how worried I am.

Make the full payments when Sulaiman Khan writes to you the details of his *ḥisāb*. I will write to you when I receive the details of the accounts of the payments made in Calcutta. But do not keep Sulaiman Khan's payment pending because of this. Inform me also so that I can write to Dr Thomas. Write to me if there is any problem so that I can write to Dr Thomas who will arrange for the payment. 8 Ṣafar, Friday.

Folio 376b. To Manik Ram.

Today, i.e. the 8th of Ṣafar, I came to know from the English letter of John Bristow that he is making all efforts for the payment of the emoluments, and that the son of Nauruz Ali Beg Khan in whose name my *tankhwāh* was fixed, is replaced. The payment in question has nothing to do with the *sarkār* of the Nawab. In fact, he owes this money to you. I did not expect this arrangement from you, and wonder how this money will be realized. Meet John Bristow and resolve this problem soon. Bristow will write to me.

Bristow also writes that the money which is due on Murtaza Khan, the *risāldār,* is also difficult to realize. It was decided at the time of the late Nawab Shuja-ud-Daula that whichever *risāldār* receives money from me would return the same when I required it. The money was made part of his [*risāldār's*] *tankhwāh* and was given by the *sarkār.* It is therefore necessary that you meet Bristow, apprise him of this and realize the money in whatever way possible. The issue of payment of everything given to the Nawab should be resolved in the presence of Mr Bristow. Give a *tamassuk* to Mr Bristow so that all dues are cleared.

You have also written that on the 4th of Ṣafar two elephants, palanquins and the other goods were dispatched from the Nawab's camp and that Mr Perceret arrived in Lucknow with the cartload of goods on the 2nd on his way to Delhi. At present there is disarray all around because of the Sikh disturbances. The people in Delhi are also scared. It is therefore not advisable that the goods come with Mr Perceret. He should halt at Farrukhabad once he reaches there and await my letter. Give him some money for his expenses so that he may stay comfortably in Farrukhabad. For the moment send him Rs 500 for the expenses. As soon as Nawab Asaf-ud-Daula proceeds towards Goraganj or Anupshahr I will write to Mr Perceret to leave Farrukhabad. Majd-ud-Daula did not want to send the *khil'at* of *wizarāt* from here. But the Emperor was insistent. Thus Majd-ud-Daula asked for Rs 20,0000 as *naẓar* but the matter settled at Rs 10,000 after negotiations. Latafat Ali Khan and Niyaz Ali Khan did not have so much money. Since I am an old servant of the Nawab I followed his instructions and handed over to them Rs 2000 that I possessed. I became the guarantor for the remaining Rs 3000 and Rs 5000. Now I have no money left for my own expenses. I thus pawned (*girvī*) the jewels. Dispatch a *hundī* of Rs 3000 and Rs 4000. I have written about this to Dr Thomas. 10 Ṣafar, Sunday, the day of occupation of the *ḥavelī* of Itimad-ud-Daula.

Folio 377b. To Mir Muhammad Husain Ata Khan.

I have not heard from you from the day I left Faizabad. I am worried about your welfare. In the meantime, I came to know that something untoward happened to your *jāgīr*. Also, that the matter got resolved due to the efforts of John Bristow. I am happy and appreciate the efforts of Bristow. Even though I was a bit worried about it I am now relieved. I have written to Mr Bristow also about it and will write again. I consider you as my friend. Keep in touch in the future but not the way you did in the past. 10 Ṣafar, Sunday.

Folio 378a. To Manik Ram.

These days your letters take a long time to reach here. I have repeatedly asked you to hand over the mail to Dr Thomas so that it can reach me quickly. The *dāk* of Nawab Asaf-ud-Daula is very slow. Earlier, three of your letters reached me simultaneously. I had strictly instructed you to write to me regularly.

I have received a letter from Ram Sundar Datt regarding the demand of my people there and about their inconvenience [because of the delay in payment], and also about his being held in captivity by them. I have replied to him. The situation there is that *pargana* Khalilganj which is in my *jāgīr* is still in the control of the people of Niyaz Beg Khan, the *'āmil*, who had been dismissed from there. Niyaz Beg himself continues to be in the camp of Najaf Khan. My deputy, Muhammadi Khan, on arrival at the *maḥāl*, was fired at by the people of the [dismissed] *'āmil* who came out of the fortress. Since Muhammadi Khan did not have enough equipment with him, he retreated to Katra in the neighbourhood. The following morning he retreated nine *kos* further into Katra. He wrote the details to me from there [Katra]. I have written about this case to Najaf Khan but I have not received any response so far. I have now procured a special *shuqqa* from the Emperor under his signature which has been sent to him through a camel-rider on the 10th of this month. I sincerely hope that Najaf Khan, who is my friend, will not cause any further delay in the resolution of this matter. But let us see what happens. I am sending you a copy of this special *shuqqa* from the Emperor which will show you how kind the Emperor has been to me. 10 Ṣafar, Monday.

Folio 378b. To Mir Sulaiman Khan.

I received your letter and came to know of the developments. I had earlier written to Manik Ram to settle the accounts. I am sure he must have informed you about this. I am once again writing to him with strict instructions. A copy of this is enclosed herewith. I hope that Manik Ram will not neglect this and soon all the accounts (*ḥisāb*) will be settled. Rest assured that I am your sincere friend and nothing is impossible. After resolving this I will write to Dr Thomas to clear off the balance. You will receive the balance from him. You will get to know verbally the details of the developments here from Niyaz Ali Khan. 10 Ṣafar.

Folio 379a. To Manik Ram.

I had written to you earlier to settle the account of Mir Sulaiman Khan. I am writing to you about the same again. It is absolutely necessary to resolve this matter. As soon as I receive the details of receipts from Calcutta I will dispatch them to you. But do not make the issue of resolving this problem contingent on the receipts. Inform me [once the problem is resolved] so that I can write to Dr Thomas for the payment of the balance. 10 Ṣafar, Sunday. Enclosed in the letter of Dr Thomas, the day of the occupation of the *ḥavelī* of Itimad-ud-Daula.

Folio 379a. To Faiyaz Ali Khan.

I received your letter and noted that Majd-ud-Daula has been overwhelmed with grief following the demise of his brother, Abul Qasim Khan. My dear, in the last two years I have been very close to him. You will know about my intimacy with him from Manik Ram and Niyaz Ali Khan. We have regularly corresponded with each other. It was because of our sincere friendship that I came here and met him. It is true that he is aggrieved for reasons you mention.But it may also be for some other reason that he has not yet recovered. For the moment I am avoiding this situation. Keep me informed about the developments there. 10 Ṣafar, Sunday.

Folio 379b. To Nawab Asaf-ud-Daula.

Niyaz Ali Khan has arrived at the court here and is busy executing your work. At the time of the award of the *khil'at* of *wizārat* to you there was demand of money from the court. I arranged for this money on his [Niyaz Ali Khan] advice. At the outset, you had directed me to look after this matter. Thank God that this has been accomplished well and that I have been of some service to you. May God give you further promotions and [may] you occupy this position and fortunes for all times to come. The rest you would know from Niyaz Ali Khan. 11 Ṣafar, Monday.

Folio 380a. To Mukhtar-ud-Daula Saiyid Murtaza Khan Haibat Jang.

Niyaz Ali Khan has arrived in the court and has made commendable efforts to obtain the *khil'at* of *wizārat.* Since I was also keen that this should be achieved and you had also written to me about it, I arranged Rs 5000 at his request. Thank God our aims have been fulfilled. May God establish Asaf-ud-Daula in this position permanently and his wealth and fortunes increase every day. Niyaz Ali Khan will apprise you of the other details. 11 Ṣafar, Monday.

Folio 380a. To Manik Ram.

Earlier I wanted to send my wild ass to an English/European (*ṣāḥib*) in Calcutta. Now I discover that the *ṣāḥib* has passed away. Therefore, if Asaf-ud-Daula accepts it you may present it to him on my behalf or else do whatever you like.

Second, *karānī ṣāḥib* has arrived in Akbarabad without my permission. He has sent a letter expressing his wish to come over here. I wrote back to him saying that I have no work for him here. Nevertheless, he reached Delhi without my permission and wanted money from me. He said that he was starving. I told him to go back to Etawah because he had come back without my knowledge and only then would I arrange for the money. I gave him Rs 30 for his travel expenses to Etawah but he did not accept it. It seems that you had given him Rs 100 before he left for this place. If you have done so it is fine. But if he goes there again and demands money from you do not oblige him.

I had written to you earlier to resolve the issue of the girl from Farrukhabad. Now you write that her father on hearing of the arrival of Mr Perceret, has disappeared. He has taken somebody's support and says he will return the money he had received [on her sale]. My dear, if you had purchased her with cash why did you not keep her safely in my *ḥavelī.* Why did you keep her somewhere else despite my repeated pleas to house her in my *ḥavelī.* This does not behove a wise person like you. It is important that you resolve the matter in whatever manner you feel fit. Once the matter is resolved, accommodate her in my *ḥavelī* under the care of Lal Khan. Do not mention that she will be brought here. I have vacated the *ḥavelī* of Safdar Jang and am now occupying that of Itimad-ud-Daula. This is for your information. You have written that the atmosphere there is a bit different. Atmosphere about what? Why don't you write clearly. I do not approve of such ambiguity. 11 Ṣafar, Monday.

Folio 381a. To Manik Ram.

Niyaz Ali Khan reached here at the ourt and made commendable efforts at getting the *khil'at* of *wizārat* for Asaf-ud-Daula. When the Emperor demanded the money I handed over to him the Rs 2000 that I had with me. I arranged the remaining Rs 3000 from the *sāhūkārs* here. I write to you so that you may recover this money from him [Asaf-ud-Daula] soon. You may give Rs 3000 to Niyaz Ali Khan.

Niyaz Ali Khan spoke very highly of all the work that you are doing for me there. I am very happy and appreciate that you are my well-wisher. I have also written to Mr Bristow and Dr Thomas about the realization of this money. Act as per their advice. You will know about the other things from Niyaz Ali Khan verbally.

I learnt that the *ḥisāb* of late Mir Lutf Ali Khan has not yet been cleared. Please clear it in the presence of Mir Sulaiman Khan and get a deed of clearance (*fārighkhaṭṭī*). 11 Ṣafar, Monday.

Folio 381b. To Najaf Khan.

I sent you a letter through Muhammad Ilich Khan after I reached Firozabad. I stayed on in Akbarabad also expecting your reply but this was of no avail. It has been one month and I am still to get your reply. I feel concerned about your welfare. I have therefore written and dispatched another letter to you on the 7th of Ṣafar through a *harkāra*. I have yet to receive a reply to that as well. I am your sincere friend and you too are my friend and [I am sure] you will attend to my letters. In future keep in touch and inform me of your welfare. Also remember me for whatever services I am capable of. You will get to know the other details verbally from Niyaz Ali Khan. 12 Ṣafar, Tuesday.

Folio 381b. To Manik Ram.

I received your letter of 9 Ṣafar on 13 Ṣafar. I had written to you earlier asking you to write to me every alternate day. You take a long time to write. You should be more regular. I have written to you in detail about the *tamassuk* of Ghulam Murtaza Khan, Nauruz Ali Khan and Nawab Muzaffar Jang. Tell Bristow the details about these and resolve this. Try to realize the money soon if you have received Nawab Muzaffar Jang's *tamassuk*. Mihrban Khan has been reinstated and he is willing to make the payment which has been due for the last fourteen months, even more.

I have written to you earlier about the pension. It is good that you have presented this before Nawab Asaf-ud-Daula and written about its payment to Bristow *ṣāḥib*. I too have written to him. You know that he is very earnest in getting the payments due to me.

I am already aware of all that you have written about the Nawab's camp. Keep writing the same way. From your letter it appears that the Nawab does not intend to come here. Write to me the details about the deployment of the reinforcement. I got to know about the departure of Mr Perceret from your letter. Earlier I had written to you and Mr Perceret. Stay on in Farrukhabad and leave only after I write to you to depart from there. I also note that Murtaza Khan has been deputed to come here. If this is correct, then after my goods are dispatched from there you and Latafat Ali Khan should stay back. Dispatch a *hundī* of Rs 500 to Mr Perceret in Farrukhabad so that he does not have any difficulty in his expenses. I had written to you about this earlier also. 14 Ṣafar, Thursday.

Folio 382b. To Manik Ram

I received your letter of 4 Ṣafar on the 11th, together with the goods. You write about the dispatch of two elephants, palanquins and other goods. I tallied the things with the list. I had written to you to dispatch some essential items like the summer clothes, the box of wine, the Chinese crockery, candlestick holders, etc. None of these has been sent. This is despite the fact that you know that I do not have these essential items with me. I am surprised why, despite my reminders, you have not sent these to me.

I have written to Mr Perceret to leave Farrukhabad with my goods and, travelling through Dhumri Aliganj, arrive in Mendu, Jawar and Brindaban, and then to come here via Chhata and Hodal. 16 Ṣafar.

Folio 382b. To Manik Ram.

I received your letter of 10 Ṣafar on the 16th. I had received earlier on the 15th the letter regarding the dispatch of the elephants, palanquins and *'amārī*. I have written to you about this. I have received Majd-ud-Daula's gifts—the *pashmīna*, etc. However, the colour of the two *thāns* of brocade is given as *qirmazī*. But only one *thān* is of this colour, the other is saffron in colour. This is just for your information.

I had written to Mr Perceret, who is in Farrukhabad, not to stay in Kol because of the disturbances there. Yesterday I told him to leave Farrukhabad, take the route of Dhumri and Aliganj and reach Brindaban from here via Chhata. This route is undisturbed. Still, I am dispatching about twenty Mewātīs to escort him.

I appreciate your sending of the *tamassuks* and the *parwānas* to Mr Bristow. Keep meeting Dr Thomas and Bristow and do as they advice. I have also written to Bristow about this. As for the money of Ghulam Murtaza Khan, which can be realized soon, get its payment done quickly. The sooner the better since I do not have much to do with him. I have written to you regularly from here and you know the details of the developments.

Resolve the case of the *wilāyatī* chariot according to the advice of Dr Thomas and Mr Bristow. As for my request of sending a person, send someone reliable and competent. You have written that no competent Bengali is available there. The man should be reliable and it is not necessary that he should be a Bengali. Send a person who you know well and about whose competence everyone is convinced. 16 Ṣafar.

Folio 383b. To Manik Ram.

I received your letter dated 4 Ṣafar which reached here along with the goods. In the enclosed details of the payment due to the people who brought them, you write that you have paid Rs 36 to the Mewātīs and Rs 33 to the *kahārs*. But the Mewātīs say that they received only Rs 26 and the *kahārs* only Rs 20, and that not a single pie beyond this has been paid.

Clear the *ḥisāb* of the elephants and the other goods that reached Delhi on the 15th. I do not know how much is to be paid. 16 Ṣafar.

Folio 383b. To Manik Ram.

I received your letter of 12 Ṣafar on the 16th. You write that Mr Perceret wanted some Telingas and therefore wanted me to send some Mewātīs to Kol so as to escort him. I have written to him not to take the Kol route and instead come via Dhumri and Aliganj, reach Brindaban and then via Chhata and Hodal to Delhi. I am dispatching fifteen to twenty Mewatis to Jawar. I have written to you about this several times.

I also note that you have handed over the pension [paper] to the *sarkār* of Nawab Asaf-ud-Daula. I note also that Bristow was over-worked and therefore the money which could have been received from the *sarkār* of the Nawab could not be realized. I know that Bristow is busy; but he is also sincere to me. Politely request him to give more attention to my work. Consult Dr Thomas also. Keep meeting them so that my work is done satisfactorily.

It will be very good if you could send the girl of Farrukhabad with Mr Perceret. But first her case should be resolved. I have written to you about this several times. You know the case and should keep me informed. 16 Ṣafar.

Folio 384b. To Mir Qasim Ali Khan.

I am pleased to get your letter. I noted that you wanted to meet me and waited for me. I did not know that you were there. As a matter of fact, I just passed through and had nobody with me who was familiar with the place. Personally, I have nothing to do here. So long as my livelihood is here I am putting up [here]. 16 Ṣafar.

Folio 384b. To Manik Ram.

The situation here is as follows: The son of Zabita Khan escaped from the *ḥavelī* of Itimad-ud-Daula on the 16th of Ṣafar. After passing about 1/2 *pās* [watch], the informers brought this to the knowledge of the Emperor. In the meantime, he had full freedom to reach his own place.

At the moment Zabita Khan along with the Sikhs has raised a commotion and plans to come over here without the Emperor's order. There is nobody at the court except Latafat Ali Khan *khwājasarā* who says that all these agitators will be punished. But I do not think that this will happen. Zabita Khan has told the Emperor that the defence against the Sikhs is his responsibility. The *vakīls* of the Sikhs have told the Emperor that if he desires they will bring to book Zabita Khan. In short nothing is clear. The only thing clear is that both the groups are in control of the country of the Emperor and have established their own *thānas*. Here in Delhi there is nothing except negligence and thoughtlessness. None of the nobles (*khudāwandān-i-mulk*) has any plan to deal with this. There is only confusion, anxiety and sleeplessness. I am surprised and worried. I do not know what there is in store for the country.

I had suggested that Mr Perceret should not take the route of Kol and should come via Mendu, Jawar and Brindaban. Preceret is expected to arrive in Mendu and Jawar within 9-10 days and then he will inform me. If in the meanwhile the condition here is stable, then it is fine. Otherwise, in the event of any disturbance, I will write to him to stay there. Write to me the details of the developments there: whether the reinforcements have been deputed and if the Nawab plans to come over here and reform the state of affairs? There is nothing left of the empire except the veneer of its name. If he wishes to keep the veneer intact he should come, otherwise even this will wear off. If this accursed group is not quelled at this moment it will be difficult to handle it in the future when it will acquire more strength. This will be bad for all of us. I have written to Dr Thomas regarding the dispatch of the *hundī*. But you should also arrange some and send it soon because I am in trouble here. 17 Ṣafar, Sunday.

Folio 385b. To Manik Ram.

I received your letter of 15th on the 17th with the *hundī* of Rs 3500. You have written that the money will be realized on payment of Rs 5 per 100. But the *sāhūkār* here wants Rs 5½ per 100. I have therefore left a few rupees with him as *amānat.* Get a letter from the *sāhūkār* there. Even when I was in trouble I arranged the money when Niyaz Ali Khan needed it for the *khil'at* of *wizārat.* I am happy and relieved that this pleased Nawab Asaf-ud-Daula. I keep the Nawab's happiness above everything else. From the letter of Dr Thomas I knew that your efforts to arrange this *hundī* have been commendable. 17 Ṣafar, Sunday.

Folio 386a. To Manik Ram.

Get back the note that I had given you in Firozabad to present to Nawab Asaf-ud-Daula. Present this [instead] to Captain Store and do as he advices. Consider this as an urgent matter. 18 Ṣafar, Monday.

Folio 386a. To Manik Ram.

Your letter of the 14th reached here on the 19th. I gather that Ghulam Murtaza Khan has taken leave from Nawab Asaf-ud-Daula and is coming here. Send the goods [with him]. I am inconvenienced in the absence of these goods. I have received the *hundī* of Rs 3500 which you sent. You had asked the *sāhū* here to cash it at 5 per cent discount. But the *sāhū* wants 5½ per cent. Get a written note from your *sāhū* so that the one here does not make any more excuses.

As for the letter of recommendation to Chandelier *ṣāḥib* for your own work, I want it to be done properly. I will do as I told you when we met in Firozabad. Rest assured that I will write to Mr Chandelier. Continue to attend to my work and resolve all related problems. I had written to you earlier about the two Indian guns and the two scarves . You had said that you would send them along with the other goods but I have not yet received them.Do not forget to send them along with the other goods. Today, the 20th of Ṣafar, the *harkāra* brought the news that tomorrow my goods would arrive in Sekandrabad. I have sent twenty *Mewātīs* and one *harkāra* to bring them here. This is for your information. 20 Ṣafar, Wednesday night.

Folio 386b. To Manik Ram.

I received on the 20th two of your letters, dated 14th and 16th, together with the paper relating to the account due on Najaf Khan, the expenses for dispatching the goods, and the details of the monthly payments to people there. I note that you have written to Mr Bristow about the case relating to the *tankhwāh* of Nauruz Ali Beg Khan. Earlier, Bristow wrote to me that you had collected this money and then loaned it to him, and that the realization of this money has no connection with the *sarkār* of the Nawab. It was precisely for this reason that I had written to you earlier. Now if you have handed over the said *tankhwāh* to Mr Bristow under the seal of the Nawab it is all right. There should not be any dispute on this account. But I know that this was not correct.

If you have a *tamassuk* under the seal of Nawab Muzaffar Jang, hand it over to Dr Thomas so that Mr Bristow can write to Abdullah Beg regarding the realization of the amount. As for the case of Ghulam Murtaza Khan, whatever you wrote is fine and there is no dispute regarding this. In my opinion it will be easier to realize the money if Rao Jaigopal and Abdullah Khan take the responsibility of the payment of money in the form of *jāidād* and *jāgīr*. Earlier, following a suggestion from Mr Bristow, I had written to you regarding this. But now it appears from your letter that this money will be returned soon.

As for the payment of your goods, I think there is no need for the *tamassuk* since you write that this is not according to the rules. But Bristow writes that he would get me the *tamassuk* from the Nawab for this money as well. Thus, in this case you do whatever Mr Bristow and Dr Thomas advise. Keep meeting them and treat this as urgent. Consult Dr Thomas also in the transaction of my business. I know that things will be easier if Mr Bristow writes to Mukhtar-ud-Daula about the payment. But he is busy being wholeheartedly engaged in my work. So if he does not write to Mukhtar-ud-Daula because of his preoccupations, there is a reason. It is not appropriate to keep reminding him of such things. Do not act on your own. Pursue the matter in such a way that the entire sum is realized early.

Try to solve the case of the girl from Farrukhabad. If it is beyond your control, tell Captain Store about it and he will help you. At any rate solve this case amicably. There is no use in perpetuating the dispute, and once the problem is resolved send her together with the slave girl and boy from Srinagar. 20 Ṣafar, Wednesday.

Folio 387b. To Mir Muhammad Ata Khan.

I received your letter of the 15th and am very sorry to know about the death of the children because of smallpox and the destruction of the household following a fire. I do not have words to express my grief. But we are all helpless before the will of God. Be calm and patient. God will compensate you with something good.

You have written to me regarding a letter of recommendation to be sent to Mr Bristow for your case. As a matter of fact I have already written to him. Rest assured and meet also Dr Thomas and Mr Store. They know your problem and will render their sincere help. Regarding your request to present your case to the Emperor here, I am willing to do it. But at the moment the Emperor and the nobles here are extremely perturbed because of the Rohilla and Sikh uprising. I will put forward your case to them at an appropriate time. 20 Ṣafar, Wednesday.

Folio 388a. To the 'amla (relevant people) of Khalilganj (who matter), the chaudhurī, qānūngo and muqaddam of pargana Khalilganj.

Be it known that the said *pargana* for the *faṣl-i-rabī'* of 1183 I have received in *jāgīr* from the Emperor. My *'āmil* will soon reach there. It is therefore instructed that you take appropriate action in protecting the revenue and that from the 21st Ṣafar, when I received the *sanad*, no single penny should be spent [anywhere else] so that there are no dues upon you. This is important. 24 Ṣafar.

Folio 388b. To Khiradmand Khan Don Pedro.

I am happy to receive your letter. You write that you have not received my reply. I received a letter of yours in Kol. In those days my *munshī* was not well and was therefore unable to write back to you. This was the reason for my negligence in not writing back. I noted that your *tankhwāh* has been suspended because of Raja Himmat Bahadur's dismissal, and that you have arrived in the Nawab's camp and need my letter. Also that you have written to Bristow and to Thomas. I am writing to Captain Store regarding your case. Meet him and keep in touch with him. He will do what is best for you to the utmost of his capacity. 24 Ṣafar, Sunday.

Folio 388b. To Manik Ram.

I received two of your letters dated the 17th and the 18th on the 22nd. I noted whatever you have brought to the notice of Mr Bristow regarding the *tankhwāh* of Nauruz Ali Beg Khan. I understand that Mr Bristow, beacuse of his preoccupation, has not given you due attention in this matter. But as I have written to you earlier also, keep meeting him. I have also noted whatever you have told Bristow about the case of Ghulam Murtaza Khan, the receipt of a letter from Rao Jaigopal, and the latter's reaction that he would take action after having examined the letter. I believe that you are doing my work.

You have written that Raja Himmat Bahadur destroyed the town of Jind(?). I had heard about this four days earlier and then received your letter where you say that there is a dispute with the people of Basant Ali Khan. It is not very clear what this dispute is about. Write clearly and in detail so that I may know.

You have also written that the owner of the big diamond has left for Benares, but that other people with one small and one big diamond would reach here soon. This is fine. Get whatever is available and bring it here. I too am on the look out here. But I am not impatient because if we search in a relaxed way it should be available at a reasonable price.

I have noted whatever you wrote about the girl from Farrukhabad. It is better that you send her along with the slave girl and the boy of Srinagar [Garhwal] and escorted by reliable people so that they reach here safely. As for the *harkāra* who came with Mr Perceret I have come to know that on the 20th of Ṣafar Perceret arrived in Khurja from where he has taken a route via Jhajjar and Faridabad. I hope that he will reach here in a day or two. [When he arrives] I will be relieved since I am much inconvenienced here due to the non-availability of goods.

Two days back I wrote to Mr Chandelier about your case in the manner that we had agreed upon in Firozabad. Mr Chandelier will be considerate to you if he has not brought a *mutaṣaddī* with him and he accepts my recommendations. But if he has his own *mutaṣaddī* I cannot say anything. In this case it is necessary for you to meet him through Dr Thomas. If he accepts you, you will have to procure a *rāẓīnāmah* [letter of consent] from me after having completed my account work. This is for your information.

I noted what you have written about the *hundī* of Rs 3500. The *mahājan* here asks for Rs 5½ per 100 but you say that it will be at 5 per cent discount. Send a note from the *mahājan* soon so that there is no demand here for more than 5 per cent discount. Also send me immediately the papers relating to the *tankhwāh* of Nauruz Ali Beg Khan and Mir Muhammad Hussain, the *sazāwal*. These are needed for the collection of the money of the Company.

You had mentioned that Dr Thomas had informed you that due to the preoccupation of Bristow he had not yet completed the papers. Get these soon. I have noted whatever you have written about the developments at the Nawab's camp. I have got the *maḥāl* of Khalilganj, near Jalesar, in *jāgīr* and this has a *jama'* of Rs 50,000. It is a good place and with due effort, the revenues will certainly be realized. 24 Ṣafar, Sunday.

Folio 390a. To Mir Muhammad Husain Ata Khan.

I received your letter of 25 Ṣafar on the 29th. Earlier I had written about your case to Bristow, Thomas and Store. I note from your letter that they have been very nice to you. I am writing to them again. Be confident and never be oblivious to the requirements of my friendship with you. Keep in touch with them and keep me informed about their reactions.

At the moment we are facing problems with the Sikhs and the Rohillas. The Sikhs are demanding money from the Emperor and nothing has been resolved. Due to this the entire business of the court is suspended. Let us see what we can do. In the meanwhile, I have obtained *maḥāl* Khalilganj, located near Jalesar, in *jāgīr* from the Emperor. This has a *jama'* of Rs 50,000. I have obtained the *parwāna* and have dispatched the *'āmil*. By the grace of the Emperor I am hopeful. Let us see what comes out. 29 Ṣafar 1190.

Folio 390b. To Diwan Manik Ram.

I had instructed you earlier to regularly send me information from there. These days there has been some delay in this. It has been four to five days since I received a letter from you and I am concerned. Hand over the letter to Dr Thomas or dispatch them through the *dāk* of Nawab Abd-ul-Ahad Khan so that I receive them without delay.

Perceret *ṣāḥib* arrived here in Delhi with the goods I had ordered on the 25th. Except for the charges to the palanquin carriers (*kahhāras*) and the bullock carts, everything which was due has been paid. Rs 2 have also been given as tip to the troopers who accompained him. Perceret *ṣāḥib* had bought a pair of oxen for Rs 40 in Mainpuri *qaṣba.* Arrange an early payment for these. The copper utensils sent by you have arrived. Three to four of them are excellent.

From the letter of Dr Thomas I learnt that you are not well. I understand that the delay in dispatching the goods may have been because of this. God is the best healer. 29 Ṣafar 1190.

Folio 391a. To Aqa Ali Khan.

I am happy to receive your letter of 29 Muḥarram on the 22nd of Ṣafar. As for the non-receipt of the opium in Azimabad, I have already written about this to the *bakhshī*, Khilak(?) *ṣāḥib.* A copy of the letter to the *bakhshī* is enclosed. Take this letter to the *bakhshī ṣāḥib* and he will give you opium, worth Rs 100, of whichever quality you want. If you do not get opium, then cash, i.e. Rs 100, will be handed over to your people. I had received your letter but because of some necessary work I did not get time to write back to you quickly. In the meanwhile your people had left. For this reason the mailing was delayed. 29 Ṣafar.

Folio 391b. To Manik Ram.

I have received two of your letters dated the 24th and one dated the 26th today, the 29th. You write that you have sent a *harkāra* to look for Perceret *ṣāḥib.* He has arrived here safely on the 25th of Ṣafar. I have written to you regarding this earler. I have noted the affairs that you discussed with John Bristow. It is proper that you visit the *ṣāḥibs* regularly and let them know whatever is required.

I am satisfied that the mirrors have been sold and the money handed over to Mr Lloyd. I have also noted the expenses incurred on the people in the *ḥavelī.* Clear all the arrears upto the month of March. In future it will be the responsibility of Mr Lloyd to make payments for the emoluments. A lot of confusion will be created if Mr Lloyd makes the payment in between. I had written to you about this earlier also. Since now very few clearances are pending, get over with them.

I have noted the case of the *tamassuks* that Ghulam Murtaza Khan had given to Rao Jaigopal and Abdullah Khan. Be alert in this matter and resolve it at the earliest. I have also noted what you have written about [raising of] the *paltans* assigned by the Emperor. Contrary to my adivce, the Emperor's people insist that I arrange their earlier emoluments also, and in future they should be paid in *jāidād*. But this is not acceptable to me and the matter is under consideration. However, the *maḥāl* of Khalilganj, with a stipulated revenue of Rs 50,000, has been given to me. I have written to you about this earlier also. I have now dispatched Muhammadi Khan as the incharge of the *amānat* and *faujdārī* of this *maḥāl*. The matter regarding the money required by the Sikhs and the *maḥāl* required by the Rohillas is also under consideration.

I have noted what you have written about the *tamassuk* of Muzaffar Jang that you have handed over to Dr Thomas. I am sure that by the end of Rabi-ul-awwal, Rs 2000 would be realized from *jāidād* of Rao Jaigopal. Be vigilant in recovering this money. Also, be alert in the matter of extracting money from Abdullah Khan. There should not be any negligence in the realization of this money.

The painters are doing nothing these days. As a matter of fact, in the absence of the masters it is difficult to get things done properly by the servants. I therefore want these artists to be sent here. Some goods left in Faizabad are also required here. Dispatch the girl (*chhokrī*) from Farrukhabad, the girl slave and the boy slave from Srinagar together with the artists and the goods. The girl's father wants some money for expenses. Since the girl is now being sent, there is no harm in making the payment. I will also tell him the amount he has taken from me. Resolve this matter at the earliest and send the girl here. Tell them to travel through Khalilganj which is located near Jalesar, from where they will be escorted by my people. I have written to Dr Thomas for the management of the *jāgīr* and the monthly emoluments. Rest assured that I will also write to John Bristow. I have noted that you will send the Indian gun and the shawl along with these people. I will write to you about the *nīlgāi* and other things later. I do not want to present the *nīlgāi* to Mirza Ali Khan. 1, Rabī' 1190.

Folio 392b. To Manik Ram.
I have just learnt from the letters from Faizabad that the matter of the Farrukhabad girl is still under dispute. Call her and do the needful as per her wishes. The matter should not be postponed any further. Also, as I have written earlier, dispatch her to me. 2 Rabī' I.

Folio 393a. To Manik Ram.
I have come to know that Basant Ali Khan, because of his enemity with Nawab Mukhtar-ud-Daula, has killed him and was punished accordingly. I came to know of this from other dispatches even though I did not receive any letter from you providing me this information. Perhaps Mirza Hasan Riza Khan will get the office of Mukhtar-ud-Daula. If this happens, it be good for us and our work will be expedited. Since I am his sincere friend and you too have good relations with him, if he gets this position see to it that he pays full attention to the work of the Bādshāh and develops close relations with Majd-ud-Daula. Establish a correspondence with him; this will be good as such and further our interests.

I discovered from the Faizabad mail the on-going fight over the Farrukhabad girl. Summon for her and resolve the matter amicably. If by any chance you are unable to do it, inform me so that I may do it properly. But if this is just mischief, then appropriate punishment should be meted out. I have written to captain Bristow as well. You should also meet him and apprise him fully about the matter. The matter should not be left unresolved any longer.

I have come to know that you have presented to the Nawab eleven pairs of oxen, one *kajkāh,* thirteen musks and 125 pieces of *zedoary* along with the animals received from the Raja of Srinagar [Garhwal]. This is fine. But I had requisitioned these items for the *Ṣāḥib-i-Kalān* [Governor-General]. Anyhow, whatever has happened has happened. Write to me in detail and send whatever is left. These things are required here including two pairs of large beams for the elephant cart. Send also the cap of the end of the old beam which was kept there for repair with Ram Sundar Datt. Apparently, the two additional caps for the handle of the peacock feather fan which earlier I had written to you to prepare in Akbarabad are ready. Find out [about them] and send them. I am concerned because I have not heard from you for so many days. Hand over the letters to Dr Thomas to be dispatched to me. 3 Rabī' I 1190.

Folio 394a. To Ram Sundar Datt.

Received your letter of 28 Muḥarram regarding the dispatch of goods to me. I am happy to know that you have dispatched these to me. In the meanwhile, with the grace of God, Mr Perceret *ṣāḥib* along with the goods has also arrived on the 24 Ṣafar.

You write that you have paid all the arrears to Bībī Jawahar. But the Bībī writes that you still owe her Rs 300. You are instructed to send to me the clearance paper of the emoluments dispatched to the Bībī without delay. 3 Rabī' I 1190.

Folio 394a. To Mirza Najaf Khan.

I have recieved the *maḥāl* of Khalilganj from the Emperor as my *jāgīr*. In view of our friendship, I consider it very appropriate that my *jāgīr* is located in the neigbourhood of your territory (*jawār-i-mulk-i-ān-mushfiq*). I therefore accepted the *jāgīr* and sent an *'āmil* to the *maḥāl*. In the world of our friendship and the unity of our interest there is no place for any strangeness (*mughāyarat*). In actuality I received the *jāgīr* because of your kindness. Now I gather that the *thāna* of Niyaz Beg Khan is established in this *maḥāl* and he himself is with you. I therefore expect you to consider my *maḥāl* as yours and instruct Niyaz Beg Khan to see that the *thānadār* does not quarrel with my *'āmil* so that I do not come to you with this case again. I hope that you will help. 4 Rabī' I 1190.

Folio 394b. To Diwan Manik Ram.

I am concerned at not having received any letter from you. I do not know the reason for this delay. In the meanwhile, many serious incidents took place there, including the assassination of Mukhtar-ud-Daula by Basant Ali Khan, the arrival of Mirza Sa'adat Ali Khan and the receipt there of the *khil'at* of *wizārat* [for Asaf-ud-Daula]. But you have not written to me about anything. This is strange because I insist on regularity in correspondence.

You must write to me the details about the arrears of the emoluments of Bībī Jawahar. Ram Sunder Datt has written to me, but she writes that Rs 300 remains unpaid. I have also written to Ram Sunder Datt about sending me her account. Get the papers from him and send them to me so that everything is clarified. In future send the daily dispatches through the *dāk* of Dr Thomas. 5 Rabī' I 1190.

Folio 395a. To Manik Ram.

I received three of your letters of the 28th of Ṣafar, 1st of Rabi and 2nd Rabi I on the 6th of this month. I have been worried about the delay in these dispatches. In future dispatch letters through Dr Thomas so that I receive them regularly. I had know even before I received your letter about the assassination of Mukhtar-ud-Daula, the subsequent punitive execution of Basant Ali Khan, the arrival there of Saadat Ali Khan and the appointment of Mirza Hasan Ali Khan as *mukhtār.* As a matter of fact, I had earlier written to you that I am happy over the appointment of Mirza Hasan Ali Khan because he is my friend and will help us in carrying out our small and big works.

Get the horse that you had obtained through Niyaz Ali Khan treated and then sell it off. It is not advisable to keep it. For the moment the price here is Rs 200. You should continue your regular meetings with Bristow and Thomas. I note that you are looking for the *'almās* [diamond]. Acquire one as soon as you can get it at an appropriate price. I have also written to you repeatedly about the *chhokrī* [girl]. I am not happy with the problems that have arisen around this girl. Summon her, act as per whatever has been agreed upon and send her to me together with the other male and female slaves from Srinagar.

Perceret *ṣāḥib* has arrived here along with all the goods. I have written to you about this several times. I have also written to you about the *hundī* and that deductions here are at the rate of Rs 5 and 4 annas, and that you should recover the extra 4 annas there.

In your second letter of 2nd Rabī' I you write that the Nawab was endowed with the office of the *wazīr* and it was agreed in the time of late Mukhtar-ud-Daula that the office of the deputyship of *wazīr, topkhāna* [arsenal] and *ghusl khāna* [inner quarters] will be given to Najaf Khan. You have written that even after his [Mukhtar-ud-Daula's] death, Asaf-ud-Daula has maintained this agreement. You also write that a letter to this effect requesting the renewal [of the agreement] has been dispatched to the imperial court. I appreciate that things have been done properly. From here also the Emperor has issued a letter with the following: the *khil'ats* of the office of deputy *wazīr* should be sent to Delhi so that it is sent to Najaf Khan from here; and that the deputyship of the *topkhāna* and *ghusl khāna* will be given to Abd-ul-Ahad Khan. I write this for your information.

I have noted whatever you wrote about about the bestowal of the *khil'at* by the Nawab upon Qutb Khan and Raja Nawal and your meeting with Chandelier ṣāḥib through Dr Thomas. Write whatever conversation you had with him. I also noted the news that the Nawab has set out towards Lucknow.

As for the money obtained from the sale of the basket of mangoes by Lloyd *ṣāḥib* which he kept and the episode of his having imprisoned Ram Sundar Datt without my permission, my dear Mr Lloyd did all this without my permission and I disapprove [of hs actions]. It is important for you to make payments to all upto the month of March so that no one is in difficulty. In future their emoluments will be payed by Mr Lloyd. After having cleared the dues of everybody, send for Ram Sundar Datt. I have written to you about this several times. Negligence is not advisable in such matters. Your account should be finalized. Carry it along when you come here. 6 Rabī' II 1190.

Folio 396b. To Manik Ram.

I have sent two rings with *nagīna* stones: one is Yamanī and the other white with a European golden rim. I have also sent the names of the *ṣāḥibs* to be calligraphed [on it]. The name of John Ware Narvenden Weldam will be inscribed on the Yamanī ring, and that of John Robinson on the white *nagīna.* I wonder if Muhammad Salah Khan, the inscriber, is in Faizabad or in the Nawab's camp. Summon him if he is in the Nawab's camp and hand this over to him. If he is in Faizabad take these over to him so that he may inscribe these names as per the calligraphic designs. He should inscribe it with care and in beautiful writing. After the rings are ready, hand them over to Dr Thomas.

As for the pension that the Nawab owes me, ensure that its arrears are used to clear the five months salary due to my people. The place for keeping the organ has not yet been finalized. Get an order from the Nawab for this. Ǵora *mistri* knows the work very well and will give suggestions. Do not keep it in the *havelī* otherwise it will get spoilt. I gather that the artists are not doing good work after I left. Since I have been ordered to stay here in Shahjahanabad it is necessary that they join me here. I have written to them a letter to this effect, a copy of which is enclosed. Hand it over Merchand when he comes here. Arrange different *sawārīs* for the Farrukhabad girl, male and female slaves and the artists and also escorts for their safety. Send them immediately via Farrukhabad and Khalilganj. It is better that they travel together. Dispatch also two *namdas*; one big sized *masnadī* and a big *namda* of high quality. I have looked in vain for good quality *namdas* here. Dr Thomas wrote to me that you met Chandelier *ṣāḥib* and that he would give you a job on the condition that you get the clearance (*rāẓīnāma*) from me stating that I have no objection [to your leaving my job]. I am thus writing to you that finish the work there and come here so that everything is clear. Since all the papers are now with me, the more time you take in clearing the account, the more delayed you will get. 7 Rabī' I.

Folio 397b. To Manik Ram.

I have received three of your letters of 28 Ṣafar and Ist and 2nd Rabī' I through the *dāk* of the Nawab. Through the different dates of these letters I learn that the *dāk* takes a long time. I therefore sent my reply to these letters through the *angrezī dāk*. In future hand over your letter to Dr Thomas so that I get them without delay. 7 Rabī' I.

Folio 397b. To Mehrchand.

I receieved your letter sent through Perceret and noted the trouble you are facing about the payments of your emoluments and the money due for the repairs of the *qit'as* [calligraphied verses]. I have written about this to Mr Lloyd. Rest assured that you will get the money from him. Second, it is necessary that you arrive here. Keep all the albums (*muraqqa's*) and *qit'as* in one box carefully so that they are safe from the dust and do not get damaged in transit. Load them together with the boxes for the Persian books and fix them there [tightly]. Also fix the cartage rates and arrive here with them without any delay. I have also written to Mr Lloyd. Follow his instructions. Travel via Farrukhabad and Khalilganj. When you reach there my people will escort you to Delhi. 7 Rabī' I.

Folio 398a. To Najaf Khan.

I have written to you earlier that Khalilganj has been assigned to me in *jāgīr*. All this is because of your kindness. Instruct Niyaz Beg Khan that his deputy should not quarrel with my *'āmil*. I have already written to you about this.

But today, the 8th Rabī' I, I received a letter from my *'āmil* stating that when he reached near Khalilganj, a large number of horsemen and *piyādas* [troopers] sprang out of the fortress and began to fight with my men. They offered resistance to my *'āmil* and placed the cannon carriage facing my men. Since my *'āmil* knows about our close relationship, he thought that perhaps the poeple of the former *'āmil* are acting in this manner because they do not know the nature of our friendship. He therefore desisted from fighting and camped at a distance from them and wrote to me. I understand that all this happened before you received my letter because I had, apprehending this, written to you about it and expected that in view of our cordial relation you would have written to [the *'āmil*]. I hope that you will now write to Ghulam Ali Beg, the *'āmil* of the *pargana* Jalesar instructing him to get the fortress of Khalilganj vacated immediately from the people of Niyaz Beg Khan and get my *'āmil* installed. Also inform Niyaz Beg Khan that there is no difference between my work and your work, and that he should write to his people to vacate the fortress and not indulge in any altercation with my *'āmil.* I shall also expect a letter from you reaffirming our friendship. This will give me immense relief. 8 Rabī' I.

Folio 398b. To Niyaz Ali Khan.

I am happy to hear about your safe return. I am sure that you will soon get an appointment with the Emperor. The news from here is as follows: Khalilganj *maḥāl* was given to me in *jāgīr*, and for the collection of the Rabī' revenue from this *maḥāl* I had dispatched Muhammadi Khan as *'āmil* and *faujdār.* Since the *maḥāl* is in the control of the deputy of Niyaz Beg Khan, who is in the service of Najaf Khan, I had written to the latter in consideration of our friendship. I had requested him [Najaf Khan] to instruct Niyaz Ali Khan to desist from any conflict with my *'āmil* and vacate the place. Muhammadi Khan informs me that despite my requests, on the 8th when he reached the neighbourhood of Khalilganj, a large number of troopers came out from the fortress to fight and arranged the cannons in line facing my men. Muhammadi Khan, because of my instructions and not having any military with him, desisted from fighting and camped at a distance from the town. I have again written to the Nawab. Write to me about the conversation you had with the Nawab. Acquire a *parwana* from the Nawab in the name of Ghulam Ali Beg with the instructions that the fort of Khalilganj should be vacated and handed over to my *'āmil.* See to it that the Nawab [Najaf Khan] issues instructions in front of the people. Consider the matter urgent so that my *'āmil* can take possession of it [fort]. 9 Rabī' I.

Folio 399a. Shuqqa enclosed with this letter.

In the meanwhile, a *shuqqa* from the Emperor regarding the case of Khalilganj was received here. I have sent it to Najaf Khan with the camel rider (*shutur sawār*). I am enclosing a copy of this *shuqqa* so that you are also familiar with its contents. This work depends on your kind attention and the old relation that I have with you. I hope things will be all right. Discuss with the Nawab whatever you think is appropriate in your understanding (*farāsat*) and think about the earliest possible vacation [of the fort]. 9 Rabī‘ I.

Folio 399b. To Ram Sundar Datt.

I received your letter and learnt about the conditions there. You had written that under instructions of Mr Lloyd, Mehrchand and others had kept you under surveillance and that you were insulted. I have written about this to Mr Lloyd and instructed him to release you. However, it is strange that you did not feel the insults when the troopers of Sayid Muhammad Khan entered my *ḥavelī* and kept you under surveillance. You faced insults at the hands of outsiders but did not even think of informing me. Now that my men are frantically trying to arrange the payments of the arrears due to my people, you are feeling insulted and even reporting the matter to me. In any case the arrears of all the employees there upto the month of March have to be cleared from wherever possible. In future this will be the responsibility of Mr Lloyd. But payments of salary upto the month of March is your responsibility. Prepare, clear and correct the accounts. Reach the camp and come here along with Manik Ram. 10 Rabī‘ I.

Folio 399b. To Muhammadi Khan, the ‘āmil of Khalilganj.

I recieved your letter of 6 Rabī‘ here through the *harkāra*. I noted the skirmish between you and the people of Niyaz Beg Khan who came out of the fort and that you retreated and camped at Katre Sherganj. Also, that since they were not ready for any settlement you went to Hathras, nine *kos* away. I also noted that you need a *parwāna* from Najaf Khan in the name of Ghulam Ali Beg, *nāib* of Jalesar, so as to be able to enter and taken possession of the *jāgīr*, [this is also needed] for them to vacate the fort and meet the expenses for the expenditure incurred.

Please do not worry and stay there. I have already written several letters to Najaf Khan regarding these matters. I have also, on 10

Rabīʿ I, sent the special signed *shuqqa* with the camel rider. I enclose the copy of these letters for your perusal. I hope that you will soon receive a letter from Najaf Khan regarding your possession of the *jāgīr* and the removal of the present *ʿāmil.* Inform me as soon as you get such a letter. In the meanwhile insist upon the *chaudhuri* and the *qānūngo* not to pay a single penny to the dismissed *ʿāmil.*

I am sending a *hundī* of Rs 300 of Deeg *sikka,* struck in the 10th regnal year of Shah Alam. This is to be cashed for your expenses at the shop of Khemkaran and Govind Rai in *qaṣba* Kol [Aligarh]. Collect the money without any discount from the shop and acknowledge its receipt. Keep me informed all the time. 10 Rabīʿ I, Monday.

Folio 400b. To Yusuf Ali.

When I was in Calcutta you had written to me to buy several things. I had subsequently bought them and handed them to Raso Sarkar. But Raso Sarkar forgot to carry them to you when he reached Faizabad and has brought them here. I will send them to you whenever I find reliable people going towards your side. 112 Rabīʿ I, 1190.

Folio 400b. To Niyaz Ali Khan.

Monsieur Delsier, brother of Chevalier, who earlier commanded a *paltan* of Shuja-ud-Daula of Awadh, has left his job and come here. Since things are not in order here, I did not feel it appropriate to recommend his employment in the court. He is reaching there with my letter. He is a reliable and worthy person. I therefore recommend that you arrange a job for him with Najaf Khan. It will make me happy. 13 Rabīʿ I.

Folio 401a. To Manik Ram.

Your letter of 4 Rabīʿ I reached here on the 11th. I noted whatever you had written about the dispatch of *khilʿat* for Najaf Khan through Qutb-ud-Din Khan, Raja Dayaram, and the departure of Nawab Asaf-ud-Daula towards Lucknow. Your letter arrived here late and I was worried. You must write in detail regularly [and send it] through Dr Thomas. I was very happy to know from a letter of Dr Thomas that you are trying vey earnestly to expeditiously resolve the case of the payment of emoluments of my people in the *sarkār.* The more you do for me the more favours you can expect from me. At any rate you should not worry. Use the arrears that you get from the court of the Nawab to resolve this issue. Clear their dues upto March and come here. If you are coming here very soon, bring along with you the slave girl from Farrukhabad, the slave boy and girl and Mehrchand the artist.

I have also noted Mir Sulaiman's demand regarding the price of the elephant. I had spoken to Dr Thomas when I met him in Firozabad and instructed him to give you whatever money you require as soon as my salary is received there. Let me know how much we owe Mir Sulaiman and I will write to him accordingly. You have written to me that I should recommend your case to Chandelier ṣāḥib. I have already written to him and he is familiar with this case. Meet him regularly and try to do my work sincerely so that he [Chandelier] should note that you are an earnest servant for your master. This is best for you.

Regarding the *tamassuk* of Ghulam Mustafa Khan, there is no news about its realization or when exactly it will be realized. Earlier I was sure that Rs 20,000 would be realized from the *rabī'* revenue of Khalilganj but now I do not think that we will get anything from there. Also the payment will be delayed for another six months. Therefore take care and write to me the details. As soon as you get this money hand it over to Dr Thomas so that he may send it to me. I need it for my expenses. The account of the realizations from Calcutta in the matter of Mir Sulaiman Khan has been sent. You [should] resolve this matter soon. 12 Rabī' I.

Folio 402a. To Mirza Niyaz Ali Khan.

I had earlier written to you recommending the case of Monsieur, Delsier, brother of Chevalier. I am happy that you introduced him to Najaf Khan. Even if Najaf Khan was kind enough to promise a *paltan*, nothing useful has been done. It is therefore necessary that you approach him so that something can be done for him. I am very happy that you are coming here [court] and I await your arrival.

I have written to you earlier about the case of my *jāgīr* in Khalilganj. I am sure that you have received my letter regarding that. I had also sent the special royal *shuqqa* with the camel rider so that you can present the case before Najaf Khan in an appropriate manner. Niyaz Beg should be strictly told that he should ask his people to vacate the *jāgīr* and facilitate its taking over by my agent or *'āmil.* This will ensure that whatever little revenue is saved will not come any longer in the control of people who have been asked to vacate the place. 12 Rabī' I.

Folio 402b. To Raja Dayaram.

On the request of some notable aquaintances of mine here, I need pure opium. I thought first to write about this to the Europeans (*ṣāḥibs*) there. Since they do not know much about opium, you should look around and aquire five to six *sers* of high quality, clear as glass opium and send it through a reliable person. As regards the payment for this opium, let me know to which *ṣāḥib* I should write so that you can get the payment from him 12 Rabī‘ I.

Folio 402b. To Najaf Khan.

[Congratulates him in a highly florid hyperbolic language on the conquest of Deeg, expressing his jubilation over his victory.]

Folio 403a. To Diwan Manik Ram.

I received your letter of 6 Rabī‘ I on the 13th and came to know about the developments there. I note that you had earlier written that you would hand over the letter to Raja Puranchand and that I should instruct his agents to bring it fast to me. My dear, I had earlier told you to hand the letter to Dr *Ṣāḥib.* But you handed them to Puranchand and thus I have received your letter in seven days while a letter from Dr Thomas written on the same date arrived three days earlier. You [should] hand over the letters to Dr Thomas.

In the case of Ram Sundar Datt, I have repeatedly told him to clear the dues upto March and that after that it would be the responsibility of Mr Lloyd and I will have nothing to do with him. But he neglected this work. Why has this problem not been solved as yet? He writes that he has no money with him while I know it well that he had enough money with him to give to the *faujdārs* and pay in advance for the *maḥals.* But to pay the people of my *ḥavelī* he has no money? Ask him to resolve this matter quickly.

Dr Thomas wrote to me that you accepted the responsibility of making the payment and wanted him [Ram Sundar Datt] to be released. He thus told Mr Lloyd to suspend his [Ram Sundar Datt's] further imprisonment.

Regarding the realizations of money from the *jāidād* of Ghulam Mustafa Khan, you had earlier written that your people would collect the payments and send them to me. But I am surprised to find you now saying that there are some problems there.

You write that the money from the revenue of the *maḥāl* Khalilganj—about Rs 5000—when collected should take care of the expenses there. But the problem is that because of the resistance of the dismissed *'āmil's* people and the inability of my deputy to take control, nothing is clear. It is doubtful if anything can be realized from the *rabī'* crop, since there is no response to the several letters, including the royal *shuqqa* that I sent to Najaf Khan. At the moment I am worried about the expenses for the intervening five to six months till the *faṣl* of *k͟harīf*. Meet Thomas and Bristow and think of ways to collect the money from there. I do not have any other source of income here. There should not be any delay because I need the money for my expenses here. Further, Majd-ud-Daula intends to visit Najaf Khan with the *k͟hil'at* and wants me also to accompany him. But I think it useless to spend my energy since I have nothing to do there. It is certain that Zulfiqar Khan is coming. So do the accounts and hand it over to Dr Thomas and rush back. There will not be any other time better than this. This is the most appropriate time because you know how loans can be coughed up. You are familiar with the entire case and also know the means to resolve it. 14 Rabī' I, 1190.

Folio 404b. To Manik Ram.

I received your letter of the 7th on the 15th. As for the case of Ram Sundar Datt, you write that he was insulted by the servents at Mr Lloyd's insistence. My dear, first, Ram Sundar Datt did not accept the responsibility of making payments. He clearly expressed his inability to do so. He instigated the people to go to Mr Lloyd to collect the money from him saying that it was he who had been sent the money and instructed by me to make these payments. They then created commotion and Lloyd was helpless. He realized that mutual respect and consideration for each other had been ignored (*pāsdarī-ye-hamdigar az miyān bark͟hāst*). He showed them my letter which stated that the payment for which he was responsible and which had been fixed by me was for only after March and that Ram Sundar Datt was to make the payments upto March. The payments thus had to be taken from him [Ram Sundar Datt]. Such being the case there is no fault of Lloyd *ṣāḥib* and he should not be accused. Since there is no money left there, make the payments upto March and come here. I will write to Mr Lloyd also. But your early presence here is essential because Najaf Khan is arriving at the court and I hope to recover from him the loan that he took from me. No one else knows the case better.

I note that Store *ṣāḥib* had taken [undue possession] your palanquin and horse. This is bad. Rest assured that I will admonish him. I also noted the difficulty you faced in the realization of money from the *jāidād* of Ghulam Murtaza Khan and Rajgopal, and that this was resolved with the arrival of a special *shuqqa* from the Emperor. Collect it quickly because there is no hope of the realizations from the *rabī'* crop from the *jāgīr* of Khalilganj. Five to six months of the rainy season will pass comfortably if the money is received from the *jāidād*. Consider this urgent and even if you have sent the *harkāra* to collect the money, be vigilant so that it may be realized soon.

I have heard that Mirza Ali Khan was unduly prejudiced regarding the Farrukhabad girl. You have not written anything about this case. Consider it urgent and necessary and write to me all the details so that I am fully informed. This may cause problems later. As I worte to you earlier, come here immediately after resolving this matter. As for your payment and correspondence with Dr Thomas, keep on doing your duty and put your heart in your work. I will recommend your case to all the *ṣāḥibs*. I have written to the Nawab several times congratualting him on receiving the *k̲h̲il'at* from the *Bādshāh* but I have not received any reply. I am surprised that despite my sincerity I am deprived of the honour of receiving a reply to my letter. 16 Rabī' I.

Folio 405b. To Niyaz Ali Khan.

I had sent earlier two letters to you through Darbari Mal, son of Diwan Kanji Mal. But I did not receive your reply since you came late from Akbarabad. I have written several times to Najaf Khan regarding the release of the *maḥāl* of Khalilganj. I have also forwarded to him the royal *shuqqa*. The *harkāras* and the camel riders who had taken this letter are still there but I am yet to receive his reply. It is well-known that I have been very sincere in serving the Nawab [Najaf Khan] and that apart from this [favour] I have never asked him for anything for myself. It is strange and unbelievable that despite all this he is not paying attention and not even replying. This delay has caused the revenue of *rabī'* to fall in the hands of the dismissed *'āmil* and things are becoming uncontrollable. I therefore request you to submit this to the Nawab in a manner that he is convinced [of the truth of our version] and issues instructions to Niyaz Beg Khan to resolve this. He should also write to Ghulam Ali

Beg, the *'āmil* of Jalesar, to assist my *'āmil* in regaining control of the *pargana*. I keenly look forward to receiving you and have the joy of meeting you. 16 Rabī' II.

Folio 406a. To Muhammadi Khan, 'āmil of Khalilganj.

I received your letter and came to know of the developments there. I have sent two letters, together with the royal *shuqqa*, through a camel rider to Najaf Khan. But I have not received any reply because these days he is preoccupied with the developments following the conquest of Deeg. It is for similar reasons that the *parwāna* for the handing over of the *jāgīrs* has also been delayed. In the meanwhile, Niyaz Ali Khan is arriving from Akbarabad. Rest assured that I will procure the *parwāna* and send it to you. Meet the *qānūngos* and *chaudhurīs* there and keep them under control. Tell them firmly that not a single penny should be paid to the dismissed *'āmil*. As for your payments, I have already sent a *hundī* of Rs 300 through the *harkāra*. Relax and do not get panicky. I have received the details of the account that you had sent: You have paid Ramji, the *jamā'adār* of the *harkāra* appointed from here, Rs 9 and 1.5 annas which is his payment upto 11 Rabī' I. Deduct this amount from their claim. Similarly, payments, at the rate of Rs 5 per head, upto 11 Rabī', I have been made to the Mewātīs employed since the 25th of Ṣafar. Make these deductions as well.

I have come to know from Ma'ad Khan Afghan that the zamindar of Hathras wants to buy the elephant you rode on to reach there. He is willing to pay Rs 22,000 for it. This elephant is not worth my *sawārī* so you can sell it. But let me know if you require another elephant for your purpose, which I could send from here. As for the elephant feed, it is as follows: 14 *ser atta* and rice with *mothī* and *masāla*. This will be sent from here through Khan *fīlbān* [elephant-keeper]. At times you may mix one to two *flūs* in the *masāla* but do not do it regularly. 17 Rabī' I.

Folio 407a. To Niyaz Ali Khan.

I have not heard from you since ages. I am surprised that you have not come here yet. I sent you three letters with the details of the developments in the Khalilganj case through Dīwān Mal, son of Kanji Mal. I am sure that you received them, but I am yet to have the pleasure of your reply. I write again that this *maḥāl* was assigned to me as *tankhwāh* and that I sent Muhammadi Khan as *'āmil* and *faujdār* there. However, the people of Niyaz Beg offered him resistance near Khalilganj and picked up a fight with him. Muhammadi Khan did not consider it appropriate to enter into a conflict with them and retreated to Hathras. Till date, i.e. the 15th day of Rabī'I, he is camped there. Ghulam Ali Beg, the deputy of Muhammadi Khan in Jalesar, told him that without a letter from Najaf Khan he will never be allowed to enter there [Khalilganj]. I thus wrote several letters to Najaf Khan and also sent him the *shuqqa* of the Emperor, but I have not received any reply from him so far. As a result of this delay the revenue of the *maḥāls* has fallen into the hands of the dismissed *'āmil.* Now there is only a faint hope of receiving the revenue of the coming year. God knows what will happen. I had asked for this *maḥāl* adjacent to those of Najaf Khan in view of the help he would offer me being my friend. But I am surprised that despite our firm friendship, he is not doing anything for me. It is obvious that I need Najaf Khan's help in nothing other than recovering my own money which is being misappropriated by others. Please submit my case to him and see that he sends instructions to Niyaz Beg Khan to vacate the *maḥāl,* and dispatches a *parwāna* to Gulam Ali Beg, the *naib* of Jalesar, to help my *'āmil* to take over the *maḥāl.* Please do something soon and inform me. It is important that some effort is made in this matter and the sooner the better.

Mulla Rahmdad Khan wants to join Zabita Khan and thus raise a *fitna.* He is approaching Zabita Khan with this intention and has established his own *thāna* in the royal *maḥālāt.* He is marching towards Shahjahanabad [Delhi] and is reported to be fifteen to sixteen *kos* from there. The people of the *paltan* are pestering for their salaries. There is no news from there [Najaf Khan's camp]. Write and appraise me of the situation through my *harkāra* who has already reached Najaf Khan's camp. Please write about your own self also and whether Najaf Khan wants to come here. Write in detail. 17 Rabī' I.1

Folio 408a. To Muhammadi Khan (*the 'āmil of the jagir*).

I received a letter from Najaf Khan which states that strict instructions have been given to Niyaz Beg Khan and that I should take possession of the *pargana.* I am sending to you this letter through the *harkāra.* As soon as the *harkāra* reaches there, take this letter and show it to the deputy of Niyaz Beg Khan and his people and manage the things. When you enter the *pargana,* be strict with the *qānūngo* and the *chaudhurī* and all the *ra'īyat* regarding the realization of the *rabī'* crop. Try to collect it as soon as possible, lest the people of the dispossessed *'āmil* take this money. Also send to the court an account of the income and expenditure receipts and the amount of money misappropriated by the dismissed *'āmil.* Write also the details and send back the *harkāra.* In the meanwhile, Niyaz Ali Khan has also arrived in the camp of Najaf Khan. Rest assured that all matters, including the collection of the necessary letters for different people, will be carried out according to our desire. 21 Rabī' I, Thursday.

Folio 408a. To Muhammadi Khan.

I have received a letter from Niyaz Ali Khan with the details of the conversation he had with Najaf Khan regarding the case of Khalilganj. It seems that Najaf Khan is not keen on releasing this *maḥāl* to us. Such being the case, it is useless for you to stay there any longer. I am aware that without the consent of Najaf Khan this matter cannot be resolved even if an army is deputed to carry out the task. Any further delay in your return would be futile. Well, whatever has happened has happened. With the grace of God, in place of this *maḥāl* we will get another one which will be free from problems.

I learnt from Ma'ad Khan Afghan that the zamindar of Hathras is willing to buy the elephant that you have for Rs 2200. Sell the elephant to someone who pays immediately so that you get the money and dispatch it by *hundī.* Yesterday, I received a letter from Najaf Khan which I redirected to you. Read it carefully and find out from its contents if there is any news of people there. Use your own understanding to find out if there is anything else [important news]. 22 Rabī'I.

Folio 408b. To Mehrchand, the painter.

I have received your letter with the portrait of the junior Bībī I noted whatever you had written about the preparation of the papers, the paintings and other matters. I had written to you earlier also to come here—so you do that now. Rest asswred that whatever you require will be done. 22 Rabī' I.

Folio 408b. To Manik Ram.

Your letter of 16 Rabī' I reached here on the 23rd. As regards the case of the imprisonment of Ram Sundar Datt and your plea that he should be sent to you, I have already written to Mr Thomas and

Mr Lloyd. I also wrote to the *khalāṣīs* forbidding them from harassing him and asked them to receive their salaries from you in the Nawab's camp. But how can they release Ram Sundar Datt and come over to Lucknow? This is a minor matter. Why don't you send the money due to them to Faizabad so that Ram Sundar Datt is released soon and that the problem is resolved.

I know that the *wilāyatī namda* is rare there. I therefore want you to buy four pieces of first grade Bahraich *namdas* and send them to me. I also appreciate what you write about the expenses for the Farrukhabad girl. Summon her father and persuade him to resolve the matter.

You have not written anything regarding the realization of the collection of money. Upto now I was hopeful about the revenue from the *jāgīr* of Khalilganj. But now this hope is gone because of the indifference of Najaf Khan. I need money for my expenses here. Get the money from the Khan in whichever manner you think appropriate. Treat this [matter] as urgent. I have also written to Dr Thomas that you are doing things sincerely regarding this matter. 23 Rabī' I Sunday.

Folio 409b. To Manik Ram.

I received your letter of 15 Rabī' I on the 21st. I am happy to know that on the 13th of this month the Nawab has ordered for the signature of Mirza Hasan Reza Khan. Things will be fine very soon. I also appreciate your regular meetings with Dr Thomas and Mirza Hasan Khan.

As for the disease of the horse and somebody's willingness to pay Rs 200, it is fine by me since I do not wish to retain this horse any longer. Send the money in whatever form you like. I noted your suggestion in the case of the imprisonment of Ram Sundar Datt in Faizabad; also your request that he be allowed to join you and that you would prepare the account of the salary of the people; and that you have already written about this to Mr Lloyd. My dear, I have already written to them about this and will do so again. But my writing is of no avail because they want their salary. It will not be acceptable to them if I write that release him and do not demand your salary. It is not necessary for Ram Sundar Datt to come for the payment of dues. It is enough that he writes to you about the money that is due and you dispatch him the desired amount so that he may clear the dues and obtain his release. If it is not proper to send the money to him then it may be sent to Mr Lloyd and he will distribute it. At any rate clear the dues upto the end of March in whatever way you think appropriate. This is the only way in which the release of Ram Sundar Datt can be ensured.

I do not approve of Mr Store taking away your *pālkī* and horse. Rest assure that I will admonish him for this. I had earlier written to you to enlist the pensioned *khalāṣīs* in the service of the Nawab, else we would loose them. But you have not acted upon it as yet. Two thousand *khalāṣīs* had gone to the *dārogha* who said that till then he had not received any instructions regarding their enlistment. They were still clamouring for their salaries. Since you know that their dues will not be more than Rs 2000–Rs 2500, why are you postponing such a small matter? Get over with the matter of the salaries quickly.

Send me four first grade *namdas* of Bahraich. I have written repeatedly to Najaf Khan and also sent him the *shuqqa* from the Badshah about the case of my *jāgīr* in Khalilganj. I have requested him to get the jāgīr released. But he has not sent me a single reply on the basis of which I can confront Niyaz Beg. Today, i.e. the 22nd, I have received a letter from Niyaz Ali Khan. He made a plea with Najaf Khan regarding this but the latter is not willing to release this *maḥāl.* Well, this is how I have been paid for my sincere friendship with him! And this despite the fact that I had asked him only for the release of my own revenue. He did not show any consideration (*murawwat*) for me. Forget about this *maḥāl.*

You had written that Mr Store and my people misbehaved with Ram Sundar Datt. Strangely enough, Gora Mistri wrote to me threatening that he would take whatever salary was due from the treasury of the Nawab. He had also written some other nonsensical (*nā-m'aqūlāt*) things. How can I be silent if he behaves in such a manner? Had he been here I would have beaten him with shoes. But Store and others stayed calm and did whatever was appropriate without even informing me.

The girl from Farrukhabad is in Faizabad. I have come to know that she does not have money for her expenses. So how can she come here? Send for her along with other people, including Ram Sundar Datt, and dispatch them to Lucknow. Clear their dues and come here with the painters, the Faizabad *chhokri* and the boy and girl slaves. But do clear all my dues because delay in money matters brings a bad name and also delays my other work. It is also in your interest that you resolve this case. 23 Rabīʻ I, Sunday.

Folio 411a. To Muhammad Riza and the others.

I received you letter (*'arẓī*) and was unhappy to know that you have been rude to Ram Sundar Dutt without informing me of his misbehaviour. You should have sent five or six persons to Manik Ram to find out the reason for delay in payment of money. Why did you misbehave with Ram Sundar Datt? Why are you troubling him? This is not in good faith. Release him without any further harassment. Let him join Manik Ram in Lucknow along with two to three people of your group. Settle the matter and get your money released. Manik Ram will then enlist you in the pension category in the service of the Nawab. Do your work cautiously and pursue the pension related cases wholeheartedly. 23 Rabī' I.

Folio 411b. To Niyaz Ali Khan.

I received your letter and noted your efforts regarding the case of Khalilganj vis-a-vis Najaf Khan. But he [Najaf Khan] insists that Niyaz Beg Khan is in command of 2000 horsemen and is in my army. Also, that he will quit in the event of any unpleasantness. I should therefore arrange my possessions, etc. by myself. In short, the Nawab [Najaf Khan] is not willing to release this *maḥāl* to me. You have also written that your consideration (*khāṭirdārī*) for Mr John and Mr Bristow stands above all other things. But in reality I wonder how you take favours to Samru and Yamin-ud-Daula and many such other things as an expression of your concern for Mr John Bristow! All this is just lip service (*hama-sakhun-i guftanī ast*).

Najaf Khan had taken a loan from me but till date there has been no talk of its repayment. In addition, I have now been virtually forced to present him Rs 25,000, the sum which was expected to be realized by me from the *rabī'* crop of this *jāgīr* as *nazr*. Since ages the Nawab [Najaf Khan] has thus been kind to me. It was in view of our friendship that I had asked for a *jāgīr* in the neighbourhood of his jurisdiction (*'āmal*). Otherwise I would have received a *jāgīr* anywhere else. But this is how Najaf Khan has repaid my old friendship. Now I have come to know that sincerity and good behaviour with nobles results only in loss and ill feelings. Anyway, whatever has happened has happened. But because I have spent a large amount on sending the *'āmil* and arranging for the *sihbandīs* there, it is necessary that you again submit to him the case so that a letter for my purpose is obtained from him and the problem of this *jāgīr* is resolved. In this way at least I will not have to bear the financial burden. But if the non-release of this *jāgīr* benefits Najaf Khan, then I will accept this in consideration of our friendship. 24 Rabī'I.

Folio 412a. To Manik Ram.

I have received two of your letters and noted your meeting and conversations with the Nawab in the presence of John Bristow. It appears that at the time of your meeting, the Nawab was not in a good mood. Therefore, the detailed submission of the problem should be postponed to the time when he is relaxed. I know that if the *parwāna* of *tankhwāh* is issued today, it takes one year for the money to be realized. So be vigilant. Present the matter to him whenever the Nawab is in a good mood. I have noted that you have deputed people for the collection of money from Jaigopal. As soon as it is ready, take it to Dr Thomas and send it to me because the time for the collection of *rabī'* crop from the *pargana* is passing off. I am sure that the people whom you have deputed will collect the money. Till date the case of the *jāgīr* has not been resolved and the revenue of the *rabī'* has been completely lost.

You have written that I must look after the interests of Majd-ud-Daula. As a matter of fact, I give them priority over all other matters. I do nothing without his knowledge and advice. The Emperor has [thus] been kindly disposed to the case of my *jāgīr*, so has been the case with Majd-ud-Daula. But nothing substantial has come out so far. The Emperor's suggestion to him that the case be resolved keeping in view the good of everybody concerned has hitherto been ignored. The strange thing is that he wears a different colour every second day. To be sure, events are taking place as per the custom of Hindustan (*anchi rasm Hindustān ast humān qism jalwagar mishawad*). I am not worried about this any more. My concern is that you must dispatch to me immediately the money of Rao Jaigopal. In the meanwhile, I sit here waiting for the air to clear. I will do whatever is required at this time. I want that at least Rs 12,000 or Rs 13,000 of Jaigopal should remain with me so that I can meet expenses for five to six months while the matter is being settled. After that I will see what happens. But for the moment even if I request for Rs 500 it is not available here.

You write that you had earlier wanted Ram Sundar Datt, with two or three persons along with the papers to be sent to you, but now, you have given up the idea because you thought that it did not appeal to me. There is no question of my disapproval of any idea which helps you clear the dues of the people without any delay. I have noted that you have sent to me the slave boy and the girl of Srinagar. Further, I am enclosing a letter for the Nawab. Keep this letter with you and deliver it to him whenever you feel that he is in a relaxed mood. 28 Rabī' I.

Folio 413a. To Mirza Hasan Riza Khan.

I am keen to meet you and wish that all these works are carried out. Regarding Manik Ram, I had written to you that he is incomparable in etiquette and obedience and is true and sincere to you in his service. I am sure that you will consider him as one of your own and will always be kind to him. Keep me informed of your welfare until we meet. Do not hesitate to write if you need anything from here. 23 Rabī' I.

Folio 413b To Muhammadi Khan.

I had sent to you a letter through a *harkāra* yesterday with instructions to set out and come here, but there is no need for any haste in this matter. Stay there without any worry, disband the new *sihbandī* and when the necessity arises, whatever is required will be arranged. In the meanwhile negotiations (*jawāb-o-sawāl*) are on with Najaf Khan. Rest assured that the matter will be settled. 24 Rabī' I.

Folio 413b To Najaf Khan.

I have received your letter regarding the case of Khalilganj with the news that you have instructed Niyaz Beg Khan to write to his *'āmil* to stay there. I notice that for the sake of Niyaz Beg you do not approve of the release of the *maḥāl* for me. With the grace of God you have such a big country and fortunes in your control that a hundred English *ṣāḥibs* can live comfortably. How can it be [imagined] that for a poor Niyaz Beg Khan there is no place other than Khalilganj. At any rate I will not deviate even a bit from what pleases you since in the realm of the nobles of high stature there is some consideration for sincerity and friendship. This is despite the fact that I—your sincere friend—accepted a *jāgīr* in your neighbourhood with the hope that I would not have to worry about its administration. Now I understand that you want to have this *maḥāl* in your control. This is fine with me. For me what matters is your happiness. If this be your wish then write to me clearly so that I can ask my *'āmil* to move out from there. In the meanwhile, I have unnecessarily spent Rs 2000 for the *sihbandī*. Well, in friendship even this is not bad. Write to me clearly since I have postponed the removal of my people from there until I receive your reply. 24 Rabī'I.

Folio 414b. To Muhammadi Khan.

I received your letter of the 16th of Rabī' I. You write that in your area the currency in circulation is of 7th Regnal year Akbarabadi and therefore on the *hundī* of Rs 300 of the 10th year of Deeg, there will be a discount of Rs 4. As per your suggestion in the letter, I have deposited the money equivalent to the discount at the market with the agent of the *sāhūkār* here.

You must have received my letter sent through the *harkāra* asking you to stay on there. Today, I have heard that another *shuqqa* from the Bādshāh stating that Niyaz Beg Khan should remove his *'āmil* from Khalilganj and the [*maḥāl*] be given over to my *'āmil* has been dispatched to Najaf Khan with Miyan Qambar *khwājasarā* who is also taking the *khīl'at* from the court to him. In addition, Majd-ud-Daula also says that Niyaz Beg Khan has been assigned a *jāidād* in Rajputana. You make the *qānūngos* and the *chaudhurīs* who come to you understand that soon things will stabilize and turn in our favour. Keep trying in your own way. I am also not oblivious [to the developments there]. Let us wait for a few days and soon we will achieve our goal. Keep the *harkāras* that you think are necessary and send the rest here. Keep me informed of the developments there. Suspend the arrangement of the *sawār* and the *sibhandī* for the moment and do whatever you think is appropriate in other matters. Retain 20 per cent of the *piyādas* that are deputed with you and take care of their expenses. We will see [what can be done] after you take possession of the *pargana.* 21 Rabī' I.

Folio 415a. To Manik Ram.

The *pargana* of Khalilganj that had been assigned to me in *jāgīr* was taken over by Najaf Khan. A special letter to this effect was sent from the royal court through a camel rider and a second letter has been dispatched today with Qambar Kwaja who is also carrying a royal *khil'at* for Najaf Khan. The Emperor is very kind to me in this matter. He asked Majd-ud-Daula to find out the reason for Najaf Khan's resistance in releasing the *jāgīr* for me. He ordered that special *shuqqa* to this effect should be dispatched. If it works, well and good. Otherwise, he said that he himself would march to help me take possession of it. But Majd-ud-Daula is indifferent these days as compared to his earlier stance. He knows it well that I am here these days in connection with my work. Until these special royal letters become effective, the revenue of the *rabī'* would have been completely lost. I am looking forward to receiving from you the money of Murtaza Khan. Collect it soon and send it here so that I can meet my expenses for the coming four to five months until the time of the [realization of] the revenue of the *kharīf*. Be careful and treat this as urgent. The dispatch of money to me at this hour is absolutely necessary. 21 Rabī' I.

Folio 415b. To Niyaz Ali Khan.

I received your letter a few days back. But I have not yet received the acknowledgement of the letter that I wrote to you on the 24th of this month. The condition here is as follows: the Emperor has not received any reply to the *shuqqa* that he had dispatched earlier through the camel rider to Najaf Khan regarding the release of Khalilganj. In the meanwhile, another *shuqqa* with strict instructions to Niyaz Beg Khan has been sent along with Qambar *khwājasarā* who is also carrying a *khil'at* [for Najaf Khan]. Still another *shuqqa* was sent instructing Qambar to negotiate the matter and report to the Emperor. I therefore write to you to speak to him regarding this matter in whatever way you think is appropriate. Request him to send a *parwāna* to Ghulam Ali Beg, the *'amil* of Jalesar, instructing him to tell my *'āmil* to take possession and dismiss the *'āmil* of Khalilganj. Issue also instructions to Niyaz Beg Khan so that he can write to his *'āmil* to this effect. Also find out whether Najaf Khan has assigned the *jāidād* for Niyaz Beg Khan in Rajputana. Negotiate in whatever manner you think is proper. Keep me informed because it is now difficult to keep the *sihbandī*. 29 Rabī' I.

Folio 416a. To Nawab Murid Khan.

I have received your letter sent through Muhammad Zaid with the request for the Emperor to release your property which had been confiscated. I am happy to know of your welfare. The fact is that I consider your work as my work. However, since I have just arrived here and am in the service of the Emperor I do not have that much connection with Majd-ud-Daula to make a request regarding all the cases. But rest assured that I will remember your case and it will be carried out at the appropriate time. Keep writing to me regularly. 30 Rabī' I, 1190.

Folio 416b To Muhammadi Khan.

I received your letter of 28 Rabī' I with two other letters from the *qānūngo* of Khalilganj, on Monday, the 1st of Rabī' II. I have noted whatever you write about the copies of your letters to Najaf Khan regarding the *'āmil* of Niyaz Beg Khan, the negotiations in this matter, and the non-receipt of the *hundī*. The condition here is as follows: Earlier a special royal letter was sent through a camel rider to Najaf Khan. Now, a second letter is being sent through Qambar *khwājasarā* who is also carrying the *khil'at* for him. Following this, still another *shuqqa* was issued in the name of Qambar *khwājasarā* instructing him to talk to Najaf Khan. Find out the conditions there and report back.

Yesterday, the 30th of Rabī' I, a letter (*'ārzi*) from Qambar *khwājasarā* to the Badshah arrived here. The Emperor instructed Majd-ud-Daula to bring this letter to the notice of my *munshī*. It says that Najaf Khan will put on the *khil'at* on Sunday and the same day he [Qambar] will talk to him about the Khalilganj problem and request him to resolve the matter. He will also see that Najaf Khan writes to the Emperor about this problem. We are thus waiting for a letter from Qambar *khwājasarā*. Further, the news is that Najaf Khan is arriving at the court. Something will be done within ten to twelve days once Najaf Khan arrives here. But for the moment you stay on there along with your two sons. Keep also with you the Mewātī *piyādas* and dismiss the rest of horsemen and *piyādas*. These will be arranged again after you take possession of the *jāgīr*.

I also learnt from your letter that one Dayaram who wanted to buy the elephant will no longer buy it because of the defect in its leg. Let me know if he is a genuine buyer and wants a better elephant. I have a beautiful swift-moving she elephant.

It is the 9th day since I gave, as per your letter, the money of the *batta* to the *sāhūkār* and he has also given me a receipt. The *sāhūkār* had written that it will be paid to you. But it could not be sent through the bill of exchange (*khokha*) because there was no one available to take it. I am thus enclosing it in this letter. Hope that you receive the *hundī* money without any delay. It is no use keeping eight *harkāras* over there. Keep whatever number is essential and send the remaining over here. 1 Rabī' II.

Folio 417. To Manik Ram.

You have been writing to me since long that the money of Murtaza Khan has been received and that it will be sent to me soon. Also, that the money from the *tamassuk* of Rao Jaigopal will be received soon, and that the people have already been deputed in his *jāidād* to collect this money which will soon be dispatched to me. I do not understand why there is so much delay. It has nothing to do with the Nawab. Also, the days for the collection of the *rabī'* crops are over—then why is there negligence in the dispatch of the money to me? You know it very well that not a single penny is available to me over here. You are also aware of my daily expenses. Again, these days there is an additional expenditure on the *sihbandī.* Thus, I am in dire need of money. I have written to you about this several times. Consider it as urgent and dispatch the money as soon as you receive this letter.

These days there has been much delay in receiving your letter also, while earlier you had promised to write to me regularly with a gap of [only] one to two days. What is the reason for this delay? Writing of letters is important because I keenly look forward to hearing about the developments over there. 3 Rabī' II, Wednesday.

Folio 417b. To Niyaz Ali Khan.

I have received two of your letters—one sent through the *harkāra* and the other through Lakshman Singh, the brother of Darbari Mal. I noted that despite your persistent submission to Najaf Khan to consider my case there has been no effect; and that something might come out when Najaf Khan is back here in Delhi. I am familiar with Najaf Khan's nature. He is a little concerned for our friendship. It is fine if something positive comes out on his arrival at the court. Otherwise I know for certain that this matter will never be resolved. Anyhow, there is no harm if you remind him of this when he starts. The reality about the consideration (*murawwat*) and friendship of Najaf Khan, as well as the sincerity and love of Majd-ud-Daula at the court is such that I am not receiving even 1/10th of their past affection for me. In sum, the wind is blowing in a different direction, and conditions here are unspeakable. When you come back here again you will yourself see the *tamāsha.*

Your suggestion that Manik Ram, in view of my friendship with Hasan Riza Khan, should stay with the latter is fine. I have therefore asked him to stay over there. But I look forward to seeing you here. When we meet we will work in consultation with each other. 6 Rabī' II.

Folio 418b. To Muhammadi Khan.

Your letter of 3 Rabī' II concerning the letter of Chhatr Singh *qānūngo* reached here on the 7th(?). I note what you say about the *sawārs* of his household being available for his work there. I have written to you earlier also that for the moment you stay on there together with two of your sons and with some people who are there. Get the *sihbandī,* the *sawārs* and *piyādas* released. It is fine, as you think, that when Najaf Khan reaches the court and I meet him, something will come out. You know that I do not have any other source of income. You should dismiss the *sihbandī* and the *mutaṣaddīs.* They can be recalled later when required. 6 Rabī' II.

Folio 418b. To Manik Ram.

I received two of your letters of the 29th and 30th of Rabī' I on the 5th and 6th of Rabī' II. You have written that the money received from the *jāidād* of Rao Jaigopal and from the *tankhwāh* of Ghulam Murtaza Khan has been used to pay the *sazāwal;* also that something has been given to Thomas and some for purposes of dispatch has been sent to the *mahājan.* I need Rs 12,000 to 14,000 for my expenses for five months. Send this money to me quickly in whatever way you like. I cannot borrow money from the people of Shahjahanabad. Do not permit any delay. But send the money in one installment. If Rs 14,000 cannot be arranged, you should send not less than Rs 12,000. This is because if money is sent in one big installment, it inspires the confidence of the *mahājan* here and facilitates the transactions with him.

I have noted that you require some *wilāyatī* clothes. I will send whatever is left with me to you through your people as soon as they reach here. I am happy to note that you have sent Rs 1212 to Dr Thomas for the payment of the monthly emoluments of the servants. The matter will now be resolved. Issue summons immediately to the Farrukhabad girl and persuade her to come over here. Something needs to be done to clear the air here and make it favourable. The business here was always carried out well. I have learnt that the Nawab is upset because now John Bristow is not doing the work the way he used to earlier. But you are intelligent and wise, [so] do things in a manner that removes the misunderstanding of the Nawab and our business is carried out soon. 6 Rabī' II.

Folio 419b. To Manik Ram.

From your two letters, dated 23 and 25 Rabī‘ I, I learnt what Mr Bristow told you and how Mirza Hasan Riza Khan represented our case to the Nawab. Dr Thomas has also written about this in detail.

The fact is that the late Nawab Shuja-ud-Daula was extraordinarily polite and cultured. Despite his unhappiness with General Smith, he never expressed it in words. He knew that if this were made public, the English officers would no longer trust him. He thus rose high in power and wealth.

In contrast, and strangely enough in the time of the present Nawab, it has all now happened despite my sincere and loyal services to him. It is the duty of his advisors to submit to him the case in a manner that the Nawab finds it convenient to admit that his remarks were just in light vein. Only then would the work move on well and the Nawab's stature too would rise high. But in the event of his persistence with the same remarks, remind him of the sums he got from me as 'courtesy' (*tawāzu‘*) and the high-grade elephants I presented to him in return for the two [average] ones which he gave. You know it well how considerate and generous with gifts I have been to him all along. You are mesmerized by the false civility of the Nawab. All his niceties are [momentary], just like the imprint on water. It is your connection with the English officers and their kindness to you which lend strength to your position. Take care of my works with sincerity and earnestness. You will gain my favour and thus will also earn the support of Bristow, Chandelier and the other officers.

Earlier, an employee of mine who looked after all my papers there, left Faizabad for Calcutta. I am worried as I do not know where these papers are now. These are important papers and have to be recovered. It is possible they are with Ram Sundar Datt. Please write to him to send you whatever English papers he has. Dispatch them to me along with the three papers I had kept with you. This is urgent. 8 Rabī‘ II, Monday.

Folio 420a. To Manik Ram.

Your letter of 2 Rabī‘ II, together with a *hundī* of Rs 2000 *ānt* was received on 8 Rabī‘ II. I had expected a reasonable *hundī*. I had written to you earlier that I required Rs 14,000 for five months' expenses and that if it was difficult to arrange this amount to send Rs 12,000 at least. You had also written that the money from Rao

Jaigopal had been collected. I am therefore surprised to receive only Rs 2000. You must send the full amount soon.

Further, from a letter from Faizabad I learnt that the problems regarding the Farrukhabad girl are yet to be resolved. This case has to be settled soon. If anyone is interfering in the matter, find out who he is and write to me. It is not proper to postpone the case any longer. Captain Store is reaching Lucknow from Bilgram. Bring the matter to his notice and he will [help you] resolve it. 8 Rabī‘ II, in the night.

Folio 421a. To Muhammadi Khan, ‘āmil.

I received your letter together with the details of income and expenditure. As for your request for money for the expenses there, I have earlier written to you to dismiss all the newly appointed people, including the troopers, the *piyādas,* the *sawārs* as well the clerks. The enquiry into the Khalilganj [*jāgīr*] is unlikely to be over in the near future, since Najaf Khan's arrival has been delayed. Unless he arrives here, nothing can be done. For the moment, you must carry out the work only with the Mewātī *piyādas.* All other people must be plainly told to leave. So long as you are there you will get Rs 60, for you and the emoluments of the Mewātīs, the two *harkāras,* etc. No additional expenses are advisable at the moment. Whenever the necessity arises, whatever is required will be arranged. At present, you should not keep more than twenty Mewātīs and two *harkāras* there. 10 Rabī‘ II, Wednesday.

Folio 421b. To Manik Ram.

Two letters of yours were received here on 10 Rabī‘ II—one of 22 Rabī‘ I along with the Mewātīs and *harkāras* who escorted the bullock-cart carrying the slave girls and the boy, and the second, of 1 Rabī‘ II which I received through the *dāk.* Together with the two slave girls and a boy, I have received five *kajkāhs,* three pieces of musk, four beams [for the elephant cart and one hundred pieces of zadoary. Cartage for eighteen days, minus Rs 12 paid in advance by you,has been paid. The four Mewātīs who had escorted the cart have taken leave to go home for twelve days for the moment. On their return, they will take back some goods to you.

From the letter of I Rabī‘ II, I learnt about your sending Rs 1212 to Faizabad for the wages of the attendants there and about the mischiefs of Ram Sundar Datt. It is good that you sent the money; all their dues should be paid soon. Keep in touch with John Bristow and Dr Thomas and complete the work. There are other works for you to do subsequently.

The problem here is that the *jāgīr* I was assigned is in the control of Najaf Khan who has advised the Emperor for another *jāgīr* for me. What would happen here next is unclear at present, particularly as Majd-ud-Daula appears to be unfavourably inclined towards me these days. In these circumstances, it is futile to expect another assignment. The Emperor's favours notwithstanding, no work can be carried out here if Majd-ud-Daula is indifferent. Anyhow, I am also not happy with him and am least worried. I have, however, to live here for four months and need twelve to fourteen thousand rupees. You must send the sum in one installment. This is the only appropriate way to maintain my position and trustworthiness in the eyes of the people here. To send the money in separate installments is not advisable under any condition. As for the collection of only Rs 100 from the *jāidād* of Nawab Abduallah Khan, interference of the people of Maharaja Surat Singh and the problem in the realization of the full sum thereof, you must try to resolve these difficulties soon and collect the full amount. You will earn more favours from me if you send me a big sum in one instance.

It is good that you have sent some money for the father of the Farrukhabad girl. I have heard that he claims he would pay off the debt he owes to me and that he would not hand over the girl. But when he was told to come over to you and pay in Lucknow, he feigned an excuse and expressed inability to pay in Lucknow. He insists on paying only in Faizabad. My dear, earlier he made a pretext of his poverty and now is arrogant enough to practically refuse to pay. Clearly, he is being mischievously instigated by someone to act so insolently. Take possession of the girl and also collect from him a written bond so that he may never have any claim over her in future and then send her here. Or else take back all the money with interests from him and close the matter. It is not appropriate to prolong the case any longer. 11 Rabī' II, Friday.

Folio 423a. To Manik Ram.

More than a month back I had written to Ram Sundar Datt about the payment to Bībī Jawahar. It seems that at the time of her departure for Azimabad, she had received a sum of Rs 1100 from him, of which, as it is entered in my account, Rs 300 were the arrears of the emoluments for the month of November, and the remaining

Rs 800 were payment in advance. But from the statement of the Bībī I learn that of this sum Rs 600 was the delayed payment to her for two months, while only Rs 500 was given in advance. There is thus a discrepancy of Rs 300 in Ram Sundar Datt's report. Investigate the matter and write to me. 13 Rabī' II.

Folio 423a. To Niyaz Ali Khan.

I am happy to receive your letter and learn about the arrival of the Nawab [Najaf Khan] from Akbarabad. Even if I know it well what the response of the Nawab will be in the matter, I have still kept the *'āmil* in Khalilganj, considering the enormous expense I have incurred so far. If he comes over to the court, fine, otherwise please bring the matter to his notice. Also find out all the details of the goods acquired in Deeg. When we meet we will discuss our plans and do what we both understand as fit. Earlier, the Nawab had agreed to have my opinion in all matters, but in no case has he sought my advice since the day I came over here. This is strange. In any case, we will discuss all this when we meet. 14 Rabī' II.

Folio 423b. To Manik Ram.

I received your letter of 6 Rabī' II on the 13th and learnt about the realization of the *jāidād* money. The sooner you send all the money in one installment, the better. I have written to you about this several times and believe you will dispatch the sum without any further delay. As for the English (*wilāyatī*) clothes, the delay in dispatching them has occurred because the Mewātīs have sought leave for twelve days to visit their homes. They are expected back any day, and then three *thans* presently available with me will be sent through them to you. Whatever you do with these clothes should be on the advice of Dr Thomas. Regarding the money of Mir Sulaiman, I have already written to you what Dr Thomas had suggested. I have noted that you have requisitioned a wild ass from Faizabad for Asaf-ud-Daula. 14 Rabī' II.

Folio 424a. To Niyaz Ali Khan.

From your letter of 12 Rabī' II, which reached here on the 14th I learnt about the conditions of the army and the people of our time. Indeed, leaders (*sardārs*) of our time are the least trustworthy. Anyhow, let the time pass, and when you meet with Najaf Khan remind him about the Khalilganj case and about how cumbersome it is to keep the *'āmil* over there. I keenly look forward to meeting you so that we share our secretly guarded plans (*markūzāt-i- bāṭin*) with each other. Try to reach here soon. As for Rs 5000 for the *khil'at*, I have sent strict instruction to Manik Ram. I will write back to you as soon as I hear from him. Do keep me informed about your welfare. 15 Rabī' II.

Folio 424b. To Manik Ram.

I have got the receipt of the sum you handed over to Dr Thomas. Well done! Do give him all the other *tankhwāh* money realized and never forget to pay him the full sum of Rs 14,000 without which I am not at ease here. Further, since long there is no news about the *tankhwāhs* of Mahbub Ali Khan, Saiyid Muhammad Khan, the son of Nauruz Ali Beg Khan and Nawab Muzaffar Jang. Mr Bristow had earlier written that he had taken a bond from the son of Nauruz Ali Beg Khan. I wonder if this money or the *tankhwāh* of the others has been received. The time for the collection of the *rabī'* season is already over. This cannot be postponed any longer.

Over here, the *mahājans* are now pressing for payment of a loan of Rs 5000 which I had taken from them to offer the *peshkash-i khil'at.* This payment has to be in cash. Consult Mr Bristow and let me know whatever he suggests. 15 Rabī' II.

Folio 425a. To Muhammadi Khan, the 'āmil of Khalilganj.

Please come over here together with the elephant and the people in your service as soon as you get this letter. Your presence at the court here is necessary for some important matters. Since Najaf Khan is around, it is time for us to present our case in an effective manner. 17 Rabī'II.

Folio 425a. To Mir Waliullah Khan.

I am happy to receive your letter. There was no letter from you for a long time, otherwise I have never delayed writing back to you. Please do keep in touch. 19 Rabī' II.

Folio 425b. To Manik Ram.

Your letter of 11 Rabī' II reached here on the 18th. Now you write that only Rs 2000 of the total of Rs 23,000 have been collected from the *jāidāds* of Rao Jaigopal, etc. and that in these *jāidāds* there is resistance by [their] people. I am surprised, as you had earlier informed me of the full payment. I have repeatedly told you how urgent it is for me to get Rs 14,000 over here. Do arrange this sum. It is absolutely necessary.

You write that since Muzaffar Jang has not yet paid Rs 16,000 and since the receipt for payment has been given to [his agent], Shah Sidq Ali, I should therefore send a letter for him to rectify this receipt. I do not think such a letter is required, for the paper you sent me shows that the payment of the entire sum of Rs 40,000 has been made. How could he have given this receipt if you had not realized the full amount? Further, Rs 16,000 due from Muzaffar Jang is from the *tankhwāh*, while the receipt pertains to the *nazrāna* sum. Think about this again; there should not be any discrepancy in these matters from our side.

Regarding the case of Abd-ul-Haq (the father of the Faizabad girl), you write that he is still to be chastened. It seems you have not yet bought the girl. What kind of transaction have you made that the matter still remains unsettled? Make him see reason, take possession of the girl, finalize the deal in writing in unequivocal terms and then send her over here. Or else, he must pay back the entire amount with interest. I have [also] written to you earlier repeatedly about the case of Bībī Jawahar. Get details of the account from Ram Sundar Datt and send them soon to me. 19 Rabī' II.

Folio 426a. To Niyaz Ali Khan.

Monsieur Delssier (?) is there in the service of Najaf Khan now for a fortnight, but he is still to be deputed along with others in a contingent, and has therefore received no emoluments. Unless he is deputed with someone, there would not be any payment. He is thus in trouble. Please see to it that he is appointed with a *risāldār* or with any other good person. I will be happy if his work is done. You will get this letter through Monsieur Delssier (?). 22 Rabī' II.

Folio 426b. To Manik Ram.

Three letters of yours, dated 11, 13 and 15 Rabī' II, reached here one after another. Since Dr Thomas has left the camp and is to join me here, the supervision of all my works has now been assigned to Mr Chandelier (?). You should submit to him, and seek his advice in all big and small matters, including the *tankhwāhs* in the same way as you did with Dr Thomas. Intimate him also about the *tankhwāh* of Nauruz Ali Khan, Murtaza as well as about the dues of Nawab Muzaffar Jang.

It is strange that in your letter of 11 Rabī' II you do not mention about the *hundī* from the *jāidād* of Jaigopal. But now after the departure of Dr Thomas you write that you have received from this *jāidād* a *hundī* of Rs 5000 to be cashed in coins minted in Bareilly. I am unhappy. Collect Rs 17,000 pertaining to the *jāidād* of Jaigopal and Abdullah Khan and hand it over, together with whatever other collections you make, to Mr Chandelier (?). It is not proper for you to be careless in this matter. As for your request for a letter from me for Shah Sidq Ali Khan regarding the cancellation of your letter of receipt to him, it is not correct in my understanding. You gave this letter to him after receiving Rs 40,000 from him. This is what you had written in the account you sent to me earlier. I fail to understand why you gave him the receipt if you had not received the full amount. In any event, it is not appropriate that there be discrepancy in our statements. We have to bear with whatever has happened. Further, try to arrange Rs 5000 for the repayment of the loan I had taken for the *khil'at* and resolve the cases of the daughter of Abd-ul-Haq and Bībī Jawahar.

From your letter of 15 instant, I learnt that Mehr Chand, the painter, has started off from there along with a cartload of goods. In the meanwhile Mr Store came here and submitted to me the account which does not show the sums you say you have paid to him. Please keep the receipts of money you have given him safe with you. We will compare the two and clarify the matter when you are here. It is no use spending time with him to inspect this account. 24 Rabī' II, Wednesday.

Folio 427b. To Manik Ram.

It has been ten or twelve days since I received your letter. I am worried. There should be no negligence in dispatching the letters. I understand that these days you may have been overworked as Dr Thomas was to leave for Calcutta. In future, however, you must send me the news of the developments there regularly. Further, arrange soon the money to pay off the loan of Rs 5000 for the *khil'at*. Several letters have been sent to you regarding this. I have also written to Mr Chandelier about this. 29 Rabī' II.

Folio 428a. To Manik Ram.

Two letters of yours, of 21 Rabī' II and 25 Rabī' II, arrived here on 1 and 2 Jumāda I. Earlier, your letters reached here regularly, but these days there has been some delay. Do send the news without fail.

I do not understand why you have given different dates of Mehrchand's departure from there in your letters. Earlier you wrote he left on 15 Rabī' II, then in your letter of 21 Rabī' II you mention he left three days before this letter was dispatched, which would mean 19 Rabī' II, while according to your letter of 25 Rabī' II he set off on 16 Rabī' II. Write the exact date.

As for the printed clothes, I appreciate and agree with you that this is a good time to present these clothes to the Nawab and that I should send them to you quickly. I am not sure, but believe the time will soon turn in my favour. I will send them with the people accompanying Mehrchand on their return and as soon as the Mewatis come back from their homes. I have no objection to these clothes being offered to the Nawab, but I doubt he would extend favours to us to facilitate our work at present. Yet I am not perturbed. A time will come when I will carry my business in a much better way. You must, however, do your best to dispatch the money as I wrote to you.

As for your query regarding the person you should submit the details of my business there after Dr Thomas' departure for Calcutta, I have written to you earlier to keep in touch with Mr Chandelier (?). I have noted that you have handed over to him the stones for the rings with the names of the English *ṣāḥibs* engraved; that the *namdas* of Bahraich are reaching with Mehrchand; and that Muhammad Ilich Khan has been honoured with *māhi marātib* and the office of *mukhtār-i kār*. Good. This is how you should keep supplying the news. I have enclosed a congratulatory letter for him. Hand it over to him and get his reply. I have also received the copy of the bond of Abd-ul-Haq, the (Faizabad) girl's father that you have now sent. 4 Jumāda I, Wednesday, the day of celebration of Nauruz.

Folio 429a. To Mir Muhammad Husain Āta Khan.

I am delighted to know of your health and welfare from your letter of 10 Rabī' I which took two months to reach here. As I wrote to you earlier, hand over the letters addressed to me to Captain Store who will then dispatch them to me without delay. You have enquired about the case of the *jāgīr* of Khalilganj. It is strange that Najaf Khan has completely turned his face, and this despite our old friendship. The letters from the Emperor with strict instructions also proved futile. I could not but help giving up the matter, but I am not hopeless. Time is never the same; as it turns in my favour things will be resolved. It is because of our sincere friendship that you thought of me and felt concerned about my problem. I never consider you separate from me. Let us be relaxed; whatever God wills shall happen.

Keep in touch with Captain Store. He will lend you utmost help in carrying out your work. Our friendship demands that you keep in touch with me and thus be a source of delight for me. 4 Jumāda I, Saturday.

Folio 429b. To Mukhtar ul-Mulk Muhammad Ilich Khan.

As your old friend and well-wisher I am delighted to know of the honours that have been conferred upon you, together with the offices of *nāib-i kul* and *mukhtār-i kār.* The late Nawab Shuja-ud-Daula was kind to you and now with the grace of God you have got further promotion. Words fail to express even in part how happy I am. The sincerity of our relations is well established. May you scale the highest position and achieve success in all that you desire. I hope that the door of correspondence between us will ever remain open, to our full satisfaction and delight. 4 Jumāda I, Saturday.

Folio 430a. To Manik Ram.

The Bahraich *namdas* that you had handed over to Shaikh Muhammad, a *harkāra,* to be given to Mehrchand and then brought over here by the latter have eventually been brought to me by the *harkāra* himself on 5 Jumāda I. The *harkāra* could not contact Mehrchand before the latter's departure. Mehrchand in the meantime has reached Dankaur Ghat, 18 *kos* from here, and is expected to enter this city in a day or two. This is just to inform you. 6 Jumāda I, Monday.

Folio 430a. To Manik Ram.

Mehrchand gave me your letter of 15 Rabī' II here on 6 Jumāda I, together with two *chaupālas* full with boxes of velvet, books and paintings, a bundle (*gāṇth*) of clothes and locked boxes (*pitārīs*) with goods from Faizabad, thirteen shawls, two Hindustani guns, two *kajkāhs,* five pieces of musks, two *man* rice for [daily] use. I have sent the detailed receipts with a separate letter through the *dāk.* 8 Jumāda I, Wednesday, sent with the Mewātīs.

Folio 430a. To Manik Ram.

Two letters of yours, one of 15 Rabī' II together with the goods brought by Mehrchand, another of 30 Rabī' II, arrived here on 6 Jumāda I. Despite your praise, the guns are not good enough to be given in gift; the prices of the shawls also do not match the quality. I have therefore kept them safe as *amānat* with me.

I wrote to you earlier and am writing again that you must soon collect arrears of Rs 17,000–18,000 from Ghulam Murtaza Khan and send me Rs 8000, keeping the rest Rs 9000 with Mr Chandelier. I need money urgently for expenses here. From a letter of Mr Chandelier I gather that your presence here is necessary immediately. Hand over this work to him and come here soon. Follow his advice in all other works. 8 Jumāda I, Wednesday.

Folio 430b. To Mir Muhammad Husain Ata Khan.

You may have received my letter of 5 Jumāda I in reply to yours. On the advice of Mr Chandelier and John Bristow I have summoned Manik Ram here to give me the final accounts and have decided then to dismiss him from the job, and never permit him to interfere in my work in future. Since you have worked with Captain Store, if you like to work for me as a *vakīl*, contact Mr Chandelier and tell him that I have suggested you and that your services are acceptable to me. Mr Chandelier then will fix up your *jāgīr* and monthly emoluments and seek permission from the Nawab to send you here to me. In case you accept this, try to reach here before Manik Ram so that he submits the accounts in your presence, and then having clarified the matter with him you can return to the Nawab's camp to look after my business there and collect the *tankhwāh* sums. Please inform me if you want this job. 8 Jumāda I, Wednesday.

Folio 431a. To Niyaz Ali Khan.

I learnt from your letter of 4 Jumāda I about your entreaties to Miyan Qambar and Najaf Khan for the *jāgīr* of Khalilganj. Please do not raise this question with them any longer. At present there does not appear to be any headway; may be in future with the grace of God we may gain in a different measure. For the moment I am anxiously waiting to meet with you. Do inform me when you plan to return and keep in touch till then. 8 Jumāda I, Wednesday.

Folio 431b. Mir Muhammad Husain Ata Khan.

Your letter of 27 Rabī' II reached here on 8 Jumāda I. You write that you have written several letters to me and that you did not get any response from me. The fact is that earlier only one letter of yours reached here and to this my reply was prompt. As regards the difficulties and the non-receipt of your *tankhwāh,* I believe that such ups and downs are part of human fortune. I pray for patience and God's grace. Following the advice of Mr Chandelier and John Bristow, I have summoned Manik Ram here to present the accounts and decided then to remove him from the job. Contact Mr Chandelier and then come here soon if you are willing to serve me as my *vakīl.* Manik Ram will submit the accounts and clarify the matter in your presence and then in two to three months you can go back and attend to my work as these *ṣāḥibs* will advise. I have also written to you a detailed letter about this on the 8th of this month. As for the development about my *jāgīr,* Najaf Khan, despite our old friendship, left me in a lurch and refused to help in getting possession of it. Desperate and helpless, I then gave up the effort [to gain it]. But with the Emperor's kindness I hope that the result will ultimately be in my favour. 10 Jumāda I, Thursday.

Folio 432a. To Shah Sidq Ali.

I am happy to receive your letter. You write that you wish for a time when all friends get together to tell their stories [of their predicament]. Verily, such meeting will bring delight to hearts, but it is also true that it could be realized only at the right time. Till then, thus, we must keep in touch and record whatever conditions we are faced with. For the moment. I am enclosing for your perusal copies of Manik Ram's report and my reply to him regarding your case. 10 Jumāda I, Friday.

Folio 432b. To Manik Ram.

Your letter of 24 Rabī' II reached here on 10 Jumāda I. You write that Mr Chandelier is pressurizing you to come over here, while, in your own assessment, you think your presence over there is necessary for my works. If you could not finish the work as yet, how do you think you can complete it now in so brief a time. Mr Chandelier's instruction to leave that place is precisely because your stay there is no longer of any use to me. Collect whatever *tankhwāh* money you can manage in twelve days. Otherwise leave this in the care of Mr Chandelier and set off for this place. I am free these days to get the details of the full accounts from you. After this whatever is appropriate will be done. Do act upon Mr Chandelier's advice faithfully.

As for the receipt to Shah Sidq Ali Khan, since you had received Rs 40,000 of *nazrāna*, as you wrote to me, and had given the receipt accordingly, how could I have written to him to consider this as cancelled? This would have amounted to breach of word. The money due from him is from the *tankhwāh*, while the receipt given to him was in acknowledgement of the payment of the *nazrāna* sum. Now that you are coming here, it is no use giving you any instruction regarding matters over there. Further, I have noted that the Farrukhabad girl is reaching here in two months time.

Send me the papers (*yāddāsht*) pertaining to my *manṣab*. Take care that these are not soiled due to the humid climate of the rainy season. It is absolutely necessary that you bring all the papers safe with you so that there is no doubt and error left in the accounts.

Further, it is useless to bring goods like clothes, etc. from there. But since in your absence there would be no one trustworthy to take care of these, they should be taken to Faizabad to be kept safe with Gokulchand *mahājan*. Gokulchand has earlier desired to purchase them. He has deputed dependable persons to contact you and collect them from you. Please take a receipt before handing them over to his agent. 11 Jumāda I Saturday.

Folio 433b. To Manik Ram.

Your letter of 7 Jumāda I reached here together with a *hundī* of Rs 3000 in tested and marked silver coin (*ānt*). I am happy to know that you have finally collected the money from the *jāidād* of Rao Jaigopal. I have written to you repeatedly to send me the money collected in one installment. But you have sent me only Rs 3000, and Rs 1000 to Mr Lloyd from the Rs 7000 collected. Rupees 3000 are still due. Further, you had written that only Rs 1000 out of Rs 11,000 from [the *jāidād* of] Abdullah Khan could be collected, while I am told that the entire money has been received. In addition, Rs 1300 are due to the people there upto April which you had committed to pay from your own but now you want to make this payment from my *tankhwāh*. You must thus hand over a total of Rs 14,300 to Mr Chandelier immediately.

Since you are leaving for this place, I have written to Gokulchand of Faizabad to take care of my goods there. Pack them all, hand them over to him when he comes, take a receipt from him, and then start for this place soon with all papers you have with you. Ram Sundar Datt should accompany you.

You have told Mr Chandelier that a sum of Rs 5200 from the *jāidād* of both Rao Jaigopal and Abdullah Khan has been received in cash in Bareilly *sikka,* while in your letter to me you mention that the collections could be made only from the *jāidād* of Rao Jaigopal. I am sad to note this discrepancy; it is not good for you. Despite my repeated warnings you refuse to give up your old habits. You committed to Dr Thomas to clear the dues of the people from your own and now you want to do this from my *tankhwāh.* You ignore my repeated reminders that I should get the money in one installment here, even though you know it well how pressing it is to have money for my expenses here. I warn you that all this does not augur well for you. 13 Jumāda I, Monday.

Folio 434b. To Gokulchand, Mahājan of Faizabad.

I have heard praises of your honesty and integrity. I am delighted. Since Manik Ram, who has hitherto been incharge of my goods is now required here in Delhi, I wish to keep them in your care. Please depute a dependable agent of yours to contact Manik Ram, ask him to show him my letter to him, collect the goods and arrange their disposal. With the proceeds of the sale I would like to buy some goods from Tanda. Mr Lloyd is my spokesman in my *ḥavelī.* These transactions should be conducted with his consultation and consent. Since there are many things to do, it is necessary that you meet Mr Lloyd in person and tell him that I have asked you to do so. Do also whatever else he wants. It is advisable that you contact Manik Ram early since I want him here immediately. Send me directly a copy of the receipt and the list of goods. I assure you of suitable returns for your efforts and services in this matter. 11 Jumāda I, Saturday.

Folio 435b. To Manik Ram.

Since it is no use bringing the goods with you over here, and since there is no one reliable enough there to take care of these, I have asked Gokulchand *mahājan,* who wanted to buy them and is an honest man, to keep them. Hand over these goods to him and take a receipt. 11 Jumāda I, Saturday enclosed in the letter to Gokulchand.

Folio 435b. To Antony Bābā Jān.

Your letter brought relief to me. I am eagerly waiting for the day to meet you. I am going to call you soon here to live with me. Keep in touch and be happy. 13 Jumāda I.

Folio 435b. To Manik Ram.

I had earlier got your letter of 7 Jumāda I together with the *hundī* of Rs 3000 *ānt,* to be cashed at the shop of Thakur Das and Sri Kishan, *mahājans* of Dharmapura. The *hundī* has been cashed and the receipt has also been sent to you by the *dāk.* This is to inform you again. 16 Jumāda I, Thursday.

Folio 436a. To Mir Muhammad Husain Ata Khan.

Your letter of 13 Jumāda I was received on the 20th. Your write that my letter took two months to reach you. The fact is that I sent you my replies within a day or two of the arrival of your letters here. You would thus soon get two letters of mine that I wrote to you on the 8th and 10th of this month.

I am sorry to hear that in the meelee ensuing in the case of Captain Store, the bearer of your palanquin was killed by the ruffians. I am, however, relieved that you crossed the Yamuna safely, have reached Lucknow and are fine. Rest assured that with the grace of God things would soon turn in our favour. Due to the rains I am held up here for the moment, but am hoping that the difficulties will be resolved with help from someone in the east or west. In this respect I am least worried and have full faith in God. I implore you also to be completely relaxed.

As I wrote to you earlier, do whatever you feel like. You can contact Mr Chandelier, convey your consent to him so that he can do the needfull for your *tankhwāh,* or you can come here straight, get the details of the accounts and then return to the camp. Please intimate your intention. 21 Jumāda I, Tuesday.

Folio 436b. To Mir Muhammad Husain Ata Khan.

I agree with the suggestion that after Manik Ram's departure you leave an agent of yours with Mr Chandelier and come over here. Get leave from the Nawab within ten–twelve days of Manik Ram's departure and start for Delhi. Since you are familiar with most of the works here your presence will be helpful. Leave the things you have with you in the care of Gokulchand *mahājan.* I have instructed Manik Ram also to do the same. Take a receipt from him. He will arrange their disposal as Mr Llyod thinks appropriate. I am told that Gokulchand is a reliable person. I have thus written to Mr Chandelier that the task of the collection of the dues of Murtaza Khan should also be assigned to him so that Manik Ram may not feign any pretext to stay over there any longer.

You know it well what a mess Manik Ram and Jugal Kishor have made of my business. Since the day Jugal Kishor left for Calcutta I have not heard from him. But I am not going to seek any explanation from him. You are wise and intelligent. Think of an effective way of obtaining all the information from him. See to it nothing is kept secret from you. This is for your information so that you could do whatever is possible. Keep in touch. 23 Jumāda I.

Folio 437b. To Manik Ram.

You write that Mr Chandelier wants you there for another one month and that your presence for my business is required over there. I think the biggest work pertaining to my business is the clearance of the accounts and for this your arrival over here is most urgent. Whatever you have done for me there is open to all. Hand over to Mr Chandelier the papers, keep the goods in the care of Gokulchand, take a receipt from the latter and come over here soon. Contact Mr Chandelier and act according to his advice; do not wait for another order from me. 23 Jumāda I.

Folio 438a. To Mir Sulaiman Khan.

I am delighted at having received your letter. I have no words to express the eagerness with which I look forward to meeting you. It is correct that Rs 7000, the price of the elephants sold through Shaikh Badr-ud-Din, have been entered by Manik Ram, as he writes to you, in my account. Its payment to you is my responsibility. But Manik Ram owes huge sum to me and I have recalled him here for clearance of the accounts. You know how much strain I am under these days. Please do not mind if there is some delay in the payment.

I have noted the way Muhammad Ilich Khan behaved with you. But I am delighted that Mr John Bristow and Mr Chandelier were of so much help. I am sending them letters of my thanks. I hope you will keep me informed of your welfare. 27 Jumāda I.

Folio 438b. To Niyaz Ali Khan.

I am extremely delighted to receive your letter and to know that you left Deeg, arrived in Palwal yesterday from Barsana and are expected today to be in Faridabad. I am keenly waiting for having the pleasure of meeting with you. 27 Jumāda I.

Folio 438b. To Antony Bābā Jān.

I am happy to hear about your health. As regards the pomegranate that you have asked for in order to use it as a preventive [medicine] for smallpox, I will send them to you as soon as they are availablle. Here too pomegranate is not available these days. Always keep me informed of your welfare. 27 Jumāda I.

Folio 439a. To Mir Lutf Ali.

I am delighted to know about your welfare from your letter. Being a friend, I keep remembering you. May God be kind to us. Please keep writing to me about your welfare. 27 Jumāda I.

Folio 439a. To Mir Sulaiman Khan.

Thank you for your letter which I had received earlier and from which I knew that you have been appointed *faujdār* of Kora. I am delighted at this news and pray that you grow in strength and position day by day. In view of our friendship, I hope that the money from my *tankhwāh* in Kora would now be realized and that this will also facilitate payment due to you. The *parwāna* [from the Nawab] for my *tankhwāh* assigned to me in Kora was issued earlier to Mahbub Ali Khan, the former *faujdār*. I have written to Mr Chandelier to obtain a new *parwāna* and send it to you. Rs 7000 that I owe you will be paid from this *tankhwāh*. All this will cement our friendship and amity. 1 Jumāda II, 1190.

Folio 439b To Manik Ram.

Your letter of 4 Jumāda II reached here on the 10th of this month. This is exactly the same as the one you wrote 27 days back on 13 Jumāda II. I had expected that you would have followed my instruction and started from there. From your letter I discover you are still stuck there and are reluctant to leave. It is in your interest that you start as I wrote to you earlier and follow Mr Chandelier's advice. 10 Jumāda II, Saturday.

Folio 440a. Request for Jāgīr.

From your benign and graceful [Excellency], I hope the *pargana* to be assigned to me under you Excellency's special signature (*dastkhat-*

i khaṣṣ) so that I could meet my personal expenses and prepare the cannon and guns, etc. 17 Jumāda II, 18th Regnal year, 1190. Request granted.

Folio 440a. Iqrārnāma [Bond of Agreement] submitted to the Mutaṣaddīs of the Royal daftar under the seal of the Emperor.

As I have been appointed by the Emperor *faujdār* of *pargana* khair, *sarkār* Kol wef. *Kharīf* of 1184 *faṣlī*, I promise that keeping in touch with the office of the royal *peshkār*, I will do the needful to administer the said *maḥāl*, assess the revenue in time in a manner which does not imply excess to the poor *ri'āyā* and leniency in the *ta'alluqa* to the defiants and thus collect each and every penny from them. Having with me Rs 55,000 against my pay claim, the rest I will send to His Excellency, or else if ordered this amount will be spent on manufacturing the flint guns to be presented to His Excellency. These words are given by me as a bond of agreement to serve as a *sanad*. 9 Jumāda II, 1184 *faṣlī* 1190 AH, 18th Regnal year.

Folio 440b. To Rao Prithi Singh

I have been assigned in *jāgīr* by His Excellency *tappa* Khair in addition to the other *maḥāls*. I have heard about your integrity and competence from Rai Kanhajasmal and wish that you come over here to meet me. I propose that the entire work be entrusted to you and that it be carried out the way it suits you. Your arrival here is urgent. 12 Jumāda II, 1190.

Folio 440a. To Manik Ram.

Your letter of 6 Jumāda II together with a *hundī* of Rs 2000 *ānt* reached me on the 14 instant. Since this *hundī*, as it is written, could be cashed only after 21 days, I will send you the receipt later. You write that you have sent to Mr Chandelier the details of the income and expenditure pertaining to the *tankhwāh* of Ghulam Murtaza Khan from the *jāidād* of Rao Jaigopal and Abdullah Khan and that they may have reached me. The fact of the matter is that I have not yet received them. Send them soon together with another *hundī* for expenses over here. As regards your [journey] to come here, your excuse of the rains is untenable. 16 Jumāda II, Friday.

Folio 441a. Copy of iqrārnāma.

Since the *faujdārī* of *tappa* Khair has been given to me wef. 1184 *faṣlī* and since the hostages of the zamindars of the villages of this *tappa* are with the erstwhile *'āmil,* Niyaz Khan, it is therefore directed that whatever dues of the year 1183 *faṣlī* they agree [to pay] in the face of the *chaudharīs,* the *qānūngos,* the zamindars and the *ri'āyā* of the said *maḥāl,* it should be collected from them. And then they should be set free and the dues collected be deposited with the imperial establishment. 25 Jumāda II.

Folio 441a. Copy of iqrārnāma.

Four per cent as *dastūr-i dīwānī* and two per cent as *nazrāna* would be deducted from the collections (*taḥṣīl*) of the *tappa* Khair wef. the beginning of *Kharīf* of 1184 *faṣlī.* 25Jumāda II.

Folio 441a. Copy of iqrārnāma.

One and a half per cent would be deducted for the *mutaṣaddīs* of *Khāliṣa* of *tappa* Khair wef. the beginning of *Kharīf* of 1184 *faṣlī.*

Folio 441a. Copy of the royal sanad.

According to an imperial order (*ḥasb-ul-ḥukm*), Imtiyaz-ud-Daula, Iftikhar-ul-Mulk Polier Bahadur Arsalān Jang has been appointed *amīn-o-faujdār* of *tappa* Khair, *sarkār* Kol, minus the *sāir* of this district (*muẓāf*) of *ṣūba* Akbarabad wef. the beginning of *Kharīf,* 1184 *faṣlī.* He should set up an appropriate administration of this *maḥāl* by chastizing the mischief-mongers and the recalcitrants, protecting the revenue payers and making adequate efforts to extend cultivation and increase habitation. The revenues should be collected in time and no penny should be spent without a proper *sanad.* May the *chaudharīs,* the *qānūngos,* the *muqaddams* and the peasants there recognize him as a regular *amīn-o-faujdār* and that all that pertains to this office is under his jurisdiction. 12 Jumāda II, 18th Regnal year.

Folio 442a. Copy of the muchalka [bond] of Harsukh Rai, 'āmil.

As I am appointed by Nawab Imtiaz-ud-Daula, Iftikhar-ul-Mulk Polier Bahadur Arsalan Jang his deputy in *pargana* Khair, in *sarkār* Kol wef. *Kharīf,* 1184 *faṣlī,* I pledge that I will manage the assessment and collection [of the revenues] in time and send to the *ḥuẓūr* reguarly whatever would be collected. No penny [from the collections] would be spent without a proper *sanad.* These words I give as a *muchalka* to serve as a proof (*sanad*) when required. 21 Jumāda II, 18th Regnal year.

Folio 442a. Copy of Ẓāminī [guarantee] of Harsukh Rai.

As Harsukh Rai has been appointed by His Highness the Nawab Ṣāḥib [Polier]his *nāib* in *pargana* Kher, *sarkār* Kol, wef. *Kharīf* 1184 *faṣlī*, I, Bhakhtmal Khatri, take this pledge that he leaves for no other place without permission and that if he does so I will present him [before you] and that in the case of my inability to do so I will be responsible (*'uhda*) for his work. These words are given as *ẓāminī* to serve as a *sanad* when needed. 21 Jumāda II, 18th Regnal year.

Folio 442a. Copy of Polier's sanad for Harsukh Rai, 'āmil of Khair

Be it known to the *chaudharīs,* the *qānūngos,* the *muqaddams,* the *ri'āya* and the *muẓāri's* of *pargana* Khair, *sarkār* kol *ṣūba* Akbarabad that the said *maḥāl* has been assigned by His Excellency in my *jāgīr* wef. *Kharīf* of 1184 *faṣlī*. I have thereby sent there Harsukh Rai as *amīn-o-faujdār*. May you treat him as a regular *'āmil* responsible for the revenues, the *ḥuqūq-i-dīwānī* and other cases (*abwāb*). His evaluations [lit. praise and complaint] in these matters will be of consequence. His duty is to keep the *ri'āyā* happy and satisfied with his behaviour, endeavour for ways to increase the revenues and habilitate the *ri'āyā*, collect the revenues in time and send them to the royal establishment regularly. He should not spend a single penny without a proper *sanad*. 20 Jumāda II, 18th Regnal year.

Folio 442b. Copy of wājib-ul-'arẓ of the vakīl of Polier.

The office of the *amīn-o-faujdār* of *pargana* Khair, *sarkār* Kol has been assigned by His Excelency to my client. I thereby request that the imperial signature is procured for the following:

Whatever is presented to ensure the welfare of the state will be conceded and the request of this slave be accepted only after investigation.

The officials and the workers: Rs 60 monthly each for measurement, Rs 22 monthly each for *peshkār*. Both in ten monthly scale as per the rule.

Exemption from *bhent* for both the persons for measurement and the *peshkār*.

Sihbandī, one hundred *sawār* and *piyāda* with Rs 4 monthly each as per the rule.

In'ām for *nānkār* of the *chaudharīs* and*qānūngos*, and *mugddamī* for the muqaddams as per the custom. The *peshkār* of the *pargana* is appointed by the Emperor himself. Explanation of the the details of the paper to the office of *Khāliṣa* is then his responsibility. This is not my people's concern.

Expenses for paper, ink, oil for lamp, carpet for *kachahrī*, sweetmeats for [distribution] on auspicious occasion, repair of the fortress.

Expenses for the *hundīs* to be dispatched to the Royal Court as per the current rate.

Expenses for shawls and turbans to be gifted to the zamindars of the villages whatever are necessary to ensure cultivation and habilitation.

Expenses for both the *'Īds, khil'ats* for the *qāẓī*

Folio 443a. Wājib-ul-'Arz from Harsukh Rai, 'āmil of tappa khair. This slave Harsukh Rai, who has been appointed *nāib* in *pargana* Khair, hopes that the imperial signature is procured for the following at the time of clarification of the accounts.

Whatever is presented here for the welfare of the state be conceded and the request of this slave be accepted only after investigation:

Expenses for sweetmeats to be distributed at arrival in the *pargana* and on Dussehra and Holi to the zamindars.

Emoluments for the *ẓāt*, etc.: Rs 60 monthly in ten monthly scale as per the rule. Rs 9 for the clerk as per the rule. Rs 9 for the *vakīl* as per the rule. Payment to the *sarrishtadār* and *fūtadār* would be from the Royal court.

Sihbandī: Requested for 250 troopers, of them Rs 4 for 150 persons as per the rule and Rs 3 for the remaining 100 troopers.

Replies to enquiry [from the *Khāliṣa*, etc] are the concern of the *peshkārs* appointed [directly] by the court.

Nānkār for the *chaudharī* and the *qānūngo*, an age-old custom.

Expenses for both the *'Īds, khil'ats* for the *qāẓī*.

Necessary people to work in the *kachahrī*.

Repairs of fortress and *kachahrī*, carpet for the *kachahrī*, oil for lamp, food for the visitors, sweetmeats for Thursday and oil for lamp for the shrine.

Turbans for the zamindars.

50 per cent exemption in *bhent* of both the seasons.

Whatever the order is for the perquisites for *'āmil.*

Expenses for gunpowder and mobilization of the troopers in the event of disturbance for chastizement of the recalcitrant *zamindars.*

Expenses for two *harkāras* to take to and bring the letters from the court.

Whatever the order regarding the *a'immadārs,* daily cash allowance holders and *milkiyān* [proprietors of land].

Folio 444b. From Harsukh Rai, 'āmil.

Before taking over the *pargana,* the money which is taken on loan from the *sāhūkār* for arranging food for the *sihbandī* will be paid back later from what would be received from the *fūtadār* (of *pargana*). But, God forbid, in another eventuality, the payment of this sum to the *sāhūkar* will be the *sarkār's* [Mr Polier's] responsibility.

Folio 444b. To Manik Ram.

I hear that you have finally decided to leave for this place. I am happy. Rest assured that I will let you go back as soon as the accounts are clarified. Please come soon with Ram Sundar Datt and the necessary papers. 27 Jumāda II, Wednesday.

Folio 444b. To Manik Ram.

Your letter of 20 Jumāda II reached here on the 27th. I am happy to know that your journey is commencing in ten–twelve days; come soon with Ram Sundar Datt and all the necessary papers. Once we are free from work you can return.

As for your request for a letter in the name of Mr Chandelier regarding your *jāgīr* and monthly emoluments, I have already sent him a letter to this effect. He has written back that since you are ready to come here, he has assured you about your *jagir,* etc. Please bring five or six *thāns* of *gulbadan* with you. you must not be worried about any work of yours. The more sincerely and faithfully you do my job, the better it is for you. 27 Jumāda II, Wednesday. 18th Regnal year 1190 A.H/1184 *faṣlī.*

Folio 445a. To Harsukh Rai, 'āmil of Khair.

I have received two letters of yours, one dispatched from Faridabad, another from Jhajjar. As regards your request for royal *shuqqas* to Khwaja Niyaz (erstwhile *amīn-o-faujdār* of the *pargana*), money for expenses and military troopers, it has been four days since a *shuqqa* and a *parwāna* of Nawab Majd-ud-Daula for the purpose have been sent to you through Fath Singh *jamā'adār* and two Tilangī watchmen. They must have reached you by now. Considering the long distance and time, the troopers have not been arranged from here. Instead, you will receive a *hundī* of Rs 200 in Delhi currency (*chalanī*) to be cashed at the shop of Kewal Kishan and Jagan Nath, the *sāhūkārs* of Khurja. Deposit the cash with the *taḥwīldār* and then arrange the troopers from amongst the people there in the neighbourhood as you feel appropriate. Meet Rao Prithi Singh and with his cooperation see to it that all the works are done satisfactorily in such a manner that I have no worries at all. Keep me informed of your requirement so that I can provide these from here. In any case, be actively busy with my works there without any apprehension. 29 Jumāda II, 18th Regnal year 1190 AH/1184 *faṣlī*.

Glossary

Ābdārkhāna: A repository of drinking water.

A'imma/A'ima: Land granted by the Mughal government, either revenue-free or subject to a minimal revenue, to learned and religious persons.

'Amal: Being in charge or in possession of, jurisdiction.

Amānat: Deposit; charge; anything held in trust; money deposited in court; among the Marathas profit derived from deposits and temporary sequestration of estates.

'Amārī: An elephant litter with a canopy.

'Āmil: An officer of government in the finance department, especially a collector of revenue on behalf of the government or of the farmer of revenue, also himself a farmer of, or contractor for, the revenue under the Mughal/Nawābī system and invested with the supreme authority, both civil and military, in the districts which he farmed.

Amīn-o-Faujdār: One who combined policing and executive power with the responsibility of supervising the measurement of land and assessment of revenues of a *maḥāl.*

Ānṭ: Scratched and marked coin.

'Arẓī, 'Arīẓa, 'Arẓdāsht: A petition; an address; a memorial; a respectful statement or representation, whether oral or written.

Aṣīl: A maidservant born free as opposed to a purchased female slave.

Āya: Foster mother.

Bādla: Silver white thread.

Bahangī: A pole with slings at either end supporting portable boxes or baskets for baggage, carried over one's shoulder.

Baqqāl: A greengrocer; vendor.

Bāradarī: A summer house.

Barāwurd: An estimate; a calculation; a monthly statement sent to the government of the revenue and village establishments of the sum payable to each person, and the increase or decrease as compared with preceding months; a statement of district disbursement.

Barqandāz: A matchlockman; guard; constable.

Basta: A parcel; a bundle; a bale; a cloth in which papers or other articles are wrapped up.

Baṭṭa: Discount on uncurrent or short weight rupees. In revenue matters it applies to the amount added to or deducted from any payment according to the currency in which it is paid as compared with a fixed standard coin.

Bēldār: A digger; a delver; one who works with a *bēl*, a pick-axe or a spade.
Bīchūba: A small tent without poles.
Bījak: A note or memorandum attached to any article of trade or transport, as a ticket, a label, a list, or an invoice.

Chakla: A large administrative division of a country, comprising a number of *parganas*. First introduced as a recognized local division in the reign of Shahjahan (1627–56).
Chalanī: Current; circulating (as a coin).
Chaudharī: The headman of a profession or trade in town; the headman of a village; a holder of landed property classed with the zamindar and *ta'alluqadār.*
Chaukī: A wooden cot; also stationary guards for protection of roads.
Chēla: A servant; a slave; a pupil; a disciple, especially one brought up by a religious mendicant to become a member of his order.
Chhukṛa: A cart.
Chhaṭka: Floral design; print.
Chūbdār: A staff or a mace bearer; servant whose work is to announce the arrival of company.
Chuktī: Settlement of a debt or bargain.
Chuktī ḍāk: Backlog of mail.

Ḍāk: Mail; a post of an establishment for the conveyance of letters and of travellers; relays of men or cattle along the road for these purposes.
Dārogha: The chief officer in various departments under the Mughal/ Nawābī government; a superintendent; a manager. In later times he is especially the head of a police, customs or excise station.
Dastak: A passport; a permit.
Dāya: A midwife; a governess.
Ḍeoṛdhī: A small mansion; an establishment of a local magnate.
Ḍēra: A tent; any temporary dwelling; or a peasant's hut.

Fard-i-Sawāl: A petition; an application. The recommendatory report of a revenue officer in former times in favour of the grant of a *zamīndārī sanad* to the persons named in the application and specifying the districts to be granted.
Faujdār: An officer of the Mughal government who was invested with the charge of the police and jurisdiction in routine executive and criminal matters; a criminal judge; a magistrate; the chief of a body of troops.
Firangī: A European Christian.

Gharī: A portion of time; the equivalent of about 24 minutes. 7½*gharis* make a *pās/pahar.*
Girah: A measure of length; one-fourteenth or one-sixteenth of a *gaz* (yard).

Gorā: Fair; white; a European.
Goṭā: A gold lace.
Gulābpāsh: A bottle for sprinkling rose water.
Gumāshta: An agent; a steward; a confidential factor; a representative; an officer employed by zamindars to collect their rents, by bankers to receive money, etc., by merchants to carry on their affairs in places other than where they reside and live.

Ḥakkāk: Cutter; polisher of precious stones.
Harkāra: Running footman; a messenger.
Ḥauda, Ḥauẓa: An elephant litter without a canopy.
Ḥavaldār: A steward to protect a village for the grain before it was stored.
Ḥavelī: Mansion; house.
Hunḍī: A bill of exchange.
Ḥuqqa: Hubble-bubble; hookah.

'Ināyat-nāma: A letter of kindness; a letter of recommendation; a written order or patent from a superior; metaphorically, also a routine letter from a person of high rank.
Iqrārnāma: A deed of assessment or acknowledgement in general.

Jāgīr: A tenure common under the Mughal/Nawābī regime in which the public revenues of a given tract of land were made over to a servant of the state, together with the powers requisite to enable him to collect and appropriate such revenue and administer the general government of the district. The assignment was either conditional or unconditional.
Jāidād: A land revenue assignment for the maintenance of troops or any other establishment.
Jama': Amount; aggregate; total in general, applied especially to the debit or receipt side of an account and to the rental of an estate; also to the total amount of rent or revenue payable by a cultivator or a zamīndār including all cesses, as well as land tax. It was especially applied to the revenue assessed upon the land alone: its special application was commonly defined by the term with which it was compounded.
Jamā'dār: Petty commander of troops; the head of any body, as *harkāras*, for instance.

Kalābatūn: A Silver thread.
Karānī: A clerk; a manager; a caretaker.
Kārchūbī: Embroidery.
K͟halāṣī: A sailor; a tent pitcher; a matross; a labourer of a superior order, employed chiefly in ships or in the army.
K͟hānsāmān: A domestic steward.

Khil'at: A dress of honour; any article of costume presented by the ruling or superior authority to an inferior as a mark of distinction. A complete *khil'at* may include arms or a horse or an elephant.
Khokha: A bill of exchange that has been paid and remains in the hands of the payers as a voucher.
Khwājasarā: A eunuch, generally the one attached to the female apartments.
Kimkhāb: Silk interwoven with gold or silver thread; brocade.
Kinārī: Silver lace.
Kos: Road measure of about two miles; also brass drum, kettle-drum.
Koṭhī: A spacious house, such as those inhabited by Europeans; a granary; a warehouse or store room; a mercantile or banking house or firm; a government factory or establishment, as the office of the local opium agent, as well as the chief or sadar factory.
Kotwāl: Urban executive officer; a town police superintendent in the Company territory.
Kumaindān: A Hindustani version of the word 'commandant', incharge of a platoon.
Kurtī: Shirt of a Company trooper.

Madira: Concentrated wine from Madira in Portugal.
Mahājan: Literally, 'great man'; a substantial merchant; in Gujarat also used for the organizing body of merchants in town.
Maḥāl: A revenue district.
Māhāna: Monthly; monthly wages.
Maḥṣūl: The produce of land; the harvest; the crop.
Man: A measure of weight of general use in India, but varying in value in different places.
Manṣab: Literally, office; dignity; a military title and rank conferred by the Mughals.
Mash'alchī: A torch or lamp bearer; a domestic servant also employed under the superior table servants to clean the plates, dishes etc.
Masnad: Throne; seat.
Mihrbānī-nāma: Metaphorically, a deed of kindness; a routine letter from a high official.
Mināsāz: A gem setter.
Morcha: Front.
Morchāl: An entrenchment for besieging a fortified place; a tower.
Muchalka: A written obligation or agreement; a bond; a deed; it is commonly applied to a counterpart covenant on the part of the properietors or cultivators of land, agreeing to the rates of assessment imposed by the government, also to an engagement under a penalty to observe the conditions of any deed or grant.
Munshī: A writer; a secretary; a term applied by Europeans usually to teachers or interpreters of Persian and Hindustani.

Muqaddam: A village headman.
Musawwada: A draft; sketch of a painting.
Mutaṣaddī: A writer, a clerk.

Najīb-o-Ashraf: Nobly born.
Nānkār: A term applied to the assignment of a portion of the land of revenue of *zamīndārī*, made to the zamīndār as an allowance for his subsistence, in lieu of his services for the maintenance of the land and for the collection of the revenues. If removed from the management of the *zamīndārī* the *nānkār* was occasionally withdrawn, in contradiction to the *mālikāna* which was always granted. In the eighteenth century the term was also applied to assignments of land or revenue made as subsistence money to fiscal and village offers.
Naqqāsh: A painter; an artist; embroiderer; gilder (of books).
Narga: Small square tent.
Nawāzish-nāma: Complimentary letters; letter of kindness; metaphorically, a routine letter from a high official.
Nazrāna: A gift; a present especially from an inferior to a superior; but the term was more particularly applied to sums received as gratuities, although in fact exacted by the state on various occasions, as fee or fines upon an assignment of revenue to an individual or an appointment or succession to office, or to a *jāgīr* or other possessions, although hereditary.
Nazr-o-Niyāz: A present; an offering, especially one from an inferior to a superior; to a holy man; or to a prince; a present in general; a fine or fee paid to the state, or to its representative on succeeding to office or property.
Niwāṛ: A broad border round a tent; also a piece sewed above a seam to strengthen it.

Pahar: The fourth part (about three hours) of a natural day or night.
Pālkī: Palanquin.
Palṭan: Platoon.
Pāndān: Betel box.
Parwāna, Parwāngī: An order; a written precept or command; a letter from a man in power to a dependant; a custom house permit or pass; an order for the possession of an estate or an assignment of revenue; a warrant; a licence; a writ; a paper of permission from a *zamīndār* to a cultivator to take up lands, leaving rent to be subsequently settled.
Pās: The fourth part of a natural day or night.
Paṭāpaṭī: Multi-coloured stripes.
Pēshkash: Tax; tribute; a fine or present to the ruling power on receiving an appointment or assignment of revenue, or on a renewal of a grant or the like.

Peshwāz: A female garment with an open front; a knee-length gown.
Pēṭh: A market; a bazaar; part of a town where shops are assembled; a trading or manufacturing town; a town attached to but distinct from a fort; the suburb or *pettah*; a banker's letter of advice announcing his having drawn a bill or hundi; a duplicate hundi or one given in lieu of another.
Piṭāra: A large basket.
Piyāda: Foot soldier.
Poṭlī: A small bundle.

Qanāt: Screen; walls of a tent.
Qānūngo: A middle-level local revenue official.
Qaul-nāma: A deed of lease; an agreement.
Qāẓī: A local judicial official.

Rāhdārī: Transit duty; a toll on goods in movement and travellers; road tax.
Rētī: Sandy ground on the bank of a river.
Ri'āyā: Plural of *raiyat,* peasant.
Rikābī (rupia): An inferior kind of rupee current in Lucknow, but not the regular coinage.
Risāldār: An officer commanding a troop of irregular horse.

Ṣaḥḥāf: A book-seller; book-binder; a librarian.
Ṣāḥib: A master; a lord; a companion; in Hindustani, the usual designation and address of a respectable European, like Mister, Sir, etc.
Sāhūkār: A banker; a dealer in money and exchanges; a merchant in general.
Sā'ir: Cess, toll.
Sālyāna: Yearly, yearly wages.
Ṣandūq: Box.
Sarā'i: A resting house; inns.
Sardār: A chief; a headman; a commander; the head of a set of palanquin bearers.
Sarkār: A large administrative division of a province; the establishment of the Nawab or a noble.
Sarpīch: An ornament of gold, silver or jewels, generally placed in front of the turban.
Saudāgar: Merchant; trader.
Sawārī: The art of horse-riding; riding.
Sazāwal: An officer appointed for revenue collection in place of a landholder or revenue farmer; a land steward; a monthly revenue collector.

Shatranjī: Carpet; floor spread.
Shuqqa: A royal order; a letter.
Ṣūbadār: The governor of a province; a viceroy under the Mughal government; an Indian officer in the Company's army holding a rank equivalent to that of captain under the European officers.

Ta'ahhud: Farming; to take guarantee; a pledge to act according to stipulated terms; an agreement.
Takhta: A plank; a platform.
Tamāsha: Spectacle; performance; looking at anything tragic or comic; an entertainment show.
Tankhwāh: Emoluments; salary; payment in cash or in land revenue; also paper relating to revenues to be obtained from the district assigned in revenue payment.
Tappū: A kind of coarse woollen cloth.
Tarka: Strings of a tent.
Ṭawāf: Going round; circumambulating (especially Ka'aba or the tomb of a pious person).
Tawāzu': Literally humility; submission; pretended kindness; empty compliment. Metaphorically payment of fee to a teacher or physician.
Thailī: A bag.
Thān: A roll of cloth/thread of specific length.
Thāna: A village/*pargana* police post.
Thānadār: In-charge of a *thāna.*
Topkhāna: An arsenal; an artillery park; a foundry for cannon; a place where military stores are kept.

Vakīl: Agent; representative or ambassador.

Wajh: Wages; hire; salary.
Warqa-i-taṣwīr: A painted leaf; final painting.
Wilāyat: A territory; an inhabited country. Used in the eighteenth century generally for Persia, Central Asia or any other European country, especially England and France.

Yasāwal: An officer of parade; one carrying gold or silver staff; a state messenger.

Ẓāmin: One who takes guarantee to make payment on behalf of a revenue farmer.
Ẓāminī: The act or the amount of guarantee.

Bibliography

Primary and Secondary works cited

Abdullah, S., *Fārsī Adab mein Hindūon kā Ḥiṣṣa,* Lahore, 1967.

———, *Mabāḥiṣ,* Delhi, 1968.

———, *Fārsī Zubān-o-Adab,* Lahore, 1977.

Abu'l Fatḥ Gīlānī, *Ruq'āt-i-Abu'l Fatḥ Gīlānī,* ed. by M. Bashir Husain, Lahore,1968.

Abu'l Fazl, *Ā'īn-i-Akbarī,* I, English tr. H. Blockman, repr: Delhi, 1989.

Alam, M., 'The Pursuit of Persian in Mughal Politics', *Modern Asian Studies,* vol. 32, No. 2, 1998.

———, Francoise N. Delvoye and M. Goborieau eds. 'Akhlāqī Norms in the Making of Mughal Governance', *The Making of Indo-Persian Culture: Indian and French Studies,* Delhi, 2000.

Alavi, S., *The Sepoys and the Company: Tradition and Transition in Northern India, 1770–1830,* Delhi, 1995.

Anderson Papers, Ad. Ms. 45432, Ad. Ms. 16265, British Library (BL), London.

Archer, M., *India and British Portraiture, 1770–1825,* London, 1979.

———, and T. Falk, *India Revealed. The Art and Adventures of James and William Fraser 1801–35,* London, 1989.

———, *Indian Miniatures in the India Office Liabrary,* 1981.

Asiatic Society of Bengal, Centenary Review (1784–1883) Calcutta 1885.

Bahar, Mohammad Taqi, *Sabk Shanāsī or Tārīkh-i-Taṭawwur-i Naṣr-i-Fārsī,* Tehran, 1319 *Shamsi.*

Barbé, E., *Le Nabab René Madec,* Paris, 1894.

Bayly, C.A. *Empire and Information. Intelligence Gathering and Social Communication in India 1780–1870,* Cambridge, 1996.

———, 'The First Age of Global Imperialism 1760–1830', *Journal of Imperial and Commonwealth History,* vol. 26, No. 2, May 1998.

———, *Imperial Meridian. The British Empire and the World, 1780–1830,* London, 1989.

———, *Indian Society and the Making of The British Empire,* Cambridge, 1988.

Bengal Letters Received, E/4/41, BL, London.

Bengal Secret Consultations, National Archives of India, Delhi.

Bhabha, Homi, K., *The Location of Culture,* London, 1994.

Bhagwān, Dās, *'Azīz ul-Qulūb,* Aligarh Ms. Abd-us-Salam Collection, 188/ 54F, Maulana Azad Library (MAL), Aligarh Muslim University (AMU), Aligarh.

Bhūpat Rāi, *Inshā-i-Roshan Kalām,* Aligarh Ms. Abd-us-Salam Collection, 109/339, MAL, AMU, Aligarh; also Nizami Press, Kanpur, U.d.

Blochet, Edgar, *Catalogue des Manuscrits Persans de la Bibliothèque Nationale,* Tome 1, Paris, 1905.

Brockington, J.L. 'Warren Hastings and Orientalism', in G. Cornall and C. Nicholson, eds *The Impeachment of Warren Hastings: Papers from a Bicentenary Commemoration,* London, 1989.

Buckland, C.E., *Dictionary of National Biography,* London, 1906.

Cannon, G., 'Oriental Jones: Scholarship, Literature, Multiculturalism and Humankind', in *Bulletin of the Deccan College,* vol. 54–5, 1994–5.

________, *Oriental Jones,* Bombay, 1964.

Cohn, B.S., 'Representing Authority in Victorian India', in B. Cohn ed., *An Anthropologist among the Historians and Other Essays,* Delhi, 1997.

________, *Colonialism and Its Forms of Knowledge. The British in India,* Delhi, 1997.

Colas, G. et F., Richards. 'Les Fonds Polier a la Bibliotheque Nationale', *Bulletin de l'Ecole Francaise d'Extreme-Orient LXXIII,* 1984.

Colley, L., *Britons Forging the Nation 1707–1837,* Yale, 1992.

Correspondence of Elijah Impey, Governor-General 1780–82, Ad. Ms. 16262, BL, London.

Deleury, Guy, 'L' ingenieur Polier', *Revue des Deux Mondes,* Oct. et. Nov. 1986.

Deloche, J. ed., *Voyage en Inde du Comte de Modave, 1773–6: Nouveaux mémoires sur l'etat actuel du Bengale et de l'Indoustan,* Paris, 1971.

________, ed. *Les aventures de Jean-Baptiste Chevalier dans l'Inde Orientale (1752–1765): Mémoire historique et Journal de Voyage à Asem,* Paris: EFEO, 1984.

________ and James Walker, Wendel's *Mémoirs on the Origin, Growth and Present State of Jat Power in Hindustan (1768),* Pondicherry: Institut Français de Pondichéry, 1991.

Dumezil, Georges, 'Preface', *Le Mahabharat et le Bhagavad Gita,* Paris, 1986.

Edney, Matthew H., *Mapping an Empire: The Geographical Construction of British India 1765–1843,* Chicago, 1997.

Enderlein, V. and R. Hickmann, *Indische Albumlaiie Miniaturen und Kalligraphien aus der Zeit der Mughul-Kaiser,* Gustav Kiepenheuer Verlog Leipzing and Weimar, 1979.

Ethé, Hermann, *Catalogue of Persian Manuscripts in the Library of the India Official Library*, Oxford, 1903.

Faiẓī Fayyāẓī, Abu'l Faiẓ, *Inshā-i-Faiẓī*, ed. by A.D. Arshad, Lahore, 1973.

Firminger, W.K., ed., *Fifth Report. Analysis of the Finances of Bengal*, Calcutta, 1917.

Francklin, W., *The History of the Reign of Shah Alam, the Present Emperor of Hindustan*, London, 1798.

Geisendorf Paul. F., ed., *Livre des Habitants de Genève (1549–60)*, Geneva: Droz, 1957.

Goetz, H., *The Crisis of Indian Civilization in the Eighteenth and Early Nineteenth Century*, Calcutta, 1938.

Gole, S. *Maps of Mughal India: Drawn by Col. Jean Baptiste Joseph Gentil Agent for the French Government to the Court of Shuja-ud-daulah at Faizabad, 1770*, Delhi, 1988.

Graffe, V. ed., *Lucknow: Memories of a City*, Delhi, 1997.

Halbfass, W., *India and Europe. An Essay in Understanding*, New York, 1988.

Hasan, S. Nurul, 'Du Jardin Papers: a Valuable Source for the Economic History of North India', *Indian Historical Review*, vol. 5, nos. 1–2.

Hastings Papers, Ad. Ms. 29138; 29135; 29139; 29140; 39903; 5346; 19233; 39891; 29170; 29177; 29167; 29163; 29129; 29151; 29143; 29159; 29233, BL, London.

Hawley, Daniel S., 'L 'Inde de Voltaire' in H.T. Mason, ed., *Studies on Voltair and the 18th Century*, Oxford: Taylor Institution, 1974, pp. 139–78.

Hodson, V.C.P., *List of Officers of the Bengal Army 1758–1834*, London, 1946.

Home Miscellaneous Series/90,/221,/191, BL, London.

India Office (IO) Maps manuscript (5). Journal contains a long description of his survey and of the people with sketches of Cheduba (85f/9), BL, London.

Irschick, E., *Dialogue and History*, Delhi, 1995.

Islam, R., *A Calendar of Documents on Indo-Persian Relations*, Karachi, 1979.

Jones, R.L., *A Fatal Friendship. The Nawabs, the British and the City of Lucknow*, Delhi, 1985.

———, *A Very Ingenious Man: Claude Martin in Early Colonial India*, Delhi, 1991.

———, 'City of Dreams', V. Graffe, ed., *Lucknow. Memories of a City*, Delhi, 1997.

Kāmwar Khan, Muḥammad Hādī, *Tazkirat al-Salāṭīn Chaghtā*, ed. by M. Alam, Bombay, 1980.

Khair-ud-Dīn Muḥammad Khān, *Tuhfa-i-Tāza or Balwantnāma*, MS. No. 607, Khuda Bakhsh Oriental Public Liabrary, Patna, English tr. F. Curwen, Allahbad, 1875.

Kieffer, Jean-Luc., *Anquetil Duperron: L'Inde en France au XVIII*, Siecle, Paris: Belles Letters, 1983.

Kopf, David., *British Orientalism and the Bengal Renaissance. The Dynamics of Indian Modernisation 1773–1835*, Berkeley, 1969.

Letters, Autographs, Manuscripts, Documents, Historiques etc. Catalogue General, Bibliotheque Cantonale of Lausanne.

'Liste des réfugiés français à Lausanne', in *Bulletin de la Société de l'Histoire du Protestantisme*, vol. 21, 1872.

Mādho Rām, *Inshā-i-Mādho Rām*, ed. by Maulawi Qudrat Ahmad, Lucknow, 1844.

Margoliouth, D.S., *Catalogue of the Oriental MS in the Library of Kings College Cambridge*, Pote (Kings) Oriental MSS; and Catalogue of the Oriental Manuscripts in the Library of Eton College, Oxford, 1904.

Marshall, P.J., *The British Discovery of Hinduism in the Eighteenth Century*, Cambridge, 1970.

———, 'Warren Hastings as Scholar and Patron', in *Statesmen, Scholars and Merchants. Essays in Eighteenth Century History Presented to Lucy Sutherland*, ed. by A. Whiteman, J. Bromley and P.G.M. Dickson, Oxford, 1973.

———, 'Empire and Authority in the Late 18th Century', *Journal of Imperial and Commonwealth History*, vol. XV, no. 2, January 1987.

Marshman, J.C., *Life and Times of Carey, Marshman and Ward: Or a History of the Seerampore Mission*, vol. 2, London, 1859.

Momin, Mohiuddin., *The Chancellery and Persian Epistolography under the Mughals, from Bābur to Shāh Jahān (1526–1658)*, Calcutta, 1971.

Mukherjee, S.N., *Sir William Jones: A Study in Eighteenth Century British Attitudes to India*, repr. London, 1987.

Murr, Sylvia, 'Les conditions de l'émergence du discourse sur l'Inde au Siècle des Lumières', in Marie-Claude Porcher, ed., *Inde et Littérature*, Collection Purusartha 7, Paris: EHESS, 1983, pp. 233–84.

Niẓāmī, 'Arūẓī Samarqandī, *Chahār Maqāla*, ed. by M. Abdul Wahhab Qazwini and M. Moin, Tehran, 1334 *Shamsi*, English tr. by E.G. Browne, London, 1899.

Orme, R., *Historical Fragments of the Mughal Empire, of the Morattoes and of the English Concern in Indostan from the Year MDCLIX*, reprint, 1974.

Parliamentary Papers 1813, vol. X, Cambridge University Library, Cambridge.

Persian Ms. in IOL, Ms Eur. D 543, BL, London.

Persian Supplements 1518, 1584, 1605, 13828, Bibliothèque Nationale, Paris.

Phillimore, R.H., *Historical Records of the Survey of India*, vol. 1, Dehra Dun, 1945.

'Polier' in Eugene and Emily Haag, *La France Protestante*, vol. 8, Paris, Cherbuliez, 1858.

'Polier' in *Dictionnaire historique et biographique de la Suisse*, vol. V, Neuchatel: DHBS, 1930, pp. 313.

Polier, A.H. *Shah Alam and His Court A.H.*, ed. by P.C. Gupta, reprint, Calcutta, 1989.

Pratt, M.L., *Imperial Eyes: Travel Writing and Transculturation*, London, 1992.

Raj, K., 'Manufacturing Trust: William Jones and the Anglo-Indian Administration of the English East India Company's Indian Territories', mimeo, 1998.

Residents proceedings of Benaras, March 1791, June 1795, National Archives of India, Delhi.

Richard, Francis., 'Jean-Baptiste Gentil collectionneur de manuscrits persans', *Dix-huitième siècle*, no. 28, 1996.

Rocher, Rosane., 'British Orientalism in the Eighteenth Century. The Dialectics of Knowledge and Government', in Carol Breckenridge and Peter Van Der Veer, eds., *Orientalism and the Postcolonial Predicament*, Delhi, 1994.

Royal Asiatic Society of Bengal (1784–1934) 150 Jubilee; and the Bicentenary of Sir William Jones (1746–1946), Royal Asiatic Society of Bengal, Calcutta, 1946.

Said, E., *Orientalism*, Vintage, New York, 1995.

Schwab, Raymond, *The Oriental Renaissance. Europe's Rediscovery of India and the East 1680–1880*, New York, 1990.

________, *Vie d' Anquetil-Duperron, Suivie des usages civils et religieux des Parses par Anquetil Duperron*, Paris 1934.

Srivastava, A.L., *Shuja-ud-daulah*, 2 vols. Agra, 1954.

Stokes, E., *The English Utilitarians and India*, Delhi, 1992.

Subrahmanyam, S., 'The Career of Colonel Polier and late Eighteenth Century Orientalism', *Journal of the Royal Asiatic Society*, 2000.

Suleri, Sarah, *The Rhetoric of English India*, Chicago, 1992.

Ṭabaṭabā'ī, G̲h̲ulām Ḥusian, *Siyar al-Muta'akhkhirīn*, vols. 2 and 3, Nawalkishor, Lucknow, English tr. Reprinted, Lahore, 1975.

Teltcher, K., *India Inscribed, European and British writing on India 1600–1800*, Delhi, 1995.

Trautmann, T., *Aryans and British India*, Delhi, 1997.

Trivedi, M., 'Encounters and Transition. European Impact in Awadh 1765–1856', in A.J. Qaiser and S.P. Verma, eds., *Art and Culture: Endeavour in Interpretation*, Delhi, 1996.

Valensi, Lucette, 'Eloge de l'Orient, Eloge de l'Orientalisme: Le jeu d'échecs d'Anquetil-Duperron', *Revue de l'Histoire des Religions*, vol. CCXII, no. 4, 1995, pp. 419–52.

Vishwanathan, G., *Masks of Conquest. Literary study and British Rule in India*, Delhi, 1998.

Zaidi, N.H., '*Inshā*' in S.F. Muhammad and S.W.H. Abidi, (eds.), *Tārīkh-i-Adabiyāt-i-Musalmānān-i-Pākistān-o-Hind*, vol. 5, Farsi Adab, Lahore, 1972.

Zilli, I.A., 'Development of Inshā Literature till the end of Akbar's Reign', in Alam et al. (eds.), *The Making of Indo-Persian Culture: Indian and French Studies*, Delhi, 1999.

Index

Harrington, 42
Harsukh Rai, 386–9
Hasan, Aqa, 157
Hastings, Warren, 3, 23–8, 30–2, 34–41, 44–6, 54, 57, 63, 96, 99, 102, 104–105, 148, 169, 175, 191, 193, 206, 220
  patronage to *pandits* and *munshis*, 37–9
  search for oriental texts, 36–40
  soft corner for Polier, 23–7
Hathras, 350, 356–8
Hay, Edward, 22
Hazrat, Mufti Ghulam (*faujdār*), 12, 98, 101, 105
Henri IV, 29
Himmat Bahadur (Raja), 340
Hindu learning, Hasting's patronage to, 37–9
Hindupat (Raja), 102, 211, 216
Hindushah, Abu'l Qasim, 47
History of India as told by Its Own Historians, 65
History of Shah Alam II, 8
Hodal, 334–5
Hodges, William (painter), 5
Holasi, 111
Humayun, 15
Hunter, 255, 275
Husain, Aqa
Hussain, Ghulam (*ḥavaldār*), 170
Hussain, Mir Muhammad, 341

Ibn Sina, 33
Ibn-al Mulaqqin, 40
Iftikhar-ud-Daula, 267
Iḥyā-i 'ulūm al-Dīn, 51
I'jāz-i Arsalānī, 1, 9–18, 27–32, 71–3, 77–9, 95
  facsimile form, 10
  format, 17
  Kishan Sahai's prefaces to, 77–9, 95
  Polier's own identification with English in, 27–32
  style of, 14–18
  use of phraseology in, 71–3
I'jāz-i Khusrawī, 79
Imad-ud-Daula, 222
Imam Bakhsh, 186, 204, 319
Impey, Elijah, 63
Imtiaz-ud-Daula, Nawab, 386
India, eighteenth century, Anglo-French rivalries in, 18–22
  book bazaar, 32–50
    Burrow, Gentil and Polier as shoppers, 43–50
    English Company in, 36–40
    missionaries shoppers, 41–2
    shopping in, 32–6
  Colonial identities in, 27–32
  images of Mughals, 65–9
  literary and intellectual ferment in, 34–5
  politico-cultural identity during, 70
  social categorization of society, 56–65
Indo-Islamic intellectual legacy, 39–40
Indo-Persian *Inshā*, format of, 17
Inshā, history of, 14
Inshā-i-Mādho Rām, 17
Inshā, writers, 14–17
Isfahan, 52
Isfhani, Fazli, 52
Isfhani, Mir Muhammad Husain, 38
Islamic intellectual legacy, 42–3, 45, 50
Islamic Museum, Berlin, 8
Itimad-ud-Daula, 328–9, 331–2, 336

Jafar, Muhammad (*chūbdār*), 100, 134
Jagan Nath (*sāhūkār*), 390